WALL STREET TO MAIN STREET

CHARLES MERRILL AND MIDDLE-CLASS INVESTORS

In *Wall Street to Main Street*, Edwin J. Perkins focuses on the spectacularly successful career of financier Charles Merrill (1885–1956), founder of Merrill Lynch, the world's largest brokerage and investment firm. The most innovative entrepreneur in the financial services sector in the twentieth century, Merrill was the central figure in the promotion of common stocks as a prudent long-term investment vehicle for middle-class Americans. With more than 100 branch offices across the nation, Merrill Lynch solicited millions of middle-class households and became famous for bringing "Wall Street to Main Street" in the post–World War II era. Today, American investors hold, either directly or indirectly through mutual funds, a greater percentage of common stocks in their financial portfolios than do the citizens of any other country. Based on archival sources, *Wall Street to Main Street* is the first biography published about the career of this major Wall Street figure.

Edwin J. Perkins is Professor of History Emeritus at the University of Southern California. He is an expert on the historical development of American financial services from colonial times to the twentieth century. His publications include five books, among them a history of the prominent New York banking firm Brown Brothers Harriman, and articles in the *Journal of Economic History* and *Business History Review*. He has testified before the United States Congress about proposed reforms of outdated financial laws.

EDWIN J. PERKINS

WALL STREET TO MAIN STREET

CHARLES MERRILL AND MIDDLE-CLASS INVESTORS

MBRIDGE
VERSITY PRESS

PUBLISHED BY THE PRESS SYNDICATE OF THE UNIVERSITY OF CAMBRIDGE
The Pitt Building, Trumpington Street, Cambridge, United Kingdom

CAMBRIDGE UNIVERSITY PRESS
The Edinburgh Building, Cambridge CB2 2RU, UK   http://www.cup.cam.ac.uk
40 West 20th Street, New York, NY 10011-4211, USA   http://www.cup.org
10 Stamford Road, Oakleigh, Melbourne 3166, Australia

© Edwin J. Perkins   1999

First published 1999

Printed in the United States of America

Typeface Ehrhardt 10½/12½ pt   *System* Penta [RF]

*A catalog record for this book is available from
the British Library.*

Library of Congress Cataloging-in-Publication Data are available.

ISBN 0 521 63029 0 hardback

For
Henry Hecht
John Fitzgerald
Doris Merrill Magowan
Charles Merrill Jr.
and
all the descendants of Charles E. Merrill

CONTENTS

INTRODUCTION

I became involved in this project through serendipity. In the late 1970s, John Garraty asked me to write a brief entry for Charles Merrill (1885–1956) for the *Dictionary of American Biography*. At that point I realized that no biography, nor much of anything else, had ever been published about the man and his accomplishments. Given Merrill's important role in U.S. financial history, his career seemed like a potentially worthwhile research project at some unspecified future date, but, without giving the idea too much thought, I put it aside.

About a decade later, I noticed in our campus newspaper that James Merrill, the prize-winning poet and younger son of the late financier, was scheduled to give a poetry reading later that week. Although deeply engrossed in writing a book on financial services that covered the period from 1700 to 1815, I decided on the spur of the moment that here was the perfect opportunity to explore the Merrill option. I arrived for the poetry reading early and sat in the front row – and a good thing, too, because within minutes, it was standing room only. During the fifteen-second gap at the end of the presentation, when no one usually knows exactly what to say or do, I rushed up and handed Mr. Merrill an envelope with a short letter inquiring about his father's papers and asking for his cooperation. He phoned me promptly the next morning, gave me the names and addresses of his brother, Charles, and sister, Doris, and encouraged me to pursue the project. Doris Merrill Magowan subsequently put me in contact with Henry Hecht at Merrill Lynch, and within a couple of months I had visited New York and gained access to the archival material.

I have been extremely lucky in my career as a historian with respect to obtaining access to unexploited primary sources: first at Brown Brothers Harriman in the early 1970s and then at Merrill Lynch in the late 1980s. I realize that other historians, among them Robert Sobel, had requested access to Merrill's papers, but they were turned down for one reason or another. I was simply fortunate enough to ask the right people at just the right time. Timing may not be everything, as the saying goes, but it can make a substantial impact on the career path of a historian. In case anyone is wondering, I received no funding from the firm or from the Merrill family; and I retained the luxury of complete editorial freedom. Thankfully, I received a summer research grant from the University of Southern California that provided the seed money to get this project off the ground.

Biographers are frequently accused of falling under the spell of their subjects and, as a result, distorting reality. Without hesitation, I plead guilty to the first accusation. Charlie Merrill had the ability to ingratiate himself with almost everybody he ever met – biographers not exempted. His informal, unpretentious manner in dealing with people of every social rank or economic level was the main factor that led me to refer to him throughout the manuscript by his casual nickname rather than his formal surname. Despite having been ensnared by the engaging personality of my subject, I do not believe that I have led readers astray by emphasizing the immense impact of Merrill's career on the institutional structure and the overall performance of the U.S. financial services sector during the middle decades of the twentieth century.

This biography focuses primarily on Merrill's business career, with only passing references to his personal life once he left college and headed for New York City. I leave for future biographers the task of producing a more complete portrait. As an entrepreneur, both in financial services and the grocery trade, Merrill was a monumental success by any standard of measurement. His ultimate achievement was primarily the product of his skill in adapting advances in marketing and management to other sectors of the economy. Nationwide chains of grocery stores and brokerage offices had similar characteristics: both organizations drew on the economies of scale and scope to more effectively reach millions of households, in partic- ular millions of middle-class households.

As the husband of three wives and father of three children, however, Charlie did not always meet the same high standards. Invariably friendly, calm, and composed in a business setting, he was often temperamental and dictatorial at home. A devilishly handsome man who exuded southern charm, he was involved in a series of adulterous affairs that led to the dissolution of at least two of his three marriages. (I heard idle speculation at Merrill Lynch that one of the reasons top management had kept a lid on the archives all these years was to prevent the public from learning about his three divorces, since divorce was considered highly scandalous behavior in respectable circles until fairly recent times.) Merrill's relation- ships with his two sons were also severely strained; neither chose to enter the business world; and both rebelled at what they perceived as the excesses of their father's lavish lifestyle. In due course, both Charles Jr. and James had successful careers of their own. James became one of the nation's most honored and respected poets. For a retrospective on his life and literary career, I recommend an article titled "Braving the Elements" by J. D. McClatchy in the March 27, 1995, issue of the *New Yorker*. Charles Jr. made his mark in secondary school education, and, in one of those cases of supreme irony, he had the pleasure of heading the charitable foundation that, over a quarter century, gave to worthy causes a substantial portion of his father's fortune. He later wrote a perceptive book about his experiences with the Merrill Trust titled *The Checkbook*.

If some scholar with an understanding of two normally rather disparate disciplines – the history of financial services and twentieth-century poetry – wanted someday to write a family biography focusing on the intergenerational conflicts between father and son, the Merrill family awaits more detailed analysis; it must rank as one of the most fractured and polarized families in U.S. history in terms of interests, attitudes, skills, tastes, and the variety of its accomplishments. In his late twenties, James wrote a jaded novel, *The Seraglio* (1957), based not all that loosely on his father's lifestyle during his final years. Charles Jr. clashed with his namesake mainly on political and social issues, and especially with respect to the proper distribution of national income and wealth.

In contrast, Charles Merrill's relations with his daughter, Doris, and her husband, Robert Magowan, were vastly more harmonious. As a child, she was his darling, and because he had different expectations for her development as an adult, Charlie never felt unhappy or frustrated about her life choices. Father and daughter remained on good terms throughout his lifetime; in periods of marital crises, Charlie often turned to Doris for solace. He occasionally revealed to her intimate details about his troubled personal relationships with Hellen and Kinta – wives number two and three – and sought her sympathy and support. Charlie mentored Robert Magowan for two decades, and the two men viewed their business careers and the management of their households from a similar perspective.

The Merrill family was extremely cooperative in helping me conduct the research for this book. I personally interviewed all three children – Doris in San Francisco, Charles in Boston, and James in Los Angeles. Over the years, several representatives of Merrill Lynch had interviewed the trio for other unpublished manuscripts, and I had access to those earlier transcripts as well. All three were open and forthright in their responses to me. I sent a number of chapters, and parts of chapters, that dealt primarily with family matters to Doris and Charles, asking them to check for errors and offer corrections. They returned everything with elaborate notes and extremely useful comments. The two siblings did not always agree with each other on every detail, but that's not surprising since many of these events occurred more than a half century ago.

Before moving on, it might be apropos at this point to explain that, although the primary focus of this book is on the involvement with Merrill Lynch, the Merrill family's most enduring business relationship has been with the grocery chain, Safeway Stores. Merrill acquired a controlling interest in the company in the mid-1920s. Son-in-law Robert Magowan became CEO of Safeway in the mid-1950s, and grandson Peter Magowan followed in his father's footsteps. When KKR (Kohlberg Kravis Roberts & Company) privatized Safeway in the 1980s, the family maintained a minority ownership position. In 1997, I had a brief telephone conversation with Peter Magowan, who now oversees the operations of the San Francisco Giants baseball team.

In researching and writing this book, I found it extremely easy to identify with the life-cycle investment strategies that Merrill advocated for middle-class households. Starting with minimal personal savings in 1973, I have been steadily acquiring a portfolio of mutual funds, and their combined value not long ago passed the half-million-dollar mark. It was all made possible by my university's defined contribution retirement program. I elected to place all my monies in common stock funds – and so should any participant in a retirement program with that option and a time horizon of ten years or longer. Based on the tried-and-true technique of dollar averaging (regular monthly contributions), investors in defined contribution plans have little reason to worry about the general level of stock prices on any given date during their working lives. Merrill was right about how beginning investors with fairly modest incomes – incomes that might never exceed the annual cutoff point for the payment of Social Security taxes – could nonetheless accumulate a sizable estate, and I am living proof of that maxim. Sensible investments in common stocks, or common stock funds, can indeed lift households from middle-class to upper-middle-class status if investors have the patience to stay the course. As it happens, my investments were in the mutual funds managed by CREF and Fidelity, not those offered by Merrill Lynch, but the investment principles remain the same, irrespective of the sponsoring organization.

With a research project of this magnitude, there are inevitably many people to thank for helping to make it all possible. Jean Cooper, in the Library Archives, at Jacksonville University, helped me locate the town of Phillips, Florida, where Merrill's parents once resided. In assessing Charlie's medical history after his first heart attack in 1944, I received sound advice from Doyce Nunis, Richard Bing, and Carol Mangione (the wife of colleague

Phil Ethington). Don Watson added some interesting information on the battle over the chain store tax in the 1930s. Sandra Vance, who has written an outstanding book on the Wal-Mart chain, read approximately half the chapters and provided useful suggestions related to both organization and style. My graduate student Tom Han gave the whole manuscript a thorough review, and Kathleen Barrett, another graduate student with a background in financial services, read one or two chapters as well. At one point, Mike Robinson showed me how to recover lost computer files. One of my oldest friends, David Heenan, a fraternity brother at William and Mary, later a successful business school dean, and subsequently the CEO of a major enterprise in Hawaii, reviewed a couple of chapters. The author of several books on modern business management, Dave is currently preparing a book on people who were perennially second in command within an organization; it includes a chapter on Winthrop Smith, who was Charlie's right-hand man (and more) at Merrill Lynch from 1940 to 1956. In fairness to all parties concerned, the firm today should be known as Merrill Smith rather than Merrill Lynch.

During the last three or four years, I participated in seminars and conferences that drew on materials in the Merrill Lynch Files. I gave informal papers at the University of Southern California, the University of California-Los Angeles, and Ohio State University; more formal presentations came at annual meetings of the Business History Conference and the Economic History Association, plus a conference of international banking historians at Berkeley in April 1997. Many scholars at these sessions offered helpful comments. Among them were Elinor Accampo, Mansel Blackford, Bill Childs, Lance Davis, Phil Ethington, Geoff Jones, Austin Kerr, Naomi Lamoreaux, Ken Lipartito, Roland Marchand, Jean-Laurent Rosenthal, Steve Ross, David Sicilia, Jonathan Silva, Ken Sokoloff, David Stebenne, Mira Wilkins, Jack Wills, and Mary Yeager. In the final stages of this project, I was the beneficiary of the extremely helpful comments of Paul Miranti, Richard Sylla, and Frank Smith, my editor at Cambridge University Press.

Three people at the firm's headquarters were absolutely crucial to my research efforts. Betty Hope had the day-to-day responsibility of maintaining the historical archives. She showed me where everything was located and helped me find many elusive items. After returning to Los Angeles, I sometimes phoned Betty, and she always cheerfully went back to the historical records to seek out whatever I might have missed. John Fitzgerald was the top-ranking executive at Merrill Lynch with whom I was in contact about this project. In the 1990s, he served as a director of the Merrill Lynch Foundation, a charitable organization. John granted me unrestricted access to the historical files. I assume he cleared the project with superiors, but I have no idea exactly who his superiors were or how high up on the organizational chart they stood. John also read most of the chapters and made recommendations for improvement. At one time an assistant to Mike McCarthy, who served as CEO after Winthrop Smith's retirement, John was extremely knowledgeable about the evolution of policies, procedures, and strategies during his long career with the firm. At no point did John, or anyone else at Merrill Lynch, attempt to censor anything I wrote. Instead, John offered a series of constructive suggestions, and I took most of them to heart.

The most valuable contributor to this whole project was Henry Hecht, and his name heads the list on the dedication page. An employee of Merrill Lynch since the early 1940s, he retired from his full-time duties more than a decade ago, but he has periodically returned to work on a series of ad hoc projects. For years Henry was on the editorial staff of *Investor's Reader*, the firm's monthly magazine that featured straightforward articles on economic and business topics. Just before retirement, he authored *A Legacy of Leadership* (1985), a brief history of the firm that integrated an informative text with hundreds of striking photographs. Henry possesses all the skills of a superb investigative journalist plus the broad vision of a seasoned historian – an unbeatable combination. I long ago began referring to him as a veritable "walking encyclopedia" with respect to any fact linked to the history of Merrill Lynch or the careers of its top executives. Occasionally, when Henry was unable to draw immediately on his unfailing memory to address one of my inquiries, he was usually able to come up with an authoritative response within just a day or two. Henry read every word of every chapter. We talked on the phone once a month, or more often, for four or five years. He saved me from scores of errors, large and small, and he polished up my prose as well. Henry is a princely man, pure and simple, and a very generous friend. He is the very embodiment of the positive values and accommodating attitudes toward the broad investing public that Charlie Merrill espoused throughout his long career.

Last, but not least – and indeed the very "mostest" – I was supported throughout the project by my wife, Judith Gladstone Perkins.

I

———————— • ————————

THE RETURN TO WALL STREET

In October 1939, only a few weeks after the Nazi invasion of Poland, Charlie Merrill boarded a train in New York headed for the West Coast. For more than a decade he had traveled to California several times every year, either by Pullman car or airplane, to consult with the top management of Safeway Stores, the nationwide grocery chain in which he had held a controlling interest since the mid-1920s. Most of Merrill's vast fortune, estimated at between $30 and $50 million, had arisen from aggressive investments in the common stocks of chain stores. These novel enterprises, which proliferated in the first quarter of the century, operated a multitude of retail outlets in one or two regional markets and sometimes blanketed most of the nation. Usually administered from a central office, or several regional offices, to take advantage of scale economies, each chain typically specialized in groceries or everyday consumer goods. The product list ranged from foodstuffs to shoes, auto supplies, and other nondurables – all selling at low, competitive prices. Because of its effective management, Safeway had emerged as one of the most successful and profitable grocery chains during the depression decade.

Over the last fifteen years, Merrill had sold off sizable blocks of his chain store securities at opportune times and realized substantial profits in most instances. He liquidated some securities near the end of the business boom in the late 1920s just before the crash of 1929 and more during a series of sharp rallies in stock prices from 1933 to 1939. But he had kept all, or most, of his common stock holdings in Safeway, and as principal owner, he influenced the appointment of senior management and participated fully in the formulation of corporate strategy. Charlie was instrumental in orchestrating Safeway's rapid geographic expansion from its headquarters in Oakland, California. By 1939 this grocery chain ranked second among the nation's leading retail food distributors, trailing only the giant A&P (Great Atlantic and Pacific Tea Company) in store locations. The close association with Safeway was one of Merrill's most enduring relationships – business or personal. In a letter to partner Eddie Lynch, Charlie revealed the depth of his attachment: "Safeway means more to me than money. I have poured my life into it."[1]

Glancing backward over the course of his business career during its first three decades, Merrill's success was linked primarily to his bold investments in chain stores, particularly his role as majority owner of Safeway. By the late 1930s, he had become better known in business circles as an aggressive retail grocer than an adventuresome financier. His once budding reputation on Wall Street had faded. Some still remembered the dashing Merrill as an upstart investment banker who had made a series of shrewd investments in securities that rose to spectacular heights, but the investment banking firm of Merrill, Lynch & Company was nearly moribund during the 1930s. The firm was one among many on the fringes of a capital market still suffering from the impact of the Great Depression.

Then, in a surprising and dramatic shift, Merrill's drift toward anonymity on Wall Street was abruptly reversed in the 1940s. He rejuvenated the old firm, contributing new capital and introducing a series of fresh, precedent-setting ideas. As a consequence, Charles E. Merrill emerged as the foremost institutional innovator in the American financial services sector during the twentieth century. How these innovative changes unfolded is the focus of this career biography.

En route to Safeway's Oakland headquarters that October, Charlie made plans for a weekend stopover in Chicago to visit Winthrop Smith, a former business associate who had worked for Merrill, Lynch in the booming 1920s. In 1939, Smith was manager of the Chicago branch in E. A. Pierce & Company's chain of brokerage offices. Both Merrill and Smith had attended Amherst College, a crucial factor in sealing their fates since the old-school connection had helped land Smith a job as errand boy and runner at Merrill, Lynch soon after graduation in 1916. Smith rose steadily in the firm and became a full partner in 1929 – an ominous year for advancement.

When the stock market crashed a few months later, the senior partners – Merrill and Lynch – decided to scale back their Wall Street activities. Not wanting to thoughtlessly and irresponsibly dismiss their partners and valued employees in an economic downswing, the two senior partners arranged to transfer their entire brokerage operations – the retail side of the business – to E. A. Pierce.

Edward Pierce was optimistic in 1930 that the U.S. economy was still essentially sound and that trading securities would remain a profitable business. By absorbing the retail operations of Merrill Lynch, he was

---

1. Engberg, "History of Merrill Lynch," ML Files.

gaining the services of many experienced and successful people. Pierce was in no mood to retrench, and in expressing that optimism, he was in solid company. President Herbert Hoover likewise believed any downturn would be short lived, and so did many other Wall Street figures. In contrast, Merrill was more cautious. Having predicted a major stock market correction as early as 1928, Charlie was less certain about future market conditions. Until he saw sure signs of an upsurge, he planned to sit on the sidelines and devote his energies to the management of his chain store investments, which totaled in the millions of dollars. Given the opportunity of continuing employment in a familiar business without interruption, a majority of the employees of Merrill, Lynch, including Win Smith, joined the Pierce organization. Most of them had few other employment options.

To complete the deal and smooth the transition, Merrill, his long-standing partner, Edmund Lynch, and a few business associates agreed to invest a total of $5 million in the recapitalized E. A. Pierce. A partnership agreement was drafted covering the next ten years. Based in part on the advice of his lawyers, who feared that he might weaken his position in any unanticipated liquidation proceedings, Charlie never sought active involvement in the management of E. A. Pierce.[2] In fact, he rarely consulted with Pierce about anything associated with the operations of the brokerage house throughout the 1930s – not even when losses started to mount because of the intractability of the depression and the distressingly low trading volume on the stock exchanges. Former business associates urged him to intervene and recommend new business strategies, but Charlie ignored their pleas. In the late 1930s, he altered the terms of his investment in E. A. Pierce by elevating his capital account to a more senior position on the balance sheet. By that date, his capital had been reduced by more than three-quarters. Charlie gave up any claim on future profits and, more important in these desperate times, limited even further his vulnerability to absorb future losses; the investment account converted to interest-only status, which from the firm's perspective became more akin to a debt liability than an equity position.

Soon after Charlie arrived at the train station in downtown Chicago in October 1939, the conversation turned to an ambitious business plan that Smith eagerly proposed. If adopted, the plan promised to save the Pierce firm from dissolution – a distinct possibility because of a lack of capital, persistent losses, and unimaginative leadership. The proposal outlined the

2. Both Merrill and Lynch actually put the investment in Pierce & Company in their respective mothers' names. I am not sure of the motivation for this, but Merrill was usually very generous toward his family and close relatives.

general terms for Merrill's reentry into the securities field as directing partner of a reconstituted brokerage house conducting operations on a grand scale. Merrill was asked to play the role of white knight; he was presented with the opportunity to rescue a firm perilously close to liquidation and abandonment. To produce a significant turnaround, however, would require the application of his substantial capital resources and management expertise. His work schedule would be sharply increased – forty hours a week at a minimum and probably much more. That meant forgoing the leisurely lifestyle of the past decade, which had been interrupted only periodically by consultations with Safeway management.

Although the scope of the sweeping reorganization plan may have taken him aback, Charlie expected a candid discussion of the clouded future of E. A. Pierce to arise sometime during that weekend. The subject was unavoidable since Merrill still had in the neighborhood of $400,000 tied up in the Pierce enterprise. The partnership agreement signed ten years before was due to expire on December 31, a date little more than two months away. Pierce had been worried for some time that several general and limited partners – not just Merrill but others as well – would elect to withdraw their financial support in light of continued operating losses and the depletion of their capital accounts over the past decade. Meanwhile, a sale of the firm's assets to new owners, or a merger with a rival brokerage house, did not seem a realistic possibility. Almost every brokerage firm in the country was losing money because of low trading volume, and no competitors had been identified as possible merger candidates. Win Smith and hundreds of employees, many of them middle aged or older, faced the unpleasant prospect of unemployment and potentially shattered lives.

In anticipation of Charlie's upcoming visit, Smith had traveled eastward several weeks earlier and reviewed the whole dismal situation with Pierce and his top aides. Smith had a definite scenario in mind for Charlie's active return to the securities field, and he wanted permission from his immediate superiors to pursue the possibility of a merger between E. A. Pierce and Merrill Lynch. (Lynch had died in 1938, and in the reorganization of the firm's affairs, which included changing from a partnership to a corporate form of organization, the comma between the principals' names had disappeared.) Smith listed several conditions that he thought might be important in formulating a package attractive enough to lure his former employer back to Wall Street. The most critical was that Charlie be named directing partner – meaning in this context that he would exercise undiluted managerial authority over personnel, strategy, and all other executive matters. With little argument, Pierce and Jerry Cuppia, his top aide, readily agreed to support the reorganization plan. If Smith could pull off a minor miracle by enticing Charlie to redirect his energies into the brokerage business and simultaneously to reallocate a healthy share of his substantial wealth into the merged firm, most of the current employees of E. A. Pierce would be able to thank heaven for a new lease on their threatened careers.

Charlie made no promises to Smith that weekend, but he agreed to give the proposal serious thought during the long train ride out to the West Coast and back. He arranged to return to Chicago in three weeks to continue the discussion over another working weekend. Meanwhile, with the help of accountants drawn from Pierce's New York office, Smith spent his time preparing projections of what the new firm might expect during its first year of operations. With prudent cost cutting, Smith was convinced that annual profits of $1 million were possible in 1940 even if trading volume failed to improve over the low level prevailing in 1939; and the profit picture would improve if trading volume increased marginally.

When Charlie arrived for his second visit, the two men devoted most of their waking hours to going over the projected financial statements. Fiddling with the numbers was something Charlie always relished. He felt comfortable reviewing balance sheets and income statements and analyzing the implications either for investment or, if unfavorable, for liquidation. Before making any major decision, and certainly one of this magnitude, he wanted to learn all the pertinent facts, pro and con. A versatile and flexible businessman, he possessed the rare gift of being equally at ease in discussing minute operating details and grand business strategies. The preliminary earnings projections heightened his interest and stimulated his competitive juices. Charlie pressed Smith about exactly how the anticipated economies would be realized without dismantling the extensive branch network that Pierce had so doggedly maintained during the depression decade.

Charlie was intrigued by the prospects but remained uncommitted. He needed more information about the Pierce firm and more knowledge about the general status of the financial markets. Having been away from the securities business for nearly a decade, he was out of touch with recent developments. There were other factors to consider as well. France and Great Britain had declared war against Hitler's Germany in September 1939, and recalling his earlier experiences during World War I, Charlie knew that major political events could have negative consequences for the securities markets. The New York Stock Exchange had closed its doors for several months after war broke out in Europe in August 1914. The same thing might happen again in 1940 or 1941, depending on developments overseas and the possibility of American involvement. These were risky times to jump into any new venture, much less a struggling enterprise that had been swimming in red ink for years.

Charlie persuaded Smith to accompany him home for the Thanksgiving holiday and then stay on in New York through December working on the proposal. Smith returned to Chicago for Christmas but came back in January to resume deliberations. "We worked late into the night for the whole month and never seemed able to get the right combination of figures that satisfied Merrill," he recalled. "It began to look very much as though Merrill was going to throw over the whole idea of a merger."[3] But Smith was too pessimistic. Charlie simply needed more time to mull over the deal and consider all its ramifications. He was fifty-four years old and had just remarried in March 1939 for the third time soon after the settlement of a drawn-out, highly publicized, and thoroughly nasty divorce. Irrespective of the circumstances, in this era most divorces were considered scandalous affairs according to the prevailing morality. Moreover, his new wife, Kinta, had every reason to believe she had married a wealthy, semiretired man who had a great deal of time on his hands for high living, travel, and leisurely pursuits. Kinta had certainly not bargained for married life with a recidivist workaholic trying to resuscitate a dying firm in a dormant securities field. Thus, personal as well as business considerations had to be taken into account.

Just days before the existing partnership agreement with Pierce was due to expire on December 31, Charlie proposed a three-month extension, which the lawyers quickly arranged. That gave him a few more weeks to gather the pertinent facts and to sort out his desires and plumb his emotions. The whole deal rested on his shoulders – what he decided one way or the other – since no other financier with sufficient resources to rescue the firm was involved in the ongoing negotiations. Employees of E. A. Pierce sat on pins and needles awaiting the news about their collective fate. Because trading in securities had been subdued for so long, brokers were accustomed to playing the waiting game – hoping for a new business boom that would someday revive the financial markets. By 1940 few employees were optimistic about the future; a change in management would save many jobs temporarily – if individuals could survive a cost-cutting campaign – but none expected their potential savior to pull rabbits out of hats even if he did choose to commit his money and managerial talents to the new enterprise. Merrill might be an astute businessman, but conditions were radically different from those in the heyday of the 1920s. Moreover, neither he nor any other business leader was in a position to deliver the ultimate panacea; Merrill did not possess the power to lower the unemployment rate, bring back economic prosperity, and increase the volume of trading on the securities exchanges.

While Win Smith and the Pierce personnel were preparing the best case for continuance and reorganization, Charlie launched his own independent

---

3. Smith, "Reminiscences," ML Files.

investigation. He arranged a meeting of the senior staff of Merrill Lynch – by 1939 a small group – in December and asked each person in attendance to submit a confidential report in answer to the rhetorical question: "What would Eddie Lynch have done?" The replies have not survived, so we can only speculate about their probable content. Had Lynch himself survived his illness in 1938 to answer in person, it seems doubtful that he would have been enthusiastic about embarking on such a risky adventure. Having become accustomed to a life of diversion and leisure after 1930, Lynch might, out of loyalty to his partner, put up some of the capital to finance the consolidated enterprise, but the possibility of his coming out of retirement and resuming an active managerial role would probably not have been in the cards. The two partners' lives had followed different courses during the depression years, and they had differing priorities. Merrill kept his hand in the management of Safeway Stores during the 1930s; Lynch hired a full-time tennis professional so that he would have immediate access to a willing opponent anytime, anywhere. Therefore, we may safely presume that the senior staff members at Merrill Lynch largely ignored the Lynch angle in preparing their recommendations either for or against the proposed merger. Whatever they wrote – whether upbeat, downbeat, or mixed – their reports failed to dissuade Charlie from pursuing the project. Although there is no evidence that their jobs were also on the line, they probably concluded that, if Charlie decided to devote more energy to investment banking and brokerage, their employment future would be brighter.

While on the West Coast in November 1939, Charlie had mentioned the merger proposal to Ted Braun, who headed an established management consulting firm based in Los Angeles. After the personal initiatives of Win Smith, Braun was probably the second most crucial person in convincing Charlie to reenter the financial services sector. Moreover, in the years that followed, Braun was the prime catalyst for the introduction of a series of internal procedures at Merrill Lynch that revolutionized the relationship between brokers and their customers in the securities field. Braun proposed to compensate brokers by paying them a straight salary, plus year-end bonuses, rather than on a commission basis, and he lobbied Charlie incessantly until he finally broke down his client's ingrained resistance. Braun's background was remote from the securities field, and his fresh perspective on long-standing, routine brokerage procedures led to the advocacy of numerous controversial concepts. His consulting firm was a leader in the use of public opinion surveys to formulate business strategies, and Merrill Lynch was among the first brokerage firms, if not the very first, to draw heavily on this type of outside expertise. In reflecting on his success as a management consultant, Braun placed the emphasis on originality: "We sold to the client a plan, or an idea, or a concept that was new, absolutely new, and which was based upon a very careful study of the client's problems and the client's market."[4] Many seasoned Merrill Lynch managers were skeptical, including Charlie on several occasions, but many of Braun's pet theories proved workable and helped to propel Merrill Lynch to the heights in the securities field in the 1940s.

The close business association between Charlie and Braun, a man sixteen years his junior, had blossomed in the mid-1930s during the rough-and-tumble political fight against a discriminatory tax on chain store outlets in California. Many states passed anti–chain store laws beginning in the mid-1920s. Enacted by the California legislature in 1935 in response to pressure from hundreds of independent retail store owners, the new law applied a $1 annual tax to a single store, $2 for a second store, $4 for a third store, and progressed geometrically to $256 for the eighth store – with all stores beyond the eighth taxed at $500 each. Because it operated so many outlets in the state, this tax threatened the profitability of Safeway Stores, which was Charlie's principal investment vehicle during the depression decade. Chain store owners across the state decided to fight back. Safeway management was instrumental in the formation of the California Chain Stores Association, a group organized to launch a political campaign to repeal the new law through the referendum process – a Progressive Era governance mechanism used extensively in California by groups of all political persuasions in the twentieth century. The association gathered a sufficient number of signatures on a petition to delay implementation of the tax until voters could decide whether to affirm the law or repeal it. The issue went on the ballot as Proposition 22 in the November 1936 election.

Braun was hired, on the recommendation of Don Francisco, executive vice president of the advertising firm of Lord and Thomas, which had overall responsibility for election strategy. Their task was to assist the California Chain Stores Association in planning a successful campaign. Braun's management consulting firm assumed the task of sampling public opinion on the tax issue and analyzing the results. He then helped design and implement a voter education program that stressed the negative impact of the tax on whole groups of citizens ranging from farmers to urban consumers. The association's advertisements claimed that the tax would lessen competition in the retail sector and lead to higher prices for consumer goods. The public relations initiative and advertising campaign avoided hyperbole and concentrated on the dissemination of reliable factual information – a tactic that appealed to Merrill's penchant for straight

---

4. Quoted from "Braun, Biographical Sketch." I obtained a copy of this pamphlet from the Los Angeles office of Braun and Company in the mid-1990s.

shooting. The catchy phrase adopted to get the voters' attention and gain their allegiance was simple and direct: "Proposition 22 is a tax on you." The election strategy worked. The chain stores won the referendum easily with 56 percent of the vote, carrying fifty-seven of the state's fifty-eight counties.

Charlie was enormously impressed by Braun's work on the tax repeal project. An imaginative entrepreneur, Merrill generated a slew of innovative ideas on his own, but he was also a good listener and open to sound advice from people he trusted. Braun joined the ranks of trusted advisers on major strategic issues after 1935, especially on anything pertaining to public relations. His lack of securities expertise was no handicap under the circumstances, since Charlie drew on Braun's keen insights to reshape the firm's policies in ways designed to satisfy the expectations of financially unsophisticated customers. In the beginning, Charlie himself had been an outsider on Wall Street; a Florida native, with a courtly southern manner, he rarely associated with the "striped pants" crowd that dominated the venerable investment banking houses – the Morgan firm, Seligman, Kuhn Loeb, and others – whose partners typically sprang from New England Protestant or Jewish origins.

In late 1939 Charlie commissioned Braun to poll public opinion in southern California about the reputation of brokerage firms in general and simultaneously to survey a narrower sample drawn from the current accounts of the E. A. Pierce branch office in Los Angeles. Braun was asked, in Win Smith's words, "to obtain a picture of what the public and the Pierce customers thought of the firm."[5] The survey produced some shocking results. Braun discovered that many customers were dubious about the veracity of the advice offered by stockbrokers, and a majority were so distrustful that they were unwilling to leave their securities on deposit with a brokerage house for safekeeping.

Braun's findings reinforced the conclusions of Elmo Roper, the pioneer public opinion pollster, who had only a few months earlier completed an independent survey at the request of the New York Stock Exchange. The creation of the Securities and Exchange Commission in 1934 to promote truth in labeling in the issuance of new securities had been one of the steps taken by the federal government to restore confidence in the functioning of the stock market, but the effect on public opinion was almost negligible five years later. Roper reported that the general public was appallingly ignorant about the functions performed by brokerage houses, and most had little faith in the honesty of stockbrokers. At least half of those interviewed did not know the difference between a stock and a bond. Many

---

5. Smith, "Reminiscences," ML Files.

people believed that brokers tried to lure investors into bad securities because they received higher commissions on transactions involving speculative stocks. A majority erroneously thought the organized exchanges made a profit when listed stocks declined in value. Given the huge decline in stock prices from 1929 to 1933 – from 80 to 90 percent in many cases – the results of the Roper poll, confirmed on a lesser scale by Braun, certainly came as no surprise to persons still actively involved in the securities field in the late 1930s. Pierce's brokers, for example, had had difficulty attracting new customers anywhere across the nation; in a defensive mood, they were hanging on for dear life to those investors still regularly trading securities in the marketplace.

Charlie reacted forcefully and emotionally to the bad news about the reputation of his friends on Wall Street. During the fifteen years that he had been involved in underwriting, Charlie had consistently advocated the wisdom of relying on high standards in dealing with customers. Rather than discouraging him about business prospects in the brokerage field – the predictable reaction of many acquaintances – the disturbing reports had the opposite effect: they heightened his interest in returning to Wall Street. He became more receptive to the challenge of reversing a bad situation and reviving the tainted reputations of old, trusted friends like Win Smith who were still employed in the securities sector; probably too he was stimulated by the chance to beat what so many knowledgeable people believed were very long odds. An avid bridge player, Charlie liked to play for small stakes even in the most casual social settings.[6] Never afraid of a calculated gamble, he aimed at coming out ahead in every sphere of life, whether leisure activities or business investments.

Finally, near the end of January 1940, Charlie told Smith that he had decided to go ahead with the merger and all it entailed, which was considerable in terms of time and money. The deal was announced in early February and scheduled to go into effect on April 1. The initial capital was around $4.5 million, with $2.5 million contributed by Merrill. A contemporary article in *Time* magazine analyzed the merger of the two firms, which had been known respectively for investment banking, the wholesale side of the business, and for brokerage services, the retail end:

> Merrill knows that no amount of capital can put an investment banker in the big leagues unless he has a nationwide security selling organization or a number of big and intimate institutional connections. . . . The Pierce brokerage chain offers Merrill a ready-made . . . organization of his own. Merrill and Pierce will have a complete two-way securities circuit. This will also provide the one thing Wall

6. Merrill's love of bridge and his insistence on playing for small stakes are mentioned in several interviews with his three children – Doris, Charles, and James – in ML Files.

Street needs to make money again: a new way of bringing business out of the sticks.[7]

To rephrase, the merged firm had the organizational capability of bringing Main Street to Wall Street – one of the firm's major strategic themes in the early 1940s. Braun reminisced years later that Charlie had grown bored in semiretirement and was "looking for trouble." Son-in-law Robert Magowan put it more bluntly and colorfully: "Merrill wouldn't have gone into this thing if Win Smith hadn't persuaded him to do it. Merrill was getting bored about 1940 after sitting on his ass for ten years. It looked like an opportunity, the only one left, and he had all the money."[8] Whether by sheer good luck or superior intuition, Charlie had, as it happened, waited for the opportune time to make a significant move back into financial services.

The Wall Street to which Charlie returned in the spring of 1940 was far different from the market atmosphere he had breathed in the 1920s. In bygone days, few people had reason to distrust the recommendations of brokers since bond prices generally held their own and stocks kept rising to new highs year after year. This earlier boom era had witnessed the first mass entry by middle-class investors into the securities markets, which heretofore had been exclusively the domain of upper-class and institutional investors like banks and insurance companies. Almost everyone was optimistic in the 1920s about trends in the economy and in securities prices; some talked as if the millennium had arrived. That naive optimism was shattered by events in the early 1930s, when stocks went through the floor. The hundreds of brokers who had recommended investments that went sour were held responsible by much of the investing public for causing the debacle. During the go-go years, when standards were vague or undefined, the majority of brokers had, in truth, tried to provide reliable advice to clients; but with few regulatory controls, too many bad apples had taken advantage of unsophisticated customers and tarnished the reputation of the whole industry – including Merrill and his fellow employees. Sickening stories of alleged fraud and misrepresentation came out in congressional investigations of stock market practices held in the early 1930s. The new securities laws that emerged offered investors more protection from questionable operations, but the unsavory publicity frightened the public. Even though stock prices climbed steadily after hitting rock bottom in 1932, trading volume on the exchanges remained low. The reputation of stockbrokers remained somewhere on a par with used car salesmen.

Charlie faced the tasks not only of reshaping the image of his own new

7. *Time*, Feb. 12, 1940.   8. Magowan, interview in ML Files.

enterprise and its hundreds of geographically dispersed employees but also of propping up the standing of rival firms, since Merrill Lynch was just one thread of the whole securities fabric. No matter how virtuously it performed, the firm was vulnerable to reversals arising from negative public attitudes toward brokerage houses. Already, the leadership of the New York Stock Exchange had launched a modest advertising campaign to reassure prospective investors about the probity of securities firms admitted to its trading floor, but millions remained skeptical, and most people still equated buying stocks with gambling. Charlie had a major selling job to do on many levels: first, with the merged firm's employees, who were understandably anxious about what their new boss was thinking, and second, with American savers who had sufficient income or other financial resources for investment in the capital markets. The challenge was great but so were the opportunities; the trick was to transfer all the knowledge he had gained from his involvement with Safeway and other chain stores to the brokerage field, and to draw on what he had learned from his experiences on Wall Street before the crash.

Once committed to the new venture, Charlie embarked on a crusade that would transform stockbrokers from rumormongers touting speculative stocks to trusted investment advisers who could assist upper middle-class households – such as the one in which he had been raised in the late nineteenth century – in accumulating a nest egg of securities over a lifetime for a secure financial retirement or a legacy for future generations. Showing other people the path to greater wealth was, from his perspective, a noble purpose. The J. P. Morgans of this world had been engaged for a century or longer in assisting persons who had already accumulated substantial wealth to maintain their financial status. Extending and broadening that concept, Merrill proposed to mold an institution that would start the process a step earlier: his firm would help individuals of modest financial resources, particularly younger people who could save systematically for twenty to thirty years, to rely on the stock market as a means of upward mobility. To accomplish that goal, he believed the brokerage field needed to shed its image as the abode of fast-buck artists and reform itself through the implementation of high professional standards – the same standards that applied to doctors, lawyers, ministers, and other trusted household advisers. Merrill Lynch would lead the way out of the darkness.

The new operating policies adopted under Charlie's direction were designed to place the well-being of the individual customer first; the broker's natural desire to drum up volume by recommending frequent adjustments in customer portfolios had to be downplayed in the new environment. The incentive to churn accounts by encouraging unnecessary trading was to be curtailed by abolishing commissions and putting all sales personnel on a fixed annual salary. What the firm accomplished in the 1940s soon set the standard for the entire brokerage sector. Perhaps as much as the establishment of the SEC, the new ways of doing business at Merrill Lynch transformed public opinion and restored public confidence in the integrity of the securities markets.

2

———— • ————

GROWING UP IN FLORIDA

In his childhood and educational years, Charlie Merrill was shaped by a mixture of southern and northern influences – both in terms of geography and family background. As an adult, Charlie projected an air of southern courtliness, with a strong element of sentimentality; yet he managed to combine these personal traits with a driving entrepreneurial spirit in harmony with old-fashioned Yankee traditions. An aggressive sales-oriented businessman, he consistently stressed truthfulness and superior customer service, while eschewing exaggerated claims and misrepresentation. His parents emphasized self-reliance and personal achievement. They preached practical values and ethical concepts; at the same time, they expected hard work to translate into improved living standards someday – if not for themselves, then for their children or grandchildren.

In his boyhood, Charlie lived with his parents in Green Cove Springs, Florida, a small town situated on the banks of the broad St. Johns River in the northeastern corner of the state, about thirty miles upriver from Jacksonville. The river flowed northward, running parallel to the coastline for more than two hundred miles before turning sharply to the east and emptying into the Atlantic Ocean just shy of the Georgia border. The county seat of Clay County and its largest town, Green Cove Springs was a modest trading center. Local farmers and orchard owners, who grew oranges, potatoes, tomatoes, and other fruits and vegetables, used the town's docks as a shipping point. Any attempt to judge Green Cove Springs strictly on the basis of its geography – that is, its seemingly remote location on the fringe of American civilization in the late nineteenth century – is inappropriate, however. A snap judgment can easily produce misconceptions about the character of this community and, in turn, lead to misjudgments about the nature of Charlie's path to prominence in the world of high finance.

A glance at a map of Florida suggests that the financier's career represents another case of an unlikely long shot who somehow accumulated untold riches – an ambitious boy from a cultural and educational backwater who overcame a series of nearly insurmountable obstacles before eventually triumphing in the nation's most competitive urban environment, namely, New York City. But that picture is inaccurate. In truth, Charlie was surrounded most of his life, for at least some part of every year, by well-educated, culturally aware, well-to-do people. He saw and heard things unfamiliar to the majority of youths living in rural America. In his teenage years, particularly, Charlie had numerous educational and social advantages, and, to his credit, he made the most of them. He was enrolled after age fourteen in academic institutions that ranked among the nation's finest. He met the right people – socially prominent, influential people – and they helped him get his career off on the right foot.

Charlie was the eldest child and only son of an upper-middle-class professional family that had aspirations for further upward mobility. Always industrious, he was employed from elementary school through college in a variety of after-school and summer jobs, several of which involved dealing with the public in a sales capacity. The supplementary income provided pocket change for minor luxuries in his boyhood and, later, covered a substantial share of his living expenses at college after his father was severely injured in a robbery attempt and the family's income declined.

Despite its remoteness, Green Cove Springs was a temporary winter home to several hundred affluent families that stood at, or near, the pinnacle of northern high society. In the post–Civil War era, improved railroad service and safer, more powerful oceangoing steamboats fostered the sustained development of tourism in sunny Florida. Initially the focus was on the northeastern corner of the state, with Fernandina, on the Georgia border, and Jacksonville, just a few miles farther south, serving as the main entry points for winter visitors. Some stayed in the local hotels and enjoyed the sunshine and warm breezes, but others traveled up the St. Johns River by steamer in search of smaller, more isolated resorts. Green Cove Springs was among the prime beneficiaries of this first flush of postwar northern tourism. William Cullen Bryant of the *New York Post* toured the area in 1873 and mentioned its spring waters in his travelogue.[1] President Grover Cleveland was a visitor in the 1880s, and press accounts of his travels publicized the resort. The author of a tourist guide published in 1882 described Green Cove Springs as a charming village with several stores plus "two large, well-furnished and finely appointed hotels and numerous pretty homes."[2] As a result of positive reports about its facilities, the town prospered during the last quarter of the nineteenth century.

Providing lodging, food, refreshments, entertainment, and other ameni-

1. Tebeau, *History of Florida*, 271.   2. Barbour, *Florida for Tourists*, 111.

ties for vacationers became one of the main local occupations. Hundreds of local citizens found employment as hotel clerks, cooks, food servers, dishwashers, bartenders, laundresses, housekeepers, and baggage handlers. Since tourists are invariably a captive market, prices were on the high side. While this vacation spot remained popular with northern visitors, the owners of local businesses reaped handsome profits. Wages for service workers were generous in season, too, because the demand for labor was high and the limited population resources in the area restricted the supply of new recruits. When the winter season peaked, able-bodied children like Charlie Merrill and his young friends could even earn respectable wages for short periods in part-time service sector jobs. The disadvantage for workers and entrepreneurs alike was that these favorable conditions typically existed only from December through March.

By the 1880s Green Cove Springs was a pricey winter resort town. It boasted a popular natural spring that gushed water with a noticeable sulfurous odor; the water rose to the surface at a temperate seventy-five to seventy-eight degrees, and local publicists touted its medicinal benefits. According to many nineteenth-century health authorities, sulfur spring water possessed curative powers. The town's leading hotel asserted in its advertising literature that the spring water was effective in treating a long list of diseases – including rheumatism, gout, scrofula, dyspepsia, paralysis, neuralgia, nervous afflictions, erysipelas, kidney disorders, and general disabilities. Another establishment, the Palmetto House, was open throughout the year and addressed its brochures to "invalids" – mostly persons with rheumatism who presumably stayed for longer visits than most pleasure-seeking tourists. Live music and street dances entertained guests at night in season. An 1875 tourist guidebook covering the entire state of Florida billed Green Cove Springs as a southern version of Saratoga Springs, the fashionable spa in upstate New York where elite society gathered every summer for horse racing and healthful dips in mineral baths.[3]

During its heyday Green Cove Springs attracted a prosperous clientele to its two or three luxury hotels and private vacation homes. The rush started after the New Year and ran through February. At its height, the town swelled to a population of two or three thousand; but fewer than a thousand local residents and invalid guests remained through the sweltering summer months. Some vacationers enjoyed the mild winter climate and spring waters for a week or two and then boarded the steamers to head back north; other more prosperous families seeking total escape from snow and frost became semipermanent residents for several months, returning

---

3. *Guide to Florida*, at end of book, no page number.

year after year to vacation homes that they owned or leased for extended periods. The Borden family, which made its fortune in the dairy business following the introduction of condensed milk, made Green Cove Springs its regular winter headquarters, and built several comfortable villas for friends and relatives along the riverbank.

Before the turn of the century Florida's winter visitors generally preferred lakeside and riverbank locations to sandy beaches, in large part because regular steamboat service to inland resort centers was more convenient than overland trips to isolated beach towns with few amenities. In 1878, the mouth of the St. Johns River was dredged to permit the entry of large oceangoing steamboats out of Charleston and Savannah. In 1886, the Clyde Steamship Line initiated through service from New York to Jacksonville. The most popular passenger vessels stopped at Jacksonville and then traveled up the St. Johns River to put in at Green Cove Springs and other resort towns on a regular schedule in season. After 1880, railroad service between Savannah and Jacksonville improved, and more visitors arrived by train – especially from Chicago, St. Louis, and other rail centers in the Midwest. Many rail travelers then boarded steamers in Jacksonville for points farther south. Few vacationers traveled much beyond Lake Winder, a resort area about 150 miles south of Jacksonville and 15 miles east of Cape Canaveral, since it was the last docking for the larger steamships. Before rail trestles crossed the St. Johns River and new track was laid parallel to the eastern coastline in the 1890s, places like West Palm Beach, Boca Raton, Miami, and other southern Florida towns were isolated, thinly populated outposts on the southern frontier.

When Dr. Charles Merrill, age twenty-six, arrived in Green Cove Springs in 1882, he functioned as physician and drugstore proprietor, a standard combination in the nineteenth century. The town's population was around 350, according to the 1880 census, with a racial mixture of approximately 75 percent white and 25 percent black.[4] One of only two or three physicians in permanent residence, Dr. Merrill soon became – along with the owners of the local hotels, saloons, and mercantile firms – one of the town's most prominent citizens. A general practitioner, he generated income from two sources. First, he provided medical care to local residents. But serving the needs of the local citizenry was not the primary rationale for his residency, however. A second source of income came from tending to the wealthy northerners who spent brief winter vacations in the town, as well as those rheumatic patients who stayed for longer periods.

4. U.S. Census (1880), Manuscript Records, Clay County, Florida, on microfilm, roll 79-126. The census listed two physicians in Green Cove Springs in 1880: Walter Calmor, age 48, born in Kentucky, and Andrew Penike, age 58, born in Florida. Whether Calmor and Penike were still in practice when Merrill arrived two years later is unknown.

Boosters of the local economy sought to gain a competitive advantage over rival vacation spots by having a competent doctor on call around the clock. A physician's presence reassured vacationers in the event of sudden illness or a serious accident. A convenient drugstore was another advantage that helped lure discriminating guests to the area. In this regard, the management of Clarendon House, the classiest hotel in Green Cove Springs, was instrumental in recruiting Dr. Merrill after his graduation from Bellevue Medical School in New York City in 1881. During their seventeen years in the town, Charles and Octavia had two children; Charlie was born in 1885 and Edith arrived in 1892. A third daughter, Mary, was born in 1902 after the family had moved to Jacksonville.

Dr. Charles Merrill was a logical candidate for employment in Green Cove Springs because he was a Florida native, having grown up in the nearby Jacksonville area. His parents were among many northerners who came south after the Civil War in search of new opportunities. The southern economy was making the difficult adjustment from predominantly slave to uniformly free labor markets. Florida had cast its lot with the Confederacy, but its contribution to the war effort had been minimal, since the state's entire population – black and white – was less than 150,000 in 1860. Blacks constituted about 40 percent of the prewar population. Except for certain spots in the northwestern sector near Tallahassee, Florida's soils had not proved conducive to cotton cultivation, and prospective plantation owners had typically bypassed the state in favor of Alabama, Mississippi, Louisiana, and Texas. As late as 1880, the majority of the 270,000 Floridians listed in the census lived within one hundred miles of the northern border; remnants of Indian tribes and a few scattered white households shared the lower three-fourths of the peninsula.

Northern Republicans like the Merrills were certainly not greeted with open arms by local residents, but because Florida was thinly settled and local boosters wanted to spur the region's laggard economy, permanent settlers from almost anywhere were tolerably accepted. Charlie's grandparents on his father's side, Riley Mead Merrill and Abigail Livermore Merrill, had come to Florida in 1870. Abigail was born in Vermont in 1835; Riley, in western New York in 1827. They were married in Angelica, New York, a village near the state's southwestern border, in 1854. Soon after the ceremony, the couple moved to Conneaut, Ohio, a small town in the state's northeastern corner, just over the Pennsylvania border near Lake Erie. Riley Merrill was a teacher and reportedly served as the principal of a secondary school. Their first child, Charles Morton (Charlie's father), was born in 1856 – on Independence Day no less. In June 1863, just before the pivotal battle at Gettysburg, Riley joined the Union army and was sent to the western front; he entered as a sergeant major and later received promotion to the rank of captain. His Ohio regiment saw action in Tennessee and marched through Georgia with General William Sherman in 1864.

Riley's first exposure to the Deep South on the march with Sherman presumably made a favorable impression. This conclusion seems warranted because just six years later, after spending a few years in the oil fields of northwestern Pennsylvania, he and Abigail bought a farm near Phillips, Florida, a small community on the southeast side of the St. Johns River about five miles from the commercial center of Jacksonville.[5] What crops they cultivated is uncertain, but corn, a southern staple, and fruits and vegetables were likely planted and harvested. An orange grove covered at least part of the property – a fact revealed by family's recollections of the hard freeze in 1877 that severely damaged the citrus trees. To supplement the family's income, Abigail may have taught in the local elementary school for a number of years.

Like many Republicans who came south after the war, the Merrills seemingly had more liberal views on racial issues than most long-term residents. For example, Riley and Abigail periodically taught Sunday School in two rural black churches in the vicinity of Jacksonville. Their instruction was not confined to Bible stories, but included a smattering of the three Rs – reading, writing, and arithmetic. Since most former slaves had been denied the opportunity to become literate, those whites who volunteered to teach black children – and a few adults – how to read and write and make basic numerical calculations helped in upgrading the educational skills of the local black population. In short, Riley and Abigail took their responsibilities to a larger society quite seriously. (Three generations later, the second of Merrill's three children rediscovered that same socially responsible path and spent most of his middle age redistributing, through a philanthropic trust fund, a portion of his father's accumulated wealth to black colleges and universities in the southern states.)

Later in life, Charlie drew on his memories of Grandfather Riley and other family members. Most of his statements to prospective biographers (none of which ever made it into print) and other interviewers, who were retained by the family or by the firm of Merrill Lynch, about the people in his past were praiseworthy and positive, and often he was effusive. Old grievances against former friends and relatives, including divorced wives, were rarely mentioned, or were glossed over. Speaking ill of a relative would have violated this southern gentleman's code of chivalrous conduct.

---

5. Phillips was eventually incorporated into the city limits of Jacksonville. This section of town has disappeared from most city maps, but Phillips Highway over the St. Johns River has kept the name alive.

To criticize the past behavior of relatives, Charlie considered disloyal and dishonorable – and in bad taste.

The more appropriate response to prying personal questions, he thought, was to frame past deeds in the best possible light, skipping over the negatives large and small. The women in his family were always the prettiest, the men handsome and accomplished, and all were dedicated and hardworking – the usual family accolades. As a consequence, we never get a rounded view of the man and his relationship with family members from the statements he left for posterity. The positive feelings he expressed in his later years do, however, sound sincere and heartfelt. By the 1950s, when most of the conversations with friendly interviewers took place, Charlie was in a magnanimous mood; he had already made his millions and had achieved great successes in his business career – so why bother to complain about past trifles and minor annoyances?

Charlie's remembrances of his grandparents fell into a predictable, syrupy pattern. The first thought that came to mind about Grandfather Riley was his striking appearance: "My grandfather Merrill was one of the most handsome men I ever saw. Snow white hair – clear blue eyes." He continued the hagiography: "This old gentleman was amazing. A dirt farmer, surveyor, school teacher, and Bible student, he was so clean that he shone; I must have inherited from this fine old man my love for cleanliness." Riley's religiosity also made a strong impression on his grandson: "Often after the noon meal he would seat himself under an enormous tree and read the Bible he knew so well. My little sister, beautiful, sweet and smart, Mary, sometimes would crawl into his lap. In my mind's eye this is one of my favorite pictures."[6] When he matured, Charlie was equally handsome, and his reputation as a lady-killer and playboy was a factor that contributed mightily to his three failed marriages. Given this revelation, it probably comes as no surprise that he did not inherit from Grandfather Riley a similarly strong attachment to the Bible or organized religion, although he remained a church member and financial contributor.

In the early 1870s, Charles Morton Merrill left Florida to enroll in Maryville College, a school located about twenty-five miles directly south of Knoxville in the town of Maryville, Tennessee. This private, coeducational institution was founded in 1819 under the sponsorship of Presbyterians, presumably as a training ground for ministers and prospective ministers' wives. The president of the college was related to the Merrills in some way, which explains why Maryville was chosen over other alternatives. Less than 4 percent of the U.S. population sought college degrees in this era, so the very fact that Riley and Abigail Merrill sent their eldest

6. Keenan, "Chain of Fortune," 20-21.

child to Maryville indicates their strong interest in the rewards of higher learning and the prospects of social betterment.

Charles graduated in 1876, and was immediately employed in a sanitarium managed by distant relatives, Rachael and Silas Gleason, in Elmira, New York. The Gleason Sanitarium attracted patients based on the reputation of the Elmira Water Cure. (Keeping this brief work experience in mind, it seems, no accident that Charles ended up four years later closely associated with another town, Green Cove Springs, that boasted the presence of its own allegedly beneficial sulfur spring.) The twenty-two-year-old Charles then began his formal medical training at the University of Michigan in the fall of 1878, and transferred after one year to Bellevue College and Hospital in New York City, where he received his medical degree in 1881.[7]

Before leaving Maryville College, Charles became engaged to fifteen-year-old Octavia Wilson, another student at the school. Like many colleges and academies in the nineteenth century, Maryville was a boarding school that combined secondary work, college preparatory education, and regular college-level courses. Because of her youth, Octavia was likely enrolled in the secondary school curriculum. Many educational institutions that sought female students, especially in the South, were called finishing schools since graduates were not expected under normal conditions to seek higher degrees; parents expected their daughters to become sufficiently well educated to converse intelligently with educated men and thus attract already wealthy or upwardly mobile husbands. How many years Octavia was in residence at Maryville is uncertain, but when she announced her engagement, Octavia was a mere fifteen years old – five years younger than her fiancé. She returned home to Mississippi in the spring of 1876 to wait out her engagement, which promised to be extended. Octavia and Charles sustained their relationship over the next seven years, mainly through the facilities of the U.S. post office, and married about six months after his graduation from medical school.

Octavia Wilson was born in October 1861 on Round Hill Plantation near Lexington, Mississippi, a town of roughly five hundred whites and four hundred slaves located fifty miles north of Jackson, the state capital, and another fifty miles east of the meandering Mississippi River. Holmes County, where Round Hill farm was located, was prime cotton country. Octavia was the oldest of eleven children; she had one younger sister and nine younger brothers. As generally happens in households with so many

---

7. Curiously, son Charlie likewise spent the academic year 1906–7 at the University of Michigan in pursuit of his bachelor's degree; he took advantage of lax rules about dual-credit course work to enroll in introductory law courses. Charlie never earned enough units to receive a college degree, and he dropped the idea of becoming a lawyer.

children, the eldest daughter spent much time and energy helping her mother with siblings; doubtless Octavia was glad for the opportunity to attend boarding school in Maryville in her early teenage years.

Edward Wilson, her father, was twenty-eight years old when Octavia was born. A native of Georgia, he worked the family's 350-acre cotton farm. There were five slaves on the premises – two males aged thirty and twenty-three plus three females aged fifty, seventeen, and thirteen.[8] The value of his farm was estimated at $6,028 in 1860, while slaves and other transportable properties were put at $11,180.[9] With aggregate property holdings of more than $17,000 (about $340,000 in 1995 prices), the Wilson household fell into the upper-middling ranks of Holmes County planters. This Mississippi county boomed in the last antebellum decade. Property values more than tripled in the 1850s, with average prices per acre for farmland climbing from $5 in 1850 to $18 in 1860.[10]

Octavia remembered her father as having great respect for education – as witnessed by her enrollment in Maryville College. He taught all of his children something of what he knew about such academic subjects as algebra, Latin, and the classics. Edward joined the Confederate army as a private and participated in several major battles in the western theater. He was captured during the siege of Vicksburg, but later returned to the Confederate army in an exchange of prisoners. After the war, Edward worked the family's cotton fields and apparently made the transition from slave to hired labor reasonably successfully. But his aggregate assets shrank by more than two-thirds during the 1860s. Property values in Holmes County dropped sharply in the postwar era. The Wilson family farm was valued at only $2,500 in 1870 (roughly $30,000 in 1995 prices), a real decline of approximately 75 percent from its prewar valuation (slave holdings were completely eliminated, of course). Ten years after the war, Edward died at age forty-two from unknown causes, leaving behind a widow and eleven children under the age of fifteen.

Octavia's mother, Emily Grace Wilson, the daughter of a local planter with total properties of over $35,000 in 1860 ($700,000 in 1995 prices), had married Edward in 1856 when she was just seventeen. While her

---

8. U.S. Census, 1860, Manuscript Records, Holmes County, p. 22. The census taken in 1860 listed the names of all persons in a household, their sex and age, place of birth, and two estimates of property – real estate holdings and other movable properties. Net indebtedness was not recorded, however, so the net worth of households is unknown. Slaves were listed separately by owners; their names were not recorded – just age and sex, as well as whether black or mulatto.

9. The personal property valuation seems high. Slaves likely accounted for less than half of the $11,000. The two male slaves were probably worth about $1,500 each; the younger females had a market value of around $800; and the older female, depending on her health and skills, was worth somewhere between $300 and $500.

10. Pressly and Scofield, *Farm Real Estate*, values for counties in Mississippi.

husband served in the Confederate army, she was left to manage the farm. Following Edward's premature death in 1875, Emily was forced to reassume those duties again at age thirty-six. Fortunately, she had blood relatives in the area to provide assistance, and as the years passed her older children were able to shoulder a greater share of the economic burden; nonetheless, these were unaccustomedly difficult times for the Wilson household. The family's long-term economic prospects were not totally bleak, however, because they still owned a valuable piece of farmland. For the short run, however, expenses were curtailed. Octavia's failure to return to Maryville College in 1876 for the fall semester was one response to a tighter family budget.

Many years later, Charlie vividly recalled summertime visits to Grandmother Emily's farm in Mississippi during his boyhood. These trips into the heart of the Deep South in the 1890s made an indelible impression on him. He bathed momentarily in the myths and frustrations of the Lost Cause. Most southern white families like the Wilsons envisioned themselves as victims of malicious, self-righteous northern politicians, in particular radical Republicans who had supported the war, advocated immediate freedom for black slaves, and allegedly masterminded a vindictive reconstruction. The war had resulted in undeniable capital losses for whites who surrendered property rights in freed slaves, and it had disrupted the income stream linked to cotton production for half a decade or more.

No matter what their actual economic status in the postwar era, whether high or low, white southerners invariably believed that their existing income level would have, and should have, been much greater if northern political leaders had not illegally interfered with southern society in the 1860s. Thus, when families like the Wilsons referred to themselves as economically disadvantaged in the late nineteenth century, they were not speaking in absolute terms but rather were assessing their situation based on hypothetical "what-should-have-been" standards; the comparison was between existing levels and the much higher levels they uniformly believed would have been realized if the southern states had been allowed to secede peacefully and undisturbed. Frequently, these disappointments fit more logically into the category of psychic losses; still, the absence of imagined luxuries was strongly felt. Most whites remained convinced that everything had been better before the war, and that damn Yankees were responsible for depleting their assets and undermining their overall quality of life.

During Charlie's periodic visits to Mississippi, Grandmother Emily entranced her grandson with idyllic portraits of life on the plantation before the Civil War. A reverence for past accomplishments, whether real or imagined, was a characteristic of the southern persona. What Charlie later half-jokingly called the "moonlight and roses" treatment was a strong component of his introduction, or more aptly indoctrination, into the persistent myths associated with his family's southern heritage. He remembered that black workers on his grandmother's farm had been given classical names – Caesar, Scipio, Cicero, and Hannibal – a tactic employed by the family to identify with the accomplishments of ancient heroes rather than dealing with modern realities.[11] One physically deformed hunchback, who was malevolently named Sherman in remembrance of the hated general, occasionally carried Charlie around the yard on his hump. Those were Charlie's chief memories of summers in Mississippi. The message about the inherent inferiority and dependent nature of freed slaves, and indeed all African Americans, was one tradition absorbed by the millions of white children growing up in southern states in the late nineteenth and early twentieth centuries – Charlie Merrill included.

Former slaves lived in the Green Cove Springs area, too, so the customs linked to race were not unfamiliar to young Merrill. Later in life, he vividly recalled witnessing the public hanging of a black man on the courthouse lawn.[12] Yet there were significant differences between Deep South states and Florida. Cotton was never an important crop in northeastern Florida, but it still dominated the economy of Holmes County, Mississippi. Grandmother Emily's farm was also more isolated from the rest of the nation than was Green Cove Springs. Few northerners had visited Mississippi since Reconstruction. In Florida, in contrast, much of the Old South mentality had been abandoned as counterproductive; the state had re-oriented much of its economy toward recreational and vacation facilities for northern tourists. Racism was still prevalent, but white Floridians no longer viewed themselves as victims of monstrous northern transgressions. A trip to Mississippi, on the other hand, was a meaningful adventure for a boy from Green Cove Springs, for it carried him back into another world – and another more rigid and uncompromising mind-set.

Friends and relatives later claimed that Charlie's romantic and sentimental behavior was linked to his youthful exposure to his mother's Mississippi roots. In truth, family members probably exaggerated the importance of those visits in shaping his personality; nonetheless, the experiences undoubtedly reinforced certain attitudes passed down by his parents at home in Florida. These early influences were reinforced in later life by his choice of marriage partners. The last two of Charlie's three wives were native southerners. Hellen, the second, was from Jacksonville,

---

11. I made a fairly extensive search of black households in the Lexington area in the 1870 U.S. manuscript census, and none of the males gave these, or any other atypical names, to census takers. These classical names were bad jokes that blacks apparently did not appreciate, and given the option, they abandoned them when slavery ended.
12. Keenan, "Chain of Fortune," 33.

and the third wife, Kinta, hailed from New Orleans; these two spouses helped to sustain the values and attitudes associated with his southern upbringing.

To balance periodic family visits to Mississippi, Grandmother Emily visited Green Cove Springs on occasion as well. "How I enjoyed her 'visits' to our house," Charlie recalled. Sometimes she stayed for months. His father "adored" his mother-in-law, according to Charlie. Whether his father really felt that strongly will never be known, but Charlie certainly got the message loud and clear that concern for the well-being of close relatives deserved high priority. As an adult, he was often charitable to relatives down on their luck, and especially those facing expensive medical bills. Charlie remembered Grandmother Emily frequently reading in bed at night; decades later he could still name some of her favorite titles, including William Prescott's *Conquest of Mexico,* a history of Spanish imperialism in the Western Hemisphere published in 1843, and James Barrie's novel *Sentimental Tommy,* which came out in London in 1896.

Grandmother objected from time to time to Charlie's foul language around the house, and her complaints prompted Dr. Merrill to discipline his son to curtail the outbursts – on at least one occasion with a "whipping so famous in the Merrill family."[13] On another occasion, his father caught him experimenting with tobacco and locked Charlie up in room for a few hours. The admonitions were ineffective over the long run, however; like many men in the first half of the twentieth century, irrespective of class origins or educational levels, Charlie smoked cigarettes regularly as an adult. The doctors tried to limit his smoking after his first heart attack in 1944, but they were only partially successful. He also had the capacity to lose his temper, although that darker side of his personality rose to the surface almost exclusively in his private life with family members rather than in business relationships, where he typically kept his emotions under tight control.

Charlie was more reticent in volunteering information about his parents. About his relationship with his physician father, next to nothing was recorded – either positive or negative. Only slightly more has come down to us about his mother. She was more reserved and standoffish than her husband, and less involved in community affairs. As a result of her family and educational background, she had developed an interest in good literature, including Shakespeare and poetry.[14] Octavia had aspirations for her

13. Keenan, "Chain of Fortune," 18, 20.
14. Author's correspondence with Doris Merrill Magowan, June 8, 1994. Charlie's second son, James, was another family member with a flair for literature; indeed, he won numerous awards for poetry and was recognized as one of the nation's leading writers during the second half of the twentieth century.

children, especially for her only son, but the limited, seasonal nature of the market for her husband's professional services left her despairing about future prospects for her descendants. There are hints that she was at least mildly envious of the comfortable status of the wealthy families that annually visited Green Cove Springs. According to Charlie's recollections, his mother often expressed the hope that he might be able to climb the ladder of success and improve the family fortunes someday, but there were no specific career goals.

One piece of motherly advice stuck in his memory: "Charlie, you can get anything in the world you want, as long as you want it bad enough."[15] Whether those were Octavia's exact words, or whether indeed she ever made such a direct, unequivocal statement, makes little difference in this context. Over time, young Charlie got the message that his obligation to himself, to his parents, and to his extended family was to make something of himself when he grew up. He was expected to become somebody his mother would be proud of – preferably in a career that had the prospect of earning a higher income than a small-town doctor practicing in a Florida winter resort. In short, Charlie got his marching orders as a youngster, and he dutifully set out to live up to the high expectations of his parents and relatives.

An average student in the local grammar school, Charlie showed little aptitude for science and no inclination to follow in his father's footsteps. In his extracurricular hours, however, he displayed a knack for the merchandising end of his father's medical practice. Charlie became a helper in the drugstore on a part-time basis almost as soon as he was able to identify items in the inventory, concoct refreshing drinks at the soda fountain, and make correct change for customers. Clerking in his father's store on Saturdays, a few hours on Sunday, and after school on weekdays became part of his regular responsibilities during his preteen years. Much later he recalled the experience:

> The hours of labor were long; the store opened at 7 o'clock in the morning and closed, theoretically, at 12 o'clock at night; as a practical matter it was open almost 24 hours every day. The turnover was so slow, and the credit losses were so large, that notwithstanding a very high margin of profit, . . . there was a very poor return on the capital . . . , and practically no return if the business had been charged the proper salaries for the efforts and time of my father and myself.

The store stocked more than twenty thousand items, he recalled, and "my best recollection is that more than one-half of these items didn't sell once a year."[16] In the 1930s, when Charlie became deeply involved in the retailing of foodstuffs and merchandise through chain stores, he adopted a

---

15. Ibid., 30.   16. Quoted in Engberg, "History of Merrill Lynch," ch. 1, p. 4.

totally different strategy – one that emphasized high volume, low margins, and cash sales over credit.

In 1898, when Charlie was twelve, the family left Florida and moved to Knoxville, Tennessee. His father's medical practice was not as lucrative as previously, and Charles and Octavia decided to try their luck in a new location. In the second half of the 1890s the tourist trade in Green Cove Springs and other resort towns along the St. Johns River began to tail off. One man alone can be pinpointed as largely responsible for the sudden and profound shift in the destination of northern vacationers: entrepreneur Henry Flagler. While most of the changes would probably have taken place eventually without his intervention, Flagler's entrepreneurship unquestionably accelerated by a decade, perhaps by as much as a quarter century, the development of southern Florida as the nation's premier winter resort.

Flagler started his business career as a partner of John D. Rockefeller in petroleum refining and made his fortune in the postwar era. In the 1880s he became enamored with St. Augustine, the oldest continuously occupied Spanish settlement in the continental United States, and decided to make the remote beach town his regular winter retreat. A narrow-gauge railroad served St. Augustine in 1874, but there was no convenient through rail service; visitors took a steamer up the St. Johns River to Tocoi, about fifty miles south of Jacksonville and twenty miles beyond Green Cove Springs, and transferred to the train for a twenty-mile trip eastward.

After 1885, Flagler set his sights on developing tourism southward along Florida's eastern coastline, starting in St. Augustine. He concentrated his efforts on the construction of railroad track southward and the erection of grandiose hotels to lure well-heeled travelers. A direct rail line to St. Augustine from Jacksonville that terminated on the south bank of the St. Johns River opened in 1883. Flagler built the famed Ponce de Leon Hotel in the old Spanish town in 1888, and it proved an instant attraction for the rich and famous. A railway bridge crossed the St. Johns River in Jacksonville in 1890 and opened southern beach towns to uninterrupted rail service from all points north. The track reached Lake Worth and the resort town of West Palm Beach along its shoreline in 1894. Immense, lavish hotels catered to wealthy Americans escaping the northern winters. The Royal Poinciana boasted 540 rooms at five dollars per day and up – mostly up.[17] Flagler introduced gambling, illegal but visible nonetheless, at expensive nightclubs in West Palm Beach in the late 1890s. "Palm Beach became the great winter mecca for the status conscious of America," according to Flagler biographer Edward Akin.[18]

Vacationers headed for Florida sunshine in the 1890s tended to bypass

17. Rinehart, *Victorian Florida*, 155.   18. Akin, *Flagler*, 155.

the little resort towns along the banks of the St. Johns River, including Green Cove Springs. Northern Florida was subject to chilly weather from time to time, including freezing temperatures, but cool days were less common in the lower third of the elongated state. Below Cape Canaveral the weather was milder, and ocean swimming in temperate water was even possible in the dead of winter at many southern Florida beaches. With his medical practice in decline because of these shifts in the tourist trade, Dr. Charles Merrill and Octavia concluded that the outlook for maintaining their accustomed standard of living in Green Cove Springs was fairly bleak. Some rheumatic patients still arrived regularly, hoping that the spring water would alleviate their symptoms, but more and more pleasure-seeking vacationers failed to return to the Clarendon House and other local establishments.

In 1897 the doctor received a brief economic reprieve. Rather than staying in town during the winter months, he accepted a position as private physician on the yacht of George W. Childs-Drexel, a grandson of Anthony Drexel, the founder of Philadelphia's original Drexel and Company (later Drexel, Morgan and Company in the nineteenth century and Drexel Burnham Lambert, Inc., in the late twentieth century). Retaining the exclusive services of medical personnel for an entire winter season was not uncommon among wealthy travelers who had elderly or chronically ill family members on board their private yachts. The salary was $3,000 for three months, which was an immense sum in the late nineteenth century; if adjusted to reflect 1995 prices, the figure translates into approximately $60,000. The drawback was that Dr. Merrill was away from home for all or most of those three months, which was not exactly Octavia's idea of a positive family arrangement. With their financial assets suddenly improved, the Merrills decided to pull up stakes and move to a more promising location.

Why the Merrills chose Knoxville, Tennessee, as their new home is not fully known. They were favorably inclined toward the area since Charles and Octavia had met at Maryville College, only twenty-five miles away. Thus, the decision may have reflected, at least in part, an effort to recapture memories of the flowering of their romance a quarter century earlier. Another important factor was the city's rapid population growth and booming economy. Knoxville grew from 8,500 in 1870 to 22,500 in 1890, and another 10,000 residents were added before the end of the century.[19] The demand for professional services rose accordingly. Dr. Merrill set up his practice very much as he had functioned in Florida: operating a drugstore to complement his medical office.

19. Deaderick, *Heart of the Valley,* 74.

How Charlie reacted to Knoxville is unknown, but few children entering their teens are typically enthusiastic about a permanent move away from cherished school friends. What is certain about his experience is that he was employed in several odd jobs that first summer in Knoxville. He sold fruit, candy, chewing gum, and other inexpensive food items to soldiers at the nearby U.S. Army camp; when the local minor league baseball team was playing at its home field, he hawked goods to spectators. He was also probably drafted to serve as a part-time clerk in his father's drugstore. In retrospect, there seems little doubt that young Charlie exhibited budding entrepreneurial talents and that this behavior was encouraged by his doting parents. Of course, many American youngsters his age were similarly active in a series of remunerative extracurricular activities, and what Charlie accomplished was not necessarily anything unusual. Nonetheless, the fact remains that he was regularly involved from a fairly young age in income-producing activities; indeed, there were few periods in his life beyond the most elementary grades when he was not employed at least part-time – after school, on weekends, and during summer vacations. Charlie rarely idled away his time at any stage in his life.

For one reason or another, the doctor or Octavia or their children, or perhaps all in nearly equal proportions, were unhappy in their new hometown. The doctor's office was in a low-income, working-class area of Knoxville, and his patients were fewer, and probably less prosperous, than he had anticipated. Nonfinancial factors also could have been important. Perhaps the Merrills just missed their friends and acquaintances in Florida too much.

Whatever the reasons, the family decided within a year to return to Florida, and Jacksonville was the choice for a second new start. Charles had grown up in the area and attended its public schools. The family had taken the steamer downriver to visit Charles's parents in nearby Phillips on many occasions during the nearly two decades of residence in Green Cove Springs. The doctor had many friends among local medical practitioners, and he anticipated finding a niche for himself in the community. His former patients in Green Cove Springs were only a few hours away by steamer, and some were expected to make a day trip to the city for professional consultations. Charles also hoped to attract patients from the tourist hotels in season, given his history of treating prosperous northern clients. The Merrills bought a home in Riverside, an affluent suburb on the southwestern edge of town along the banks of the St. Johns River, in 1899.

Jacksonville was not hurt as severely as the small river resorts by the southward expansion of the railroad network in the 1890s, and in general, the city's economy had boomed in the last quarter of the century. The population rose from just under 7,000 in 1870 to more than 25,000 by the end of the century. Jacksonville possessed a fairly diverse occupational base, and it still attracted a loyal clientele to its hotels and amusements during the winter months. The famous St. James Hotel, opened in 1869 with five hundred rooms, was constantly being upgraded, including the addition of electric lights in the late 1880s, and it remained a local landmark and the destination of thousands of discriminating guests. But the city's continued rapid growth as a tourist mecca had been thrown into question by the increased popularity of newer resorts in St. Augustine and south Florida. Nonetheless, fashionable hotels continued to spring up in Jacksonville. At the turn of the century, for example, Henry Flagler authorized the construction of the Continental Hotel, with the aim of making it the city's most exclusive and expensive resort hotel.

Jacksonville had certain characteristics in common with Green Cove Springs, although everything was on a much grander scale. Florida's largest city had numerous medium-priced and luxury retail shops in its downtown section to appeal to the throngs of winter visitors. It was not strictly a typical southern town in the late nineteenth century, and its northern guests made it something of a cultural crossroads. Whether they arrived by water or rail, Jacksonville was usually the first stop of travelers entering the state. Although situated on the periphery of the Deep South, the city's residents embraced most of the basic tenets of white southern culture in this era, including a firm belief in the virtue of agriculture over industry, the importance of maintaining a sense of honor in personal and business affairs, and a certainty about the racial superiority of European stock to African Americans.

Charlie spent two rather uneventful years attending the area's public schools. At fourteen, he graduated from the elementary school in Riverside and entered Duval High School near the center of Jacksonville in the fall of 1900. Outside the classroom, he held a variety of part-time jobs to earn extra money for sundry entertainments and teenage self-indulgences. His most remunerative employment was as a newsboy for the *Florida Times Union*. Charlie had a regular delivery route and occasionally sold newspapers to the general public on street corners and places where large crowds gathered on weekends and holidays. Family legend has it that among his regular customers were a group of prostitutes who entertained clients at a local bordello and who reportedly gave him ten cents each week in tips for prompt service.

In May 1901, two years after the Merrills had returned to Florida, Jacksonville was devastated by a huge fire that consumed many of its prime business and residential districts. The flames leveled more than two thousand buildings, including the St. James Hotel and Flagler's recently constructed Continental Hotel, which was due to open the next month. About one-third of the city's residents were left homeless. The entire Riverside area, where the Merrills lived, was spared. Jacksonville's political and economic leaders rallied to rebuild, but they decided to concentrate on creating from the rubble a more diversified economic base. Tourism as a goal was not abandoned, but, on a relative scale, less emphasis was placed on reestablishing the purely seasonal aspects of the economy. Civic leaders could see the handwriting on the wall: the beach resorts farther south were destined to lure the majority of northern tourists now that the rail network was proceeding down the coastline.

The fire destroyed several public schools and severely disrupted the educational system. The lower and upper grades were temporarily consolidated into functional buildings. Duval High School, which Charlie had attended during that year, was one of the schools damaged by the fire. So that he could escape the anticipated fire-related disruptions in the local public schools, the Merrills decided to send Charlie to the college preparatory academy operated in conjunction with Stetson University in De Land, Florida, a small town about one hundred miles south of Jacksonville and twenty-five miles inland from the coast along the St. Johns River. Like many professional households, they possessed the financial resources to afford the added expense of private education.

Educational facilities had been erected on the site in 1883 by Henry De Land, a wealthy New Yorker, who was attracted by the mild climate and who later decided to build a fancy resort hotel, a surrounding service community, a preparatory academy, and a college – all in his own image.[20] Unable to generate sufficient tuition income to live up to the founder's lofty aspirations, Deland Academy and College was rescued by John B. Stetson, the prominent Philadelphia hat manufacturer, who became its new benefactor in 1889. Once he gained financial control, the Philadelphian changed the name to Stetson University. Despite the adoption of the more pretentious "university" title, Stetson retained the preparatory academy as an integral part of the institution. Like many boarding schools in this era, the preparatory division offered some military training for male students, including uniforms and a regimen of marching and drilling.

Charlie did not head for Stetson in the fall of 1901 faced with the prospect of attending school with total strangers. Joining him was Sam Marks, a school chum the same age from Jacksonville. Occasional roommates at Stetson over the next two years, Charlie and Sam remained good friends and periodic social companions for the rest of their lives. When Merrill died in 1956, Sam Marks was one of five trustees named to

20. Varnum, *Florida*, 71.

administer his trust fund. Indeed, many of the friends that Charlie acquired at the four different schools and colleges he attended between 1901
and 1907 played continuing roles in his personal and business life. Charlie
had a friendly, outgoing personality; always a master at informal networking, he used old-school ties to good advantage over the years.

In the fall of 1902, the Merrill family was struck by tragedy. The doctor
was the victim of a robbery and savage beating on a street not far from his
home in Riverside that left him incapacitated for the rest of his life. Two
black men from Jacksonville ventured into the suburbs and stalked Dr.
Merrill one night when he went out for an after-dinner stroll. Hit on the
back of the head with a heavy object by one attacker, he fell to the ground,
and a second man stomped on his throat. The robbers stole his wallet and
left him for dead. Dr. Merrill was found lying motionless in the street
later that night by another black man who alerted the doctor's neighbors.

Dr. Merrill's skull was fractured and his condition critical. Octavia
immediately called Charlie home from Stetson because the physician in
attendance thought the end might be near. Luckily, that prognosis was
overpessimistic. Within a few days, Charles, then forty-six years old, came
out of his coma and began the slow process of recovery – a recovery that
was never complete. What made the situation even more difficult for the
family was that Octavia, now forty-one, was expecting the birth of their
third child within weeks. A second daughter, Mary Drexel (named after
the wealthy family that had engaged Charles for the winter season a few
years earlier), was born in early November. Seventeen years younger than
Charlie, Mary never lived with him for more than a few weeks in summer;
she was more like a niece than a sister.

Charles's head injuries threatened not only to take his life but to undermine his economic and social standing as well. Confined to a wheelchair
for months, he lost patients to other physicians. Friends were sympathetic
about his plight, but rumors circulated that his mental processes and
consequently his medical skills had been impaired. Unable to work, his
income plummeted, and the family had to live off accumulated savings.
Octavia was busy caring for the new baby and Charles was away at school,
so neither was a prime candidate for contributing significantly to replacing
lost household income. Discouraged, the doctor closed his Jacksonville
office in 1903, moved the family across the St. Johns River to his father's
farm in Phillips, and contemplated his clouded future.

Within a few months, the doctor decided to return to an environment
that he knew well and in which he had previously prospered – the winter
resort town that catered to the well-heeled. Thanks to Flagler's visionary
entrepreneurship, West Palm Beach was rapidly emerging as the nation's
most exclusive winter mecca, and Charles decided to try his luck there.

Some of his former patients in Green Cove Springs regularly wintered in southern Florida, and through their recommendations and other referrals, he hoped to rebuild his medical practice. He also invested in local real estate, and the property rapidly appreciated in response to the population boom in the area after 1905. A few months after his arrival, he sent for his wife and daughters – Edith, age twelve, and baby Mary.

Money had suddenly and unexpectedly become a crucial issue in the Merrill household. From its secure upper-middle-class lifestyle, this professional family had swiftly fallen a notch or two, and the possibility that lower-middle-class status, or even impoverishment, might one day be its fate seemed all too real. To help make ends meet, Octavia opened and managed boarding houses, one for whites and another for blacks.[21] Family members subsequently remembered the frightening impact of this financial crisis, and they generalized from that experience to portray the Merrill family as a household that had struggled economically for years – a modified version of the rags-to-riches American dream. Debunking that myth does not detract by any means, however, from the serious difficulties confronting the Merrills in the aftermath of Charles's injuries. The fears were real in light of the family's diminished income, and there were no guarantees about the future.

Meanwhile, Charlie was finishing his second year at Stetson. All indications suggest that his two years at the school were rewarding, both socially and intellectually. He engaged in a series of pranks and had several disciplinary sessions with school authorities, but nothing seriously detrimental marred his record. Dancing was forbidden on the Stetson campus, a fundamentalist Baptist institution. Sometimes he and his buddies illicitly attended dances sponsored by a local Episcopal church; if caught by school officials, the boys were subject to rifle marches and other minor punishments for breaking the rules.

For reasons not fully clear, the Merrills concluded that Charlie should not complete his senior year at Stetson but transfer instead to one of the more established, elitist prep schools in the north. Perhaps they believed the curriculum at Stetson was insufficiently demanding, or they might have been concerned that the general reputation of the school, which had been in operation for only two decades, was too weak. Southern schools, at whatever level, were rarely considered beyond the region's borders as much more than second rate. Charlie was not a ball of fire in the classroom, but his academic record was sufficiently respectable to suggest that with a little more polishing and with more prestigious credentials, he might gain admission to one of the nation's premier private colleges or universities,

---

21. Merrill, *The Checkbook*, 6.

all of which were located in the North. His teachers at Stetson wrote sufficiently persuasive letters of recommendation to get him admitted to his new preparatory school: Worcester Academy in Massachusetts.

The fundamental reason for Charlie's transfer to Worcester was his family's burning ambition that he be given every opportunity to succeed in a financially rewarding career – preferably one of the recognized professions. Many of Dr. Merrill's northern patients had touted the necessity of a superior education for any young man who wanted to make his mark on the world. Inasmuch as Charlie showed little interest in medicine or religion, some family members had their sights set on a possible legal career. His teachers at Stetson believed Charlie had the intelligence and sufficient training to survive in the more demanding curriculum of most northern preparatory schools. Since colonial times, southern families had sent their sons northward to complete their education. Princeton was an early favorite because it was less distant than most prestigious northern schools. By the early twentieth century, when Charlie Merrill went north, certain prep schools had established long-standing reputations as feeders for a specific group of colleges and universities. Worcester Academy, for example, directed many of its graduates to Amherst College and the Ivy League schools.

The seventeen-year-old Charlie left in the fall of 1903 to attend prep school in Worcester, Massachusetts; he never resided in Florida again on a permanent basis, although he did purchase several vacation homes in the area over the years. During his college years, he only returned to Florida during breaks in the school calendar. Years later, after he had made his millions, Charlie developed a palatial waterfront resort complex called "Merrill's Landing" in West Palm Beach, where his parents had moved soon after his father's misfortune, and Charlie spent some of his time in southern Florida on a regular basis for the rest of his life.

3

A NORTHERN EDUCATION

When Charlie left for his senior year at Worcester Academy, just a few weeks short of his eighteenth birthday, he was primarily a product of southern culture. Except for one year in Knoxville, he had only occasionally been away from Florida and had never traveled to a northern state. His longest trips had been summertime visits to Grandmother Emily's cotton farm near Lexington, Mississippi – a community set squarely in the Deep South. Charlie was not, however, the typical southern teenager. He had grown up experiencing a milder version of southern culture – one that had been softened by outside influences.

In the first place, Charlie was continually exposed to northern influences in his family. His paternal grandparents were Yankees who had migrated to Florida after the Civil War. They had retained many customs and attitudes, which they passed down to the two succeeding generations. Moreover, Florida was less parochial than most states below the Mason-Dixon line because so much of its economy was oriented toward attracting and catering to winter visitors from the North. Sophisticated northern tourists reinforced the common view, conceded by most knowledgeable southerners, that established northern schools generally provided a superior education for young men seeking advancement in fields other than plantation agriculture.

By 1907, when Charlie ended his formal education without having earned an undergraduate degree, he had become more northern than southern, both in manner and orientation. He spent one year at Worcester Academy, two years at Amherst College, and a year at the University of Michigan. Over this period, his rougher edges were polished and honed. Traces of his southern upbringing remained, but, all and all, Charlie had assimilated into a clubby, class-conscious society that granted high status to men who achieved success in the pressure-packed world of business. Increasingly acculturated, he was eager to complete his immersion by joining what eventually became known as the "eastern establishment." A small cadre of business and political leaders, virtually all white Protestants educated at elite northern universities and colleges, mostly in New England, the so-called establishment exerted enormous power in shaping national events, both in politics and on the economic front, in the middle decades of the twentieth century.

Charlie's educational career did not start out grandly, however. His year at Worcester Academy was thoroughly miserable. Coming to a new school to complete the senior year would be a difficult transition for any teenager even under the most favorable conditions. Unlike his time at Stetson, where his hometown chum Sam Marks was also enrolled, Charlie knew no one at Worcester before his arrival and soon realized that he had little in common with most of his new classmates. His southern accent was distinctive and branded him straightaway as someone intellectually and socially suspect. His academic training was not as sound as that of other students, which reinforced the negative stereotype. At Worcester, Charlie was always playing catch-up in his studies.

Elitist, all-male New England prep schools were modeled on their English counterparts. The sons of wealthy and upper-middle-class families dominated, with a sprinkling of scholarship students from professional households with inadequate financial resources – such as the Merrills. Most students were carefully attuned to social and class origins in selecting friends and forming cliques. Charlie was predictably the target of ostracism and snobbery because of his southern background and, to compound the problem, because he was the recipient of financial aid. His housing assignment was a small room at the top of the stairs on the dormer floor of the residence hall, where he lived in cramped quarters with other students on scholarships. Today millions of students at private high schools and universities receive financial aid with little stigma attached, but less tolerant attitudes prevailed in the early twentieth century at elite prep schools in New England. The Merrills did not possess the wealth and family background that most of Charlie's classmates esteemed simply as a matter of course. In this class-conscious, inbred environment, he felt inferior – financially, intellectually, and socially.[1]

In this era few people felt the need to apologize for blatant discrimination directed toward other races, genders, religions, cultures, or classes. Blacks, women, Catholics, and practicing Jews were not welcome at the school.[2] Worcester had enrolled its share of southerners over the years, so

---

1. According to Charles Merrill Jr., his father frequently spoke about the constant humiliation he felt at Worcester and at Amherst, in large part because of his scholarship status. Author's correspondence with Charles Merrill Jr., April 9, 1994.
2. Some students who were at least partially Jewish in terms of ethnicity did attend Worcester in this era. Take, for example, Clarence Dillon, one of Merrill's Wall Street rivals in the 1920s.

Charlie's origins were not entirely exotic; nonetheless, like most newcomers from below the Mason-Dixon line, he was a fish out of water during his first year in the school.

To earn extra money to cover at least a portion of his living expenses during the school year, Charlie became the campus sales representative for a men's clothing company. This type of agency arrangement was not unusual at private boarding schools. Several clothiers that catered to prep school and college students, but that had no accessible retail outlet, signed agreements with students living on campus. Working on commission, they solicited orders based on flyers and catalogs from fellow students; it was a riskless financial arrangement for agents because they made no investment in inventories. Selling clothes also gave Charlie the opportunity to meet a cross section of the student body and make new friends, and he did make some headway over the course of the year, particularly with younger students in the lower grades.

In addition to pursuing his studies and his part-time sales job, Charlie participated in school athletics. The prep school ideal was to nurture young men both in the classroom and on the playing field. Most educators believed organized sports were character builders. Weighing under 130 pounds, Charlie was a second or third stringer on the football team, and he only occasionally took the field in games against outside opponents. On the baseball team, he was the regular centerfielder, which suggests reasonably good running speed and a decent throwing arm. His batting average and run production in this "dead" ball era, which meant few home runs, are anybody's guess.

By the spring of 1904, Charlie had not accumulated enough academic units to earn a diploma. A very unhappy young man, he investigated opportunities to start afresh at a new school the next fall.[3] Worcester officials agreed to grant his degree in absentia so to speak, if he successfully completed his first year of college at some approved institution of higher learning. Charlie momentarily considered applying to the architectural school at Cornell University in Ithaca, New York. In the end, he accepted the advice of mentors at Worcester to apply to Amherst College, a liberal arts institution located about fifty miles away in a rural setting near the center of the state.

That summer Charlie did not return home to join his family but re-

---

Dillon's father, Samuel Lapowski, was a Polish Jew who arrived in the United States in the 1860s and married the daughter of recent Swedish immigrants who were Lutheran. Their three children were all raised as Protestants. Samuel Lapowski changed his name to Dillon, his mother's maiden name, after the turn of the century.

3. Merrill felt little attachment to Worcester Academy and gave the school no substantial monies. He sent his older son to Deerfield, where his old friend, Frank Boyden, was headmaster, and his younger son to Lawrenceville.

mained in the northeast to earn money for the upcoming school year. A train ride to Florida was long and costly, and Charlie decided that he could ill afford to spend either the time or the money. Instead, he had lined up a potentially lucrative summer job through Heath White, a Worcester classmate, who had worked as a waiter the previous summer at a resort hotel on Peaks Island, three miles off the coast just outside Portland, Maine. Charlie felt comfortable in the resort environment because it resembled the atmosphere in Green Cove Springs. Other college students were likewise employed in various service-sector jobs on Peaks Island, and they formed a friendly peer community. Charlie later remembered, in particular, the attractive young women who worked on the island for the summer months. The vacationers, almost exclusively from upper-class households, were similar in most respects to the tourists who came to Florida in winter. As compensation, Charlie received room, board, and modest wages. Augmenting these were the often-generous tips from satisfied customers. Charlie saved eighty dollars over the summer – roughly sixteen hundred dollars in 1995 prices. That money was enough to cover most of his living expenses at college during the first semester, which the college catalog estimated at ninety for students on limited budgets.[4]

Today, Amherst College ranks as one of the nation's elite small colleges, on a par in terms of the academic credentials of its student body with the leading colleges and universities in the northeast, including the Ivy League schools. In the first decade of the century, when Charlie attended, its reputation was solid, but the college had not yet reached the level of other top schools with regard to the rigor of its overall academic program. Amherst College was established in 1821 as a private, all-male institution (women attend today) under the sponsorship of traditional Congregationalists who were concerned about the repeated exposure of young men to immoral and unorthodox urban influences at many of the other prominent colleges in the region. It was planned, in particular, to serve as an alternative to Harvard, where students living in Cambridge had easy access to Boston's nontraditional ministers and free-thinking intellectuals. In that more cosmopolitan setting, there were also more taverns and prostitutes to lure the weak-willed into decadence and immorality. Parents who wanted to protect their vulnerable sons from these temptations were predisposed toward Amherst.

Gaining admission to Amherst in 1904 was not difficult for candidates with the proper background. An applicant's prior educational training was

---

4. The cost of attending Amherst in 1904–05 was estimated at $291 on the low end of the scale and $400 on the high end, with more desirable housing and a more expensive diet accounting for most of the price differential.

the most important factor and a critical barrier for many potential candidates. A young man needed exposure to some of the key elements of a classical education, which the New England prep schools invariably provided. In addition to testimonials about their good moral character, all new students were expected to have a solid foundation in Latin, Greek, English, mathematics, and history. Depending on whether the candidate planned to major in the arts or the sciences, he also needed to demonstrate proficiency in a mix of collateral courses, including French, German, physics, and chemistry. Entrance examinations were administered on campus in June and September, with test scores reported two weeks later. In addition, there was an alternative method of gaining admission, as specified in the catalog: "from certain preparatory schools of approved standing, certificates of fitness to enter College are received in place of entrance examinations."[5] This latter route is how Charlie gained admission.

Worcester was one of the recognized feeder schools for Amherst. Its teachers were respected by Amherst officials, and their recommendations were sufficiently positive to get Charlie admitted. He was granted financial aid in light of his father's diminished earnings after the robbery and beating. Tuition was $55 per semester – $110 annually. Amherst had $12,000 available annually for scholarships, and it made awards between $50 and $150 based on financial need.[6]

In the early twentieth century Amherst was a tight community of 400 to 500 students plus around forty faculty: a Camelot largely detached from the troubles of the world. Nearly half the student body hailed from Massachusetts, while one-fifth came from New York. Charlie was one of a handful of students from the southern states, and the only enrollee from Florida during his two years at Amherst. The college's curriculum was fairly impressive; it mixed many of the elements of a classical education – Greek, Latin, and philosophy, for example – with numerous modern courses such as astronomy, botany, economics, geology, and public speaking. The college had thirty departments offering courses, the majority staffed by a single instructor. Most professors had some advanced training. Several had traveled overseas, particularly to German universities, for graduate work. Teaching, not scholarly production, was the primary mission of this faculty.

5. Amherst Catalog, 1904–5.
6. In the introductory essay to *The Checkbook*, Charles Merrill Jr. states that the sale of two lots in West Palm Beach provided the money for his father's tuition to Amherst in 1904. Whether the family paid full tuition is uncertain since the sources are inconclusive. According to Jencks and Riesman, *Academic Revolution*, 138, Amherst and Berea in Kentucky are two colleges with a long tradition of offering comprehensive financial aid packages to needy applicants, including scholarships, loans, and employment opportunities. Such financial considerations may explain why Charlie's mentors at Worcester were so keen on his applying to Amherst.

Following the hallowed tradition of in loco parentis, administrators provided, at least in part, substitute parental guidance and discipline for students living away from home. Student behavior was governed by a long list of rules, which most students resented as impingements on their personal freedom. At Amherst all students were required to assemble for morning chapel Monday through Saturday at 8:15 sharp. On Sunday, they attended the church of their choice in the surrounding area. Students were allowed only a few unexcused absences from scheduled classes. Those who accumulated too many demerits for absences and tardiness were subject to severe penalties, including suspension for a semester or even expulsion.[7]

Extracurricular activities were an important aspect of student life in this era. Amherst professors typically served as advisers to students working on the campus newspaper or the yearbook and to clubs of all varieties. Faculty families periodically invited students into their homes, which were adjacent to campus, for refreshments and small talk. They also acted as chaperones at dances and other social functions. The primary goal of the institution was to provide comprehensive training, in and out of the classroom, for young men seeking advancement in professional or business careers. Despite the paternalistic overtones, the system was generally successful in preparing students for careers; most Amherst graduates left ready to assume adult roles.

The intellectual and social interchange between students and faculty at Amherst made a deep impression on Charlie. Years later, he fondly remembered faculty members in glowing detail. Like most of his peers, he had a stereotypical view of professors. From the student perspective, most academicians were knowledgeable persons who displayed peculiar habits or obvious eccentricities. Some were chronically absentminded; some cultivated long beards or groomed themselves differently than other adults; others behaved oddly at times, and so on. What stuck in Charlie's memory were the interesting stories about his former professors – not malicious gossip but anecdotal accounts of humorous statements and out-of-the-ordinary events. But his respect for the faculty was sincere. He later gave the college $300,000 to construct eighteen apartments in five buildings on the east side of the campus for younger members of the faculty.[8]

To overcome the disadvantages of its isolation from city life and to stay competitive with rival institutions, Amherst allowed fraternities on campus

---

7. Surprisingly, neither the college catalog nor the student handbook listed any regulations regarding alcohol consumption on or off campus, nor did they state any rules with regard to entertaining women in the dormitories or nearby fraternity houses. Freshmen were not allowed to smoke on the streets of Amherst village before February 22, however.
8. Merrill stipulated that the apartment complex provide a playroom for children, a large common room with a kitchenette for entertaining other faculty and students, and a laundry room.

– a point of no small consequence in the life and career of Charlie Merrill. According to educational and social historian Helen Horowitz, the hedonistic and anti-intellectual attitudes of the majority of students who joined fraternities had seriously undermined the scholarly mission of most all-male and coeducational colleges and universities, especially the private institutions, by the end of the nineteenth century.[9] In the long-drawn-out battle between faculty and students over the purpose of higher education, students, at least where men were present, had mostly triumphed. At Amherst, President Edward Hitchcock tried to eliminate fraternities from the campus in the mid-nineteenth century, but the effort failed.[10] In an attempt to steer students away from excessive drinking and idleness, Hitchcock promoted myriad extracurricular activities, including athletics and numerous societies.

The emerging collegiate culture that student leaders, most of whom were fraternity men, carved out was antithetical to scholarship beyond the maintenance of minimal standards. As a rule, only the independents, non-fraternity members, who were generally denigrated by the majority as grinds – in the 1990s we casually call them nerds – genuinely sought to expand their store of knowledge. Most fraternity men doubted if the standard curriculum would be of much value in the larger business world that they planned to enter after graduation. As a consequence, they avoided the challenges of difficult course work and tried instead to enroll in gut courses taught by the most lenient graders. Many directed their energies into extracurricular activities – sports, musical societies, drama clubs – plus informal socializing.

Because relatively few students were concerned with high grade point averages, the competition for grades was less in evidence than it is today. Professors handed out As and Bs sparingly, and they assigned Ds, Es, and Fs with little hesitation.[11] Most turn-of-the-century students believed that earning a so-called gentleman's C was perfectly acceptable and, indeed, in most cases, preferable; it signaled that the student had been sufficiently responsible to stay current with the class, but that he had not gone over-board and tried to outshine his classmates. Since many professors showed little mercy in grading exams and assigned work, the fear of flunking out was constant for students with weak backgrounds or poor study habits. According to Horowitz, most men believed that cheating was acceptable

9. Horowitz, *Campus Life*, 3–55. The intellectual life at all-female institutions, in contrast, was typically more challenging, particularly in the northern states.
10. Horowitz, *Campus Life*, 38, 53.
11. The grade of E was common on transcripts in the early twentieth century; today it would be the rough equivalent of a D− or F+ grade. At Amherst College, an E was insufficient to earn hour credits for course work.

behavior if the goal was to avoid probation or dismissal for inferior performance. Only students who aspired to postgraduate work had a strong incentive to achieve a high grade point average. Meanwhile, students who were not burning the midnight oil had more free time for athletics, clubs, and socializing with classmates and girlfriends.

Charlie had a respectable, if unspectacular, academic record during his two years at Amherst, although he demonstrated noticeable academic improvement his sophomore year. He maintained just above a C average during the 1905–6 school year; two less than satisfactory marks turned up on his transcript – E grades (50 to 59 percent, not passing) in French and physics courses. The second year he moved up into the C+ to B− range overall, with passing marks in every course he attempted. The Amherst curriculum was surprisingly modern, meaning not overwhelmingly classical. For example, Greek language courses were no longer required. In addition to Latin, which was still a mainstay, Charlie took courses in English, French, German, mathematics, physics, chemistry, physiology (biological systems), history, biblical literature, and public speaking. His only A grade was earned in the first semester of chemistry during his sophomore year; but something went wrong in the second half of the course sequence because he dropped to a D in the spring term. His best subject was English, where he started with a C in the fall of 1904 but earned solid Bs over the next three semesters. Charlie also earned Bs in mathematics, public speaking, history, physiology, and German. In this era before grade inflation, Charlie's overall record at Amherst was reasonably satisfactory, and it was especially satisfactory for a young man who was active in fraternity life and other extracurricular activities.

Either as a result of his training at Amherst, or perhaps simply as a result of cumulative polishing, Charlie developed outstanding writing skills that made him an effective communicator in business correspondence and in-house memos. He thought logically and systematically, and his prose was clear and concise – as well as sparkling and humorous on occasion. His solid performance in the only math course on his transcript is not surprising since he eventually developed a real knack for analyzing complex financial data. Without any formal education in business subjects, which were not considered legitimate academic subjects at most elite colleges and universities, he later discovered that he was able to digest an enormous amount of information related to income statements, balance sheets, and a whole array of financial instruments. Educators have justified liberal arts curricula for generations because of their ability to teach students how to think critically and analytically in a wide range of real-life situations. That philosophy certainly seems to have lived up to its promise in the education of Charlie Merrill.

Charlie joined the Chi Psi house within a few weeks of arriving on campus. His acceptance by fraternity members was a welcome change from his cool reception at Worcester. Charlie soon became a fraternity man par excellence – in both the more positive and more negative connotations. Wine, women, and song plus undying loyalty to fraternity brothers were high priorities in his life. He loved the hedonistic culture of college life. The first year he lived in a dorm, but the next fall he moved into the Chi Psi house, where Edward "Suds" Sudbury became his closest friend. Charlie took all the hoopla about brotherhood very seriously.

He loved a good party, with lots of booze and plenty of opportunities for flirting with sexy, entertaining women. He was blessed with the handsome good looks to attract a constant parade of female admirers. Men enjoyed his conversation and companionship as well. A classmate recalled: "He had a friendly manner, was companionable and interesting – and had a 'million-dollar' smile which was unaffected, a ready one, a wide grin."[12] Charlie succumbed frequently to social diversions throughout his life. Even after his first heart attack at the age of fifty-nine, and long after his third and final divorce, he relished the companionship of attractive women, whether married or single. Through it all, however, and despite his frequent partying and entertaining, he rarely allowed liquor or alluring women to divert his attention from the demands of business affairs.

To cover some of his expenses, Charlie was employed at several jobs during the school year. Following up on his profitable experience as a representative for a clothing firm at Worcester Academy, he signed an agreement with Renison & Coe in nearby Springfield that called for a sales commission of 15 percent, with one-third of that figure paid in clothes for his personal wardrobe. Thus, irrespective of tight finances, he was invariably well dressed and sported the latest styles. During his second year at Amherst he earned a tidy sum that paid a substantial share of his annual expenses.[13] In addition, he worked as a waiter. The college did not operate dining halls for students; they were required to make boarding arrangements with local families. Charlie persuaded a woman living about a mile and a half from campus to provide food service for about two dozen students, mostly his Chi Psi brothers. He waited tables and received free meals as compensation.

All-male Amherst was distant from any big city, but students still had

12. Keenan, "Chain of Fortune," 63.
13. Keenan, "Chain of Fortune," 64, lists Charlie's earnings in the 1905 school year as $1,300, but that seems far too high under the circumstances, for it converts into more than $25,000 in 1995 prices. Maybe the correct number was $130, which converts into around $2,600 in 1995 prices, or perhaps, alternatively, his sales volume was $1,300, which would have produced commissions of nearly $200 ($4,000 in 1995 prices). The latter two numbers seem more in line with the probable upper limits for a part-time sales position.

opportunities for a social life with the opposite sex. Two so-called sister schools, Smith College in Northampton and Mount Holyoke College in South Hadley, single-sex colleges that enrolled young women, were within ten miles of Amherst. An electric street railway connected Amherst with Northampton, Holyoke, and surrounding towns. Their proximity made it relatively easy for Charlie and his friends to arrange dates for weekend dances and other social occasions. The automobile was still an expensive novelty in 1904, and few students possessed such ostentatious luxuries.

Generally speaking, female students took their studies more seriously than did college men, in part because alcohol and athletics were less important in their daily lives. Some young women were extremely studious and avoided the social scene altogether. Others were devoted to their books during the weekdays and sought diversions on weekends. A third group was more interested in the extracurricular and social attractions of college life and had little time for classwork. A fair share of the most serious students at these private colleges used their knowledge to pursue careers in teaching, social work, and other professions that did not blatantly discriminate against women.[14] Because combining a career with marriage and a family was culturally unacceptable for most American women, these female college graduates rarely married.

For the majority of young women, however, the college experience was a time to enjoy their freedom and search for a husband. Weekend trips to nearby men's colleges were common. A fair number of postgraduate marriages to the "right" people were the result of this periodic intermixing of students at Amherst, Smith, and Mount Holyoke, which was exactly the outcome that many parents had anticipated. Charlie fell in love with Marie Sjostrom, a student at Smith, during his sophomore year – not an uncommon occurrence; they became engaged a year or so later and came within an eyelash of marrying.

His relationship with Marie, a pretty blond, consisted mainly of a series of weekend dates usually centered on some organized function at the college – an athletic contest or a dance. Women students who arrived for the weekend typically stayed in approved rooming houses, where the hosts were expected to enforce strict rules about visitation and late hours. While some young women were sexually active, few were genuinely promiscuous. The majority were determined to maintain their virginity until marriage, or at least until the announcement of their engagement. Charlie took Marie to the sophomore hop and junior prom at Amherst, as well as numerous fraternity parties.

---

14. Horowitz, *Campus Life*, 193–219. On the other hand, women at coeducational schools were more likely to marry and less likely to pursue careers after graduation.

During the Christmas break in his second year, Charlie received news about the death of his little sister Mary, who had just turned three, in West Palm Beach from diphtheria. He was spending the vacation with the family of Suds Sudbury in Mount Vernon, New York, when word arrived on January 2, 1906. After her death, family members became convinced that, if they had still been living in the Jacksonville area, where medical facilities were more accessible, little Mary would likely have been saved. The story is pertinent because many years later Charlie recounted the story to his son Charles, who had expressed liberal political leanings and had questioned his father's rationale for accumulating such enormous wealth. In a letter that defended his upper-class status and lifestyle, Charlie remarked, "The fact my father knew how to save his daughter's life, and yet, because of limited finances did not possess the equipment, crushed him." Then he added the punchline: "Money, of course, is not everything, but, my friend, emergency after emergency comes up in this world of ours, in which for a few brief moments, at least, and maybe longer, money is the equivalent of everything."[15]

In truth, given the state of medical knowledge in 1906, nothing more probably could have been done in Jacksonville to fight Mary's illness than in southern Florida, or anywhere else in the world for that matter. Proven drugs or treatments did not exist. Family members felt guilty about Mary's early death, and their escape into an "if-only" fantasy was one way to relieve the pain; it also gave them an outlet for expressing their frustration at falling out of the ranks of the upper middle class. Of course, these considerations in no way invalidate Charlie's central argument: that adequate financial resources in a medical crisis and access to the best hospitals can often make a significant difference in the treatment and cure of the seriously ill.

In the second semester of his sophomore year, Charlie became involved in a confrontation with powerful alumni who played a continuing role in overseeing affairs at the Chi Psi house. A fraternity brother was found guilty of cheating on an examination, and in accordance with college rules, the student was immediately expelled. Several members of the governing committee for the local Chi Psi chapter, all of whom were Amherst graduates, plus several current members of the house wanted to expel the offender from the fraternity as well. Clarence Birdseye Sr., a New York lawyer and father of the frozen foods innovator, spearheaded the movement for expulsion; the aim presumably was to make an example for other undergraduates who might be tempted to wander from the straight and narrow. Charlie was incensed; he thought these purists were merely adding

---

15. Keenan, "Chain of Fortune," 79.

insult to injury for no good reason. He believed that, by turning their collective backs on a fallen brother, members would be acting in direct violation of their initiation oath to support each other in good times and in bad. Joined by Suds Sudbury and a few others, Charlie fought the proposed expulsion from the fraternity.

A compromise solution emerged. The guilty party was suspended for five years, rather than irrevocably thrown out of the fraternity. Charlie claimed a de jure victory, but in reality it represented no victory at all since it was doubtful that someone five years older, by then in his mid- to late twenties, would choose to return to the fraternity. Charlie lost some friends over the issue and incurred the wrath of certain members of the Chi Psi governing board. Birdseye supposedly made it widely known that he would prefer that Charlie not return to Amherst for the fall semester, although there is no evidence that he exercised any influence with school officials on that score.

The issues surrounding the cheating case at Amherst are important because they reveal how Charlie responded to situations that brought into conflict competing principles. Which principle took precedence in this instance was the question – society's condemnation of cheating on exams, or Charlie's personal loyalty to friends while simultaneously upholding his pledge of eternal brotherhood? In the spring of 1906, Charlie chose the latter. There probably is no simple explanation for this choice, although several are worth consideration. First, Charlie might have cheated on occasion himself and felt sympathy for a fellow student who unfortunately had been caught red-handed. Second, even if he had never cheated, he almost certainly knew others in the fraternity who had, and he may have believed that censuring one person when so many others were equally guilty was hypocritical.

A third possibility is that Charlie may have felt the new honor code was too strict and uncompromising. Amherst adopted this system of student self-monitoring in 1904 in imitation of codes at West Point Academy, the University of Virginia, and a few other schools around the nation. It relieved professors from being solely responsible for preventing cheating. At most institutions students were required not only to live up to the code in their own conduct but were also honor bound to report any suspected violations by peers. Students appointed to an honor council adjudicated most of the alleged cases of cheating, as well as cases of lying and stealing, and those found guilty were in most instances summarily dismissed from the college, frequently without the possibility of subsequent reinstatement. Like everyone at Amherst, Charlie had been required to sign an agreement acknowledging his acceptance of the honor code as a condition of enrollment at the start of his sophomore year. Students particularly objected to provisions obligating them to turn in the names of suspected friends to authorities, claiming that the rules converted them into perpetual spies. Thus, Charlie's defense of his fraternity brother against powerful alumni and some members of Chi Psi who took the honor code very seriously was perhaps a rebellion against the honor code's exceedingly moralistic demands.

Lastly, he may have taken into account the motives of the cheater. If, for example, the student was simply trying to avoid flunking out of school and seeking thereby to continue the enjoyment of the multiple benefits of college life, then Charlie might have seen the cheating as justified. Horowitz's conclusions in *Campus Life* seem apropos in this context: "College men placed a high value on mutuality, on the bonds that united them with each other and against the faculty." With regard to students who broke the rules, "they refused to judge each other as they were judged and offered mutual aid to those threatened with being caught and sympathy for the convicted."[16] Charlie certainly had sympathy, although it should be noted that his dispute was not with college officials but strictly with the membership of his own fraternity.

Years later, when Charlie reflected on his stance during this episode, he expressed regret at his actions. He concluded in retrospect that he had backed the wrong set of principles; the maintenance of high standards for truth and honesty should have taken priority over dreams of perpetual brotherhood. Birdseye and the others had not acted maliciously and improperly after all in their efforts to rebuke a dishonest member of Chi Psi. Once Charlie had become involved in the securities field, where standards of truthfulness were decidedly low in many quarters, he realized the importance of scrupulously sticking to the high road in all matters, large and small.

When school ended in the spring of 1906, Charlie headed for West Palm Beach to be with his family. He spent that summer working in journalism. His father had suggested to the owner-manager of the *Tropical Sun,* the local newspaper, that he take a long vacation in Arizona to seek relief from tuberculosis. In addition, he had nominated his son as a suitable replacement.

Charlie got paid $17 per week – about $340 in 1995 prices – to act as managing editor, reporter, occasional typesetter, and business manager. In his free time, he played baseball three times a week with the local semiprofessional team. Although he had absolutely no journalistic experience, he

16. Horowitz, *Campus Life,* 13.

did a creditable job, and the word soon got around about his solid performance. Years later he recalled the outstanding training that he had received at the newspaper; moreover, he explained, "I learned human nature."[17] At summer's end, Charlie had several employment opportunities in journalism. "I am about the luckiest boy you ever heard of," he wrote Suds Sudbury in September.[18] "I have the offer of a position as business manager of the Greenville, Miss. *Daily Times* at $75 (per month) to begin with and double if I make good." He added, "Greenville is a town of 20,000 population, the second largest in Mississippi, and the *Times* is a good daily." Charlie also had the option of staying in West Palm Beach with the *Tropical Sun* or taking charge of a trade paper in Miami. The job offers were tempting, but he and the family decided that he should continue his pursuit of a college degree.

In the fall, Charlie did not return to Amherst but transferred instead to the University of Michigan in Ann Arbor, where his father had spent the academic year 1878–79. His extended family, particularly on his mother's side, played a major role in the decision to transfer. Grandmother Emily Wilson convinced Charles and Octavia that her grandson was born to be a lawyer, and she backed up her strong opinions by raising most of the funds necessary from relatives in Mississippi to pay full tuition at Michigan. What made the school so attractive was a special program that allowed juniors and seniors to enroll in introductory law courses that counted simultaneously toward their bachelor's degree and a law degree. Amherst had no law school. Michigan's academic reputation in the early twentieth century was certainly equal to and probably higher than that of any other school that Charlie had ever previously attended.

The decision to attend Michigan was a strategic career move, dictated in large part by Dr. Merrill's inability to recover completely from injuries sustained three years earlier and to resume earning an income that would support an upper-middle-class lifestyle. Octavia had taken over the management of two boarding houses, one catering to whites and the other to blacks, in order to help make ends meet. Money was short, but the situation was not desperate. If things had been worse, Charlie would have been pressured to drop out of college and take one of the positions open to him in journalism. Instead, the extended family decided to pool its resources so that he could remain in college, but hereafter with a specific career goal in mind: the law. Charlie reluctantly agreed. He had no personal aspirations to become a lawyer. That profession was chosen because other options – physician and minister in particular – seemed uninviting. Charlie was willing to enter a legal curriculum, and that was a satisfactory

17. Hecht, *Legacy of Leadership*, 18.   18. Keenan, "Chain of Fortune," 86.

response for ambitious family members who held the purse strings. Despite the flap at Chi Psi, there is no evidence that Charlie wanted to transfer from Amherst to another school. In his letters to fraternity brothers over the next year, he constantly expressed his sorrow at his failure to return for his junior year. Moreover, his sweetheart, Marie Sjostrom, was still at Smith College.

When Charlie left for the University of Michigan in late September 1906, his personal financial situation was stronger than at any time in the preceding three years. He had saved almost $200 ($4,000 in 1995 prices) from the newspaper job, enough to cover most of his living expenses for the entire year. Not having to apply for scholarship aid put him in a more positive frame of mind. When he arrived in Ann Arbor, he sauntered over to the local chapter of Chi Psi and signed up for a room in the fraternity house. He moved into a ready-made community, and it took only a few weeks for him to feel at home. To earn extra money, he accepted the job of chapter steward, which entailed ordering food and supplies. Since it meant spending a fair amount of money – enough to feed everyone living at the house for the entire year – the position carried important responsibilities. Unlike the dining system at Amherst, fraternity men at Michigan hired a cook and ate their meals at the house. Charlie had moved into a white-collar position at the college level. No more waiting tables for him – and no more attempts to compete in intercollegiate sports, either.

Charlie subsequently claimed that the year at Michigan was his happiest at any school. That assertion may seem surprising in light of his poor academic performance, but what he probably had in mind was his carefree social life with male friends – all the beers he drank at the fraternity house and with members of two drinking clubs, Pipe and Bowl and later the Friars. He wrote to Suds Sudbury that the demands on students at Michigan were greater than he had previously experienced, which may have reflected the natural progression from lower-division courses to more difficult upper-division courses and introductory law courses. Charlie performed well enough in the first semester, but his grades plunged in the second. He did not earn satisfactory grades in three out of five courses. His expanding circle of friends over the course of the year was detrimental to his study habits. Equally important, Charlie was not stimulated by the law school curriculum. Whether he was officially suspended from school or left of his own volition is not clear. Two years later, he returned to Michigan for the summer school session to make up the deficiencies from that disastrous spring semester of 1907. Charlie never finished his senior year and therefore failed to earn a college diploma, although he later received honorary degrees from several schools, including Amherst College.

Meanwhile, his mind was fixated on Marie Sjostrom, who was in her junior year at Smith. They corresponded regularly. That spring he traveled by train to Amherst to take Marie to a Chi Psi dance. In June she came out to Ann Arbor for the commencement dance at the Michigan chapter. At some date along the way, Charlie and Marie became formally engaged. His fiancée's father was a prosperous textile manufacturer in the New York City area. The tentative plan was to marry when Marie finished her studies at Smith in June 1908. By then Charlie expected to nail down a position that would support a wife and family. The likely starting point was with his prospective father-in-law's textile mills.

But Charlie was in no hurry to enter the job market that June. As a summer lark, his uncle Augustus Wilson landed him a job as center fielder on the baseball team in Shaw, Mississippi. This small town was located fifty miles northwest of Grandmother Emily's farm near Lexington and twenty miles northeast of Greenville, the busy river port that rested on the eastern bank of the Mississippi River. Uncle Augustus had influence in the regional business community; it was he who had found an opening for Charlie with the Greenville newspaper at the end of the previous summer. Shaw's baseball team was unaffiliated with any of the teams in the major leagues. The competitive level was low – Class D on the minor league scale and probably not much beyond the stronger intramural teams at Amherst and Michigan at the turn of the century. In a region where entertainment was scarce, the Shaw team drew respectable crowds to its games. Management offered Charlie $25 per week ($500 in 1995 prices), and he took the next train out of Michigan bound for Mississippi. Charlie finished the season, and then headed for New York, where his prospective father-in-law had a job with the family textile firm waiting for him. The future looked promising.

Reflecting back on his college days, Charlie always identified more with Amherst College than with the University of Michigan. He spent two years at the former and only one, plus a summer, on the latter's campus. His academic record at Amherst had been respectable, but not so at Michigan, which may have colored his thinking. When he thought of his deep attachment to Amherst, he identified mostly with the many good times at the fraternity house than with what he had learned in the class-room. The Chi Psi experience at Amherst, and at Michigan for that matter, had an enduring impact. In 1916, when he hired Winthrop Smith to work as an office boy for the newly formed Merrill, Lynch, the applicant's main qualification was that he had been a member of Chi Psi at Amherst. That was a sufficient introduction and recommendation for Charlie. In addition to valuing the rewards of its social atmosphere, he deeply respected the school's academic reputation, which improved steadily over the years. His second son, James, was later educated there and earned high academic honors.[19] Charlie always considered Amherst College his alma mater, and later in life he donated generously to its endowment.

For the next four decades, New York became Charlie's home, and it was there that he made his fortune. Charlie was a prime example of an outsider – mostly southerners, midwesterners, and second-generation immigrants – who came to the nation's financial center with fresh ideas and the determination to succeed in the business world. In making this transition from southern to northern culture, Charlie was by no means a singular phenomenon. Many contemporaries likewise escaped the limitations of the agricultural southern economy and shifted their talents to the industrially and commercially oriented northern states. New York City – more so than close-knit Boston or Philadelphia – was open to ambitious southerners.

Other prominent financiers in the first half of the twentieth century had southern roots. For example, Clarence Dillon, who headed the prestigious investment banking house of Dillon Read in the 1920s and 1930s, was a Texan, born three years earlier than Merrill in 1882, who attended Worcester Academy a few years before Charlie, arriving in 1897. After graduating from prep school, Dillon went to Harvard to earn his undergraduate degree.[20] On Wall Street, Dillon underwrote gilt-edge bonds and arranged their sale to wealthy individuals and large financial institutions; Merrill advocated common stocks for the portfolios of upper-middle-class investors. Both were southerners with northern educations who became major innovators in the nation's most active market for long-term capital. Dillon became a Wall Street insider who was well respected by his peers. Merrill, in contrast, was viewed by many of the very same people as a pretentious upstart with too many well-intentioned, but impractical and potentially dangerous, ideas. In the end, of course, Charlie had the greater impact because he democratized and thereby revolutionized the U.S. capital markets.

19. Charles Jr. chose Harvard University instead of Amherst, much to his father's disappointment.
20. Sobel, *Life and Times of Dillon Read,* 34, 224. Charles McCain, who succeeded Dillon as senior partner in the 1940s, was a native of Arkansas who graduated from Yale in 1904.

4

———— • ————

THE LURE OF NEW YORK

When he headed for New York at the end of the 1907 baseball season in Mississippi, Charlie's immediate career plans were in the hands of his prospective father-in-law. The legal curriculum at Michigan had not inspired him. He had ruled out a career in law, or in any of the acknowledged professions, and family members had to accept that decision. Charlie was determined instead to enter the world of business, where the variety of positions and opportunities was so much broader. In this era there were thousands of manufacturing firms producing many different items, retailers and wholesalers in every line of merchandise, and financial services of all types. Business had less social prestige overall than the recognized professions, but its income potential was greater, especially if a young man could start out headed in the right direction.

Charlie's main strategy for achieving economic success in 1907 was to marry into money. Marie Sjostrom's family was hoping for an ambitious and talented son-in-law who might develop the skills to perpetuate the family fortune. The arrangement, so to speak, seemed mutually beneficial to all parties – the Merrills and the Sjostroms. When he got off the train in New York City, a job was ready and waiting. Charlie was no schemer, far from it, but the odds were good from the outset that any young Smith student with whom he became romantically involved would come from an upper-middle-class or possibly even a wealthy household. Marriage into an influential and well-to-do family was one of the outcomes anticipated by parents who sent their sons and daughters to the elite New England private schools. By marrying well, Charlie would be virtually guaranteed an upper-middle-class lifestyle, and possibly more. During their engagement, which would be lengthy because Marie planned to finish her senior year at Smith, Charlie hoped to put some money in the bank and perhaps help out his mother in shouldering the financial burden of caring for his disabled father and sister Edith in West Palm Beach.

Robert Sjostrom was a successful textile manufacturer who owned six

mills in the New York metropolitan area. His enterprises were administered from a central office in lower Manhattan. By 1907, Sjostrom spent
much of his time at his residence in suburban New Rochelle, about twenty
miles to the northeast, and left day-to-day operations to hired managers.
Charlie began as an office boy at fifteen dollars per week – an entry-level
position with low pay. If Charlie performed his duties faithfully, Sjostrom
promised rapid promotion and sharp increases in salary.

Charlie's living quarters those first few months in New York were
modest and in accordance with his wages. He lived in a fourth-floor room
in the Chelsea area of mid-Manhattan, a place that was so small, he "had
to get into it with a shoe horn."[1] His Irish landlady took four young men
into her home. For a room, plus breakfast and dinner, he paid $6.50 weekly
– more than 40 percent of his income. The Chelsea location was no random
choice. Charlie selected Chelsea because the Sjostrom family kept a winter
apartment in the Endicott Hotel just a few blocks away. At the hotel he
could conveniently visit Marie and members of her family when they were
in town.

Sometime during his first year in New York, Charlie met Eddie Lynch,
his future business partner. Both swam regularly at the Twenty-third
Street YMCA, where dues were low; they ran into each other by chance
one day and started to chat about mutual interests. Just six months older
than Charlie, Lynch had attended Johns Hopkins University in Baltimore,
his hometown. He began his career as an office boy with Liquid Carbonic,
a manufacturer of soda fountain equipment, then progressed to bill collec-
tor, and finally to salesman. He too was living on a modest salary, plus
commissions. Soon after their first meeting, the two young men agreed to
become roommates, with Charlie moving into Lynch's more spacious quarters on West Thirty-sixth Street. Their personalities were vastly different
yet surprisingly complementary. Charlie was gracious and outgoing; Lynch
was blunt and assertive. Perhaps they speculated about joining forces in a
business venture one day, but made no plans. Each was following a different career path. Charlie's future was tied to the Sjostrom clan.

Charlie proved his worth straightaway, and within a year Sjostrom had
named him credit manager for the six mills under his control. In retrospect, it was a momentous appointment in that financial services remained
Charlie's specialty for most of his long career. His primary duties were
borrowing money from commercial banks to cover seasonal requirements
and extending credit to customers, both wholesale and retail, who placed
orders for textiles. As his responsibilities grew, his salary escalated. By the
end of 1908, Charlie was making $100 per week, over six times his starting

---

1. Keenan, "Chain of Fortune," 106.

salary. Adjusted to reflect money values in the mid-1990s, he was earning in the neighborhood of $100,000 annually at the tender age of twenty-three. As intended, he shared his good fortune with his family. Dutifully, he saved $1,700 and sent it to his parents to pay off their mortgage.

In the spring of 1909, Charlie's career plans took a sharp detour. Almost a year after her graduation from Smith, and nearly two years after their engagement, Marie remained hesitant about going through with the marriage. Perhaps she feared leaving home or had undergone a change of heart. Whatever the case, Marie and Charlie quarreled and broke off their engagement. Within days, he either quit his job with Sjostrom's enterprises or was asked to resign. Textiles were not his future. Years later, at Robert Sjostrom's death in 1937, Charlie wrote a touching sympathy note to his widow: "I came to New York alone and friendless, except for the Sjostroms. Robert, from the start, took me to his heart, watched over me and trained me, as if I were his son . . . ; he gave me, in two years, not only the rudiments of business, but a post-graduate course as well." To a business associate, he said: "The two years I worked for Mr. Sjostrom turned out to be the equivalent of a university course in business in general, and credits, finance, cost accounting, and administration in particular."[2]

At loose ends after the breakup with Marie and the loss of his job, Charlie decided to return to the University of Michigan for the summer session of 1909. The purpose was not to reassess his decision regarding a possible legal career. Mainly, he just needed a place to get away from social and business pressures and some free time to calculate his next move. He also wanted to clean up his clouded academic record that remained from the spring semester of 1907. Several months in Ann Arbor seemed an inviting change of pace. A relatively high salary over the past year had permitted Charlie to save a substantial sum that would easily cover tuition and living expenses. Since he no longer needed money to help in establishing a new household, he could afford to attend the university with no financial strain or need for part-time employment, a welcome change from the years at Worcester and Amherst.

Near the end of the summer, Charlie remembered conversations with Fred Bale, a recent Amherst graduate whom he had met in New York through the informal alumni network, about possible employment opportunities. Bale had taken a job with George H. Burr & Company, a firm that bought the accounts receivable of other businesses or made secured loans against accounts receivable, and he had successfully solicited Charlie as a customer. Usually called factors, these firms provided short- to intermediate-term financing for manufacturers and merchandisers who were

2. Keenan, "Chain of Fortune," 114.

typically undercapitalized and therefore had difficulty borrowing from commercial banks. Charlie had met George Burr briefly on several occasions while working for Sjostrom's textile mills. He wrote Burr to ask about any openings at the firm but had received no answer, and temporarily gave up the pursuit of that option.

Returning to New York in the fall of 1909, he moved into a room with Bob Underhill, another former Amherst student, and started pounding the pavement and scouring the want ads looking for a job. Although he had accumulated a fair amount of experience over the preceding two years, he was willing to start out near the bottom of the career ladder once again. Employment opportunities were few, and he had little luck for several weeks. The rejections he received were humiliating, and memories of these frustrations produced a soft spot in his heart for others who had once been successful but had lost their livelihood because of personal tragedies or a weak economy.

Racism cost him one job opportunity. The credit manager of Hygrade Silk Mills was looking for an assistant, and the pay at $35 weekly (more than $35,000 annually in 1995 prices) was certainly respectable. Because the man was black, Charlie declined. Later, he cited his southern background as an important factor in passing up the position, but many northern whites were equally unwilling to take orders from minorities, or white women for that matter, who had risen to a position of authority.

When Charlie returned to his rooming house one afternoon in October, he learned that Fred Bale had left a message about something new opening up at George Burr. The owner had decided to diversify by creating a bond department. Burr had hired an experienced Chicago banker to run the new department, but on the train trip to New York, the prospect had caught pneumonia and soon died. Needing someone in a hurry, Burr offered Charlie the job of manager at $25 per week plus 10 percent of profits. Charlie's career on Wall Street was launched. Thereafter, there were more continuities in his life. Among them was the presence of Lillian Burton, whom Burr had hired as secretary for the deceased Chicago banker; she stayed on to assist Charlie. Burton served as Charlie's personal secretary; she was a regular part of his life for decades, longer than any of his three wives. On the advice of his mother, who always urged him to dress for success, he found a new tailor, E. R. Van Sickle, who kept him handsomely attired for the next half century.

Burr's motive for expanding into investment banking was to help some of his regular customers, to whom he routinely provided short-term advances against accounts receivable, in strengthening their capital base. One firm in particular, a radiator and plumbing supply company named McCrum-Howell, was deeply in debt to George Burr and the sale of bonds to outside investors was envisioned as a possible bailout. Monies raised in the capital market could be used to reduce the short-term loans to Burr. But McCrum-Howell was too small and its balance sheet too weak to attract the attention of an established investment banking house. Burr decided to take the initiative and see what might be accomplished through diversification into a broader range of financial services.

Charlie was placed in a difficult spot. He was being asked to attempt to sell to individual investors the long-term debts of small- to medium-sized companies, most of them family owned, and none with a previous record of issuing and redeeming interest-yielding bonds. Today, we would likely call debt obligations in this category "junk bonds" because of the high-risk element. Junk bonds, which became popular investment vehicles in the 1980s, are debt obligations that fall below "investment grade" in the rankings of the major independent bond-rating services.

Another serious handicap was that few employees at George Burr, including Charlie, had any experience in the investment banking field. As it happened, Lillian Burton, whose previous secretarial position had been with a firm that regularly lured unsuspecting clients into questionable transactions through misrepresentation, probably knew as much as anyone about marketing securities. Often called bucket shops, these unscrupulous securities dealers told customers that their orders had been properly exccuted, when, in fact, the monies had been diverted for other purposes.[3] Because the fraud laws were lax or nonexistent, prosecuting the guilty was difficult. Rumors were rife about hot investments, and securities salesmen were rarely held accountable for providing customers with erroneous or deliberately false information.

Burton showed Charlie some of the advertising literature, mostly direct mail solicitations, that her previous employer had used to attract new accounts. Charlie was intrigued by the potential effectiveness of these marketing tools. He received more encouragement from Rudolph Guenther, an owner of Albert Frank-Guenther Law, an advertising agency that solicited clients in the financial services sector. Another maverick, Guenther played an important role in supporting and promoting Charlie's career aspirations over four decades.

The decision to embark on an aggressive advertising campaign was a milestone. Bold promotional techniques were generally frowned on at that time by the leading securities firms. The majority of the established investment banking firms in the early twentieth century – J. P. Morgan,

---

3. An anonymous reader for Cambridge University Press stated that at least some so-called bucket shops were, in truth, legitimate businesses that dealt in stock options; their customers were allegedly fully aware of the risky nature of these transactions. This claim certainly sounds plausible, but unfortunately I am unaware of any corroborating sources.

Kuhn Loeb, Kidder Peabody, and Goldman Sachs, just to name a few –
did almost no advertising to attract new clients. They simply listed their
names in "tombstone" style on formal announcements of new issues. The
most prestigious firms with the major share of the underwriting commissions were placed at the top in large letters, with other participants listed
in descending order of importance in progressively smaller type. Most of
the established firms periodically ran advertisements in newspapers and
financial journals that provided limited information about the location of
their offices and the range of services normally rendered, but they rarely
tried to attract new customers with detailed information, either about
investment principles or specific securities.

The Morgans and their lesser peers had built their reputations gradually,
normally over decades, and depended on word-of-mouth recommendations
and referrals by influential people. Along with professionals in medicine,
law, and accounting, the leading investment bankers not only disdained
advertising but argued further that aggressive marketing by others was
fundamentally unethical because such promotional materials allegedly led
to lower professional standards. Ironically, such twisted logic was itself
unethical behavior in a market-oriented economy because the underlying
purpose was not the protection of the public from fraud but rather the
maintenance of what amounted to de facto cartel profits through tacit
noncompetitive agreements. The taboos on aggressive marketing tactics
discouraged the entrance of new competitors into the investment banking
field. The code of silence and the perpetuation of public ignorance about
the functioning of financial markets operated in the best interests of the
leading firms. Only by dealing with an established investment house could
an investor obtain access to critical information and avoid the risk of
dealing with unprofessional, untrained, and possibly crooked investment
advisers. Without advertising, new faces had a difficult time getting started
in this field; meanwhile those firms that dared to break the unwritten rules
were cited by competitors as undignified and probably disreputable. It was
a no-win situation for most outsiders and that suited the established investment bankers just fine.

Charlie decided to buck tradition. He elected to use various techniques,
including advertising, to sell bonds for which he believed a market existed
if only a means could be found to tap into it. He sought savers who wanted
higher returns and who accepted the greater risk of default. Charlie saw
nothing inherently wrong with the direct solicitation of potential investors,
so long as he provided accurate, up-to-date information. No get-rich-quick
schemes received his endorsement. With Guenther's assistance and counsel, Charlie experimented with circulars, newspaper advertisements, and
prompt follow-up letters to interested respondents. Because Burr's opera-

tions were on the outer edge of the larger bond market, the owner was prepared to risk the disdain of the powerhouses in the investment banking field.[4]

In the November 1911 issue of *Leslie's Illustrated Weekly*, Charlie published a magazine article on investing, under his own name, that enunciated many of the principles he preached for the next four decades. Addressing himself to "Mr. Average Investor," he stressed the importance of knowing a customer's financial circumstances before embarking on any investment program. Certain investments completely appropriate for people in their twenties, for example, would not be right for the elderly, and vice versa. Was the customer's goal growth or safety – or some mixture? Knowledge about a customer's comfort zone with regard to risk was also important. In time, these ideas became more formally institutionalized when Merrill Lynch pioneered the "Know Your Customer" rule for brokers and sales representatives. In the same article, Charlie endorsed the concept of broadening the market for securities by appealing to more upper-middle-class investors in hundreds of towns across the nation: "Having thousands of customers scattered throughout the United States is infinitely preferable to being dependent upon the fluctuating buying power of a smaller and perhaps on the whole wealthier group of investors in any one section." In 1911, his ideas were mere dreams, but those dreams eventually came true.

The willingness to adopt unorthodox and untraditional promotional techniques was one of the hallmarks of Charlie's career on Wall Street, beginning with his entry into the securities field in 1909 and lasting until his death in 1956. A few firms on the periphery of the market – some honest and some dishonest – also placed a great deal of emphasis on the marketing aspects of the investment business in the first decade of the twentieth century, so Charlie was by no means the sole innovator, but over the long run he enjoyed more success than competitors, especially in the 1940s and 1950s after Win Smith brought him back to Wall Street. How he functioned in this regard before the Great Crash of 1929 hardly caught the attention of the larger investment banking houses, but the marketing policies that Merrill Lynch pursued in the 1940s altered forever the character of the securities business. These later policies were not fundamentally different from those he had adopted early in his career, but they were carried out on a much grander scale and had a vastly greater impact. In short, the lessons Charlie learned about the importance of an effective marketing program during the three and one-half years that he managed the bond department for George Burr were put to good use in later years.

---

4. For another account of the power of advertising in the financial services sector, see Wyckoff, *Wall Street Ventures*, 96–97.

In addition to his discovery of the power of advertising, two other significant events occurred during his tenure with Burr. First, he hired Eddie Lynch, his former roommate, as a securities salesman. Lynch had continued working in sales for Liquid Carbonic and had been reasonably successful. He was earning roughly $75 per week in commissions ($75,000 annually in 1995 prices) when Charlie convinced him to agree to $25 per week plus commissions, the best Burr would authorize under the circumstances. Lynch decided to accept the challenge of shifting into a completely new field where the earnings potential seemed greater over the long run. At Charlie's insistence, he spent the first two weeks at his desk trying to learn as much as possible about securities. Once he had gained a little knowledge, Lynch went out making calls on prospective customers, many of them cold calls to skeptical listeners.

Lynch was persistent and effective. One story about his pursuit of a potential customer – a story perhaps embellished over time – is worth repeating because of its future implications. Lynch supposedly arrived at the offices of Diogenes Balsam, a Brooklyn necktie manufacturer, around midmorning and presented his calling card to the secretary on duty. She told Lynch that Balsam was extremely busy and had no free time that day; Lynch insisted that he would wait and take his chances. Hours allegedly passed, yet Lynch waited patiently in the anteroom until five o'clock that afternoon. Finally, he caught up with the elusive Balsam, who was about to leave for home, and after a brief conversation, they struck up a friendship that was mutually rewarding for many years.

The Balsam episode is critical because that contact, in turn, helped cement Charlie's lifetime involvement with chain stores as an investment vehicle for himself and his loyal customers. Balsam's firm was a major supplier of inexpensive neckties to the McCrory chain of five-and-ten-cent stores. A year or so later, Balsam introduced Charlie to John McCrory, who was looking for ways to bolster capital resources. Subsequently, Charlie sponsored an offering of securities for the McCrory chain, and over the years he became one of the firm's major stockholders.

Chain stores that retailed foodstuffs, drugs, and inexpensive consumer goods had existed since the late nineteenth century, but their popularity increased rapidly during the first decade of the twentieth century. The entrepreneurs who founded these chains took advantage of economies of scale and introduced standard operating procedures throughout their systems. They purchased inventories in bulk at low prices and passed a large share of the savings on to consumers, mostly middle-class households. These companies were expanding in every way possible – number of stores, sales, and profits. Charlie was too young to have been in on things at the very beginning, but he jumped on the bandwagon fairly close to the start of the parade. He recognized the growth opportunities and took advantage of the general neglect of the chain store sector by most other financial services firms. He recalled years later: "When I was a credit manager for a large manufacturing firm, it came to my attention that our best customers from the standpoint of stability, volume of orders, prompt pay, etc., were the chain stores." He added: "The chains . . . offered standard merchandise to the public at substantially lower prices than were obtainable elsewhere; I became convinced then that there was a wonderful opportunity for any business that could cut loose from obsolete methods, on the one hand, and not attempt to profiteer on the public, on the other."[5] Over the next three decades, he concentrated his energies on providing the capital to fund the expansion of his chain store clients from town to town, state to state, and occasionally across the nation. A true believer in the future of mass retailing, Charlie steadily acquired common stock in many of these firms, and he became extraordinarily rich in the process.

In their formative years, most chain stores financed their expansion from retained earnings. Commercial banks were willing to lend short-term money to finance inventories, but term loans, with maturity dates spread out over several years, were impossible to obtain. The elite investment banking houses demonstrated no interest whatsoever in raising capital, either bonds or stocks, for these novel enterprises, or indeed for any strictly retail ventures; railroads, governments, and some industrial securities were the mainstays of investment bankers. Because of their difficulty in securing external financing, most chains grew steadily but not spectacularly. One positive aspect of their measured growth was that their ratio of debt to equity was typically low and the burden of interest payments light.

For someone who made honesty and full disclosure his bywords during a long career on Wall Street, the sad irony is that Charlie's very first underwriting effort for George Burr was tainted, and perhaps fraudulent from the outset. Charlie was totally in the dark. In this era, long before the Securities and Exchange Commission required a formal prospectus from the issuers of new securities, the information available to investors and the general public about the true financial position of business enterprises was woefully inadequate. Even diligent salesmen often knew little about the current status of the companies they recommended because not much current information was available. Independent audits by reliable accounting firms of the financial statements of the issuers of stocks and bonds were rare. When critics alleged that investing in securities was akin to gambling, there was an element of truth in their accusations. "Buyer beware" was the universal rule. Prior to World War I, only a small

---

5. Quoted in Engberg, "History of Merrill Lynch," ch. 2, p. 2.

percentage of the total U.S. population owned corporate securities, and most investors were reasonably sophisticated people who recognized the trade-off between reward and risk. Sleazy operators sometimes suckered the unwary into worthless investments, but, overall, dishonesty in the securities field was not a serious public menace because of narrow markets.

Charlie's first assignment was to sell a series of bonds issued by McCrum-Howell, one of Burr's customers that was having difficulty retiring its outstanding short-term debt. Burr assured the new manager of the bond department that the issuer was a profitable company with a promising future that simply needed an infusion of new capital to fortify its balance sheet. After the bonds had been sold to investors, Burr convinced Shearson Hammill, a leading brokerage house and securities dealer in unlisted stocks, to maintain a market for the firm's common stock. McCrum-Howell's financial statements showed profitable operations in 1910 and 1911. In addition to his other investments, Charlie bought about $20,000 of the firm's stock, mostly on margin with money borrowed from a loan officer at Mechanics and Metals Bank.

One day out of the blue in the spring of 1912, more than two years after the successful bond underwriting, Burr called Charlie into his office to pass on the bad news that McCrum-Howell was on the verge of bankruptcy. The published financial reports had all been manipulated. Based on this inside information, Charlie tried to sell before the news got out, but miscommunications with his broker cost him a substantial sum of money. Even worse, many of his customers, some of whom held both the bonds and common shares of McCrum-Howell, were also at risk. He immediately wrote each customer a personal letter expressing his regret about giving them such poor advice. He suggested they purchase other securities that he believed would soon make up for their losses, and his recommendations were generally sound.

Charlie was exceedingly angry about what had happened in connection with McCrum-Howell because he soon came to believe that Burr knew, or should have known, the sorry state of affairs all along. Charlie concluded that the bond issue in 1909-10 had been initiated strictly to bail out George Burr & Company, with complete disregard for the welfare of investors. Burr had misled him, and he in turn had misled his valued clients for more than two years. Charlie found his employer's irresponsible attitude reprehensible, and within a year, he left for another position. Privately, he vowed to create a firm of his own one day with colleagues whom he could implicitly trust.

While things were moving forward at George Burr, there were important developments in Charlie's personal life as well. In the fall of 1909, his sister Edith, now eighteen, arrived in New York City to enroll in Miss

Bangs and Miss Whiton's School for Girls, a two-year institution in upper Manhattan. His mother instructed him to look out for his sister's welfare, and he immediately assumed the role of protective older brother. Charlie arranged an invitation for Edith to a Chi Psi dance at Amherst, and he periodically took her to parties at the homes of his employer, George Burr, and his employer's son, Courtney Burr. But Edith grew progressively unhappy in New York City and longed to return to familiar surroundings in West Palm Beach.

In the middle of her second year, Edith announced her intention to drop out of school. Octavia was willing to yield to her daughter's wishes, but Charlie resisted. In his relations with his mother, he naturally had grown more independent and assertive. He outlined his views on Edith's proposed withdrawal in a letter to Octavia dated January 20, 1911:

> The point is that you have agreed to send her to school for a year and have entered into a contract to pay the full year's tuition; and if you don't pay it, I will. I don't believe in doing things any other way. The only asset poor people have is the common variety of honesty, and that entails living up to written obligations. The very idea of letting Edith go down there to impose on you and leaving school at this stage of the game is preposterous. . . . It makes me fairly sick to think of how hard it was for me to go through school and of the thousands of girls who haven't anything and are working their fingers off to learn something and then Edith, with everything that anybody should desire, not taking advantage of opportunities that are fairly thrown at her. She has acted deceitfully in this matter as far as I'm concerned, and anybody, to keep my admiration and respect, has to make good once in a while.[6]

Charlie won the argument. Edith stayed in school for the spring semester, and he sent Octavia the money to attend her daughter's graduation ceremonies in June 1911. He was never asked to reconcile, however, two seemingly contradictory statements in the letter to his mother: one implying that the Merrill family was poor and therefore had to make honesty its special virtue, and another suggesting that Edith had been blessed with everything she ever needed or wanted. This illusion of family poverty, even in the face of evidence to the contrary, was persistent, and it may have been an important psychological factor in driving Charlie to the heights of the financial world.

About a year later, in March 1912, at a dinner party hosted by Courtney Burr, Charlie met the woman who soon became his first wife and the mother of two of his three children. Elizabeth Church had graduated from Briarcliff, a school on the Hudson River north of New York City, the previous spring, and was living with her married sister. Born in Columbus,

6. Keenan, "Chain of Fortune," 129.

Ohio, to a cultured family with diverse talents and interests, her father, Samuel H. Church, had been successful in both the business and academic worlds. Beginning as a telegrapher for the Pennsylvania Railroad, Church worked his way up to a vice presidency and subsequently wrote a history of the firm. He became president of Carnegie Institute in Pittsburgh, a school with a strong scientific and engineering curriculum; in the twentieth century it merged with another local institution to form Carnegie-Mellon University. Samuel Church wrote a biography of Oliver Cromwell, as well as several novels and plays. Eliza's mother died when she was nine, and when relations with her new stepmother deteriorated, she moved to New York to live with her older sister Ruth. A shy and retiring personality, nearly the opposite of Charlie, she was pretty and possessed some talent as a pianist. A wife's role at that time was to help her husband get ahead in the business world, and in that regard Elizabeth was eminently successful.

After a whirlwind romance and a very short engagement – no repeats of the drawn-out situation with his previous fiancée – Eliza and Charlie were married in a Roman Catholic ceremony at the Vanderbilt Hotel on April 8, 1912. For their honeymoon, they chose Hot Springs, Virginia, the site of the Homestead, a lavish resort hotel in the Appalachian Mountains. After a week, Charlie received an urgent telegraph from Burr asking him to return to New York as soon as possible to follow up on a lead for a possible underwriting.

Burr had heard from a Chicago banker that Sebastian Kresge, the principal stockholder in S. S. Kresge, a chain of variety stores headquartered in Detroit, Michigan, was seeking capital for expansion. The chain had opened more than fifty stores by 1910; it had added thirteen stores in 1911 and had plans for another twenty in 1912.[7] Charlie traveled to Detroit, where he met with Kresge and outlined his proposal for underwriting $2 million in preferred stock plus ten thousand shares of common stock. The proceeds from the preferred stock would provide virtually all of the capital for expansion. The common stock was largely a sweetener, with shares reserved for the underwriters and their favored customers at prices below market values. The Kresge deal was Burr's and Charlie's first opportunity to handle the distribution of securities for one of the rising chain stores. Burr knew he did not have the resources to handle the underwriting alone, so he approached Hallgarten & Company, one of the city's second-tier investment banking houses with good connections in European markets, to discuss a joint offering. The senior partners at Hallgarten were glad for the opportunity to participate in the Kresge underwriting. They were willing to allow Burr's firm to distribute a fair allotment of the

7. Lebhar, *Chain Stores,* 399.

securities and to share in the profits, but because of the unsavory reputation Burr had acquired as a result of the McCrum-Howell failure, they were unwilling to permit George Burr & Company to appear in any public announcements of the underwriting. They were concerned that any connection with Burr would tarnish their reputation.

Burr came back to the office and discussed the situation with his sales manager. Charlie suggested a reverse offer: give Hallgarten all the profits, with George Burr retaining the right to be named as the primary underwriter in all advertising and press releases announcing the transaction. By forgoing profits in this instance, Burr could begin the process of reestablishing his firm's reputation. If the Kresge distribution went well, other chain stores might be drawn to Burr for additional offerings. Hallgarten agreed to this arrangement, and the success of the Kresge underwriting boosted the prestige of George Burr, and, of course, it helped Charlie's reputation on the street as well. He personally subscribed to one thousand of the common shares and soon made a handsome profit. The Kresge underwriting was a major breakthrough. From 1912 forward, Charlie's destiny was tied to the fortunes of the burgeoning chain stores.

While Charlie was negotiating the Kresge underwriting, Eliza was busy decorating their apartment at 13 West Eighth Street in Greenwich Village. That summer they often visited friends in Oyster Bay, Long Island, where they swam, played tennis, and danced at the exclusive Seawanhaka Club. A year later Charlie and Eliza decided to give up the city for the suburbs. They rented a house in Montclair, New Jersey, and Charlie became a commuter. He bought a sporty car that cost $1,200 – more than $24,000 in 1995 prices. He learned to play golf and took up bridge. His golf game improved so that his handicap dropped to only eight strokes. Charlie's love of card games, especially bridge and poker, was also sustained over the years; he was a highly competitive bridge player, and later in life, when he had more leisure time, almost a compulsive player in the evenings. His younger son, Jimmy, recalled that his father usually insisted on playing for money even in casual games with men or women "just to keep it interesting."[8] Charlie always paid opponents promptly for his losses, and he insisted on collecting from the losers even if only a few cents were exchanged at breakfast the next morning.

One day in the summer of 1913, Rudolph Guenther, who regularly proselytized Wall Street figures about the importance of advertising and who had found a convert in Charlie, was asked by Herb Dillon, a partner at Eastman Dillon, to recommend someone for a position in sales. Eastman Dillon was one of the city's leading underwriters, boasting numerous

8. Author's interview with James Merrill, Los Angeles, April 1989.

prestigious accounts. Charlie's name was among the first to come to Guenther's mind. He knew that Charlie was still angry with Burr about the McCrum–Howell bankruptcy and was frustrated by his failure to convince his employer to boost his participation in underwriting profits above 10 percent. In his three years at George Burr, Charlie had generated more than $750,000 in commissions and profits, but his aggregate compensation, salary, and participations totaled no more than $100,000 – around $2 million in 1995 prices. He wanted a larger slice of the pie. Burr's resistance prompted Charlie to begin looking around unhurriedly for the right opportunity to transfer to another firm, preferably one of the establishment houses. Dillon told Guenther the job paid $50 per week plus commissions, a modest compensation package, but Guenther thought $100 was the minimum his young friend would even agree to consider. Charlie subsequently met with Dillon and convinced his host to raise the offer to $125 per week. The shift in employment was a sharply upward career move in terms of the pecking order on Wall Street, but it was downward in terms of administrative responsibilities. When Charlie left George Burr, Lynch assumed the vacant position as sales manager of the bond department.

The new job at Eastman Dillon did not work out as Charlie had hoped. Conflicts with Herb Dillon were frequent and distasteful. Dillon was unwilling to allow Charlie the same free rein that he had exercised under Burr. This old-line investment house dealt almost exclusively with railroads, governments, and select industrial firms, whereas Charlie's main successes to date had been with innovative, but unconventional, chain stores in the retail sector. Eastman Dillon had tradition on its side; Charlie was by habit nontraditional. He also got into a nasty dispute with Dillon over the firm's plan to participate in an underwriting of an issue of Chalmers Motors stock. Charlie's contacts in Detroit, mainly Sebastian Kresge and his business associates, were dubious about the fledgling automobile manufacturer's prospects. Charlie told Dillon that he could not in good conscience recommend the stock to customers. That stance was not what Dillon wanted to hear from a subordinate only recently hired to help generate more sales. Hat in hand, Charlie went back to Burr and tried to get his old job back. His former employer smugly turned him down.

The situation at Eastman Dillon went from bad to worse. In a general reorganization and cost-cutting campaign, Herb Dillon reduced Charlie's guaranteed weekly draw from $125 to $75. One day Dillon surprisingly handed Charlie a file on McCrory Stores, and asked his opinion about participation in a possible underwriting of bonds or preferred stock for the variety chain. Charlie gave the firm, and retail chains in general, a ringing endorsement and asked for the opportunity to help negotiate the deal and supervise distribution of the securities. He thought Eastman Dillon had an opportunity to earn between $200,000 and $250,000 in commissions and fees, and he saw up to $50,000 in it for himself. Dillon coldly rejected Charlie's presumptuous initiatives, telling him that the McCrory proposal had arrived at the office long before his employment date; Charlie therefore had no right to expect a share in the underwriting commissions if the business was eventually undertaken. As it turned out, nothing happened in terms of Eastman Dillon's involvement. Charlie kept the McCrory file in his desk drawer and waited for a more opportune time to act.

Frustrated by his inability to exert much influence with the senior partners at Eastman Dillon, Charlie decided to make another bold move – a move that might propel him forward into greater riches or one that might backfire disastrously. In late December 1913, he outlined the proposal to Herb Dillon. Charlie would resign his current position, giving up his regular salary, to operate independently, but he would remain on the premises. He just needed office space and access to telephone lines. Under this arrangement, he would continue to trade his customers' securities through Eastman Dillon, thereby generating brokerage commissions for the partnership. Because Charlie had retained a number of loyal customers during his four years as a broker and underwriter, Dillon agreed to the plan. For his staff, Charlie retained Lillian Burton, his faithful secretary who had moved with him from Burr to Eastman Dillon, and one male assistant. On January 6, 1914, the firm of Charles E. Merrill & Company was launched.

5

OFF TO A FLYING START

In just over three years – starting from the day Charlie headed out on his own as a securities broker and aspiring investment banker and continuing until the date of his decision to volunteer for military service in World War I – his new enterprise made steady progress in terms of trading volume, new issues, and profitability. Without specific plans about where to concentrate his energies, he pursued whatever opportunities came his way. As a rule, Charlie focused his talents on those sectors of the economy that had demonstrated a potential for exceptional growth. Within a few years the firm's principal interests stretched to three diverse industries: chain stores – both grocery and general merchandise chains; automobiles – both assembled vehicles and auto parts; and motion pictures – the production and distribution of silent movies as well as the manufacture of raw film in a joint venture with the Du Pont Company. Chain stores and motion pictures were the big winners; the firm's association with automotive manufacturing was less successful.

What this otherwise diverse group had in common was that all were relatively new industries that had arisen in the first quarter of the twentieth century. For investors, there were high risks associated with these ventures. Losses were sometimes an unfortunate reality, but, to compensate, the potential for huge capital gains was also present. Most of the corporations Charlie sponsored proved successful, although some ran into serious trouble and filed for bankruptcy. Luckily, the numerous sound investments more than offset the occasional losers.

Like many young hotshots on Wall Street with bold visions (past and present), Charlie struggled at first, survived difficult times, and eventually prospered. Early on, Eddie Lynch was recruited as a business partner. In the division of responsibilities, Charlie, who was a proven master at the art of calm persuasion, took the initiative in pursuing corporate clients. Lynch was often cast as the tough negotiator in discussions with lawyers and other financiers. In this complementary duo, Charlie was the outgoing personality who brought in new business, whereas the introspective Lynch probed for the rough spots and ironed out the details.

When Charlie entered the securities field just before World War I, the financial sector was extremely varied in terms of the number of firms involved and the services provided. The institutional maturation of U.S. capital markets had been an ongoing process since the nation's founding. The techniques of sophisticated trading in securities – including stocks, bonds, and options of all varieties – had been well known for more than a century. At the pinnacle of the investment community were the elite private bankers who dealt primarily in new issues of gilt-edge bonds and preferred shares, and less often in common stocks. They were typically located on Wall Street, with the exception of a few houses headquartered in Boston. Their main customers were wealthy households, commercial banks, and insurance companies that were interested foremost in the preservation of capital and a fixed stream of income. The interest and dividend yields associated with these securities were low – in the range of 2 to 5 percent with no possibility of annual increases. At a time when the inflation rate was low, bonds and preferred stocks were reasonably good investments for buyers interested in maintaining the purchasing power of their portfolios.

The elite firms frequently formed incestuous syndicates to distribute securities widely in the U.S. market and overseas. Their profits arose almost exclusively from the underwriting fees that corporate clients paid to float new issues. Customers were expected to hold securities – whether bonds, preferred stock, or common stock – for the long term. Informational asymmetry dictated that common stocks were appropriate investments only for those with access to superior knowledge, such as managers and underwriters, or, alternatively, speculators who were highly insensitive to risk. As a consequence, the House of Morgan and its near peers did not maintain extensive facilities for those who wished to trade securities regularly on secondary markets. Indeed, the partners in these firms did nothing to encourage any activities even remotely connected with speculation, and trading per se was considered speculation by most contemporaries. When customers periodically pressed the elite houses to suggest prudent investments in common stocks, the recommended securities were invariably the issues of firms listed on the New York Stock Exchange, and all were well-known companies immediately recognizable to investors and the general public.

In the retail sector of the capital markets were brokerage houses. They dealt with traders and speculators of all varieties on a daily basis; many brokerage firms had facilities for arranging trades in commodities as well as securities – plus put and call options. Unlike investment banking houses, brokerage firms were geographically dispersed and could be found in almost every large to medium-sized city across the nation.

At the turn of the century, stockbrokers had a somewhat unsavory reputation. Their regular customers were investors primarily interested in seeking capital appreciation from investments in securities, whether short term, intermediate term, or long term. Many brokerage houses performed nothing much beyond transactions services for customers; their sales personnel acted as intermediaries in arranging trades of securities on secondary markets. Many firms were locally owned and managed. Several houses maintained chains of branch offices, usually concentrating on a specific region such as the South, Midwest, or Northeast; none were nationwide in scope. Brokers that were not official members of the New York Stock Exchange, and other major exchanges, usually had standing arrangements with member firms to handle trades on a split commission basis. For example, in 1914 and 1915, Merrill Lynch channeled all its trades on the NYSE through cooperating brokers.

The brokerage niche in the financial services market included persons with varying ethical standards in regard to customer relations. Some brokers were scrupulously honest; others revealed various shadings of truthfulness. Some, without malice, casually lured investors into speculative common stocks by holding out the prospects of rapid price appreciation based on rumors that they never bothered to confirm – often because they did not have access to the staff resources necessary to launch investigations. Many brokers never blatantly lied, but on the other hand, they never told customers the whole story either, avoiding any mention of potential negatives on the horizon. The overwhelming majority of these questionable investments never lived up to expectations, leaving buyers with diminished income and depleted capital. During sharp downturns in the securities markets, investors in the stocks of shaky companies often lost heavily. Many stocks that were actively traded were unlisted on the major exchanges; normally issued by small to medium-sized firms, these securities changed hands on the so-called Curb Exchange (the predecessor of today's American Stock Exchange) and in atomized over-the-counter markets throughout the nation. In New York and elsewhere, some of the brokerage houses that concentrated on the securities of smaller companies had solid records in terms of picking winners and helping their customers increase the value of their portfolios. Indeed, one of the key problems facing aggressive investors who sought capital gains and increased dividends was how to isolate the honest and sincere brokers from the irresponsible con men who were only interested in churning accounts.

Another group of securities firms operated between the polar extremes of the elite private bankers and ordinary commission brokers. Some of these firms had a dual focus. While these hybrids aimed at generating a steady return from the performance of routine brokerage services, their principals were constantly on the lookout for opportunities to earn underwriting commissions on new issues of securities for small to medium-sized enterprises that did not qualify for listing on the NYSE. Once a new issue had been placed with investors, these hybrid firms sometimes agreed to maintain an active secondary market for the securities in question. These so-called market makers held inventories of specified securities and were always prepared to accommodate trades based on their quoted "bid and ask" spread.

The key reason for Charlie's early success was that his firm became involved in activities that financial experts today would designate as merchant banking.[1] The partners not only acted as financial intermediaries in bringing together underwriting clients, syndicates of wholesale securities dealers, and retail customers, they also acquired substantial blocks of their clients' common stock, becoming thereby partial owners of the companies that the firm's salesmen were simultaneously recommending to investors. When several of these companies prospered and their common stock skyrocketed, the partners earned considerable profits. During the first fifteen years of operations, which covered the entire period that Lynch was active in the firm, the partners' escalating wealth arose primarily from merchant banking activities.

Brokerage evolved as a handmaiden that complemented and reinforced the more lucrative underwriting and merchant banking activities. Charlie was optimistic from the start, but he had not anticipated that underwriting would so quickly overshadow the brokerage end of the business. While an energetic broker could earn a decent income from small commissions on a large volume of transactions, few people on Wall Street ever accumulated a sizable fortune unless they branched out into other more lucrative areas of high finance. Despite the secondary role of brokerage, however, Charlie

---

1. The generally accepted meaning of the term *merchant banker* has altered significantly since the eighteenth and nineteenth centuries. Originally it referred to firms that combined mercantile activities with the provision of financial services, typically in connection with international trade. Baring Brothers was the most prominent English firm in this category. Brown Brothers, based first in Baltimore and later New York, ranked for much of the nineteenth century among the leading Anglo-American merchant banking houses; the partners were involved in the import and export of English and American goods, the issuance of letters of credit to American importers trading throughout the world, and the purchase and sale of foreign exchange in the United States. By the last quarter of the twentieth century, however, the term *merchant bankers* was used to refer strictly to financial services firms that assisted corporate clients in raising capital and simultaneously took a substantial ownership position in those same corporations. In most of Europe, but not in the United States, commercial banks were frequently allowed by law to engage in merchant banking activities. In the 1920s Merrill, Lynch and similar firms were known in New York simply as brokers and investment bankers, but, given the scope of their activities, they would meet today's criteria for designation as merchant bankers.

never overlooked or underestimated the importance of adding and servicing retail accounts. The expeditious handling of transactions for customers who regularly traded securities was always a high priority. Investors seeking a sounding board about what securities to buy or sell received the most accurate information available, which was often skimpy no matter how conscientiously pursued. Customers desiring to invest in common stocks were also given realistic advice about the probable timing of any prospective capital gains.

The "commission" business, as it was known at the time, generated modest revenues and profits at Merrill, Lynch. Its significance was that it kept the sales force, which consisted of only three or four men full time in the 1910s, in communication with persons who regularly invested in new issues of securities. Indeed, the provision of superior service for retail accounts was viewed as a critical element in the partners' overall plan. Even if the revenues earned from brokerage were limited, without eager investors to call on for the placement of new issues, Charlie would have found it impossible to arrange underwriting contracts with corporate clients. Wholesaling securities (underwriting) and trading securities (retail brokerage) were complementary activities at Merrill, Lynch. Attracting new retail accounts and keeping existing customers satisfied became standards used in evaluating the effectiveness of promotional advertising and sales personnel.

The firm's policies in handling customer accounts reflected Charlie's innovative approach to serving the needs of unsophisticated investors in middle- and upper-middle-income households. Most of his ideas were not original in 1914, but few investment houses in the U.S. market had adopted a similarly comprehensive set of policies and principles. In addition to an emphasis on truthfulness, full disclosure, and the avoidance of exaggerated claims, the partners encouraged salesmen to steer a portion of their customers' funds into the common stocks of companies with a reasonable prospect of above-average increases in sales, earnings, and dividends. The goal was to assist customers in increasing their wealth over the years, not merely the preservation of capital. At the same time, customers who insisted on avoiding the risks associated with common stocks were likewise highly valued and never unduly pressured to alter their portfolios, since the placement of new issues of corporate bonds and preferred stocks was invariably a key component of the firm's underwriting business. The Merrill partners aimed at serving every possible type of customer – from the extremely conservative to the avowed speculator.

In April 1916, Charlie spelled out in a memorandum some of the principles for sales personnel that he stressed throughout his career in the financial services sector:

> From conversations that I have overheard over the telephone between one or two of our salesmen and their clients, I notice a very unfortunate tendency to dwell upon the profits that a customer is likely to make on a certain transaction and not upon the merit of the issue as an investment. . . . There is no more dangerous lie in the world than a half-truth and quite a few of the exaggerated statements that I have overheard have been half-truths. . . . Some people around the Street are inclined to wonder why Merrill Lynch & Co. have made good; but very few of these people realize that the personal customers of Mr. Lynch and myself implicitly rely on anything we tell them. . . . The thing for you to bear in mind is that once you get a customer's confidence in the integrity and honesty of the house, you have already paved the way for a string of repeat orders. . . . We have no objection to doing business in all kinds of securities – investment, semi-investment and speculative – but what we do particularly object to is to turn an investment issue into a semi-speculative issue without our consent or approval, and vice-versa. . . . Please bear this in mind and remember that in every sale you are either increasing or destroying a good-will which up to this time has been our most valuable asset.[2]

These concepts, and others that concentrated on the dangers of misrepresentation, were repeated again and again in sales meetings and training sessions.

Generally speaking, Charlie sought the middle road between dull conservatism and rampant speculation. In flyers mailed to regular customers and prospective new accounts, he advised investors who had not reached retirement age to maintain and constantly build an investment portfolio that had a reasonably good prospect of rising in value over the long run. Investors holding a diversified portfolio of common stocks of growth-oriented companies with sound management could look forward, he assured the fainthearted, to accumulating substantial wealth over a period of fifteen to twenty-five years. A true believer, he dutifully followed his own advice and recruited others to join the parade, including his partners, employees, and retail customers.

During the first four months of 1914, Charles E. Merrill & Company generated a sufficient volume of trading commissions to show a respectable profit of $6,700. With conditions improving, Charlie gave up the rented space at Eastman Dillon in May and leased a larger office on the seventh floor at 7 Wall Street. Simultaneously, he persuaded Lynch to leave Burr and pool their talents for a second time. Lynch arrived with a list of satisfied investors who had been recruited during their years with Burr. By October 1914, the proprietorship had become a partnership – retitled Merrill, Lynch & Company (with the comma). Charlie arranged to increase the firm's capital from $15,000 to $50,000 by offering a few well-

2. Memorandum in ML Files.

chosen outside investors limited partnerships expiring in two years; the financial terms were payment of 6 percent interest plus a 10 percent participation in net profits.[3] Acting on behalf of the partnership, Lynch was admitted as a member of the New York Stock Exchange in the first half of 1916.

The partners' first major underwriting initiative became, inauspiciously, a narrow escape from disaster. The culprit was the outbreak of war in Europe. From his short tenure at Eastman Dillon, Charlie had retained a keen interest in the McCrory chain of five-and-tens. By 1914 the chain had more than 110 stores in the eastern half of the United States. One of Lynch's regular customers, necktie manufacturer Diogenes Balsam, helped to arrange a meeting with CEO John McCrory. Pointing to his successful financing of the Kresge chain in 1912, Charlie convinced McCrory to authorize the issuance of $2 million in preferred stock to shore up the balance sheet and finance further expansion. The proposed underwriting fee was access to one-fifth of the company's outstanding common stock. Since the partnership did not possess the resources to handle this transaction without the cooperation of another investment house, and perhaps two or three members of a syndicate, Charlie's next task was to locate cosponsors of the proposed new issue. He contacted more than thirty mid-sized firms in New York City, but all declined for various reasons.

Undaunted, Charlie took the train to Chicago and recruited S. W. Straus & Company, a regional investment house with experience in real estate bonds. The financial package for McCrory was increased to $2.5 million, with half in first mortgage bonds and half in preferred stock. Straus agreed to handle the placement of the bonds for a mere 2 percent of the chain's common stock. That left Merrill, Lynch with responsibility for the distribution of $1.25 million in preferred stock, and if they accomplished that, the partners would be eligible to acquire up to 18 percent of McCrory's outstanding common stock. Charlie explained the situation to his mother: "I have been working almost every night and twice on Sunday, and just now am almost petered out. The new firm is making money – about $500 in April and over $2,500 in May. I have just closed a wonderful piece of business that will either make us or break us."[4]

Lynch salesman Sumner Cobb, who had attended Amherst College, and Charlie spent the next few weeks contacting prospective customers. By early July investors had subscribed to the entire $1.25 million in preferred stock. But just a week or so later political rumblings in the Balkans caused investors to become fearful about the prudence of making new financial commitments. The outbreak of war in August unleashed a

3. Merrill to Hume, May 5, 1914, ML Files.   4. Keenan, "Chain of Fortune," 165.

huge selling wave on Wall Street, and the New York Stock Exchange closed its doors, not to reopen again for several months. A majority of the subscribers to the McCrory offering canceled their orders. The deal was put on hold.

The partners tried to survive slow times by living off the commissions from over-the-counter trades. They put themselves on a draw of only $100 per month. Cobb, the third salesman in addition to the two principals, left to accept a job with Converse Rubber. Charlie, Eliza, and daughter Doris, just six months old, moved out of their rented house in Montclair to save money. Eliza packed up Doris and went to live temporarily with her sister in Ohio. Charlie sold his car and moved into a small apartment. Meanwhile, to keep the partnership afloat, Charlie convinced Gates McGarrah, president of Mechanics and Metals Bank, where he had borrowed several years earlier to finance his purchase of securities in McCrum-Howell, to advance the partnership approximately $20,000 despite the absence of adequate collateral. "If he had refused me that loan," Merrill later recalled, "I think I would have given up and gone home to raise watermelons. I walked out of McGarrah's office with tears of gratitude in my eyes." He added: "Is it any wonder that to this day we have maintained an active account in that bank?"[5]

When the New York Stock Exchange reopened for limited trading in December, the crisis had passed. Business as usual resumed in February 1915, when all limits on trading ended. Because of investor optimism about the prospects for corporate profits on war orders from Europe, volume was heavy. The partners handled a flood of brokerage transactions in the early months of 1915. Eliza and Doris returned from Ohio, and the family rented an even larger house in Montclair. From this low point in the fall of 1914, Charlie's career soared from peak to peak over a period of four decades. Never again would the lack of adequate financial resources be a serious impediment to his ambitions.

With the financial markets returning to normal, Charlie turned his attention again to the McCrory chain. The underwriting was restructured, and this time the transaction went through without a hitch. The original enterprise was split into two separate corporations: McCrory Stores, the operating division, and McCrory Real Estate, which held store properties. Straus & Company in Chicago found investors for $725,000 in mortgage bonds to finance the real properties. Merrill, Lynch assumed responsibility for the placement of $1.25 million of 7 percent cumulative preferred shares in McCrory Stores. A sinking fund was established to retire the preferred

5. Quoted in Lewis, "Lynch Biography," 51.

stock on a regular schedule, which meant that its status was more akin to long-term debt than permanent equity.

Charlie again sought out a cosponsor for the preferred offering on Wall Street. In May 1915, John Prentiss, a partner at Hornblower & Weeks, agreed to a participation for 20 percent of the profits. This Boston-based investment house was a second- or third-tier firm, not in the same league with the elite private banking houses, but nonetheless respectable.[6] Hornblower & Weeks's willingness to form a syndicate with Merrill, Lynch lent credibility, as well as capital, to the McCrory underwriting. Charlie hoped that some of the cosponsor's good reputation would rub off and make it easier for him to attract cosponsors when future opportunities arose. The names of the various parties in underwriting syndicates – whether they were perceived as upright, conservative firms or those firms with somewhat speculative tendencies – were extremely important in Wall Street circles. Charlie believed in aggressive purchases of the securities of untested firms in growth sectors of the economy, yet he wanted to avoid acquiring the reputation of a plunging speculator – and walking that fine line was always a challenge.

While negotiations with McCrory were ongoing, Charlie devoted some of his spare time to organizational matters. Several business trips from 1912 through 1915 to Michigan to confer with Kresge and later McCrory had led to valuable contacts with investors in Detroit, a city that had recently emerged as the center of U.S. automobile manufacturing. One of the investors in the earlier Kresge flotation had been Charles Mott, who held a substantial block of shares in General Motors. To serve accounts in this area more effectively, Charlie decided to open a branch of Merrill, Lynch – essentially a small, one- or two-person office – in Detroit. Edward Ewing MacCrone, a Michigan native, was initially named to head the branch, but he left, or was eased out, within a few months. Before departing, MacCrone sold $100,000 worth of preferred stock to officials of rival S. S. Kresge, who presumably knew from their own experiences the wisdom of investing in the securities of competitive chains. MacCrone's replacement in August 1915 was Harold Matzinger, who had formerly worked with the partners at Burr and who had recently married Charlie's sister Edith.[7] In 1917 the firm opened another branch in Chicago to serve

6. Hornblower & Weeks was an established brokerage house that had only ventured into underwriting new issues in 1912. Some of its initial public offerings had performed poorly; in taking a chance with Merrill, Lynch, it was getting involved in a deal which many contemporaries believed was another risky proposition.

7. With regard to the employment of Merrill family members by the firm, Matzinger was one of two prominent exceptions. Neither of Charlie's two sons expressed any interest in following in their father's footsteps. Doris's husband, Robert Magowan, was brought into the firm, however, and he eventually became CEO of Safeway, as did Charlie's grandson Peter Magowan.

retail customers, and in the immediate postwar period it added new offices in Los Angeles and Milwaukee. The West Coast connection was unusual for a New York firm, and it served as an early indication of Charlie's grandiose visions of future possibilities.

In retrospect, the decision to expand geographically, which seemed at the time a practical response to unfolding events, was important in terms of its impact on future operations. The origins of this strategic decision are unknown, but it seems reasonable to assume that, because Charlie was exchanging views with ambitious retailers who had opened stores in hundreds of communities, the idea of imitating this branch system in the financial services sector had certainly crossed his mind. He had already been convinced of the sound logic of chains of retail stores that sold medium-priced goods in high volume on low margins. Why not offer services, rather than products, based on the same general principles in the brokerage field? The concept was not original, since several brokerage houses had already opened offices in more than one city within regional markets; still, it probably would not have occurred to anyone at the time that Charlie would someday carry that organizational strategy to its logical conclusion: a nationwide network with more than one hundred brokerage offices.

To help sign up subscribers for the McCrory shares over the summer of 1915, the firm rehired Sumner Cobb and recruited part-time sales personnel. An advertising campaign in newspapers and financial journals was launched. The partners wrote detailed personal letters to their best customers explaining the merits of an investment in McCrory's preferred stock. Subscriptions moved slowly, but the entire issue was finally placed. In the end Merrill, Lynch accounted for 90 percent of total sales; Hornblower & Weeks generated only 10 percent of sales, but that firm received 20 percent of net profits – the prearranged division. Commissions earned were sufficient to pay off the debt to Mechanics and Metals Bank and leave the new partnership with a handsome profit.[8]

The partners not only earned an underwriting fee, but, as part of their total compensation package, they also received valuable contingent benefits – namely, options to buy McCrory's common stock at fixed prices above the current market. If the retail chain was able to use the funds wisely and

---

8. In "Chain of Fortune," Keenan states that the firm made $300,000 in profits on the McCrory underwriting, but that figure seems much too high under the circumstances. The issue totaled only $1.25 million. Maybe a researcher compiling facts on the firm's history added a zero and compounded the error by putting a comma in the wrong column; if the figure was only $30,000, which seems a possible explanation, it would have represented 2.4 percent of the preferred stock flotation. Alternatively, the higher number might have included the capital gains that arose from exercising options on McCrory common stock, in which case, $300,000 overall does not seem beyond the realm of probability.

build on its prior successes, and if, in turn, its common stock caught the attention of investors, Merrill, Lynch stood to reap large capital gains by exercising its option rights as common stock prices climbed. As it happened, the chain continued to expand and earn record profits, and the partners eventually accumulated a large block of its common stock that on paper was worth millions of dollars.[9]

Another long-term business relationship was with the Kresge chain. Charlie had managed an underwriting for Kresge three years earlier when he was still learning the ropes at George Burr. With the McCrory success behind him, Charlie seized the opportunity to renew old acquaintances.[10] He met with Kresge in Detroit in November 1915 and presented a proposal to raise additional capital. The chain had expanded to more than 130 cities and towns in the Northeast and Midwest, and management wanted to continue its torrid growth. Charlie and the principals worked out a plan to issue $2 million in preferred stock plus 100,000 shares of common. Hornblower & Weeks immediately stepped forward to act as a cosponsor on this second joint underwriting. When the news spread on Wall Street, the partners at Burr and at Hallgarten were undoubtedly chagrined to learn that they had lost a valued corporate client.

The solicitation of other investment bankers' regular clients was considered ungentlemanly behavior by the elite houses. Relationship banking – business conducted in a cordial atmosphere among friends that paralleled the unbreakable ties of marriage – was considered the proper way of conducting business between a corporate client and its financiers. Some successful bankers considered any interference by outsiders in an ongoing business relationship to be inherently unethical. The firms at the top of this oligopolistic pyramid preferred the comfort of stable relationships, and they were unwilling to countenance the behavior of more aggressive competitors, most of whom they pejoratively labeled as speculative. Corporate clients who were dissatisfied with their previous underwriters were, on the other hand, always welcome in the offices of the elites, but the initiative had to be taken by the prospective client, not the passive investment banker. If, for example, the Morgan partners had, by chance, heard rumors about Charlie's aggressive pursuit of Kresge, they undoubtedly would have turned up their collective noses.[11] But Merrill, Lynch was still an incon-

---

9. Charlie's ties with the McCrory Stores ended in the early 1930s, when the chain nearly went bankrupt. Cordial relations with Kresge, another early client, also ceased over time.
10. Sebastian Kresge and John McCrory were partners in the variety store business for about a year in the 1890s. After the split, they independently built successful chains. Thus, it seems likely that Kresge, in addition to Balsam, was instrumental in facilitating the 1914 meeting between Charlie and McCrory.
11. Chernow, *House of Morgan*, and Carosso, *The Morgans*, reveal just how seriously these codes of behavior were taken in their outstanding books on the Morgan firm and its Wall Street

sequential house from the perspective of the elites in 1916, and few, if any, had any knowledge of the origins of this minor underwriting. Later, in the 1940s, the flagrant breaking of outdated, aristocratic taboos would become one of the hallmarks of Charlie's second career on Wall Street.

In other transactions involving chain stores before the U.S. entry into World War I, the partners again broke new ground. For the first time, they raised capital for chains specializing in groceries, and they negotiated their first corporate merger. The firm's increasingly visible link to chain store financing had caught the attention of the partners of Cassatt & Company, brokers and investment bankers in Philadelphia. In the late spring of 1916, Cassatt recruited Merrill, Lynch to join a syndicate organized to issue securities for Acme Tea Company, a grocery chain headquartered in Philadelphia with more than four hundred stores in eighty cities. In a second underwriting with Cassatt in late 1916, Merrill, Lynch sponsored the issuance of securities that financed the merger of two large grocery chains in the New York metropolitan area, Jones Brothers Tea Company and Grand Union Tea Company. The underwriting totaled over $10 million, and it caught the attention of business reporters at the *New York Times,* who proclaimed on December 8, 1916: "The transaction ranks with the largest chain store deals in recent years." After consulting with Rudy Guenther, who focused on the development of creative advertising for firms in the financial services sector, Charlie decided to spend nearly $2,000 to telegraph – rather than use the slower mail – reprints of the *Times* story to dozens of out-of-town newspapers. The money was well spent, since a number of large orders for securities arrived from distant points over the next few weeks. In short, within three years of its founding, Merrill, Lynch was recognized on Wall Street as a firm with substantial expertise in the fast-growing chain store sector of the economy.

A second industry that attracted a fair amount of Charlie's attention in the late 1910s was automotive manufacturing. Many of the firm's corporate clients in this sector proved unprofitable and ultimately failed. By 1915 the automobile industry was still sorting out the winners from the losers in what was becoming an increasingly oligopolistic field. Henry Ford was on top of the mountain with roughly half the industry's annual sales and huge profits. General Motors had already taken a firm hold on the number two slot with about one-fifth of the market. Numerous firms on the fringes struggled to capture a respectable share of the remaining one-quarter or so of the market. Because Ford had the bottom end of the auto market

---

peers. Ironically, Morgan Stanley, one of the successor firms after the breakup dictated by new banking laws in the 1930s, became very aggressive in mergers and acquisitions in the 1970s and 1980s.

wrapped up with the Model T, other manufacturers concentrated either on mid-priced or high-priced vehicles. As a rule, the elite private banking houses had remained leery of the aspiring manufacturers of the horseless carriage. In 1910, Lee Higginson & Company, a second-tier Boston-based firm, raised the capital required to rescue General Motors from impending bankruptcy, but other conservative houses were reluctant to assist in raising funds for expansion.

Through the Kresge connection in Detroit, Charlie had opened several accounts for automotive executives who aimed to diversify their investment portfolios by including the securities of chain stores. Because these entrepreneurs were themselves deeply committed to a relatively new industry, they had little hesitation about allocating a portion of their personal investments to other growth-oriented sectors of the American economy. Most automobile manufacturers sold their products through broad dealer networks, and their executives were comfortable with the concept of distributing consumer goods through hundreds of retail outlets. Charlie got involved in Saxon Motors as a result of the efforts of Lee Counselman, an industry veteran previously associated with Chalmers Motors, a moderately successful small-scale manufacturer that traced its origins back to 1905.[12] In 1915, Counselman was vice president of Saxon, a firm headed by Harry Ford (no relation to Henry). The company wanted to raise approximately $6 million to build an assembly plant and execute a marketing plan for an automobile with a powerful engine and a luxurious interior.

In November 1915, Merrill, Lynch underwrote an issue of securities for Saxon Motors. The stock was offered to customers as a speculative investment because the company was not an established automotive manufacturer. When the new plant was ready to start assembling vehicles, the company had a backlog of orders. Then a series of disasters struck. The recently completed plant burned to the ground. The building was fully insured, but management was unwilling to wait for its reconstruction to start production of the existing model. The company rented space in several locations and went ahead with the assembly of what turned out to be an inferior automobile. By the time the plant was rebuilt, Harry Ford had died. Charlie, Lynch, and Counselman tried to lure Walter Chrysler, a vice president at General Motors then in charge of the Buick division, to Saxon Motors by offering him an annual salary of $35,000, a large jump over his existing salary. But Chrysler declined. Over the next few years things went from bad to worse at Saxon Motors; in 1922, the company fell

12. Rae, *American Automotive Industry*, provides a good overview of the industry in its formative years. Rae cites Hugh Chalmers as an automotive entrepreneur who was effective in terms of salesmanship but who lacked organizational skills, and thus ultimately failed.

into receivership and never recovered. Years later Charlie concluded that he had mishandled the negotiations with Chrysler. He lamented that if he had had the foresight to offer Chrysler 20 percent of Saxon's common stock, he probably could have recruited the man who was destined to create a company that rose to preeminence as a member of the Big Three.

A second missed opportunity in the automotive field was a chance to participate in an initial public offering of securities for Fisher Body Corporation. Matzinger, the manager of the Detroit branch office, was on good terms with the six Fisher brothers. Fisher Body had been one of Michigan's largest carriage manufacturers in the late nineteenth century before it shifted to automobiles in 1908.[13] Tightly held by the Fisher family, the company was a major supplier to General Motors and other automotive manufacturers. At a meeting in Detroit, Charlie, Lynch, and Matzinger reached a tentative oral agreement regarding a proposed underwriting with family members, but company lawyers and other outside financial advisers dissuaded the brothers from continuing negotiations on the proposal. How close Charlie actually got to clinching the Fisher deal is difficult to judge based on the surviving evidence. Just a few years later, in 1919, the Fisher brothers sold a majority interest in their company to General Motors for more than $25 million.

Another project linked to the automotive industry was closer to home. Spicer Manufacturing Company, located in South Plainfield, New Jersey, was a parts supplier for vehicle assemblers. By 1916 it was one of the nation's largest producers of universal joints, drive shafts, and axles both for cars and trucks. Charlie was introduced to Spicer management through the partners of Cassatt, the same Philadelphia house that had drawn Merrill, Lynch into grocery chains. Spicer did well during the war years, but its Sheldon Axle division drifted into financial difficulties late in the decade. To protect their valued customers from heavy losses on their investments in the company's securities, the underwriters were called on to assist in the reorganization by helping to establish a $500,000 revolving fund to pay the most pressing debts and provide sufficient leeway for recovery. As a result of this second sour experience, Charlie lost his initial enthusiasm for the automotive field.[14] No matter, however, because plenty of other opportunities arose for the firm in chain stores and, curiously, in motion pictures.

Charlie's business career was interrupted in 1917 and 1918 when, in a burst of patriotism, he volunteered for military service. This decision was

---

13. Chandler, *Pierre S. du Pont,* 465.
14. Spicer, renamed Dana, remained one of the firm's underwriting clients from the 1920s through the 1940s and 1950s.

not impetuous or out of character since he was a lifelong supporter of U.S. military preparedness. Believing that the United States might enter the European conflict at some point, he had made inquiries about the Civilian Officers Training Program at Plattsburg, New York, as early as 1916. When Congress voted to declare war on Germany in April 1917, the partners decided to run an advertisement in the *New York Times* encouraging the public to subscribe to the Liberty Loan drive, and they pledged to handle all subscriptions "without profit or commission of any kind whatsoever." Merrill, Lynch was the first investment house, or at least among the very first, to offer to perform government business during the war on a gratis basis. After the advertisement appeared, officials of the New York Stock Exchange summoned Charlie for a mild lecture about the impropriety of failing to consult in advance with the Business Conduct Committee, which exercised jurisdiction over the advertising of member firms. This run-in with exchange authorities was premonitory because conflicts with the Wall Street establishment over rules and regulations became commonplace during later periods in the firm's history.

Despite Charlie's fervent desire to join the crusade, the partners initially agreed that in the interest of perpetuating the business, only one of them should volunteer for military service, and Lynch was the logical choice because he was still a bachelor. But Lynch failed the eye examination and was rejected for officer training. Charlie immediately mailed an application to the officers training camp at Fort Myer in Arlington, Virginia. After hearing nothing for several weeks, he took the train to Washington to investigate the status of his application. He learned that the army had more applicants for officer training than it could process and that priority was being given to persons with some previous military training. Inventively, Charlie cited his sophomore and junior years at Stetson; Stetson had a military department, and he had occasionally marched around the grounds in uniform. Another important fact was that, by traveling to the training camp from New York on his own initiative, Charlie had demonstrated his seriousness and eagerness for military service. The army's personnel officers decided to admit him to the program forthwith.

Charlie was thirty-two when he entered the army in the summer of 1917. After completing his initial military training at Fort Myer, he was commissioned a first lieutenant and assigned to cooks and bakers school at Camp Lee in Petersburg, Virginia. His previous experience as food manager for the fraternity house at the University of Michigan may have been a factor in the army's decision to assign him to such routine duty. Why he was not sent to the financial corps, given his background, remains a mystery. Boredom at cooks and bakers school led him to seek a transfer to the air corps division, and he reported to the School for Military Aeronautics at the University of Texas in Austin in February 1918. Charlie was the oldest aviator in his group. His flight training was at Kelly Field near San Antonio, and from there he was ordered to Carstrom Field near Arcadia, Florida – his home state.[15] The airfield was about one hundred miles northwest of his parents' home in the Palm Beach area, and he occasionally flew over to visit them. In a letter to his daughter, Doris, Charlie later recalled "the expression on my father's face – relief, pride and love – when I climbed out of the plane that brought me from Arcadia to Palm Beach."[16] He also got up to Jacksonville to visit boyhood friend Sam Marks on weekends. Much to his chagrin, Charlie learned that he was not among those scheduled for shipment overseas; instead, the air service needed him to train others to fly pursuit aircraft. His relatively advanced age compared to other pilots and the fact that he had a family at home were likely taken into account in the army's decision not to send him to Europe.

Meanwhile, Lynch, who had maintained his enthusiasm for participation in the Great War, enlisted in a cavalry unit as a private in the spring or summer of 1918. The army's rules about wearing glasses had been relaxed – at least for privates, if not officers. Lynch was still learning how to ride horses in combat situations when the armistice was announced in November; like Charlie, he never left American shores. Who actually managed the firm during the six months or so that Lynch was away is not clear from surviving records, but sales personnel continued to handle brokerage functions for regular customers as best they could. Key members of the secretarial and backroom staff were still employed when the partners returned in late 1918.

The eighteen months that First Lieutenant Charles Merrill spent in the army were a golden opportunity to observe firsthand the managerial policies of a large bureaucratic organization with a clear, unambiguous goal: winning the war. All his previous experience had been with small or medium-sized organizations. What he learned from this military detour that later proved useful is difficult to assess with any certainty, but Charlie had a chance to note the strategies that motivated large groups of people who were focused on a common goal. In the attempt to carry Merrill,

15. Eliza moved into a house near Kelly Field during Charlie's flight training. Other young officers often came by the house in the evenings, and she entertained them by playing the piano and singing. According to Charles Jr., his father later spoke about those months in Texas as among the happiest of their marriage. Author's correspondence with Charles Merrill Jr., April 9, 1994.
16. Quoted in Keenan, "Chain of Fortune," 226.

Lynch and its customers to new heights and greater wealth, Charlie had, from the outset, revealed aspects of his missionary zeal; the military experience probably reinforced his earlier tendencies. What was new was that the army was a prime example of how a large organization, albeit a non-profit entity in this instance, could achieve great success with a sound master plan and proper direction. One thing can be said for certain: nothing that happened in 1917 and 1918 had a negative impact on his future business career.

While he was temporarily distracted by the air corps, Charlie continued to ponder how the partnership should recoup after the fighting had stopped. Based on the firm's performance before the United States entered into the war, he was exceedingly optimistic about future prospects. In one prescient letter to Lynch in 1918, Charlie expressed some of his thoughts in a series of short, clipped sentence fragments:

> Must have higher class help. More efficient. Must get organized for average business of 10,000 shares per day. More help or better and faster, or better system. . . . Put out weekly review of stock market through syndicate of news-papers. . . . Must have real sales manager. Retail. And some real salesmen who will get outside the office and stay outside. No ticker hounds. We could use 20 good men right away.[17]

When he left the army and headed back to his home in Montclair and his career on Wall Street, Charlie had every right to take a great deal of pride in his civilian accomplishments. Not yet thirty-five, he was already wealthy, and he had his sights set on even greater riches. Enriching himself through merchant banking strategies, and in the process helping others to enhance their wealth through the performance of investment banking and brokerage functions, were activities he enjoyed immensely. For Charlie, work and pleasure were often simultaneous pursuits.

His partnership with Lynch, despite occasional tensions and personality conflicts, had worked out satisfactorily on balance. He had developed a tremendous loyalty to Lynch – a loyalty that persisted long after the latter's death in 1938. With American troops headed home, Charlie had no hesitation about plunging ahead at an equally fast pace in the postwar era. The firm had become an acknowledged specialist in handling the securities of firms in a sector most other investment houses had imprudently ignored, chain stores.[18] Their loss was Charlie's gain. Off to a flying start, he hoped

---

17. Quoted in Keenan, "Chain of Fortune," 231–32.
18. Goldman, Sachs underwrote an issue of securities for the F. W. Woolworth variety chain sometime in this period – thus Merrill Lynch was not alone in financing these ventures. Other investment firms were never as strongly committed to the chain store sector, however.

to increase his stature in the eyes of observers who informally determined the rankings of the most influential investment houses on Wall Street. Merrill, Lynch still had a long way to go to reach the top echelons, but the partners were headed in the right direction.

6

THE BOOMING TWENTIES

The 1920s were enormously prosperous years for Merrill, Lynch and its two principals. Although underwriting contracts revived at a disappointing pace in the immediate postwar years, the number of transactions quickened in the middle of the decade. In addition to the financial rewards associated with these ventures, the partners took great satisfaction in underwriting issues for two of their former employers in the manufacturing sector – Robert Sjostrom's Patchogue-Plymouth Mills, Charlie's first employer in New York City, and Liquid Carbonic, where Lynch had started his career. These transactions, in particular, were welcome because they demonstrated that the partners' former associates retained a great deal of respect for their financial judgment.

Before the end of the decade, Merrill, Lynch had served as underwriter for the securities of more than seventy different companies. Generally speaking, the partnership sponsored the securities of entrepreneurial enterprises that had sound management and a growth orientation with respect to sales and profits. In many cases corporate clients were making their initial public offering of securities. Only one of the varied underwriting clients ran into serious financial trouble in the 1920s – not a perfect record, but still respectable considering the volume of transactions and the element of risk associated with initial public offerings. Retail customers who bought and held the securities sponsored by the partners had every reason to be thankful for the dividends and capital gains over the long term.

Like many of his contemporaries of the war years, Charlie was optimistic and sometimes ebullient about the future of the U.S. economy and the prospects for the securities markets in the upcoming decade. The federal government's aggressive bond campaign had drawn a significant number of middle-class households into the financial markets for the first time. "I venture to predict that we will sell government bonds before the war is over to 8,000,000 to 20,000,000 people," he told Lynch at one point. "People who start buying bonds from motives of patriotism," Charlie added, "will continue to do so because they are the most convenient form of safe investment."[1] And, indeed, with the exception of one deep, but short, postwar recession, the economy continued to move ahead at a steady pace from 1919 to 1929. Inflation and unemployment remained low, real wages rose, and corporate profits kept climbing.

The general public became participants in the financial markets for the first time in the 1920s, and common stocks caught the attention of investors, many of whom were unseasoned and unsophisticated. The number of stocks listed on the New York Stock Exchange doubled between 1915 and 1925 – from just over 500 issues to more than 1,000. The number of individuals holding equities jumped between 1910 and 1930 from fewer than 2 million to perhaps as many as 5 million.[2] The market value of all stocks on the NYSE climbed from $4 billion in 1901 to $60 billion in 1929. With prices climbing, trading volume increased – rising, for example, from 260 million shares in 1922, to 450 million shares in 1925, and to over one billion shares in 1929.[3] The number of issues listed on out-of-town exchanges and quoted regularly in over-the-counter markets went up as well. New brokerage firms and small to medium-sized investment banking houses proliferated. Meanwhile, many firms already in financial services broadened the range of their activities. Several of the leading commercial banks in New York City created subsidiaries to underwrite securities. Before the decade ended, commercial banks had siphoned off up to one-half of the business in government and corporate bonds from the elite private houses.

In light of its sponsorship of the securities of McCrory and Kresge before the war, Merrill, Lynch had established itself as a leading financier of the neglected chain store sector. Charlie hoped to build on that base and get off to a fast start in 1919, but prospective clients were hesitant. Fears of a postwar recession, which soon became a reality, put the brakes on the expansion plans of many chains. As a consequence, just three of the firm's twenty-five underwritings from May 1919 through December 1922 financed chain stores. Kresge, a former client, sold a $3 million debt issue in 1920. Two new clients were J. C. Penney and G. R. Kinney, the latter a fast-growing chain that retailed low- and medium-priced shoes through

1. Quoted in Keenan, "Chain of Fortune," 239.
2. Many sources cite as many as 10 million probable equity holders in 1930, but over the course of this project, I have grown increasingly skeptical about a figure that high. First, there were no reliable statistics on ownership patterns in the 1920s; second, a 1950 Roper survey, which was conducted using fairly systematic methods, listed only about 6 million shareholders. Common sense suggests that there were probably not 4 million additional investors in stocks in 1929. Indeed, I suspect that 5 million is the upward bound number. The number of active brokerage accounts in 1929 was around 1.5 million.
3. Sobel, *Great Bull Market*, 102.

more than one hundred stores by 1921. The former was an organization begun by James Cash Penney and two partners, whom he later bought out, in Kemmerer, Wyoming, in 1902. The chain had grown to nearly two hundred outlets by the end of the war. In July 1919, Merrill, Lynch, with a one-third participation, and G. H. Burr, the partners' former employer, agreed to underwrite $3 million in preferred stock for J. C. Penney & Company.

In the negotiations with Penney, Charlie heard in detail about two managerial policies that left a deep impression – and had future implications. In the nineteenth century, most country stores made it standard practice to extend liberal credit to retail customers to generate sales, which meant that owners needed extra working capital to finance accounts receivable as well as inventories. Moreover, a certain percentage of customer debts proved uncollectable and had to be written off against profits. Penney flouted convention and insisted on cash payment in all transactions. To compensate for the absence of credit, prices were kept low. What Penney gave up in terms of profit margins, he expected to recoup with high volume. Prices were so competitive that his outlets, initially called Golden Rule Stores, soon gained a foothold in many towns and small cities.

The other innovative policy in the Penney organization that impressed Charlie greatly was its profit-sharing program. The founder allowed managers in the field to become part owners of their respective stores and thereby to participate in the profits earned within their locality. The plan represented a compromise between two extremes. Some retail firms owned and administered hundreds of stores from a central headquarters; others were essentially coordinating agents for a multitude of locally owned franchises. This incentive program produced a cadre of loyal, ambitious store managers, thus providing a viable solution to what economists identify as the principal-agent problem.[4] The arrangement at Penneys blended elements of central control and local initiative. As a rule, store managers received only modest salaries, but through the profits accruing from partial ownership, they could boost their annual income substantially. Charlie endorsed both concepts – cash sales and some form of profit sharing at the local level – and variations on these themes would be implemented at Safeway Stores after he assumed control.

Whenever underwriting was slow, the firm depended on revenue from the performance of less glamorous, but still important, financial functions. Having become familiar with the operation of the commercial paper market during their years with Burr, the partners established a similar department at Merrill, Lynch. It dealt in short-term notes payable to bearer, usually

4. My thanks to reader Richard Sylla for calling my attention to the principal-agent issue.

with maturity dates of 60 to 180 days; the issuers were companies in need of extra working capital to supplement their outstanding loans from commercial banks. Many companies that issued commercial paper through Merrill, Lynch were also underwriting clients, and the performance of a range of collateral financial services helped to cement the relationship.

A second source of revenue was the performance of routine brokerage functions for retail customers at the firm's seven branch offices. For most of the 1920s the firm maintained two offices in New York City, in downtown and uptown Manhattan, as well as outlets in Chicago, Detroit, Los Angeles, Denver, and Milwaukee. The number of people employed in the two New York offices grew to more than forty by 1930, while out-of-town employees totaled fifteen to twenty. During the decade, twelve employees were welcomed into the partnership as junior members, including Winthrop Smith, who joined the firm after his graduation from Amherst College in 1916.

For four years, starting in 1919, the partners underwrote the securities of several companies linked to petroleum production and refining in the Southwest. Charlie's interest in the region had been piqued by his flight training in Austin and San Antonio in 1918. As was true in many of the partners' business transactions, a personal connection was a factor in their entrance into this industrial sector. Charlie had hired Louis McClure, a classmate at the University of Michigan and fellow member of the Friars, a campus drinking club, to work for the firm in New York. With business slow in the first half of 1919, McClure left for the rapidly developing oil fields of Texas and Oklahoma. A few months later, in October 1919, he was instrumental in arranging the underwriting for an issue of preferred stock for Panhandle Production and Refining. Overall, the partners sponsored nine issues of securities for six different oil companies through 1922 with an aggregate value of more than $14 million. But the partners' interest in this industry soon waned. Lynch, who was especially active in the negotiations with petroleum companies, found his attention diverted by pressing duties in motion pictures in the early 1920s.

The one underwriting deal that went sour for the partnership in the twenties was associated neither with petroleum nor with chain stores, but rather with manufacturing. In the summer of 1920 the firm underwrote an issue of $1 million in preferred shares for Waring Hat Manufacturing, which had a plant in nearby Yonkers. The manufacturer had weathered the postwar recession with minor losses, and its future looked encouraging to most analysts. In addition to recommending the company's securities to retail customers, the partners increased their investment in Waring Hat's common stock in 1923. Merrill, Lynch's commercial paper department handled debt obligations for the company on a regular basis.

Then, unexpectedly, the partners learned that the valuation of Waring Hat's inventory was highly inflated. Charlie tried to save the company by attempting to arrange additional financing, but other creditors refused to participate, arguing the futility of investing further in a faltering enterprise. In the end, everyone took a bath. The partners lost heavily on their investment in Waring Hat's common stock. Retail customers who had bought the preferred shares sponsored by the firm suffered as well. Charlie softened the blow somewhat by offering customers with sizable losses the opportunity to buy stock in the Ginter Company, a grocery chain later renamed First National Stores, at the underwriter's price – a figure well below the prevailing market.[5] Most investors who accepted the offer to buy Ginter stock at a discount eventually recouped the losses associated with the collapse of Waring Hat.[6]

As the anniversary of the firm's opening approached in January 1924, Charlie took the occasion to draft for staff and friends a broad statement that summarized its accomplishments to date. Always a strong believer in the value of publicity – the opposite view of most of his peers on Wall Street – Charlie mailed the message to every retail customer and arranged for its release to the business press. "During the past ten years we have sponsored, issued, wholesaled or retailed many millions of securities. . . . Our business is to serve all classes of security buyers." Nonetheless, he observed, "The great American fortunes have been made by shareholders

5. Under the more restrictive rules introduced in the 1930s, the practice of allowing certain classes of customers or individuals to acquire new issues of stock at discount prices was made illegal. By applying modern ethical standards, we could probably accuse Merrill of acting in an underhanded manner in the aftermath of the Waring Hat disaster. But I doubt seriously if anybody in the 1920s thought there was anything improper about a brokerage house trying to do a small favor for customers who had been burned by the firm's bad advice on a previous investment. Merrill certainly did not think he was doing anything wrong; on the contrary, he believed he was doing the right thing under the circumstances.
6. At least one dissatisfied customer sued the firm for misrepresentation in the Waring Hat underwriting. The Business Conduct Committee of the NYSE somehow got involved, and members requested the privilege of inspecting the underwriting books in the possession of Merrill, Lynch. The committee was irked by the firm's failure to respond instantaneously to its request, and Charlie was summoned to explain the delay. He told the committee that he and his partners believed they needed time to consult with the firm's lawyers before responding affirmatively. Winthrop Burr, chairman of the committee, was angry about the partners' allegedly disrespectful behavior, and he lectured Charlie for nearly an hour about the power and responsibilities of the NYSE and its various committees. Charlie suspected that the real motive for his summons was a lingering resentment over the advertisement that Merrill, Lynch had run in 1917 offering to handle government bonds on a no-fee basis without consulting the same committee in advance. The partnership had been called before the Business Conduct Committee on that occasion as well. In this earlier episode, Charlie had referred to some members as "old fogies" with respect to their attitudes about the appropriateness of advertising. Whatever the case, he drafted a four-page memo describing his meeting with the committee in October 1925. Charlie finally offered his apologies, and that seemed to satisfy committee members who seemed primarily interested in humbling anyone who challenged their authority in any way.

and not by bondholders." With that thought in mind, Charlie informed readers that the partners had dutifully followed their own prescription for accumulating wealth: "For our part we have invested a certain definite percentage of our own money in all the concerns financed by us. By far the larger part of our present resources has come through a faithful adhesion to this policy." Moreover, Charlie explained, "In addition to the money originally invested, we have put in, at times, management, supervision, counsel, and financial support in emergencies. It is our policy to stand behind our companies." He ended by exclaiming that "so far as we know, this is the first complete statement ever put out by a house of issue – covering a ten year period." More than fifteen years later, Merrill Lynch broke precedent once again on Wall Street by becoming the first privately held firm to voluntarily release the partnership's income statement and balance sheet for public scrutiny.

While his business career was progressing by leaps and bounds, Charlie's private life was in disarray. Not long after the birth of Charles Jr. in 1920, he and Eliza began to quarrel more frequently, and the chasm between them widened. Charlie developed something of a dual personality as the years passed: invariably calm and collected in a business setting, at home, he could be argumentative, dictatorial, irascible, and demanding. After the war, Charlie made an essentially unilateral decision to move the family from Montclair to a triplex at 471 Park Avenue in the heart of Manhattan. He also bought a weekend retreat in Westhampton on the southern shore of Long Island and a vacation home in Palm Beach near his parents' residence. Charlie wanted to reap more of the tangible benefits of economic success. But Eliza was uncomfortable in the family's new environment. She preferred the quiet, suburban atmosphere of northern New Jersey to high-pressure Manhattan, given its inhabitants' obsession with moneymaking and their proclivity for heavy drinking and late-night parties. Eliza found these social diversions distressing; her husband found them stimulating.

Entertaining friends and business associates a few days during the week and almost every weekend was a way of life that Charlie enjoyed immensely. The fraternity house atmosphere of his college days was recreated on a minor scale in Manhattan and on Long Island during the summer months. Good food, flowing liquor, a rubber of bridge, and lively, informal conversation about business affairs were his amusement and relaxation. Eliza's trepidations aside, their rising standard of living and free-spending lifestyle merely reflected the norm for a household headed by an ambitious financier who was rapidly ascending to the top of the business world. Despite his heightened status among his peers on Wall Street, Charlie generally avoided socializing with members of the elite investment banking houses who were generally products of Ivy League schools – the "striped pants crowd," as he derogatorily referred to them. Instead, he preferred the company of colleagues employed at Merrill, Lynch, executives of the enterprises that the firm had financed, corporate lawyers who had participated in these deals, and old chums from his school days – plus their wives if they were married. Understandably, Charlie felt more at ease with other nouveaux riches than with the silver-spoon socialites who came from stuffy eastern money.

In partying around Manhattan and when out of town for business or pleasure, Charlie frequently encountered attractive women who shared his enthusiasm for an active social life. Wealth, power, a small measure of fame, and handsome good looks, in combination, have since the dawn of civilization made it relatively easy for prosperous men to turn their sexual fantasies about younger women into reality. Charlie was not immune to these temptations when opportunities arose. In time he entered into a series of extramarital affairs that contributed to the breakup of his marriage.

By the summer of 1924, he and Eliza were living apart. Charlie moved into the Hotel Marguery. Divorce was less common at that time, in large part because family law was so rigid and restrictive. In many states, including New York, only adultery or extreme cruelty was recognized as a legitimate reason for granting a divorce. As a result, couples living in New York that wished to avoid the embarrassment of an unpleasant public trial were forced to establish a temporary residence for one spouse in another state where the laws were more flexible. Florida fit that category. Eliza took Doris and Charles to Jacksonville to establish legal residence and file the appropriate papers. Sam Marks, Charlie's boyhood friend, handled the divorce, which became final in February 1925, ending thirteen years of marriage. After the divorce, Eliza moved back to New York City, thereby allowing Charlie to act as a parent to Doris and Charles on a fairly regular basis.

The number thirteen has long been considered unlucky in Western societies, and Charlie's prolonged experience with the state of matrimony offers proof that an element of truth resides in this fanciful yet enduring superstition. After Eliza, he was subsequently married to two other women – also for roughly thirteen years each, give or take a few months.[7] Indeed,

---

7. James Merrill cited his father's three marriages in "The Broken Home," originally published in 1966: "Each thirteenth year he married . . ." The poem was reprinted in a collection of Merrill's work titled *From the First Nine: Poems 1946–1976* (1981), 140. Many of Merrill's works focus directly or indirectly on his father's private life.

with only a few intervening months, Charlie was married for thirty-nine consecutive years to three different women – a remarkable marital record even by the relaxed standards of the late twentieth century.

Not a man to waste time in matters of the heart after his frustratingly long engagement to Marie Sjostrom, Charlie, now thirty-nine, married Hellen Ingram, fourteen years his junior, just a few weeks after the divorce from Eliza became final. A Jacksonville native like himself, she had a budding career in journalism when they met. She began as a music and society reporter for the *Florida Metropolis*, later renamed the *Jacksonville Journal*. In 1922, at age twenty-three, Hellen demonstrated her own entre-preneurial bent when she became the owner, editor, and publisher of a weekly magazine called *Silhouette*. The publication ran stories about social events, concerts, and other entertainments; its pages included book re-views, fashion reports, and feature-length articles. Within two years the magazine was distributed along Florida's eastern shoreline from Jackson-ville southward. Miami became Hellen's residence and publication base, reflecting the city's status as the state's main vacation resort.

In the summer of 1924, when the tourist trade was slow, Hellen enrolled in journalism courses at Columbia University to improve her publication skills. Having learned through a mutual friend in Jacksonville that Charlie had separated from Eliza, she contacted him soon after her arrival, and within a short time they had begun dating. Despite the age gap, they had much in common; they shared southern roots and had rather similar backgrounds. For example, Charlie was familiar with the journalism field since he had worked as a jack-of-all-trades on a weekly newspaper in the Palm Beach area during the summer months between his sophomore and junior years at college. Hellen was energetic, pretty, artistic, and full of life; equally important, she appreciated the demands and rewards of the business world. She seemed to be just the person Charlie was looking for at this stage in his life. After Hellen returned to Miami that fall, Charlie arranged several trips to southern Florida to visit his parents in West Palm Beach and pursue his new romance. Under pressure, Hellen agreed to marriage as soon as his divorce was final. They were united at her family home in Jacksonville in February 1925. Lynch arrived from New York to serve as his business partner's best man. Charlie had acquired a trophy wife to complement all of his other expensive possessions. He took Hellen to Europe for a belated honeymoon in the spring.

The couple established a household on West Eleventh Street in Green-wich Village – not far, ironically, from where Charlie's first marriage had begun. He spent more than $50,000 on remodeling and furnishings, in-cluding the purchase of at least one costly original painting to please his bride. Hellen became pregnant a few months after their marriage, and in

March 1926 their first and only child, James Ingram Merrill, was born. Hellen broadened Charlie's social horizons. She was imaginative, articulate, and enjoyed socializing with a variety of new friends and old acquaintances. Hellen mixed reasonably well with his cronies from the office – at least for the first ten years of their married life – and she introduced him, in a casual way, to a more artistic and intellectual crowd – the actors, writers, editors, musicians, and painters who also made New York City their home. High finance and high culture were the lifeblood of Manhattan, and the Merrills were participants in certain aspects of both worlds – although business and finance always took precedence.

Not long after Charlie and Hellen were married, he bought a spacious estate in Southampton, a summer resort town about one hundred miles east of the city on the southern shore of Long Island. The house was called "The Orchard" in deference to the bountiful apple trees on its outer grounds. A large frame structure with numerous bedrooms on the second and third floors for weekend guests, it possessed, in addition to the standard living quarters, a conservatory, a music room with an organ, and other luxurious amenities. A staff of seven or more – cooks, a butler, maids, and chauffeurs – was required to keep the household functioning. All the house servants were African Americans, since they were the employees with whom Hellen felt most comfortable in light of her southern upbringing. Albert Jaeckel, the firm's top lawyer and someone Charlie had known since a visit to Williams during his sophomore year at Amherst, owned a summer home in the area, and that proximity was probably a factor in the decision to acquire this magnificent piece of real estate. The Orchard was Charlie's weekend home from late spring through early fall for the next twenty years; after his heart attack in 1944, he would spend many weekdays there as well.

Charlie's real estate spree did not end with residences in Manhattan and Long Island. He purchased for the astronomical sum of $500,000 (around $5 million in 1995 prices) a four-thousand-acre plantation called Wildwood, located ten miles north of Greenwood, Mississippi, on the Tallahatchie River. The *New York Times* reported on October 21, 1927, that the new owner planned "to restore Wildwood to its former grandeur." This middle-age indulgence was on a scale that only persons with surplus wealth can readily afford.

The location of the plantation provided the rationale for its selection. The great house was located less than fifty miles northeast of his grandmother Emily's farm in Holmes County. He had visited the family farm often in the summer during his youth. As business manager of his newly acquired cotton fields, Charlie installed Jefferson Wilson, a close relative on his mother's side of the family. The plan was to spend time at his

Mississippi retreat on a regular basis, escaping the constant business pressures of New York; but after the initial visit to arrange the purchase, Charlie and Hellen rarely returned. Southern Florida became, instead, his favorite winter vacation spot. The Mississippi farm hardly paid its own way, and he sold the property at a loss in 1938. Charlie's underlying motivation for buying Wildwood was to participate, if only from afar, in the aristocratic tradition of the great southern planter. Charlie felt a need to demonstrate to his mother and her relatives, plus his new bride and her relatives, that while he may have gone north to make his fortune, he still retained a warm place in his heart for the lost cause of the Confederacy and his southern heritage. Of course, he never stopped to ponder for a moment, nor did anyone around him in the 1920s and 1930s, the extent to which these revered traditions were based on exploitation and a false sense of racial superiority. After his death, however, his oldest son and namesake took a different approach to the family's social obligations. Charles Jr. was instrumental in directing a portion of his father's trust fund into predominantly African American colleges and universities in the southern states.[8]

In addition to the profits arising from financing firms in the manufacturing and retailing sectors, Charlie also realized substantial capital gains from the firm's singular investment in the motion picture industry. In 1921, the partners acquired a controlling interest in the American division of Pathé Frères Cinema, the internationally prominent French movie studio, and five years later they surrendered their position to a group of investors at a handsome profit. The Pathé venture was radically different from previous merchant banking transactions. In this instance the partners went beyond acting merely as passive, outside investors. From the outset, Lynch was an active participant in the day-to-day management of the company, which was also headquartered in New York. In addition to the financial rewards, there were nonpecuniary returns as well. The studio connection presented opportunities for socializing with movie stars and famous directors, and the partners thoroughly savored their exposure to the glamorous lifestyles of celebrities in the entertainment field.

Like retail chains and automobiles, motion pictures had emerged in the late nineteenth century. After the turn of the century, numerous movie producers at home and abroad were active in releasing films for American audiences. Since language was no barrier in the silent era, many films shown in the United States were European imports. Pathé Frères began producing films in Paris in 1896 and soon emerged as one of the world's

8. Merrill, *Checkbook.*

largest and most prolific studios. By 1905, the French firm had established a broad distribution network for its films in the United States.[9] Along with such pioneers as Edison, Vitagraph, and Biograph, Pathé was among the group of independent producers who formed the Motion Pictures Patents Company (the so-called Trust) in 1908. Two years later the French firm strengthened its commitment to the U.S. market when it acquired production facilities in New Jersey and began making movies specifically targeted at American viewers. In 1911, the company introduced its highly acclaimed newsreel to movie audiences. The Pathé newsreel was a staple in American theaters for decades – until TV news programs dictated its obsolescence a half century later. The enormously popular *Perils of Pauline* serial was another of the company's successful projects.

The outbreak of World War I severely disrupted film production in France and other European locations. The disruption, in turn, led to a major restructuring of the studio's organization in the United States. A separate business entity called Pathé Exchange, Inc., a wholly owned U.S. subsidiary of the French parent, was incorporated in January 1915. Precisely how Merrill, Lynch became associated with this enterprise remains obscure. The partners were approached in 1915, soon after the creation of the new U.S. subsidiary, by Paul Fuller, a lawyer working in the New York office of the French law firm Coudert Frères. Fuller had met the partners during legal proceedings connected with the securities of another client. He offered to place both men on the American subsidiary's board of directors for the generous annual salary of $50,000 each. Since neither partner had any previous experience in the film industry as producers or financiers, the rationale for their recruitment at such stupendous salaries – on the order of $1 million annually in 1995 prices – is unfathomable. Extant sources indicate that the partners were retained to function as financial watchdogs for the French parent, but others with superior credentials in the movie industry and with lower compensation expectations were almost certainly available. Pure speculation suggests that profits were perhaps so high in the U.S. market, and French executives were so accustomed to throwing money around, that few thought the remuneration for the partners' service on the board was in any way excessive. Whatever the case, Fuller arranged this sweetheart deal for the two principals, and it led to their deeper involvement in motion pictures as time passed.

Pathé operated profitably throughout the war and during the postwar period. Lynch remained on the board from 1915 to 1921, but Charlie resigned when he entered the army in 1917. Like chain stores, movie theaters catered to the growing American middle class; by the end of the decade the retail distribution network included thousands of theaters in cities and towns across the nation. Millions attended screenings on a weekly basis. Pathé was a major producer and, more important, one of the largest wholesale distributors of films in the U.S. market. Its feature films starring comedian Harold Lloyd were extremely popular with moviegoers. In the five months from September 1920 to January 1921, before the acquisition by Merrill, Lynch, the company released eighteen full-length features.[10] Through its thirty-three branch offices from coast to coast, the company arranged rentals to independent theatrical exhibitors of feature films and shorts – both the studio's own productions and hundreds of movies by other producers – plus its regular Pathé newsreels.

Persistent and unresolvable disagreements with the management of the parent company in Paris led executives in the American subsidiary, primarily President Paul Brunet and General Manager Elmer Pearson, to investigate the potential advantages of gaining financial and legal independence. Again, lawyer Paul Fuller was a key figure in convincing Merrill, Lynch to negotiate the split with the French company. A precedent for Wall Street involvement in financing the operations of the film companies already existed. In 1919, the esteemed investment banking firm of Kuhn, Loeb had sponsored an issue of $10 million in preferred and common stock for Famous Players-Lasky Corporation, then one of the largest and most successful movie studios.[11]

Since Lynch was the most knowledgeable partner about the situation at Pathé, in 1921 he went to Paris, where he spent three months hammering out the details of the divestiture agreement with officials of the French company. This transaction was the boldest in the firm's history because the partners were not merely assuming a minority position, as had been true in all past financial deals, but were actually bidding to acquire majority ownership. The purchase price for the company's U.S. assets was between $6 and $7 million. The largest item in the contract was the assumption of the American subsidiary's outstanding debts, somewhere in the range of $4 to $5 million. The balance sheet for the new company listed $2 million in bonds, $2 million in preferred stock, and two classes of common stock – 100,000 shares of Class A common and 10,000 shares of Class B common, the latter with the right to elect two-thirds of the board of directors. Both the bonds and preferred stock were convertible into Class A common stock,

---

10. Grunning, *Wid's Year Book: 1921–1922*, 316.
11. Hampton, *History of the American Film Industry*, 243.

a sweetener that enhanced their marketability with investors seeking immediate income as well as the possibility of future capital gains.

Generally speaking, Charlie had a penchant for issuing senior securities with convertibility features or with warrants attached that permitted future purchases of common stock at favorable prices. With these extra inducements, all parties contributing to a given firm's capitalization could share in the prosperity if management could generate healthy profits. In the Pathé deal, Merrill, Lynch took 51 percent of the Class A stock and all of the Class B stock, giving the partners unchallenged control of the new company. The firm's cash outlay was between $350,000 and $750,000; recollections vary on the amount invested, but irrespective of the actual total, this transaction would prove extraordinarily lucrative over the next five years.

No sooner was the deal consummated than Lynch, in checking the Pathé accounts after returning from Paris, discovered that Paul Brunet had been guilty of either mismanagement or outright fraud. Brunet was released, and Fuller was named president of Pathé Exchange – now essentially a figurehead position. Lynch became chair of the board of directors and for all practical purposes assumed the duties of CEO. Pearson remained as general manager and second in command. In this instance, the partners' merchant banking activities had drawn them into the administration of a company in a sector of the economy far removed from financial services. From this date forward, Lynch devoted up to half of his time and energy to the management of the film company. Charlie's input at Pathé was irregular; he made no significant alteration in his normal work pattern, concentrating on financial services linked primarily with chain stores.

Under Lynch's stewardship Pathé performed exceedingly well. In 1925, the company earned $1.4 million on net assets of $8.6 million.[12] The Class A common stock received a listing on the New York Stock Exchange, which testified to its generally high quality. The stock traded in the range of $70 to $80 in early 1926, reflecting a moderate price–earnings ratio of 10 to 12.[13] The bonds went up, too, tripling in price from just under $1,000 to around $3,000 because of the convertibility feature. The partners periodically liquidated portions of their inventory of securities in a rising market – except for the Class B voting stock, which was held intact. With Merrill, Lynch in control of the board of directors, the company concentrated on film distribution, a business conducted through strategically

---

12. Alicoote, *1927 Film Year Book*. The stocks of eleven film companies were listed on the NYSE in 1925, including Famous Players-Lasky, First National, Fox, Loew's, Metro–Goldwyn, Universal, and Warner Brothers. The industry leaders in 1925 were Famous Players-Lasky with profits of $5.7 million and Loew's at $5.2 million.

13. *New York Times*, Jan. 3, 1926.

located exchange offices in more than thirty American cities, and the production of newsreels and weekly serials. After most of its box office stars of the 1910s signed with other studios, the company curtailed the production of costly full-length features to only five or ten annually.

The divestiture agreement with the parent in 1921 included one provision that soon emerged as an unanticipated bonus. The American firm retained the patent rights to a process developed by Pathé Frères in France for the manufacture of raw film stock. Thousands of reels of this raw stock were shipped annually to the United States. When Congress passed a protective tariff on imports of raw film stock in the early 1920s – a law that gave Eastman Kodak a near monopoly in the U.S. market – the partners' access to the patent rights for the French process suddenly became a valuable asset. Lynch sought a domestic manufacturer with the capability of producing raw stock. The Du Pont Company, which had diversified from gunpowder into a full range of chemicals in the first quarter of the century, had been trying for years to develop a film product that would be competitive with Eastman Kodak, but without much success. The two companies joined forces, with one supplying the patent rights and the other the expertise and productive capacity. The Du Pont-Pathé Film Manufacturing Corporation was a joint venture capitalized at just over $2 million with a plant located in Parlin, New Jersey. This company was another profit maker. The partners subsequently sold their equity position to Du Pont – again at a sizable gain.

In 1926 changing conditions in the mass entertainment market led the partners to reassess their position in motion pictures. To remain competitive, knowledgeable advisers counseled, they needed to raise huge sums of new capital to fortify Pathé. Since the end of the war, the major studios had been engaging in vertical integration, and the industry as a whole was becoming increasingly oligopolistic. The leading producers and distributors had extended the scope of their enterprises to include theatrical exhibition. The motion picture industry, in short, had adopted the same strategies as other big businesses. Independents – whether in production, distribution, or exhibition – were feeling competitive pressures at every level. Many theaters drawn into the national chains were obligated to screen the entire annual output of one major studio, leaving less room on their schedules for outsiders like Pathé Exchange to find exhibition outlets.

Pearson, the general manager at Pathé, told Charlie that Merrill, Lynch needed to make a decision soon about whether to improve the company's strategic position. The partners had to decide, Pearson advised, whether to compete with other integrated film studios on their own terms by investing in a chain of theaters or, alternatively, quit the business. Pearson estimated that the cost of acquiring a competitive chain of theaters would be approximately $150 million – an enormous sum.[14] The discussions about the future of Pathé were, in retrospect, a critical point in the firm's history, because a decision to go forward would have had tremendous repercussions.

A commitment to Pathé had to be judged not merely on financial merits alone but also in terms of how such a decision would impact the partners' business careers over the long run. Any concerted effort to build and operate a chain of theaters would have likely transformed both men into full-time movie moguls. Lynch was already halfway into the movie business, whereas Charlie had remained largely on the sidelines. Functioning as an executive in the entertainment field was not how Charlie had envisioned his future. He was attracted by the concept of a nationwide chain of outlets that offered consumers all varieties of goods and services, but first movers in the film industry had already taken a strong position in the theatrical market and Pathé would have to start from scratch. If they did decide to expand forward into exhibition, the amount of money required would have necessitated a corporate restructuring so severe that the partners' power to control the board of directors would almost certainly have to be relinquished to outsiders. Given these considerations, Charlie voted to sell.

Negotiations for the sale of the partnership's Class B stock were conducted with Blair & Company, a Wall Street house representing a group of investors that included Joseph Kennedy (later chair of the Securities and Exchange Commission and the father of a future U.S. president) and Cecil B. DeMille, the famous producer-director. The sale price for the firm's entire 10,000 shares of Class B stock was $2.9 million; most of this money was pure profit since the cost basis of the shares was negligible.[15] In subsequent years the new owners merged Pathé Exchange with other enterprises in the entertainment field to create RKO, a fully integrated company that competed with the established Hollywood studios in the 1930s. How many millions the partners actually realized in net profits from their investment in Pathé is uncertain – although the rate of return was undeniably astronomical. The partners benefited, first, from the regular dividends paid on the profits earned from 1921 to 1925; second, from the

14. The amount of capital invested in the motion picture industry rose dramatically from $120 million in 1924 to $850 million in 1930. Movie palaces, some costing more than $1 million, became popular in major cities. After 1927 the cost of converting theaters from silent to sound was expensive. The data on capital invested come from Wasko, *Movies and Money*, Table 2.1, p. 31.
15. Merrill to Robert Lewis, Jan. 10, 1949, ML Files.

periodic liquidation of bonds, preferred stock, and Class A common stock; third, from the joint venture with Du Pont in the manufacture of raw film stock; and, last, from the sale of all the Class B common stock in 1926.

The Pathé interlude was important, too, because it gave Lynch the opportunity to make his business relationship with Charlie something more akin to a two-way street. Charlie had created the firm in 1914, and he had taken the initiative in arranging most of the transactions involving chain stores. But Lynch made Pathé his personal bailiwick, and the success of the venture helped to cement the strong ties between the two partners.[16] Through the film company, Lynch had a chance to return the favor by contributing significantly to Charlie's wealth and power.

The firm's deepening involvement in the management and administration of a second thriving enterprise in a heretofore unfamiliar field during the early 1920s also set an important precedent, one with major implications in the next decade. In the first instance, Lynch's attention was diverted from a concentration on the challenges of high finance. In the second instance, Charlie was the partner who actually sailed off into uncharted waters. As a consequence of two unrelated events – his escalating involvement in the affairs of Safeway Stores and the effects of the stock market crash in 1929 – Charlie essentially abandoned financial services in 1930 and redirected the course of his business career.

In the mid-1920s, executives of the leading chain stores brushed aside their postwar fears and launched into a new round of geographic expansion. The popularity of the automobile as the preferred means of local transportation aided the chains in their pursuit of sales and profits. The effect on consumption was most dramatic in rural areas, where farm families could drive an inexpensive Model T to town on a regular basis to shop for products they previously had gone without or ordered from catalogs for mail delivery. Meanwhile, households in urban areas used the automobile to shop more frequently as well. Wherever they resided, consumers found it less inconvenient to travel an extra mile or two to save a few cents on the purchase of staple goods from low-price chains. The impact of the automobile on retailing strategies was probably most evident to contemporary observers with respect to Sears, Roebuck; in the mid-twenties the giant retailer shifted away from its strictly catalog orientation and began opening hundreds of stores in towns and cities throughout the country.[17] Charlie was an important figure in financing the expansion of retail

---

16. Lynch was on the Pathé board of directors as late as 1928. Wasko, *Movies and Money*, 83.
17. Tedlow, *New and Improved*, 259–343. Montgomery Ward, the major competitor in catalog sales, failed to expand into retail outlets until after World War II.

chains in this period. The firm handled a large number of sizable under-writings, and the partners began to receive more recognition from peers in the investment field. By the end of the decade, Merrill, Lynch had moved out of the shadows to rank as a legitimate second-tier firm in Wall Street circles. In an article published in the *New York Evening Journal* on May 10, 1924, Charlie championed the securities of retail chains. These stores were successful, he argued, because they were "gradually narrowing the gap between the producer of merchandise and the consumer." He added: "For years this country has suffered serious economic loss due to the high cost of distribution." In a booklet prepared for existing accounts and prospective customers in 1925, Charlie stressed the importance of these companies in the overall economy. He pointed out that the aggregate sales of twenty-two leading retail chains "was equal to 50% of the total motor output, to nearly 100% of the total petroleum production and to 100% of the bituminous coal production." Charlie was proud that his firm had contributed to this growth by helping to finance companies that had 5,800 retail outlets and sales of $520 million. The list of chain stores that became new clients of the firm after 1922 included Diamond Shoe, Lane Bryant, Lerner Stores, National Tea, Newberrys, Peoples Drug, Walgreen Drug, Western Auto, and, of course, Safeway Stores. The Safeway connection, which began in 1926, requires much explanation, and that discussion must be deferred to the following chapter.

In an important memorandum drafted in 1929, Charlie reflected on his experiences with the chains:

> I can say with honesty and sincerity, that the executives of the large chain store corporations rank among the highest, if not the highest, as to downright charac-ter. The men behind the big chain store industries, in every instance, without a single exception, as far as I know, began life under modest circumstances . . . ; that they have been able to keep their heads, retain their sanity, hang on to finer ideals, and retain affection for and a deep desire to help those in the ranks, speaks volumes for these men.

The executives at Safeway fit this pattern: "The main strength of the Safeway Company lies not in the locations of its stores, its warehouses, or any of its great tangible resources – it lies in its men. As we are faithful to this trust, and alive to responsibilities to the stockholders, and to the consuming public, we will continue to grow and prosper." In explaining the increased listings of chain stocks on the exchanges, Charlie remarked: "I believe that the popularity of chain store securities is due to the fact that the public in general believes that chain stores will be the main factor in solving the problem of distribution." After citing the pioneering work of efficiency expert Frederick W. Taylor, Charlie attributed the rise in security values "to the fact that in America both capital and labor have . . .

demonstrated what can be done to increase and improve production by eliminating waste, by invention, by superior organization, better methods, and team work." He continued: "Just as Henry Ford is the most conspicuous exponent of mass production, so will some individual stand forth in the chain store field as the leader in the science and art of mass distribution."[18] Charlie never lived to see the day, of course, but in the 1980s Sam Walton, the founder of Wal-Mart, became by far the nation's wealthiest business leader. Like Kresge, McCrory, and Penney before him, this Arkansas entrepreneur also rose from modest circumstances; in the post–World War II era, Walton made his fortune in retailing through discount merchandising. In short, another of Charlie's foresightful predictions came true.

In early 1928 Charlie sensed that stock prices were probably reaching a peak and that prudent investors would be wise to review carefully the status of their portfolios. Few other financial experts and prominent economists had the same stark premonition of the possibility of a huge sell-off in the near to intermediate future. Others on Wall Street occasionally had doubts about how long the bull market might last and how high prices could climb, but most quickly dismissed their reservations. Corporate earnings kept rising and stock prices kept soaring.

Once Charlie became convinced of the danger of a sharp correction, he never relented. In a form letter to Merrill, Lynch accounts sent out over his signature and dated March 31, 1928, Charlie sounded the public alarm.[19] Eighteen months before the onset of the sharp downturn in stock prices, Charlie told investors that most of the companies the firm had underwritten had little funded debt on their balance sheets. The absence of debt was a sensible policy under the circumstances, and he recommended that retail customers take heed. "The advice we have given important corporations can be followed to advantage by all classes of investors. We do not urge that you sell securities indiscriminately, but we do advise, in no uncertain terms, that you . . . lighten your obligations, or better still, pay them off entirely." Customers who listened carefully fared better than other unwary investors over the next three or four turbulent years.

Some of his partners, including Lynch, believed that Charlie was being too pessimistic, but he overcame their resistance, either through patient persuasion or the exercise of raw executive power. The firm liquidated a healthy share of its portfolio of stocks, although the partnership still held many millions of dollars of securities in the companies that it had financed.

---

18. Memorandum drafted by CEM, Jan. 3, 1929, in ML Files.　　19. Letter in ML Files.

In a memorandum for employees drafted several weeks later, Charlie defended his policies: "We try to run our business in a safe and high-grade manner, giving our customers the maximum of protection at all times." The customer response to his recent letter had been positive: "the average margin . . . comes nearer being 40% than 25%." As a result of portfolio adjustments, the firm had "considerably more than ten million of our own money free and clear." He boasted that the firm was "just as safe and strong as any of the big national banks" and that no active stock exchange house was currently "stronger in proportion to its liabilities." Charlie was slightly premature in his assessment of the precarious state of the stock market, but as in so many instances in the past, he knew exactly what he was talking about.

During the last few weeks of Calvin Coolidge's term in office after the election of Herbert Hoover in November 1928, Charlie played the Amherst card to obtain an interview with the outgoing president at the White House.[20] Coolidge was Amherst's most famous alumnus, and Charlie had already started giving his alma mater substantial sums of money, so the old school connection was strong. Coolidge concurred with his guest's dire predictions about future trends in the financial markets. With call money at 7 to 8 percent and stocks yielding only around 3 percent, they agreed that either interest rates or stock prices had to tumble by 50 percent to create a new equilibrium. Charlie made a sincere, if modest, effort to induce Coolidge to join the partnership at an annual salary of $100,000 or 10 percent of profits after he left office in March. When the president protested that he knew next to nothing about investment banking, Charlie explained that his new duties would consist largely of public relations. As a new employee, his first task would be to use the press and radio to warn Americans about the dangers of excessive debt and irresponsible speculation. Coolidge politely declined the lucrative offer.

Months passed after Charlie's initial salvos about deteriorating conditions, yet the stock market kept roaring ahead. The Dow-Jones average for industrial stocks climbed for the fifth year in a row in 1928, rising just under 50 percent – the largest jump of the decade. The founder's fears seemed unwarranted to many listeners, including the majority of his partners. But Charlie persisted with his doom-and-gloom scenario. He believed further liquidation of the firm's holdings was in order. In lighthearted moments with his immediate family and trusted friends, Charlie stated that he was so certain about coming events that others vehemently denied that maybe he "needed to consult a psychiatrist."[21]

20. The details of the Coolidge connection are outlined in Griffis, "Saga of Wall Street," 77–80.
21. Author's correspondence with Charles Merrill Jr., April 9, 1994.

In late 1928, while away on a business trip, Charlie sent Sumner Cobb, a junior partner in the firm and long-time employee, a sharply worded letter expressing his unhappiness with the foot-dragging in New York. He cited a list of investments totaling $46.6 million, and he wanted implementation of a plan of systematic liquidation, starting with $7 million over the next thirty days. "This is official and urgent," he told Cobb. "Regardless of the whys, wherefores, serious objections or any other reason, I want to clean up and do it now. . . . If I had the exclusive say, I *would sell everything*, except about 90,000 [shares of] Safeway." He added: "Get up a *mammoth*, live wire sales campaign to embrace every office and every man – set quotas, commissions prizes; enlist dealers, pools, papers, and take all steps necessary to move the stuff – both good and bad." Charlie's patience was wearing thin. "Nobody seems to give a damn and I don't like it one little bit," he told Cobb. "You and Ed know my feelings, and you must let me decide when enough is enough."[22]

While in Palm Beach to attend his father's funeral, Charlie wrote a lengthy letter to Lynch on February 25, 1929.[23] He laid out his position in extremely strong language. "The financial skies are not clear; I have many reasons for this opinion . . . the Federal Reserve Banking System has issued warning after warning that a storm is gathering." He continued: "Anybody not 'money drunk' can read these signs if he will." Upset that so many of his associates remained unconvinced, Charlie wrote: "I do not like the apathetic and indifferent attitude that seems to be prevalent in the New York office. . . . Why there should be any resistance to turning a very substantial amount of this profit into cash is an absolute, unending, insoluble mystery to me." The objection tendered by some that, by taking huge profits on stocks currently held, the partners would become liable for income taxes at high rates and at an inopportune time, Charlie dismissed as misguided thinking.

A crisis in the partnership was potentially at hand. Continuing the assault on his internal foes, Charlie accused Lynch of abetting the resisters: "You do not come out flat-footed and say that you oppose liquidation, but I notice that you do not liquidate, and you do not let anybody else liquidate. It just seems too bad to me that you and I should be pulling at cross-purposes, and not together at a time when we are prosperous . . . ; business ceases to be of any interest when I must carry an intolerable burden of worry and anxiety." He presciently continued: "Many fine reputations have been built up in this era of extraordinary prosperity, which will not stand the acid test when troublesome times are here."

Charlie ended the letter on an ominous note that reflected his growing frustration:

22. Merrill to Cobb, no exact date but late in 1928, ML Files.   23. Letter in ML Files.

If I am wrong in insisting upon liquidation, then that is a luxury which I can afford, and in which you, and all of my partners, should indulge me. . . . I prefer as you know, to have harmony rather than friction; I would like to feel my wishes are respected, and are carried out without the necessity of resorting to stronger and more objectionable methods. It seems to me, I am sorry to say, that nothing I can say or do, if my requests are couched in polite and reasonable terms, has any effect. This, to me, is an intolerable situation . . . ; it is not only your privilege, but it should be your duty to carry out a sane, reasonable plan for our mutual protection, and do it at once.

The message did not have the desired effect, despite all of his threats and pleadings, so Charlie took action after he returned to New York. Lynch left for a European vacation in late spring. Charlie not only adjusted the partnership's balance sheet to reflect his prudent views, he also used his power of attorney to restructure Lynch's personal holdings. After months of brow-beating, Lynch finally acceded to Charlie's demands. He wrote from Paris: "I don't agree with your thinking, but I will not disagree with your actions. If you wish, sell all of my holdings."[24] If Lynch felt resentment over his partner's intrusion into his affairs, he had every reason to be thankful a few months later.

When the crash came in October 1929, the firm was prepared, having large reserves of ready cash on hand. Forewarned was indeed forearmed. Charlie had proved correct in his assessment of market conditions – probably more correct than even he had envisioned, given the magnitude of the downswing over the next three years. His partners, employees, and hundreds of loyal retail customers remained forever grateful for his wise counsel; he helped many of them avoid huge capital losses in a prolonged bear market that would drop more than 85 percent from its all-time high in September 1929 to its lowest point in March 1932. Charlie's reputation as a market forecaster was etched in stone after the crash and remains to this day one of the hallmarks of his career on Wall Street.

Charlie was not alone in his assessment of stock market conditions, but he was among the earliest and loudest voices crying in the wilderness. Moreover, he did not use his superior intuition merely to feather his own nest through secrecy, deceit, or manipulation. He never engaged in short selling the stocks of companies that his firm had underwritten, although he knew they were at risk.[25] (In short selling, a speculator borrows a stock certificate from a third party, sells it for cash, waits for an opportunity to repurchase at a lower price, and returns the certificate to the lender – retaining the profits if the market had fallen during the interim.) While

24. Quoted in Hecht, *Legacy of Leadership*, 42.
25. Lynch may have engaged in some short selling after the crash, but he may not have profited since the market recovered some of its losses over the next six months, climbing sharply from the low in November 1929 to the high in April 1930.

brokers with most other firms were encouraging customers to borrow more money to buy more securities, Charlie instructed his sales personnel to advise investors to exercise caution with regard to acquiring stocks on margin.

The firm had reduced its vulnerability in a sharp downturn, but Charlie retained a substantial number of shares in a select group of the companies that the partners had financed. The stocks of more than twenty-five companies with a market value of $30 million were listed on the partnership's balance sheet in January 1930.[26] The stocks of just four companies accounted for more than 85 percent of the total: $14.8 million, Safeway Stores; $5.4 million, MacMarr Stores; $4.6 million, McCrory Stores; and $1.1 million, National Tea. The large positions in the equities of Safeway and McMarr remained because the partnership had assumed a controlling interest in these two grocery chains on the West Coast, and Charlie wanted to maintain his voting power in forthcoming elections for the boards of directors. He had the voting strength to select the CEOs for both companies, and he planned to stay in complete control for the foreseeable future. As a consequence, those stocks were exempt from the pruning of the investment portfolio that occurred in 1929. Safeway and McMarr were the remnants of the partners' highly successful strategy of functioning as merchant bankers.

After dropping steadily for three weeks, the stock market rebounded over the next five months. Following a low of 248 in November, the Dow-Jones industrials rose to 294 in April – a climb of 18 percent. Many contemporaries breathed a sigh of relief, believing that the sell-off was

---

26. A consolidated report of securities held by the firm shows a bottom line of $47 million – a discrepancy of $17 million with the number listed in the text. I arrived at the $30 million figure by multiplying the number of shares held in various companies by the bid price listed in the *New York Times* for January 23, 1930. The most likely explanation for the difference is that the extra $17 million was held as collateral covering customers' margin accounts; these securities were financed largely through bank loans and did not reflect the partners' equity. In an earlier letter marked "confidential" from Merrill to Lynch in February 1929, the market value of securities on hand was listed at $32.6 million, with $25 million linked directly to Safeway Stores. Subtracting the loans outstanding against these securities of $3.7 million, the partners' equity was $28.9 million in early 1929. Years later, in an interview with representatives of the firm in 1982, Robert Magowan asserted that Merrill and Lynch each ended up with from $50 to $100 million when the original firm entered a decade of dormancy in 1930, with a mix of financial assets in cash, bonds, and stocks. Magowan claimed that their respective stock portfolios had declined on the order of 70 percent by the low point in 1932. The Dow-Jones index rebounded through early 1937 – climbing an astonishing multiple of 4.75 – to reach 63 percent of its 1929 high. My intuitive guess is that Merrill's capital gains exceeded his losses during the 1930s because he held substantial amounts of cash after 1928 that were available to invest in stocks at rock bottom prices. According to Magowan, business was so slow at Merrill Lynch just prior to the merger with E. A. Pierce in 1940 that the firm's capital account totaled only about $2 million; see Engberg interview with Magowan, Nov. 19, 1982, ML Files.

merely a short-term correction rather than the beginning of a bear market. But Charlie remained dubious about the long term. Indeed, he was so pessimistic that he decided to curtail drastically his involvement in the financial services sector. On February 3, 1930, the firm announced that the brokerage portion of the business, namely, the six branch offices, had been transferred to E. A. Pierce, already the nation's leading brokerage house in terms of number of offices. Most of the employees in the six branches, primarily sales personnel and support staff, agreed to join the Pierce organization and continue in their current positions. Some of the junior partners at the main office also accepted an invitation to join Pierce, including Sumner Cobb and Winthrop Smith, two men who had been with Charlie almost from the very start.

Announced in the press as a sale of assets, the arrangement was closer in its dimensions to one of the firm's earlier merchant banking transactions. Pierce took over the bulk of the firm's property and personnel, but Charlie and Lynch received no payment in return. Instead, they and their departing juniors agreed to invest $5 million in E. A. Pierce to strengthen its capital base. The two principals put up $1.9 million each, and their former partners contributed $1.2 million. Charlie believed strongly in the concept of a large-scale, geographically diversified brokerage house with thousands of retail accounts. Pierce had been in the securities business since 1901 and had established an outstanding record as managing partner of the firm that bore his name after 1926.[27]

Merrill, Lynch was not formally dissolved in this shake-up. A skeleton staff moved into much smaller quarters at 40 Wall Street. The new strategy was to restrict future operations to investment banking. Henceforth, there would be no retailing of securities and no merchant banking commitments. The partners planned to continue underwriting securities for former corporate clients at the wholesale level and to join syndicates with other houses when opportunities arose. But the search for new corporate clients ceased. The retrenchment proved sensible as events unfolded, since the number of companies going public for the first time in the depressed 1930s was minuscule.

Lynch went into quasi retirement. With millions in the bank and millions more invested in safe bonds and preferred stocks, he spent most of the next seven years, until his untimely death in 1938, living a life of leisure and luxury. He came to the office occasionally, as did Charlie, and sometimes they met with executives of companies that the firm had financed in the past. Business and recreational activities increasingly overlapped. Deals were arranged on tennis courts, on the golf course, at the

27. For a capsule biography of Pierce, see Hecht, *Legacy of Leadership*, 34.

country club. Charlie joined from time to time in his partner's hedonistic pursuits.

Charlie's dramatic decision to shift careers from financial services to groceries at the age of forty-four was based on several considerations – both negatives and positives. The main negative was that he had lost confidence in his partners as a result of their foot-dragging in 1928 and 1929 with regard to the realization of paper profits on investments in common stocks. His goal was to emphasize safety in uncertain times; they were driven more strongly by greed and the avoidance of income taxes. Even Lynch had proved recalcitrant. Although Charlie ultimately prevailed, the stress of constant conflict with his business associates had tried his patience. He never wanted to go through a similar experience. Henceforth, he wanted total control of an enterprise, with no dissenting partners.

The main positive was that at Safeway and allied chains, he would be able to exert virtually unchallenged power over policy decisions. Since the purchase of Safeway stock in 1926, he had developed enormous respect for M. B. Skaggs, the executive he had recruited to run its operations on the West Coast. Increasing amounts of Charlie's time in the late 1920s had been spent in overseeing the management of Safeway. In 1929, he deepened his commitment to the grocery sector by investing additional monies in another West Coast chain that came to be known as MacMarr Stores. Unafraid of airplanes since his days in the military, he was one of the nation's first bicoastal businessmen, traveling regularly from New York to California and back. Charlie enjoyed the people and the challenge in the grocery field. To date, he and Skaggs were in almost complete agreement on strategic issues.

Having financed numerous chains over the years, Charlie was ready to try his hand at orchestrating the administration of one of these vast enterprises, and perhaps two or three. In a partial division of assets with Lynch following the downsizing in 1930, Charlie assumed ownership of most of the stock in Safeway and MacMarr. His career on Wall Street seemed over, but his energy level was as high as ever. Charlie was eager to test his entrepreneurial skills in a new territory – both occupationally and geographically.

7

THE SAFEWAY DECADE

Starting in 1926 and continuing for much of the rest of his life, Charlie was the entrepreneurial force behind Safeway Stores. During his sabbatical from Wall Street in the 1930s, the grocery chain became the primary focus of his attention during his working hours. From the mid-1920s through the early 1930s, he assumed responsibility for providing the financial expertise to accommodate Safeway's dynamic growth, which occurred largely through mergers with and acquisitions of other regional chains. His vision was consistently expansive. In 1933, the grocery chain reached its high point in terms of number of outlets with 3,265 stores nationwide, ranking third behind A&P and Kroger.[1] Luckily, groceries were only slightly hurt by the depression, since most households sought to maintain existing diets. With incomes reduced and unemployment rife, Americans were more prone to frequent the grocery stores that sold staples at discount prices.

Safeway was the partnership's second significant acquisition of a major company in an unrelated, nonfinancial sector. Indeed, the bulk of the funds to finance the transaction came from the sale of the Class B common shares of Pathé Exchange, the firm's first major merchant banking acquisition. Charlie preferred foodstuffs to celluloid. As events unfolded in the early 1930s, his exit from motion pictures appeared extremely foresightful. Movie theaters were hurt badly from 1930 to 1933 by the economic contraction. But movies rebounded after the election of Franklin Roosevelt, and attendance records during the remainder of the depression decade soared. In contrast to their sharp curtailment of purchases of durable goods, American consumers apparently decided that regular entertainment and a hearty diet were two necessities in household budgets.

The chain that became known as Safeway Stores was begun by Sam Seelig in Los Angeles in the years before World War I.[2] Southern Califor-

---

1. Lebhar, *Chain Stores,* 397. Lebhar actually lists 3,400 stores at the end of 1932, but internal sources indicate that his data, although close, was slightly off.
2. Cassady and Jones, *Changing Competitive Structure,* 14–23.

nia was the nation's most rapidly developing urban economy after the turn of the century. The population of Los Angeles rose from just over 100,000 to nearly 600,000 between 1900 and 1920.[3] After the war, the Seelig chain became deeply indebted to its main grocery wholesaler, a company owned by W. R. H. Weldon. In a swap of stock for debt, Weldon assumed control of the chain and changed the name to Safeway, leaving Seelig in charge of retail operations. In preliminary discussions with Joseph Merrill (no relation to Charlie), who was on the West Coast seeking new underwriting clients, the owner expressed interest in selling out for the right price. Weldon saw himself chiefly as a wholesaler and was anxious to transfer managerial authority over the retail end of the business to outside investors. The West Coast grocer told Charlie at one point that he was extremely distrustful of Seelig and wanted to sever ties as soon as possible. A deal was soon struck. The price for 80 percent of the outstanding stock of Safeway Stores, which had 330 outlets by the end of 1925, was $3.5 million.

The grocery trade underwent a profound realignment in the 1920s. Through the first two decades of the century, the sale of foodstuffs in urban areas remained predominantly a function of small independents. Local owners relied on equally independent wholesalers to supply their inventories. The range of products available for sale was extremely limited by modern standards; for example, consumers patronized butcher shops for most of their meats and bought fresh fruit and vegetables from local vendors. In his book *New and Improved: The Story of Mass Marketing in America*, historian Richard Tedlow has identified this atomistic system as the initial phase of the marketing and distribution of goods in the U.S. economy. In the second phase of development, grocery entrepreneurs internalized markets, integrated wholesaling and retailing, and expanded geographically at a meteoric pace. The Great Atlantic and Pacific Tea Company led the way.

By 1920, A&P had more than 4,500 stores, most of which, despite the misleading broad name, were located east of the Mississippi River. Its closest competitor was Acme Markets, based in Philadelphia, with fewer than 1,300 stores. Large chains combined accounted for less than 6 percent of total food sales in retail stores in 1920. A decade later, however, the five largest chains, which now included Safeway Stores, had increased their market share fourfold to more than 25 percent.[4] The chains drew customers with lower prices that were made possible in part by scale efficiencies and in part by reducing services – eliminating credit sales and free home delivery.

3. Friedricks, *Henry E. Huntington*, 8.   4. Tedlow, *New and Improved*, Table 4.3, p. 196.

Charlie was able to accomplish something in groceries that had proved elusive in motion pictures – getting in very close to the ground floor in an industry undergoing dramatic change and marching swiftly toward larger business units. A&P had first-mover advantages, but within the second tier of fledgling competitors, Safeway quickly gained equal status. Whereas other grocery chains operated primarily in the East and Midwest, Safeway had a strong presence in the western states. This positioning was advantageous because the western regional economy, which included California, was growing at the fastest clip in the nation.

Charlie's first important task was to recruit a capable CEO to run the chain. Neither he nor Lynch seriously contemplated moving west to assume those duties, so the administrative system that had worked so satisfactorily with Pathé was not an option. One person with strong recommendations from peers in West Coast retailing was Marion B. Skaggs, the owner-manager of a grocery chain based in Portland, Oregon. The average annual gross sales of his stores at $84,000 ranked among the highest in the trade. In June 1926, Charlie checked into the Benson Hotel in Portland and conducted eight days of intense negotiations with Skaggs. His strategy was to orchestrate a merger of the Safeway and Skaggs chains, which were roughly equivalent in terms of the number of stores.

Initially skeptical of the fancy dress and refinement of emissaries from Wall Street, Skaggs discovered that he had a great deal in common with Charlie with respect to background, outlook, and burning ambition. Skaggs recalled: "We were both raised in the country . . . had a lot of self-confidence . . . and were both quite independent." He added: "During the years we worked together, the mutual respect and confidence established in those first eight days were never marred." At one point Skaggs offered the ultimate compliment: "With me, Charlie Merrill – in addition to being smart, quick, honest – always did more than he promised all through the years of our association."[5]

Charlie was determined not to repeat the mistake he had made in trying to lure automobile executive Walter Chrysler to Saxon Motors a few years earlier. A high salary alone would not be a sufficient inducement; he planned to allow Skaggs to maintain a substantial equity position in a proposed merger of the two chains. Two proposals were laid on the table. For the Skaggs properties, Charlie offered $7 million outright – a combination of cash, bonds, and preferred stock – or, alternatively, $1.5 million cash plus 30,000 shares of common stock in the merged company. Skaggs jumped at the latter option. He also agreed to serve as CEO, but insisted on total control of operations without any interference from outside direc-

---

5. Quoted in Keenan, "Chain of Fortune," 325.

tors. Charlie consented to a five-year voting trust giving Skaggs full authority in operational matters. Oakland, California, a point just about midway between Portland and Los Angeles, was chosen as the location for the new corporate headquarters. In praising Safeway's progress in a memorandum drafted in 1929, Charlie cited the CEO's outstanding leadership qualities. Not only was Skaggs effective as "a buyer, assembler, and distributor of foodstuffs," Charlie observed, but "his ability to absorb information, recognize improvement when he sees it, and adapt himself" was a similarly admirable trait.[6] Marion Skaggs became one of Charlie's most trusted business associates from the mid-1920s until the West Coast grocer retired from Safeway in the 1940s.

Born in Missouri into a household headed by a father who worked as an itinerant minister and part-time storekeeper, Skaggs left college to join his brother in operating a small restaurant, confectionery, and meat market in Diamond, a village in the southwest corner of Missouri near Joplin.[7] After a brief stint in Oklahoma, in 1915 he purchased for just over $1,000 his father's equity in a grocery store in American Falls, a small town about thirty miles from Pocatello, in southeastern Idaho. Six years later Marion Skaggs owned more than fifteen stores in Idaho and Montana.

Skaggs operated in a fashion similar to that of J. C. Penney, who had started in variety stores in neighboring Wyoming a decade earlier. Like that nontraditional entrepreneur, Skaggs sold only for cash; no credit to customers meant the absence of slow and uncollectible receivables. Low prices produced high turnover and outstanding profits. Skaggs recalled: "You could open a pretty good grocery store for $3,000 and a big one for $5,000; . . . our goal was $100,000 annual sales per store, with a 15% gross and a 5% net profit, so that it was not unusual to make a 100% return on the investment." Another similarity with the Penney organization was the profit-sharing plan for employees. In addition to a base salary, local managers received 30 percent of the net profits of their stores, and they had the option of investing in nonvoting shares of the parent company – shares that kept rising in value because of the company's extraordinary profitability. This incentive package attracted a group of talented and industrious store managers. By the early 1920s, Skaggs had moved his headquarters to Portland, where he branched into grocery wholesaling to complement his retail operations and lower costs. Merging with a Utah chain established by one of his relatives, the Skaggs chain managed more than three hundred

6. Merrill, memorandum on Safeway and chain stores, Jan. 3, 1929. ML Files.
7. Diamond is only fifty miles north of Bentonville, Arkansas, where Sam Walton launched his chain of Wal-Mart stores in the post–World War II era.

stores in Oregon, Montana, Idaho, Nevada, and northern California by 1925.

With Skaggs in charge of operations, Charlie began searching for other merger candidates near and far. In this role, he had the opportunity to perform the duties that he knew best, and for an enterprise in which he and his partners at Merrill, Lynch had a major financial stake. Safeway provided the perfect vehicle to combine his intimate knowledge of capital markets with his unquenchable interest in retailing on a grand scale. Pathé had been only a fortuitous digression for Merrill, if not for Lynch; groceries were more engrossing and more challenging. In the 1920s Charlie transferred all that he knew about high-powered finance to the promotion of mass retailing; a decade later, when he returned to Wall Street to promote financial services for the middle class from coast to coast, the transfer process was just the reverse. Charlie kept learning about successful business practices throughout his life, and the lessons kept paying off – not only with respect to his personal wealth but also with reference to his impact on the institutional development of the U.S. economy.

Charlie and Skaggs agreed that the company needed to expand rapidly to maximize opportunities for economies of scale in wholesaling and retail distribution. Internal growth would be too slow for what they had in mind, so the implementation of a plan to arrange mergers with other established chains was the logical step. Empire building became the order of the day. Over the next few years, Charlie negotiated a series of mergers of existing chains with Safeway Stores.[8] The search focused on chains with good locations and high sales volume per outlet. Charlie began in southern California with the Chaffee chain, but soon became active in the southeastern and southwestern states. In 1927, Sanitary Grocery, a chain based in Washington, D.C., and Bird Grocery Stores, headquartered in Kansas City, were absorbed. Charlie worked at a frantic pace. During a short stopover in Arizona between trains, he made a hasty deal to acquire the local Pay'n Takit chain. Most transactions involved the swap of stock certificates, with little cash changing hands.

The initial public offering price of Safeway common stock in the over-the-counter market was $226 in 1927; a five-for-one split in 1928 brought the adjusted price down to under $50.[9] After Skaggs agreed in 1929 to renounce the five-year voting trust with two years still to run, Charlie

---

8. The 1920s witnessed the second merger wave in U.S. history. Not just grocery stores but many other enterprises were involved.
9. See article on Merrill in *Investor's Reader*, Oct. 19, 1953, pp. 14–20. Stocks priced under $100 per share typically attract greater trading volume than more expensive securities, which explains the frequency of stock splits in financial circles.

arranged listings on the New York Stock Exchange for the preferred and common stocks of Safeway Stores. The common climbed above $115 before starting a steady decline in the second half of 1930. According to a financial statement prepared by employees in January 1930, Merrill, Lynch held about 20 percent of the company's outstanding common stock with a market value of $14.8 million.[10]

Other chains added to the Safeway system included Piggly Wiggly stores in the western half of the nation, Sun Groceries in Tulsa, Knoblock Brothers in Baltimore, Newway Stores in El Paso, and the MacDonald chain in Canada. From a core of 670 stores on the West Coast in 1926, Charlie had multiplied the number of outlets nearly fourfold to 2,660 by the end of 1929. Annual sales per store at $91,000 were the highest in the food industry by that date. Despite its tremendous growth, Safeway was still less than one-fourth the size of A&P, the industry leader in annual sales volume and number of stores.

After encountering resistance from one prospective merger candidate in the Northwest, Charlie decided to carry his commitment to groceries a step further by organizing an independent company that paralleled Safeway in some locales. Ross MacIntyre had expressed his eagerness to join forces with Charlie in a grocery chain, but he was unalterably opposed to assuming a subordinate position to CEO Marion Skaggs within the Safeway organization. MacIntyre had been a vigorous competitor of the Skaggs chain in the Portland market, and he had no intention of suppressing that rivalry to accommodate the preferences of New York investment bankers. Charles Marr, the owner of a chain based in Spokane, Washington, had similar negative feelings about merging with Safeway. His entrepreneurial ambitions whetted, Charlie and his new assistant, Lingan Warren, convinced MacIntyre and Marr to merge in 1929, creating a new company called appropriately MacMarr Stores. The company's common stock traded on the Curb Exchange, the forerunner of the American Stock Exchange. In January 1930, the market value of the common shares held by the partnership was $5.4 million. Charlie anticipated uniting the new company with Safeway at some future date, but he was content to wait for a more opportune time. Skaggs had no objections to the interim arrangement. In the early 1930s, after Skaggs had stepped down as CEO, Charlie negotiated the absorption of the MacMarr chain by Safeway.

10. The number of common shares in the firm's portfolio was 126,386, and the bid price in the *New York Times* in late January was $117. In the early 1950s the market value of the shares held in 1930, after a 3-for-1 split in 1945, was roughly $15 million – meaning that, after the sharp decline in the early 1930s, it took more than two decades for the common stock to fully rebound and surpass the previous high. The company remained profitable throughout the 1930s and 1940s, however, and paid a steady dividend to investors.

Ling Warren was Charlie's most important business associate during the 1930s. He was a late arrival, having joined the Merrill, Lynch staff in 1928. A few years later, he was named CEO of Safeway, when Skaggs, who was in failing health, became chairman of the board of directors. In his relationship with Charlie, Warren filled the spot left vacant by Lynch, who, like so many of his peers on Wall Street, was frustrated by the persistence of the depression. Meanwhile, Lynch and his wife remained close allies of the Merrill family, and they contributed indirectly, but nonetheless significantly, to the breakup of Charlie's second marriage by introducing to their friends a woman who became Charlie's lover and, in time, the third Mrs. Charles Merrill.

Warren came to the firm, as had so many others, through personal connections – what today we call networking. On a visit to Jacksonville in the early 1920s, Charlie met Warren, who owned a local lumberyard. Charlie was impressed by Warren's credentials and urged his fellow Floridian on several occasions to consider a move to Wall Street. When Charlie's involvement in the grocery business on the West Coast deepened, he concluded that he needed someone to act as his emissary and liaison officer with Skaggs, with other executives at Safeway, and with the principals of prospective merger candidates across the country. Charlie finally convinced Warren to accept a position with the firm; after a few weeks of training in New York, Charlie sent his new employee to the Northwest to work out the details of the MacMarr deal. Merrill, Lynch ended up with 40 percent of the common stock in the merged enterprise, which was about a one-third greater participation than Charlie, Lynch, and Skaggs had originally anticipated. Warren got most of the credit for the favorable outcome – "either by good luck or good management," was Charlie's overall assessment.[11]

Warren's chief assets were his business success on a local scale plus his Florida residence and southern background. Indeed, the two most important adults in Charlie's life from the late twenties through the mid-thirties – Hellen and Ling Warren – shared a common regional heritage. Hellen and Charlie divorced in the late 1930s, but Warren stayed with Safeway into the 1950s. By shifting from a career emphasis on financial services to groceries and by spending more daytime hours at his Southampton estate, which, given its African American staff, resembled a southern mansion, Charlie was able to escape from certain aspects of life in Manhattan that still seemed alien to him. Meanwhile, he was drawn to California as a prime location for capital investment because the climate and growing economy were reminiscent of his home state – only on a grander scale.

11. Merrill to Lynch, personal and confidential, Dec. 21, 1928, ML Files.

Having acted as an entrepreneur first in financial services and then in grocery chains, Charlie added a third, unrelated sector to his list of new ventures. In 1932 he introduced *Family Circle,* a free weekly periodical distributed at the checkout counters of several major grocery chains. Magazines aimed at women readers interested in the latest fashions and sound household advice had proved popular in the United States since the middle of the nineteenth century.[12] In the first three decades of the twentieth century, *Ladies' Home Journal, Women's Home Companion,* and *McCall's* were among the best-selling monthly publications. They featured a mixture of romantic fiction and nonfiction articles focused on the household, including cooking, child care, sewing, fashion, and the latest conveniences in domestic services. The magazines were distributed primarily through the mail, and the revenues that kept them afloat came from advertisers promoting their brand goods. Subscription rates were typically low to generate large circulations and thereby maximize the exposure of consumers to advertisements.

In what by now had become a familiar pattern, Charlie first became interested in publishing through personal connections traceable to northern Florida. In this regard, Hellen's brief stint as the shoe-string publisher of a weekly aimed at Florida tourists, a career cut short by marriage, played an important role in pointing her husband toward an innovative concept in a new market. Hellen facilitated Charlie's introduction to Harry Evans, who had been a sportswriter for the *St. Augustine Evening Record* in the 1920s. An avid golfer, Evans met Clair Maxwell, who headed the old *Life* magazine, at a tournament, and later received an offer to join the magazine's staff in New York. Hellen supposedly arranged a round of golf that included Evans, Ling Warren, and Charlie; soon thereafter, serious conversations about a possible business venture in publishing were under way.

Both men brought something fresh to the discussions. During visits to San Francisco, Charlie had noticed a small publication featuring shopping news and advertising that was given out in the city's leading department stores. Why not introduce something similar in grocery stores, he wondered? Meanwhile, Evans had observed during his short tenure at *Life* just how much of the typical advertiser's money was wasted because blanket coverage in national publications was necessary to reach that segment of the total readership with a potential interest in purchasing a given product. An old adage in advertising was apropos in this context: every agency readily admitted to prospective clients that up to half of the money spent on a broad advertising campaign was probably wasted, but unfortunately

---

12. Waller-Zuckerman, "Marketing the Women's Journals" and "The Business Side of Media Development."

no one was ever able to determine with much accuracy which half of the budget genuinely attracted paying customers and which half was frittered away. Advertising in general paid, proponents asserted, but determining which media outlets were most effective for specific products remained a guessing game.

Charlie's own experience with direct-mail solicitations for new brokerage accounts, dating back to before World War I, had been extremely positive. He had been converted to the power of advertising long before his peers in financial services were even willing to concede the legitimacy of such nontraditional activities. Among the other factors that influenced Charlie's decision to go forward in publishing were his fond memories of summer months as a substitute newspaper editor in West Palm Beach between his sophomore and junior years at college. The journalistic bent persisted throughout his career and helps to explain the public relations strategies that he implemented at the reinvigorated Merrill Lynch in the 1940s.

From discussions between Charlie and Evans arose the idea of a weekly woman's magazine given away at the checkout counters of the leading grocery chains. Research suggested that members of urban American households visited a nearby grocery store approximately twice per week and that women did most of the family shopping. The magazine would be supported strictly by advertisers whose featured items could be found on the shelves of the grocery chain in question – no other items would receive exposure. The advertising dollars so often wasted in reaching an inappropriate and unresponsive audience could be spared entirely. To put it more crudely, advertisers buying space would be promised "more bang for their buck" in a highly focused publication with a targeted readership.

Charlie tried to interest Skaggs in making *Family Circle* a division or subsidiary of Safeway Stores, but the CEO was skeptical. Skaggs knew groceries, not publishing, and he passed on the opportunity to invest company funds in the project. Charlie decided to go ahead with his own capital. In certain respects, *Family Circle* was the riskiest of all his entrepreneurial ventures since he was starting from scratch in a field in which he had no training or background – although the amount of money involved was not substantial given his total net worth. Charlie relied heavily on Evans as managing editor to make the magazine a success. In a departure from past business practice, this venture was pursued as a personal investment transaction and therefore disassociated from his investment and merchant banking activities at Merrill, Lynch, which still functioned with a skeleton staff.

The first issue of *Family Circle* appeared in September 1932 at three chains along the East Coast. Customer reaction was positive, and increased sales of advertised goods demonstrated the magazine's impact on shoppers.

Within a month, circulation had reached 350,000; two years later, distribution passed 1.3 million weekly. Skaggs had been unwilling to invest Safeway capital in *Family Circle,* but he was enthusiastic about allowing its distribution at company stores. Indeed, Safeway became a major purchaser of advertising space in Charlie's magazine. The large chains discovered that *Family Circle* was an ideal way to promote at low cost their own private-label brands. The chains enjoyed larger margins on house brands than on items from their regular outside suppliers. Publishing profits were more elusive than circulation growth, but the magazine moved into the black in 1937, five years after its founding.

In 1946, the editors altered their distribution strategy and for the first time began asking readers to buy the magazine. The price was a mere five cents (less than fifty cents in 1995 prices). The magazine was simultaneously enlarged and sold on a monthly basis. By this date, Charlie was not deeply involved in policy making. He turned managerial control over to Palmer Leberman and Jack Schaefer, two trusted associates from the publishing world. During the early 1950s *Family Circle* sold at checkout counters in fifteen chains with more than 7,500 outlets; monthly circulation was more than four million copies, ranking seventh among major American magazines. Annual advertising revenues topped $12 million. In 1954, two years before his death, Charlie sold a controlling interest in *Family Circle* to Leberman and disposed of the remainder of his stock to other officers and employees of the magazine for an undisclosed sum. Charlie had taken a major risk in starting a new enterprise during the depths of the depression, but with foresight, talented business associates, and determination, he had enjoyed a measure of success in the publishing field.

After peaking at 3,400 stores in 1932, the expansion of Safeway Stores ground to a sudden halt. The depression finally took its toll. Charlie's acquisition of additional chains was suspended. The retail market became more competitive in the mid-1930s as the gap in consumer prices between the chains and independents narrowed. Meanwhile, Safeway passed Kroger to move into second place in aggregate sales volume. Charlie bragged in February 1933: "It is generally conceded that Safeway is in a class by itself in having fully 80% of its stores modern and up to date in every respect."[13] The new emphasis under CEO Ling Warren was on internal improvements; management sought more effective cost controls and superior delivery systems for existing outlets. A new type of grocery store with expanded product lines and more convenient customer self-service became popular with shoppers in the 1930s, and Safeway was in the vanguard of

13. CEM to Skaggs, Feb. 20, 1933, ML Files.

the movement to high-volume supermarkets. As a result of closures and consolidations, the total number of stores in the chain declined about 10 percent. A&P, by comparison, reduced the number of its outlets by 40 percent – to under 10,000 over the decade. By 1939 the average store in the Safeway chain had annual sales of $130,000, up more than 40 percent from a decade earlier, and still the best performance among major competitors.

Like most other companies during the depression years, Safeway and the other leading grocery chains assumed a defensive stance. The goal was to maintain existing profits rather than to reach higher ground. Safeway remained profitable and paid a regular dividend. The lowered growth expectations were reflected in the prices of the company's outstanding securities. From early 1930 to 1935, Safeway common stock fell from approximately $115 to $35, a decline of 70 percent. The market value of Merrill, Lynch's holdings in Safeway during this period plummeted from more than $10 million to just over $4 million, wiping out a large share of the huge paper profits recorded before the 1929 crash. By 1940, the common had rebounded to $45, selling at a respectable but unspectacular price-earnings ratio of 10 or thereabouts. Charlie held on to his securities throughout these difficult times and even added more shares to his portfolio at low points in the 1930s. His faith in the future of Safeway Stores was unshakable.

Before leaving the discussion of Charlie's activities at Safeway and *Family Circle*, we should examine for a second time an important episode, first discussed in Chapter 1, that shaped the course of subsequent events. In the mid-1930s, Safeway Stores became engaged in a public debate over the survival of chain stores in California. The political attack on chain stores had its origins in the first decade of the twentieth century; the movement escalated as the depression deepened. In the end the chains thwarted most of the discriminatory legislation generated by the controversy. With hindsight the threat was probably exaggerated, but to participants in the contest, including Charlie Merrill, the outcome was very much in doubt.

Critics of chain stores argued that outsiders – persons from beyond a given locality – had targeted small and medium-sized retailers for extinction. The discussion rarely addressed the benefits or advantages to consumers that arose from shopping at the chains, which priced goods lower than local competitors. Independent retailers saw their livelihood under attack, and unable to compete with the chains on the basis of price, they organized politically to legislate the interlopers out of existence. The history of government involvement at the local, state, and federal levels in the American economy is long, varied, and often filled with ambiguity, but one consistent strain has been the effort of persons with a vested interest in the maintenance of the status quo to drive innovators from the marketplace through discriminatory legislation.

Independents initially appealed to local pride and encouraged shoppers to freeze out the chains by refusing patronage. When that tactic failed, they organized trade associations and became a powerful lobby in state capitals, where legislators were typically responsive to the demands of small business owners. The debate was a mixture of economics and social justice, but at the heart of the matter was the conflict between the consumer's right to purchase quality goods at low prices and the right of local businessmen to preserve their position of economic, political, and social leadership in small towns across the nation.

The most common form of discrimination against the chains was an escalating tax on businesses that operated more than two or three retail outlets within state borders. The leading grocery chains with thousands of stores were the most vulnerable to the effects of anti–chain store legislation. In the eastern half of the United States, A&P, Kroger, and other leading grocery chains were at the forefront of the fight to prevent the enactment of discriminatory laws against chains.[14] In the western states, that task fell largely to Safeway Stores. As early as 1931, Warren was corresponding with Charlie about "the advisability of adding to the Safeway staff at headquarters a man with political experience, who would be qualified to set up an organization in every state to defend the company against tax legislation."[15]

In 1935, independent grocers convinced the California legislature to enact a progressive tax on chain outlets that threatened to cost Safeway upwards of $650,000 annually in additional taxes. Before the act took effect, Charlie and Safeway officials mobilized the other chain store operators in the state. They filed petitions that delayed implementation of the law until California voters had a chance to decide its fate in a statewide referendum.

In 1936, the electorate voted resoundingly to repeal the tax, vindicating the efforts of Safeway and other chains to continue giving consumers the benefits of the lowest prices for household staples. Charlie's children later recalled that one of their father's favorite refrains after the success of the referendum was to boast that, if he ever got to heaven, it would be because he had acted to save the citizens of California a few cents on every quart of milk.

Although it was certainly not obvious to participants at the time, the

14. Tedlow, *New and Improved*, 182–258.   15. Warren to CEM, Nov. 16, 1931, ML Files.

most important aspect of the anti–chain store fight in California was that it introduced Charlie to Ted Braun, the public relations expert from Los Angeles. Braun surveyed public opinion throughout the state, and based on the accumulated data, he was instrumental in designing an election campaign that triumphed. Educating farmers and urban consumers about the relevant facts over a period of months – and not just in the final weeks before the vote – was an important element in that successful strategy. Charlie was extraordinarily impressed by the tone and tenor of the campaign, and Braun became a key outside adviser after the financier's return to Wall Street in 1940.

While concentrating his energies on Safeway in the late 1920s and early 1930s, Charlie was called upon to help solve a financial crisis at one of his very first clients in the chain store sector – McCrory Stores. One of the company's problems was that, contrary to the advice of many retail experts, Charlie included, McCrory's had signed long-term leases for store locations at fixed sums. Management thought it had wisely provided for the future, but exactly the reverse proved true. The persistent deflation of the 1930s drove up the real cost of its leases to untenable levels. The variety chain was devastated by the depression; its profits turned almost overnight into substantial losses. Unable to renew its revolving bank credit, the company went into bankruptcy and receivership in 1930.

Charlie was an interested party because Merrill, Lynch held over 70,000 shares of McCrory common stock with a market price of more than $65 at the end of 1929. Three years later the same stock had dropped through the floor to a mere $2 per share. Legal authorities appointed Charlie to the committee assigned the task of restructuring the finances of the threatened variety chain. He recommended renegotiation of the leases with payments based on current sales volume rather than fixed sums, and other committee members concurred. Most landlords were willing to alter the lease terms because the alternative was losing a tenant in a period when the demand for commercial space was weak. Charlie also helped to recruit Charles Green, an executive at S. H. Kress, a competing chain with more than two hundred outlets, to become the new CEO. McCrory emerged from bankruptcy under this plan and soon returned to profitability. But the glory days had passed. By 1940, the common stock had climbed to $15 per share – seven times its low point in 1933 but a far cry from the $65 price it had commanded a decade earlier. As a result of the controversial bankruptcy proceedings, John McCrory, the founder, and Charlie parted on bad terms. A few years later he had a falling out with Sebastian Kresge, another of his original clients. Charlie made lasting friendships with most of his business associates, but there were exceptions.

In the mid-1930s Charlie's marriage to Hellen began to break down. The problems were similar to those that had undermined his relationship with Eliza. Conflicts abounded over his rootless lifestyle and his relations with other women – some sexual, others merely flirtatious but nonetheless vexing. Hellen recalled their life together: "He always had more women friends than men friends. He is naturally attracted to them and when 'courting' is unsurpassed."[16] His wife's artistic outlook and Charlie's hard-boiled business demeanor were no longer capable of easy compromise. Moreover, Hellen, now in her mid-thirties, had matured and was no longer overwhelmed and intimidated by her husband's great wealth and exalted position. She had a mind of her own, and she resented his efforts to control her life and that of their son, Jimmy. Arguments over child rearing were frequent. Charlie had rigid opinions about what was best for the children. Hellen believed her husband was too much of a disciplinarian.

Charlie had an old-fashioned view of the rights and privileges spelled out in the marriage contract: the husband commanded, and while the wife and children had the right to protest, they ultimately obeyed or took the consequences. A household, he thought, should be managed in a fashion similar to a profitable business enterprise, an idea that reflected in some ways his own upbringing. A frustrated autocrat, he was increasingly discontent at home. In a revealing letter to Doris in May 1937, Charlie explained:

> You know, I am sure, of my devotion to Hellen, and happiness when everything is going just right. What causes me untold concern, however, is my lack of confidence in my ability to continue to stand in the future the sudden squalls and violent storms which, in the past, have shaken me almost to the breaking point. I have held the position of leadership in every important activity with which I am connected; this long continued role has led me to expect loyalty and cooperation from all who willingly enlist under my banner. . . . I cannot tolerate insubordination, or resistance, either open or passive.[17]

As it stood, Hellen and Jimmy were often insubordinate and resistant to his will; consequently, they became expendable.

While Charlie and Hellen were still together, he did have the pleasure of seeing his only daughter married to a man of whom he heartily approved. Robert Magowan met Doris at a party at her father's house in Palm Beach in 1934, when she was twenty years old. The couple were married in Southampton in June 1935. A graduate of Harvard University, Magowan started his business career with Macy's department store in New York, but left for a better position at N. W. Ayer, one of the nation's

---

16. Hellen Ingram, "An Old Wives' Tale," 1954, a 28-page manuscript in ML Files.
17. CEM to Doris Magowan, May 27, 1937, ML Files.

pioneer advertising agencies, where he was working when he was introduced to Doris. After the Magowans' Cuban honeymoon, Charlie took his
son-in-law under his wing and sent him to San Francisco to learn the
grocery trade. Over the last two decades of his life, Charlie's relationship
with Robert and Doris was the most personally satisfying of all his associations with family members. His mother, Octavia, had died in 1933, and
his sister Edith succumbed prematurely in 1936. Neither Charles Jr. nor
Jimmy ever indicated any interest in following in their father's footsteps,
but Magowan, already involved in the business world, identified with his
father-in-law's general outlook on life. Charlie molded Magowan to be his
successor. After a stint with Safeway, Magowan soon transferred to Merrill, Lynch in New York, where he spent more than a decade and a half.
Magowan returned to Safeway as CEO, replacing Ling Warren, in 1955.

Another celebratory moment came in 1936, when Charlie, Hellen, and
Jimmy moved into a new house in Palm Beach designed by the architect
Howard Major. "Merrill's Landing" was a palatial vacation home, with
outlying structures, on an inland waterway. In similar fashion to his estate
on Long Island, there were numerous rooms for overnight guests. In a
cheerful mood, Charlie described his new residence to Doris: "The house
and grounds are lovely; I have never seen anything like it in Palm Beach,
or for that matter, anywhere else. No one single feature stands out, but the
grounds, house and furnishings are in such harmony that the entire effect
is one of beauty, comfort and dignity."[18] A year later, he was still singing
its praises. "The place in Florida," he told Doris, "has been a godsend. I
go down there pretty badly shot to pieces, and after three or four days, I
begin to snap out of it."[19] In stark contrast to the pleasure he derived from
his new home, Charlie's relationship with Hellen was deteriorating daily.
By the spring of 1937, they were irreconcilably at odds, and by the end of
the year they had separated.

At some point in the mid-1930s, Charlie began an affair with Kinta Des
Mare, who became his third wife. He met Kinta through Signa Lynch,
who had married Eddie Lynch in the 1920s. Signa was a native of New
Orleans, and Kinta was a hometown acquaintance. According to one
source, Charlie was attracted by Kinta's "beauty and warmth."[20] She
possessed a more compliant, less challenging personality than Hellen.
Charlie wanted a more subservient female companion at this stage of his
life, not someone so competitive and independent. As his wife, Kinta was
perfectly happy to cooperate in organizing their social life around the

18. Quoted in Keenan, "Chain of Fortune," 471.
19. CEM to Doris Magowan, Dec. 6, 1937, ML Files.
20. Transcript of interview, Nov. 10, 1955, with Henderson, who worked as the head gardener at
    the Orchard in 1930s and 1940s, in ML Files.

provision of nighttime and weekend entertainment for friends – mostly Charlie's friends – who were frequent guests at their homes in Southampton and Palm Beach. Charlie, now fifty-one, led an active life, including golf and tennis in the daytime, followed by dinner parties and bridge at night. Kinta was thirty-five in 1937; the age gap was about the same as between Charlie and Hellen. "Cute and shapely . . . a showpiece," nephew Merrill Matzinger remembered; she was someone "to keep house and self elegant for friends to admire."[21] Kinta was essentially Charlie's second trophy wife, although not a younger model.

Hellen was infuriated by the affair with Kinta. At first, she refused Charlie's request for a friendly divorce. Later, she agreed to a divorce but asked for a substantial financial settlement, including possession of one, or both, of the couple's homes in New York and Florida. Charlie's net worth had been reduced substantially from its high point in 1929 by the decline in stock prices, but his assets still totaled in the millions and his income held up surprisingly well because companies like Safeway continued to pay handsome dividends.[22] With prices falling, Charlie's earnings from investments purchased more luxuries than in the 1920s.

The effort to keep their marital squabbles hush-hush and out of the New York newspapers failed. The scandal became public in what seemed at the time lurid detail – meaning hints of adultery. In that era, adultery was a serious civil offense and one of the few grounds for granting a divorce in New York courts.[23] Charlie was angered by Hellen's behavior after their separation. He complained to Doris that he could not understand her "campaign of vilification against me" nor her "ostrich like stupidity, avarice and cruelty."[24] After more than a year of legal maneuvering, Hellen consented to a divorce that stipulated a generous financial settlement. Charlie retained ownership of the Orchard and Merrill's Landing. Still impetuous and unwilling to waste any further time in the pursuit of happiness, he married Kinta in Pensacola in March 1939, just a month after his divorce from Hellen became final. Their marriage was, according

---

21. Transcript of interview of nephew Charles Merrill Matzinger, Oct. 20, 1955, in ML Files.
22. There are no precise financial records for the 1930s, but I have estimated from various sources that the income from Safeway securities alone was at least $500,000 annually and possibly more, depending on how many additional shares were bought at declining prices after 1930.
23. In the transcript of an interview with Ned Magowan, Robert's brother, there is mention of Hellen's "indiscretions," which presumedly allude to sexual affairs with persons unknown. Whether such affairs occurred before or after her separation from Charlie, or indeed were mere rumors, is unverified by any other information in the files. My interpretation of these events, based on the general tone and context of Magowan's recollections, is that Charlie's lawyers were planning to file a countercharge of adultery against Hellen in the event she tried to use the infidelity issue to damage him in any legal proceedings.
24. Typed excerpts from letters from CEM to Doris, Oct. 29, 1937, and Jan. 14, 1938, in ML Files.

to all reports, reasonably fulfilling for five years – that is, until his first heart attack; failing health thereafter altered drastically his lifestyle and undermined his relationship with Kinta.

Still grieving over the recent deaths of his mother and sister and in turmoil over the triangle with Hellen and Kinta, Charlie endured another tragedy a year before his remarriage that affected both his personal life and his business affairs: Eddie Lynch died in May 1938, just a week short of his fifty-third birthday. During a voyage across the Atlantic, Lynch was afflicted with blood poisoning. He survived the trip but died of septicemia a few days after arriving in London.[25] In acknowledging the condolences that poured in, Charlie told one correspondent: "Eddie's death has been a terrific blow to me. For 31 years Ed and I were the best of friends and for 29 of these years the closest of business associates."[26]

Charlie's words were sincere, but, in truth, their closeness in business affairs had steadily dissipated over the last decade – although personal ties were tightened in 1936 and 1937 after Charlie started dating Kinta. Their drifting apart began in the mid-1920s when the partners sold their interest in Pathé Exchange and reinvested the profits in Safeway Stores. Lynch had been deeply involved in the management of the motion picture company, but he remained on the periphery of the venture into groceries. Previously a workaholic, Lynch never found a business project after 1926 that aroused his interests; in the 1930s, nothing much except tennis and other recreational activities consumed his time.

The long contentiousness over reducing the partnership's exposure to a possible downturn in the stock market in 1928 and 1929, a debate in which Charlie and Lynch took opposite sides, was another factor that loosened the bonds between the two men. Other problems periodically arose. In a sharply worded memorandum in April 1929, Charlie accused Lynch of misconduct and disloyalty during the course of negotiations with a prospective underwriting client.[27] After downsizing in early 1930, the partnership did not aggressively seek new underwriting clients. Lynch was for all practical purposes retired over the last eight years of his life; he managed his investment portfolio but did little else to participate actively in business affairs.

In the reorganization of the firm after Lynch's death, Charlie steadfastly refused to drop the name of his long-term associate from the masthead.

25. The facts related to Lynch's death were revealed in the author's correspondence with Doris Merrill Magowan, June 8, 1994.
26. Quoted in Hecht, *Legacy of Leadership*, 30.
27. CEM to Lynch, April 10, 1929, ML Files. The discussion centered on efforts to line up possible merger candidates for First National Stores, a grocery chain. Lynch's actions were shameful, according to Charlie, and had caused the partners to "lose their own self-respect."

When legal advisers explained that according to state law in New York, only the living could appear in the title of a partnership, Charlie told them to search for some means of circumventing the statute. The inventive lawyers argued before government officials that by dropping the comma between the two names and converting the existing title into the name of an ongoing business enterprise rather than living persons, the partnership should be allowed to continue with only slight modification. The new formal title thus was Merrill Lynch & Company, virtually the same as in the past except without the comma. Ironically, Lynch, who contributed nothing to the revival of the firm in the 1940s, was memorialized and immortalized for the major accomplishments of others who followed in his wake – and all because of the sentimentality and loyalty of the man who had been his business partner for almost a quarter of a century.

Contrary to Charlie's proclamations in 1938 that he did not know "how he would get along" without his former partner, Lynch's death was one of the important elements that set the stage for Charlie's renewed interest in the financial services sector. With Lynch out of the picture, Charlie was in a position to insist on complete control of decision making without having to worry about whether someone else in the firm might interfere with the direction or implementation of his policies. Win Smith, his confidant after 1940, did not possess the financial resources to challenge Charlie in any substantive way. Pierce, the other senior partner, had been on the verge of bankruptcy, and he was content to defer to Charlie on all important matters. The prospect of a quiet atmosphere at the apex of power suited Charlie just fine. At midlife, he had had his fill of uncompliant wives and uncooperative business associates. At a resuscitated and expanded Merrill Lynch, he could do what he wanted, when he wanted; meanwhile, he could listen to the opinions of the other principals only when he believed their counsel made a positive contribution. Tolerant of dissent when policies were under review, he was intolerant of foot-dragging once a decision had been made – usually by himself. Contrary to the historical dictum that "power corrupts" and in time "absolute power corrupts absolutely," after his return to Wall Street, Charlie used his superior position more in the fashion of an enlightened monarch than a tyrant.

8

REFORM ON WALL STREET

During the depression years, when Charlie had largely withdrawn from the financial services sector and refocused his energies on Safeway Stores, the U.S. capital markets underwent one of the greatest transformations since their emergence in the 1790s. A series of New Deal reforms altered dramatically the investment climate on Wall Street. Although most of the nation's leading financiers opposed the federal government's enhanced supervisory role, the new regulations were for the most part in harmony with principles that Charlie had expounded throughout his career. He had long advocated regulations and procedures that would make investment bankers, the stock and bond exchanges, securities dealers, and brokers more accountable to small investors and less beholden to narrow special interests.

Although frequently at odds with the Old Guard that set the rules for the New York Stock Exchange during his first career on Wall Street, Charlie was not instrumental in promoting the reform agenda in the 1930s, either publicly or in private. E. A. Pierce, who assumed control of Merrill, Lynch's branch offices in 1930 and later became a business partner in the grand merger a decade later, was deeply involved in the debate over the propriety of new regulations, however. Nothing in the historical record suggests that Charlie was ever critical of Pierce's efforts to improve conditions for the investing public during these turbulent years.[1]

Given the important changes in the 1930s, a review of the federal government's reform program is apropos here because its enactment was another critical factor that paved the way for the spectacular success of Merrill Lynch after Charlie's return to Wall Street in 1940. Until the fourth decade of the twentieth century, government regulation of the

---

1. In contrast, Edmund Lynch was an outspoken opponent of New Deal regulation, a strong defender of the NYSE, and a severe critic of President Roosevelt. See Griffis, "Saga of Wall Street," 142.

financial services sector was haphazard. Some sectors were heavily supervised, others hardly at all. Commercial banks had been subject to governmental oversight at both the federal and state levels from the outset,
beginning with legislative charters for the Bank of North America in the
1780s and the First Bank of the United States in the 1790s. Insurance
companies, initially ignored by legislative bodies, were forced to comply
with a host of new regulations at the state level in the late nineteenth and
early twentieth centuries. Investment banking and brokerage, in contrast,
escaped close scrutiny, although this financial sector was never totally
neglected. During the early nineteenth century, for example, the state of
New York passed laws governing transactions in what we call today financial derivatives – puts, calls, and all varieties of option contracts.[2] After
decades of relative inattention, public oversight of the investment sector
rose steadily from 1880 to 1920, and the impact was much greater than
depicted in most published accounts of the evolution of legislation governing U.S. capital markets.

In response to the rise of large transportation and industrial enterprises
after the Civil War, governmental units at all levels expanded the scope of
their regulatory activities. By the 1910s, most states had established commissions to oversee the operations of the public utilities operating within
their borders. Included under the rubric of public utilities were companies
that provided citizens with basic services – water, electricity, and gas; and
in a second category were corporations that provided rail transportation.
Mounting concerns about the rate structure of these assorted utilities led
public commissions to investigate the capital structure of regulated enterprises and, in turn, to exercise greater influence over the composition of
their capital structure. In the 1920s the federal government joined the
states in monitoring more carefully the issuance of railroad securities. Prior
to World War I, the link between railroad securities and the rise of U.S.
capital markets was extremely close; as late as 1910, more than 90 percent
of the listed issues, stocks and bonds combined, on the NYSE represented
the indebtedness of railroad companies.[3]

The weaknesses in U.S. securities laws were associated primarily with
the unregulated sectors. The rules governing the security issues of industrial and service sector firms that were neither banks nor utilities and of all
foreign issuers, whether corporations or national governments, were comparatively lax. Several factors were important in explaining the lack of
governmental oversight. Until the 1890s the issues of large industrial firms
were few in number, and they rarely traded on the larger exchanges. The

2. Werner and Smith, *Wall Street*, 100–101.
3. Data gleaned from official NYSE lists; complete index, vols. 1 to 10.

same held true for the bonded debt of foreign governments. While issues in these categories increased steadily after the turn of the century, they did not constitute a majority of the listings on the NYSE until sometime in the 1920s.

Until the third decade of the twentieth century, only a small percentage of the population owned securities. Most holders of stocks and bonds in the nineteenth century were reasonably sophisticated investors who were capable of determining the risks and rewards associated with traded securities. Cautious households with substantial wealth typically arranged the purchase of securities through investment banks that had a long-standing reputation for soundness and probity. Following the conservative advice of the partners in such venerable houses as J. P. Morgan, Kuhn Loeb, and their near peers, risk-averse savers generally restricted their investments to government and railroad bonds, with perhaps a sprinkling of high-yielding preferred stocks issued by the leading railroads. In performing their essentially fiduciary role, most financial advisers to upper-class households stressed not the potential for capital gains but the preservation of principal and the generation of a modest income stream.

Although some corporate issuers had established a solid record of dividend payments on their common stock, persons who opted to invest in these securities were normally prepared to assume the risk of potentially volatile price swings and an inferior position relative to creditors in any future bankruptcy proceedings. Indeed, most investments in common stocks during this earlier era were, by their very nature, considered at best mildly speculative. Only railroad stocks and the common stock of large industrial enterprises such as U.S. Steel received the qualified endorsement of the leading investment banking houses.

Equities were risky investments because they were subject to manipulative trading schemes fostered by greedy traders. Groups of speculators periodically organized pools to drive a given stock to an uncharacteristically high or low price; they hoped to realize handsome short-run profits before the stock returned to its normal price level. Adventurous traders who sustained substantial losses in common stocks, either because of bad corporate results or because of the speculative activities of insiders, received little sympathy from lawmakers and the general public. The victims of stock manipulation usually took their medicine without resort to the American legal or legislative systems.

Another important factor that deterred the federal government's oversight of the capital markets was that the organized exchanges in major cities had adopted private codes designed to protect investors from most – but not all – essentially fraudulent activities. The exchanges supervised what were fundamentally auction markets, in which a single specialist acted as the sole intermediary in matching buy-and-sell orders for a particular issue. The commissions permitted to specialists and brokers for providing these transaction services were fixed and uniform for every stock issue irrespective of volume. The New York Stock Exchange, which traced its history back to the late eighteenth and early nineteenth centuries and was the nation's leader in terms of trading volume, set the tone for other regional exchanges. Access to the trading room was restricted to qualified members of the exchange, and applicants had to meet certain criteria to gain admission: primarily minimum capital requirements and recommendations from prominent businessmen regarding their good reputations. Members caught flagrantly manipulating stock prices were subject to temporary suspensions or permanent expulsion. Wash sales – offsetting buy-and-sell orders that produced high volume and were designed to draw unsuspecting outsiders into trading a given security – were strictly forbidden. In addition, the governing boards of the exchanges screened the securities proposed for regular trading to make certain that the issuing companies were bona fide enterprises in sound financial condition.

Generally speaking, the stock exchanges exercised the powers of self-regulation in a responsible manner, the complaints of critics notwithstanding. Their procedures were intended to protect innocent investors from outright fraud, although lax rules regarding their members' participation in questionable techniques such as corners and bear raids provided ample ammunition for skeptics. (In corners, traders continuously purchased shares of a targeted stock in an effort to drive the issue to extremely high prices before unloading their holdings; in bear raids, traders borrowed shares of a targeted stock and sold them continuously in an effort to drive the price of an issue down to extremely low levels before discharging their obligations at huge profits.) The majority of losers in these speculative binges were other traders who were also members of the local stock exchange, not unsophisticated outsiders. The occasional news reports about fortunes gained and lost on Wall Street made dramatic headlines, but there was no loud public outcry for legislative reform.

The weakest link in the securities field was the so-called over-the-counter market for stocks and bonds. Securities traded over the counter were issued by smaller firms without an established record of earning capacity. Many were new ventures just getting off the ground. These inherently speculative issues did not qualify for listings on the exchanges; therefore, the rules and regulations governing their issuance and trading were not well defined. In this loosely organized market, one or more brokerage firms typically announced their willingness to expedite trading in a given stock; in facilitating transactions, the brokerage firm functioned more as a dealer than a true auctioneer. Because of low volume and the irregularity of orders, dealers normally sold stocks out of inventories on hand, periodically replenishing supplies when inventories ran low. In quoting rates to prospective buyers, brokers in the over-the-counter market did not usually reveal what percentage of the price represented the underlying value of the security and what percentage represented the markup or sales commission.

Most brokerage firms active in the over-the-counter market had varying commission schedules for different classes of securities. As in most real estate transactions today, the broker received more compensation for negotiating a sale out of his employer's inventory than for arranging transactions through third parties. To generate more trading volume in certain issues, the managers of brokerage firms periodically offered their sales personnel the opportunity to earn higher-than-normal commissions on transactions in thinly traded stocks or highly speculative issues. Customers were rarely told the source of any stock recommended for purchase; they were rarely told whether the stock came from the dealer's inventory or from third parties. In general, the commission structure in the over-the-counter market did not encourage individual brokers to provide the most forthright, disinterested financial advice to the investing public.

Prior to the twentieth century, the states exercised jurisdiction over securities dealers and brokers in the over-the-counter market almost exclusively through antifraud laws. If sales personnel grossly misrepresented the investment quality of a security issue, the guilty parties could be pursued through the courts. Unfortunately, several years usually had to pass without the payment of interest or dividends before a fraudulent transaction was objectively confirmed; by then, little money, if any, remained to reimburse the unsuspecting victims. In the typical fraudulent transaction, unscrupulous brokers targeted unsophisticated investors and lured them with dreams of huge profits in a short period of time. Many inexperienced people with surplus funds available for investment were unable to assess properly a salesman's grandiose claims that sounded "too good to be true." So-called bucket shops were the worst offenders. These scam artists promised tremendous profits on invested funds, but they never had any intention of actually acquiring legitimate securities for their gullible customers. Many of the reforms subsequently enacted to curb the abuses on Wall Street had the greatest impact on unsavory firms on the fringes of the capital markets – firms that had no legitimate connection with the New York Stock Exchange or with any of the nation's organized exchanges.

In the United States, the legal environment with regard to the sale of worthless and misrepresented securities was essentially reactive rather than proactive and preventive. The guilty, if they could be found and brought to court, received punishment after financial losses had become an undisputed reality. Meanwhile, reputable investment firms and the officials of leading stock exchanges did not advocate the passage of protective legislation because they relied on the uncertainties associated with over-the-counter markets to retain the allegiance of existing customers who were reluctant to invest in unlisted stocks. In retrospect, the attitude of the leading figures on Wall Street was self-serving and irresponsible because sensible protective measures were readily at hand and clear precedents for their implementation already existed. In England, mounting public concern about the lack of accurate and truthful information linked to the huge volume of corporate securities issued in London, the world's foremost capital market in the nineteenth century, led Parliament to enact the Companies Act in 1844.[4] Strengthened in 1900, British law required the release of pertinent financial information about the corporate issuer and its bankers coinciding with any sale of securities to the general public. A company's directors and its investment bankers could be held personally liable for any lack of thoroughness and diligence in providing accurate information to potential investors. British law did not prevent, or actively discourage, the sale of securities to finance speculative new ventures, but it did require that investors be reasonably informed about the risks associated with different classes of securities. These precautionary measures helped to cement London's position as the world center of international finance. One of the main goals of reformers in the United States during the first quarter of the twentieth century was to bring the rules and regulations applicable to new issues of all stocks and bonds up to the higher standards that had been in force in Great Britain for more than half a century.

High standards for the securities of regulated industries already existed in the United States by the 1920s. Railroad commissions in several states and the Interstate Commerce Commission at the federal level had the power to subpoena and make public on a regular basis the financial statements of the companies under their purview. Banks and utilities were similarly monitored by various public agencies.[5] Since a large percentage of the securities listed on the major stock exchanges through the 1910s had originated with the railroads, banks, and utilities, the practical differences between disclosure policies in Great Britain and the United States were actually less acute as late as 1925 than in the last stages of the great bull market, when a flood of unregulated industrial stocks and foreign bonds were granted listings on the organized exchanges.

4. Edwards, "Company Legislation," 1–6.
5. See Ayres, "Governmental Regulation"; Ripley, "Public Regulation"; Baskin and Miranti, *History of Corporate Finance.*

The most serious effort to reform the laws applicable to unregulated securities prior to the New Deal reforms emanated from a seemingly unlikely point: the state of Kansas, a locale distant in space and culture from the nation's leading financial centers. In response to recurring reports about a flurry of financial losses linked to bad investments, the citizens of Kansas reacted decisively to restrain the activities of the growing number of brokers peddling worthless stocks. Too many sleazy salesmen were succeeding in selling wheat farmers pieces of paper that proved no more valuable than a frivolous claim on the "wide blue sky." In 1911 the state legislature approved a new set of rules and regulations that went further in many respects than comparable laws in Great Britain. Kansas's comprehensive blue-sky regulations required not only the registration of all new issues, with accompanying financial statements, but also the licensing of brokers and dealers. State officials were granted unprecedented authority in administering the rules. First, they had the power to deny licenses to sales organizations and sales personnel suspected of deceptive practices. Second, officials could deny authorized brokers the privilege of selling any security within the state whose merits seemed questionable, including otherwise legitimate issues that seemed "not to promise a fair return."[6]

Over the next two decades, other states passed different versions of blue-sky bills designed to protect local investors from some of the worst abuses of securities fraud. Often overlooked in historical accounts of the blue-sky movement was the critical fact that the tight rules were directed almost exclusively at the speculative, over-the-counter sphere of the securities market. Securities issued by companies already listed on the nation's stock exchanges were invariably exempted from registration requirements at the state level. As a consequence, the leadership of the New York Stock Exchange and other prominent exchanges did not feel terribly threatened by the movement to extend the arm of state governments into this marginal sphere of the capital markets. On the contrary, stronger laws with regard to unlisted securities were generally welcomed because they indirectly encouraged investors to restrict their transactions to a smaller universe of listed stocks and bonds. In short, Wall Street's opposition to government regulation was not all-encompassing; the main objection of the financial elite was to any interference in the functioning of their private domain – the organized exchanges.

A second important regulatory development, infrequently mentioned in discussions of the background for New Deal financial reforms, was congressional passage of the Transportation Act of 1920.[7] The law gave the Interstate Commerce Commission expanded powers. ICC officials were

---

6. Carosso, *Investment Banking*, 164.   7. Hoogenboom, *History of ICC*, 112–18.

granted, first, the right to receive advance notice of any intended issuance of securities by the nation's railroads and, second, the power to review the accompanying financial documents and allow or disallow all proposed transactions. William Z. Ripley, an activist economics professor at Harvard University, was a leading proponent of reform. Railroads were still the overwhelming providers of passenger and freight services, and the public had become increasingly involved in their operations and financial affairs. During World War I, the federal government seized control of the railroads in an effort to improve the efficiency of the war effort. In 1920, the fear of overcapitalization, which many concluded would put upward pressure on fares and rates in order to raise sufficient revenues to meet interest obligations, led Congress to grant its premier regulatory agency these extraordinary new powers. Although the new rules affected their role as financial advisers to the nation's railroads, investment bankers on Wall Street were rarely consulted in the formulation of this revolutionary piece of legislation. Both shippers and railroad executives, who were at odds on many other issues, saw considerable merit in granting the ICC authority to regulate access to the capital markets; since these rivals agreed, that section of the bill sailed through congressional committees with little opposition and became law without controversy in 1920.[8]

The ICC's ability to deny railroad executives the privilege of issuing new securities was similar to the authority granted to regulators in the Kansas law. Because the majority of corporate bonds and a healthy percentage of the preferred and common stocks listed on the nation's exchanges were associated with the railroads as late as the mid-1920s, the discrepancies between British and the U.S. securities laws were, from a practical standpoint, less significant than many contemporaries and subsequent historians have supposed. The Transportation Act of 1920 was, in many ways, the model and unrecognized predecessor of the securities reforms of the 1930s.

Congressional hearings into the causes of the stock market crash were delayed for several years because many experts expected a rebound within a period of months. Precipitous legislative action was deemed unnecessary and unwise. Volatility in stock prices was a recurring event, and few were unduly alarmed about the situation in late 1929 and throughout most of 1930. Indeed, in the six months following the sharp sell-off in October 1929, most stocks recovered up to one-half of their recent losses. From its low point of 198 in November, the Dow-Jones industrial average rose

---

8. Kerr, *American Railroad Politics*, 224. The issue had been controversial during the first decades of the century.

nearly 50 percent to 294 in April 1930. From that point, the bears took control and prices steadily plummeted. The Dow fell 33 percent in 1930, 52 percent in 1931, and another 23 percent in 1932. Between its high in September 1929 and its low in July 1932, the popular market average had dropped 89 percent.[9]

Exactly how many investors were significantly hurt by the stock market's sharp decline is unknown. During the first three decades of the century, the number of investors in common stocks throughout the nation had steadily increased, and ambitious brokers successfully solicited more clients among upper-middle-class households that had previously avoided the capital markets. In an effort to embellish the story by exaggerating the extent of the disaster, some historians have suggested that the number of investors drawn into the great bull market might have climbed as high as 10 million by 1929. More careful analysis of the available data indicates a lower figure – on the order of 3 to 5 million.[10] Whatever the true number, several million upper-middle-class families that had not previously owned securities felt the negative effects of the tailspin, and they demanded that their elected representatives take action to remedy the alleged abuses.

President Herbert Hoover and leading Republicans in Congress agreed early in 1932 to launch an investigation into the stock market with an eye to possible reform. Many critics focused on the general practice of short selling on the exchanges.[11] Some purists argued that short sales were inherently unethical and ought to be prohibited; others believed short selling had contributed significantly to the market decline and needed to be more tightly controlled. Defenders of the status quo countered by claiming that short sellers actually promoted price stability; they contended that short sales acted as a restraint on speculative increases in stock prices and thus acted to dampen the influence of overoptimistic bulls. During the congressional investigation, which continued into 1933, it was revealed that Albert Wiggin, the president of the Chase National Bank, one of the largest commercial banks in New York City, had sold short the stock of his own institution in the summer of 1929 and had profited to the tune of $4 million after the crash.[12] While subsequent reforms did not outlaw short sales as a recognized trading strategy, CEOs and other leading officers were prohibited from using this technique to profit from declines in the stock prices of the companies they actively managed.

The leading spokesman for Wall Street interests during the congres-

9. Data from Farrell, *Dow Jones Averages.*
10. Sobel, *Great Bull Market,* 74. Firms that were members of the NYSE reported 1.5 million customer accounts in 1929. This figure does not include the accounts of nonmember firms that dealt in over-the-counter stocks and securities listed on other regional exchanges.
11. Seligman, *Transformation of Wall Street,* 9–18.	12. Brooks, *Once in Golconda,* 104.

sional hearings in 1932 and 1933 was Richard Whitney, president of the New York Stock Exchange. Whitney was simultaneously the managing partner of a medium-sized firm that concentrated on railroad and utility bonds. His brother, George Whitney, was an influential partner in the prestigious investment banking house of J. P. Morgan. In several appearances before Senate committees, Richard Whitney stoutly defended the NYSE against the attacks of critics. Federal legislation was unnecessary, he argued; the exchanges were fully capable of enlightened self-regulation. At one point the unflappable Whitney met with skeptical investigators in his New York office and coolly informed them: "You gentlemen are making a great mistake. The exchange is a perfect institution."[13]

Before the decade had ended, the high and mighty had fallen. Richard Whitney was indicted for embezzlement – a deceit inflicted not on the general public but on his trusting friends at the NYSE, including his brother, George.[14] Finally exposed after years of deception, Richard Whitney pleaded guilty, and a judge sent him upriver to Sing Sing state prison. Ironically, among his many creditors during the 1930s was E. A. Pierce, which had lent him a substantial sum, reportedly as high as $100,000 against good collateral.[15] Whitney's ignominious departure in April 1938 represented the final surrender of the Old Guard on the NYSE to the spirit of reform; thereafter, the primary responsibility of the exchange was to the investing public rather than to private floor traders. In retrospect, Richard Whitney's sudden departure was another of the key events that signaled to Charles Merrill that a return to Wall Street might be appropriate and timely.

The congressional investigation of securities markets and the nation's major exchanges resumed in the early months of 1933 after the election results from November 1932 had been tallied. Incoming president Franklin Delano Roosevelt had campaigned for reform of the capital markets, and he recruited a team of lawyers headed by Felix Frankfurter, a professor at the Harvard Law School, to draft new legislation.[16] The comprehensive reform program proceeded in several directions. First, commercial banking and investment banking were institutionally divorced. During the early twentieth century, some of New York's leading commercial banks had formed subsidiaries – contemporaries called them affiliates – to engage in

---

13. Brooks, *Once in Golconda*, 198.   14. Chernow, *House of Morgan*, 421–29.
15. Brooks, *Once in Golconda*, 208. Since Pierce's loans were fully secured, the firm suffered no losses on the Whitney account. The major losers in bankruptcy proceedings were numerous unsecured creditors who were members of the NYSE, including J. P. Morgan for a sum reportedly on the order of $500,000.
16. Included in the group of lawyers recruited by Frankfurter was James Landis, who later became commissioner of the Securities and Exchange Commission. For an analysis of Landis's role in the reform movement, see McCraw, *Prophets of Regulation*, ch. 5.

underwriting new issues of securities, and by the end of the 1920s these affiliates had captured roughly half of the bond market. In addition to railroad, utility, and industrial bonds, several bank affiliates were prominent sponsors of the bonds of foreign governments, particularly of shaky governments in South America. Unfortunately for the underwriters and their clients, in the wake of the broadening world depression, many of these foreign issues defaulted soon after issuance. Critics of the increasing mixture of commercial and investment banking functions, especially Senator Carter Glass of Virginia, a former secretary of the treasury in the Wilson administration, were extremely vocal in claiming that the imprudent activities of bank affiliates had contributed significantly to the crash.

Although these unfounded allegations have been largely discredited by financial historians in recent years, contemporary political leaders were uncertain about what had caused the long series of economic disasters from 1929 to 1933, and they bowed to the pressure tactics of Senator Glass and his allies to separate by law the two financial services.[17] Financial institutions that had been involved in both commercial banking and the securities markets were required to choose one sector or the other in 1934; thereafter, all commercial banks were prohibited from underwriting securities for corporate clients and foreign governments. In assessing the implications of the divorce of commercial and investment banking for Charlie Merrill's career, the main effect was that it prevented aggressive commercial banks from diversifying into securities and providing additional competition to brokers and underwriters after the revitalization of Merrill Lynch in the 1940s.

The second and third thrusts of reform were aimed at increasing the flow of financial information to the investing public and, simultaneously, at raising the ethical standards applied to underwriters, brokers, and dealers. The loose models for legislation were the updated version of the original British Companies Act, the broad powers granted to federal regulators at the ICC in the Transportation Act of 1920, and the numerous blue-sky laws that state legislatures had enacted in the first quarter of the century. In testimony before congressional committees and in journalistic releases, most Wall Street representatives opposed the reform movement. Conservatives claimed that new federal laws might cause the collapse of capitalism; others argued that tightening the rules at the depth of the depression would act to impede economic recovery. Rarely has such a large group of otherwise intelligent people been so blind to what was truly in their own best interest – and, of course, the best interest of a multitude of

17. The literature on this subject is succinctly summarized in Benston, *Separation of Commercial and Investment Banking.*

investors at home and abroad. Many of the leading financiers in the 1930s had a mind-set more attuned to the narrow, elitist capital markets that had prevailed before World War I. Out of touch with new realities, they could not adjust to a shifting market that had attracted millions of upper-middle-class households to stocks and bonds in the 1920s. Convinced that they had been duped, these unsophisticated investors now demanded greater accountability and more protection from unscrupulous salesmen.

The two most prominent exceptions to this broad indictment of Wall Street figures were Paul Shields, who had been a partner at Merrill, Lynch in the 1920s, and E. A. Pierce.[18] They were the managing partners of two competing firms that concentrated on providing customers with routine brokerage services – trading previously issued securities on secondary markets. Such institutions were typically called commission houses by contemporaries, and their profits were linked directly to the volume of trading by thousands of customers, large and small, both on the organized exchanges and over the counter. Shields and Pierce, as did many of the managing partners of other commission houses, understood that only by restoring public faith in the fairness of the market mechanisms could brokerage firms expect to retain the loyalty of trusting clients and, in turn, maintain volume. Taking a more comprehensive view of the problems facing Wall Street than did most of their peers, Shields and Pierce realized that more complete public disclosure of financial information and the proper labeling of the risks associated with specific securities would benefit all participants in the U.S. capital markets in the long run. Laws requiring greater disclosure had not harmed the London capital market, nor in the United States had ICC regulation damaged the popularity of railroad securities.

Pierce and Shields had other motives for supporting the federal government's reform program. Their two firms, as well as other commission houses, had long been at odds with the entrenched leadership of the New York Stock Exchange. The three key groups working daily on the NYSE floor were the specialists, private traders, and various representatives of the commission houses. The specialists were essential because they took responsibility for keeping auction markets functioning for the security issues assigned to them. The private traders, who had proliferated in the nineteenth century and entrenched themselves in the first quarter of the twentieth century, were primarily speculators and arbitrageurs. They took advantage of inside information and easy access to the specialists' stations on the NYSE floor to reap handsome profits with little risk. In their own

18. For a nutshell discussion of Pierce's career and his role in the reform movement, see Brooks, *Once in Golconda*, 198–202.

defense, private traders claimed that, on balance, they played a positive role in the market by smoothing out price fluctuations, but the commission houses that served millions of investors were dubious about the traders' assertions and wanted their activities more tightly controlled. Because private traders generated a substantial volume of daily activity, they were usually supported by the specialists in conflicts with the commission houses.

Although the commission houses held a majority of the seats on the NYSE by the 1930s, archaic voting rules gave the traders and specialists combined the power to reelect annually the exchange president and other officials who set the trading rules and governed daily operations. The presidential incumbent was always a current member of the exchange, and he performed only limited duties without financial compensation. Shields and Pierce hoped that the federal government's oversight of the nation's stock exchanges would eventually lead to a more democratic governance system at the NYSE. While their goals were thwarted in the mid-1930s by Richard Whitney and his conservative friends, by the end of the decade, the commission houses, with their network of nationwide branch offices, had the upper hand in the power struggle on Wall Street. The presidency of the NYSE became a full-time salaried position, and nonmembers were eligible for election. Following these internal reforms, the presidents of the exchange placed the interests of the investing public and the broad Wall Street community ahead of the selfish goals of the private traders.[19] When Charlie Merrill returned to the financial services sector in 1940, the leadership of the NYSE acted more in unison with his aggressive efforts to attract upper-middle-class investors to participate more broadly in the capital markets.

In two important bills passed in 1933 and 1934, the federal government extended its involvement in the capital markets far beyond the railroads to include all other issuers of securities.[20] The key provision was the requirement that issuers, aided by their investment bankers, submit in advance a prospectus to governmental authorities that included a detailed description of the securities proposed for issuance and, in addition, accurate information about the company's current financial condition. From the date of submission, the authorities had twenty days to review the prospectus for omissions and errors; during this waiting period, they were empowered to issue stop orders to halt the release of any securities not meeting the standard of full disclosure. The main goal was truth in labeling. Question-

---

19. Sobel, *N.Y.S.E.*, 40–70.
20. For a detailed discussion of the politics of the reform movement, see De Bedts, *New Deal's SEC*, and Parrish, *Securities Regulation and the New Deal*.

able securities issued by shaky companies were not rejected, but they had to be described as clearly speculative in the formal prospectus, and not depicted as safe and secure investments.

Initially, the Federal Trade Commission was given the responsibility for regulating the capital markets. In 1934, Congress created the Securities and Exchange Commission to assume those duties, and Joseph Kennedy, to whom Merrill and Lynch had incidentally sold their controlling interest in Pathé in the mid-twenties, became its first commissioner. Kennedy was one of the few business leaders who had supported Roosevelt in the 1932 presidential election. Unlike the broad powers granted to the ICC in 1920, SEC administrators could not disapprove the issuance of securities that seemed imprudent or unlikely to provide investors with an adequate return. In this respect, the U.S. securities laws enacted in the mid-1930s were similar in spirit to the precedents set by the British Companies Act.

The new securities laws also gave federal officials the power to intervene in the governance of the NYSE and other exchanges across the nation. They used this authority sparingly, however. The clubby atmosphere prevailing at most exchanges was left generally intact despite the fears and predictions of many conservative critics of government intervention. The SEC mandated that the governing boards of the exchanges strengthen their rules with regard to prohibiting the formation of insider pools organized to manipulate stock prices. It also insisted on the abandonment of the investment bankers' practice of reserving a limited number of shares in new stock issues for business associates and prominent politicians at below prevailing market prices. The high-profile names on several preferred lists at J. P. Morgan had been embarrassingly exposed during congressional hearings.[21] By the end of the decade, government and NYSE officials were generally cooperating in an effort to restore investor confidence in the fairness of the securities markets and in the wisdom of holding and trading the common stocks of the nation's leading corporations.

Securities dealers and individual brokers were required to register with the federal government. Congress escalated the legal penalties applicable to both firms and individuals for violations of the law. The blue-sky laws at the state level had been ineffective against interstate scams. After 1933, firms faced stiff fines and the possibility of suspension or closure for failing to comply with the new federal laws. Any registered salesperson suspected of making misleading statements to customers became subject to criminal, not merely civil, prosecution. Judges were encouraged to sentence con-

---

21. For information on people on the preferred lists, see Seligman, *Transformation of Wall Street*, 34–35, and Chernow, *House of Morgan*, 370–73. Among the names on the list kept by J. P. Morgan were former president Calvin Coolidge, U.S. senator William McAdoo, Standard Oil president Walter Teagle, and Chase National Bank president Albert Wiggin.

victed violators to at least some time in prison; the worst offenders were banned from working in the securities field for the remainder of their careers. These harsh penalties were adopted to serve as a stern deterrent to sales personnel and other white-collar employees who were presumably averse to the prospect of enduring the shame of a term in jail or prison. Deceitful practices were not entirely eliminated, since several violators were caught almost every year thereafter; the tougher rules put bucket shops out of business and sharply curtailed the instances of fraud and deception in the securities field.

In 1938, Congress passed the Maloney Act to extend the power of the SEC to regulate the decentralized over-the-counter markets. The National Association of Securities Dealers (NASD), formed in the late 1930s, worked with the federal government to apply the same ethical standards to brokerage firms that were not formal members of the organized exchanges. Another purpose of this voluntary organization was to promote greater uniformity in the various state securities laws that paralleled or overlapped the new federal regulations. By 1940, membership in NASD had reached approximately 2,900 firms across the nation.[22]

E. A. Pierce and other commission houses struggled to survive the depression decade. Like most of his financial peers in the aftermath of the 1929 crash, Pierce believed the economy would rebound within a reasonable period of time, and he hoped to take advantage of the temporary disruption to gain competitive advantage. In 1930, following the investment of $5 million by his new limited partners – Charles Merrill and Edmund Lynch, in their respective mothers' names, plus a few of their business associates – Pierce had capital resources of $15 million at his disposal. In addition to his assimilation of the retail offices of Merrill, Lynch and most of their personnel, Pierce acquired other small chains for his growing organization, including the offices of Logan & Bryan on the West Coast.[23] By the late 1930s, the Pierce firm boasted offices in forty cities; they were concentrated in the mid-Atlantic and Midwest states, but also included six outlets on the West Coast, an office in Denver, and three in Canada.

Surprisingly, the sharp decline of nearly 90 percent in stock prices from 1929 to 1933 did not affect the volume of daily trading in a proportional manner. Because stockbrokers made their living from negotiating trades, irrespective of the level of prices, most were not overconcerned about the consequences of the economic downturn on commission revenues. During the prior decade, trading volume on the NYSE had risen from 230 million

22. Loeser, *The Over-the-Counter Securities Market,* 118.
23. Hecht, *Legacy of Leadership,* 44.

shares annually in 1920 to 445 million shares in 1925 and 1.2 billion shares in 1929. From that high point, volume dropped to 812 million shares in 1930, 576 million shares in 1931, and 425 million shares in 1932. After Roosevelt's election, trading volume climbed to 655 million shares in 1933 – a figure more than 45 percent higher than in 1925. Stock prices also jumped in 1933, after three years of horrendous decline. Industrial production rose in 1933 and 1934, and the economy seemed to be recovering from the depths. Pierce and his employees breathed a joint sigh of relief, but their optimism was misplaced.

During the public debate over the viability of broadening federal regulation of the securities markets in the mid-1930s, conservative critics had predicted that more government oversight would be detrimental to the overall health of the capital markets. To reiterate Whitney's famous taunt, How could anyone possibly improve an already perfect institution like the NYSE? In light of events over the next decade, the skeptics had expressed valid concerns. Except for an upswing in 1936 and 1937, trading volume dropped steadily through 1942, and brokers suffered a continual deterioration in their earnings. Volume fell by one-half in 1934 to 324 million annual shares, and in 1938 it took a five-year nosedive. The final count for 1940 – a mere 207 million shares traded on the NYSE – was lower than the comparable figure in 1905, when the number of listed issues was vastly smaller. The stock market was on the ropes and getting weaker year by year.

Given the lack of trading activity, it is little wonder that persons associated with E. A. Pierce, as well as the partners and employees of competitive commission houses, were on the verge of financial collapse in the final months of 1939. Although the U.S. economy had been improving since Roosevelt took office in 1933, with the exception of a dip in 1937 and 1938, more customers were closing their brokerage accounts than opening new ones. Pierce's vision of a nationwide chain of brokerage houses was in serious jeopardy. Profits had evaporated and losses were mounting. In a defensive move, Merrill shifted his investment in the Pierce firm from an equity position to creditor status. E. A. Pierce, having worked so diligently to promote the reform program both in Washington and on Wall Street, now heard the echo of skeptical voices still defending the status quo before the crash and stridently complaining about the ill effects of Roosevelt's New Deal. Winthrop Smith, the manager of the Chicago office, and his counterparts throughout the branch network were not generating enough commission revenue to cover the rent and other fixed expenses. The ten-year partnership agreement was expiring in early 1940, and Pierce & Company was forced to consider the prospect of dissolution. The situation was bleak. Then, of course, Charlie Merrill reentered the picture.

In retrospect, Pierce bravely held the fort through exceedingly difficult times. He kept the firm alive until Charlie could return with the capital and managerial skills to convert Pierce's nationwide chain of offices into what became, in time, one of the nation's – indeed, one of the world's – most successful business enterprises. The financial benefits accrued not just to the partners in Merrill Lynch, Pierce, Fenner & Beane (later Smith), but to thousands of its employees, as well as to millions of thankful customers who prospered with the revival of U.S. capital markets.

9

THIRD CAREER: NEW STRATEGIES ON
WALL STREET

Any claim to immortality in Wall Street annals for Charles Merrill must rest on what he accomplished in his third and final career as the CEO of the nation's largest and most profitable brokerage house – a firm that, after several mergers, boasted the long title of Merrill Lynch, Pierce, Fenner & Beane. Critics jokingly dubbed the firm WE THE PEOPLE, but the partners embraced the label and boldly advertised it to proclaim their commitment to serving the investment goals of middle-class households. From the date Charlie returned to Wall Street in early 1940 until his death in 1956, he spearheaded a host of innovative strategies that had a tremendous impact on American capital markets and on the overall character of the nation's financial services sector. In time, these policies and procedures affected capital markets around the globe. All previous figures of any major significance in the history of U.S. capital markets – from Alexander Hamilton in the late eighteenth century to J. P. Morgan in the early twentieth – had made their reputations by sponsoring the issuance of new securities that directly financed the operations of governments or the expansion of business enterprises. And, indeed, during his first sojourn on Wall Street from 1914 to 1929, Merrill had followed that familiar path to substantial wealth, plus a modicum of fleeting fame. His successes came primarily in merchant banking, an offshoot of investment banking. He held large blocks of common stock in many of the companies that he had financed.

Prior to Merrill Lynch's ascendancy in the 1940s, the provision of routine brokerage services had never been a pathway to leadership in the elitist world of high finance. Even the acknowledged leaders in the brokerage field in the 1920s – men like Paul Shields and E. A. Pierce, for example – had never held high status or exercised much power, formal or informal, within Wall Street circles. Unlike the concentrated investment banking market, retail brokerage was a highly competitive, decentralized business, with numerous outlets in virtually all large and most medium-sized cities coast to coast, plus offices in a few relatively small towns with a quorum of prosperous residents. Whereas the most successful investment bankers earned huge fees, sometimes running into the hundreds of thousands of dollars, for negotiating large transactions that closed within a few days or weeks, commission brokers charged their retail customers only a few dollars for arranging irregular trades of a few hundred shares of common stock. There was little glamour and only modest income potential associated with the secondary market for the typical employee. Most securities brokers earned incomes sufficient to support a middle-class or upper-middle-class household, but few accumulated the means to move into the most expensive neighborhoods. Only the key partners in the leading brokerage firms were moderately wealthy.

By the 1930s, most enterprises in the U.S. financial services sector, by tradition or law, were involved in a limited range of activities. The leading investment banking firms in the United States were unintegrated, single-function enterprises. Overwhelmingly wholesalers, most disdained brokerage and provided only limited transaction services – usually arranging trades on an ad hoc basis strictly for their best customers. None of the prominent investment banking houses in New York or Boston tried to expand and diversify their range of services by creating a branch network of complementary brokerage offices. In contrast, numerous firms with origins in the brokerage field periodically attempted to upgrade their status and income through an expansion of services. The most ambitious partners in brokerage houses that possessed a strong capital base or had access to reliable financial resources often made the effort to attract investment banking clients. Firms on the periphery of the capital markets generally entered the field by underwriting new issues of securities for small and medium-sized business enterprises – the types of corporate issuers that the leading investment bankers consciously avoided. Indeed, firms that acted as market makers and brokers were the underwriters of virtually all the securities traded in the atomistic over-the-counter market. But these firms rarely got the chance to act as underwriters for blue-chip issues – railroad bonds and other securities listed on the New York Stock Exchange.

The institutional and organizational separation of brokerage and investment banking functions persisted for so long because many financiers who successfully climbed into the second or third tier of the investment banking field tended thereafter to downgrade the performance of routine brokerage transactions services. Brokerage was mundane and generated modest revenues. Charlie Merrill more or less conformed to that pattern in the 1920s; once his investment and merchant banking activities proved extremely profitable, his interest in the brokerage side of the business steadily waned. The firm kept in operation most of the branches it had opened before 1920, but the emphasis was no longer on expanding retail operations.

When he returned to the financial services sector in the 1940s, Charlie drew freely on his experiences in both of his previous business careers. His familiarity with financial instruments and his devotion to sound investment principles were qualities of continuing value. Yet, in many ways the years he had devoted to Safeway Stores were equally as important as what he had accomplished on Wall Street before 1930. Like retail food sales, brokerage generated small returns on each transaction, and the maintenance of high volume was essential for profitability. The most vital concepts that Charlie had learned at Safeway and subsequently transferred to the revitalized Merrill Lynch were those associated with the sound management of a large chain of geographically dispersed outlets with thousands of employees. Safeway owned and operated more than three thousand stores during most of the 1930s. When Charlie and Lynch had managed the partnership in the 1920s, the organization was small enough that Charlie knew almost everyone he employed. At Safeway, the scale and scope were vastly greater; Charlie knew only a fraction of the employees, and he communicated regularly with just a handful of the key executives. Other executives ran the day-to-day operations; Charlie only participated in discussions focusing on persistent problems and grand strategies for the retail food chain.

The goal at Safeway was to generate high volume by giving customers good value for their hard-earned money. The customer base for the chains, and all competitors in food sales, was all-inclusive in terms of social status and income levels. The grocery chain sold good-quality staples in no-frills stores at low prices. Over the years Charlie came to believe that the same approach could be applied to the delivery of brokerage services and that the customer base could be enlarged to encompass the American upper middle class.

When he assumed the role of directing partner of the revitalized firm in 1940, Charlie faced challenges on three fronts. These challenges were interrelated in terms of the basic principles to be applied, but the locales and audiences for his intended message were different and thus required varied approaches. First and foremost, Charlie wanted to create a new and revolutionary corporate culture for the brokerage house and its hundreds of employees. The emphasis henceforth was on providing superior customer service at reasonable fees to a broadening customer base, and that goal was to be accomplished through the mutual cooperation of brokers, researchers, and backstage clerks. Since there were no models in the brokerage field, many of the business practices that Merrill Lynch adopted were original and unprecedented.

The second task was to lobby, cajole, and take whatever means were necessary to wake up other participants in the slumbering securities sector to new realities of the mid-twentieth century. In a business in which public confidence was absolutely crucial to success, Charlie needed to boost the image and even the performance of competitors so that his own firm could prosper in the long run. Profitable brokerage required high volume, and an upsurge in trading activity was unlikely if other firms adhered to outdated traditions and self-defeating behavior. In short, Charlie sought competitive advantage, but he had no plans to destroy rivals. Indeed, he hoped that other brokerage houses would in time adopt many of his institutional innovations and thereby also contribute to the rejuvenation of Wall Street.

In the early 1940s, all brokerage houses needed more customers. As it stood, low volume meant that almost every firm was losing money. Consequently, Merrill Lynch set out not to steal large numbers of existing accounts from other brokers but rather to attract new customers. Charlie realized that everyone in the securities field needed to pull together to restore the public's confidence in stocks and bonds as investment vehicles and, second, in the securities markets as organized institutions in which fair play and honesty prevailed.

The third challenge was to draw a much broader swath of the general population into the stock market and turn more citizens into committed investors. Charlie's plans went beyond luring back all the disillusioned participants who had been lost during the depression years. His concept was much bolder. The new strategy was to solicit accounts from the millions of upper-middle-class American households that had never participated actively in the stock market. Charlie aimed to convince hundreds of thousands of reluctant neophytes to trust his firm and its employees to provide sensible guidance in building greater wealth through a systematic investment program. Statistics gathered by the NYSE indicated that roughly one million U.S. households maintained active brokerage accounts in 1940. The staff at Merrill Lynch concluded that the potential market over the next decade was approximately double that figure. The opportunities for growth were inviting, and in response the partners made a tentative commitment to open branch offices in twenty new cities over the next several years.

Charlie hoped to alter the image of brokerage houses by making them a haven for cautious people interested in prudently investing their savings in stocks as well as bonds. During the nineteenth century and well into the twentieth, stodgy investment bankers had concentrated on assisting the wealthy in preserving their existing assets by recommending investments in government and corporate bonds. In an ambitious departure from that limited goal, Charlie planned to offer households on a lower economic plane the opportunity to improve their status through regular investments in common stocks with growth potential. The annual total return on common stocks on the New York Stock Exchange had averaged approximately 10 to 12 percent over the long term, which meant that sums invested in any given year multiplied at least tenfold over a quarter century. If, for example, an investor saved $300 to $500 yearly for two decades and, by age forty, accumulated a portfolio of common stocks worth $10,000, the value of those securities and their accumulated dividends, disregarding taxes, would likely rise to at least $108,000 by age sixty-five and to $175,000 by age seventy. Within a generation, middle-class households could conceivably climb a notch or two on the economic scale and join the upper middle class, while families already upper middle class could aspire to climbing into the very highest echelons.

By the late 1930s, millions of Americans, probably the majority, were convinced that any investment in common stocks was closely akin to gambling; that is, persistent losses were the likely outcome for all except the unusually knowledgeable and lucky. Moreover, millions could not distinguish between common stocks and commodity options with respect to their risks and rewards. To alter these perceptions, Charlie knew, would require the wide dissemination of information about the fundamental character of stocks and about the functioning of the securities markets. Not everyone could be persuaded, of course, but if potential investors would listen attentively and take the lessons to heart, they were likely to reap tangible benefits over a lifetime. And, of course, the other beneficiaries from an upswing in trading would be the thousands of employees of the many firms in the securities sector and the partners with invested capital.

While lawyers were working out the details for the merger of Merrill Lynch and E. A. Pierce, Charlie and his closest associates, including Win Smith and son-in-law Robert Magowan, spent long hours in February and March 1940 preparing for a conference in New York City at which they intended to reveal their ambitious plans for future operations to the assembled managers of their chain of brokerage offices. To assist in the planning process, Charlie commissioned Ted Braun, whose management consulting firm was based in Los Angeles, to make a thorough analysis of the Pierce branch in southern California.[1] Braun and Charlie had become friends and confidants during the long and bitter political battle to prevent the Califor-

---

1. Merrill, Lynch was not the first firm to draw on the services of outside marketing experts. Another prominent brokerage house with a chain of branch offices, Fenner & Beane, hired a consulting firm to survey customers in 1935, and the partners also arranged a branch managers meeting in New York to discuss the results. See *Proceedings of First Managers Convention, Fenner & Beane*, 1935, in ML Files. In 1941, Merrill Lynch and Fenner & Beane merged.

nia legislature from imposing punitive taxes on Safeway Stores and other large chains.

Braun's organization studied the Pierce office from two perspectives. First, he engaged accountants to conduct an internal review of the revenues and costs associated with servicing different types of brokerage accounts. Second, Braun hired a group of interviewers who, discreetly, without revealing the name of the client, surveyed the attitudes and opinions of a broad sample drawn from the nearly three thousand customers who maintained accounts at the Los Angeles office. The questions ranged from sweeping inquiries to questions narrow and concise; interviewers sought customer views about the capital markets in general and about the performance of the Pierce branch and its personnel in particular. What Braun discovered mirrored the conclusions of the Roper poll that had been conducted earlier on behalf of the NYSE. Most customers expressed doubts about the fairness of the system to outsiders like themselves, and, not surprisingly, they were suspicious of the trustworthiness of stockbrokers as an occupational class. On the other hand, most customers gave generally high marks to Pierce brokers in the Los Angeles office, which indicated that criticisms of the capital markets were generic and did not reflect negatively on the quality and reputation of the firm's current employees. (To cite a reasonably good analogy from the world of politics: most Americans routinely tell pollsters that, while they deeply distrust the U.S. Congress as a political institution, they usually retain a great deal of confidence in the honesty and abilities of the representatives from their own district and state.)

Based on his review of the Los Angeles branch, his discussions with top management at the expanded Merrill Lynch, and his experiences with other firms in the goods and services sectors, Braun proposed one of the most unconventional ideas in the history of the American financial services sector. To longtime participants in the brokerage field, his proposal was thoroughly revolutionary in its implications – a concept almost as radical as Marxism itself. Braun recommended that individual brokers no longer be compensated by paying them a percentage of the commissions linked to specific transactions (at Pierce the split to brokers was 28 percent of the gross commission). Instead, brokers would receive fixed annual salaries that reflected their overall contributions to the profitability of the firm. The existing compensation system was relatively easy to administer because it pinpointed and rewarded the activities of sales personnel; the new system would be much more challenging because branch managers would be asked to apply subjective standards to determine how much each employee was contributing to the overall performance of the branch.

No firm on Wall Street had ever implemented such an unorthodox compensation policy, and when Braun initially floated the concept, some old pros were incredulous that such a preposterous idea had been seriously discussed. The talk about a shift to salaried positions reinforced the doubts of many old-timers at Pierce that someone like Braun, a total outsider who admittedly knew next to nothing about the investment business, could possibly develop workable ideas for success in the brokerage field.

If Merrill Lynch genuinely wanted to differentiate itself from other brokerage houses, Braun argued strenuously, the firm needed to inaugurate a dramatic new policy that addressed the lingering concerns not only of existing customers, but more important in the long run, the fears of millions of potential customers. Merely proclaiming that its brokers were more honest than rivals and were more dedicated to meeting the financial goals of investors was unlikely to translate into anything more than a marginal competitive advantage. Braun's polls suggested that almost everyone who had ever dealt with a brokerage house had wondered at times about whose welfare was paramount whenever the broker recommended either the purchase or the sale of securities. Was the broker merely seeking to earn the commission linked to a proposed trade, or did he genuinely believe the transaction was in the customer's interest? These suspicions about a broker's motivation were inevitable, Braun stressed, so long as the broker was compensated based on a commission basis. The only effective means of altering the fundamental relationship between brokers and their customers was to eliminate completely any incentive to churn individual accounts.

Charlie, whose experience was primarily in the investment banking field rather than in the secondary markets, was initially equally dubious about the new compensation proposal, but Braun wore him down. In correspondence years later with Lou Engel, who headed the firm's advertising department, Charlie recalled the circumstances:

> Of all the policies suggested by Ted Braun this was the toughest one of all for me to adopt. . . . I remember distinctly telling Ted Braun that I would not work for a firm that did not pay a commission. [After a pause,] Ted leaned back in his chair, relaxed and said: "This point is the keystone of all my suggestions. If you do not adopt it, it's no use talking about any of the rest."

After Charlie had ceased his opposition and become an advocate, he "too had a difficult time in selling this policy to my partners." Looking back on the events of the preceding fifteen years, Charlie concluded: "I think that of all our policies, this is the most important one."[2]

---

2. Merrill to Engel, Dec. 8, 1954, ML Files.

The two-day conference of branch managers convened at the Waldorf-Astoria Hotel in New York City at ten o'clock on Wednesday morning, April 3, 1940. Pierce opened the proceedings and quickly introduced the new directing partner – Charles E. Merrill. Charlie began by discussing the rationale for the meeting and the strategic planning that had preceded it. He told listeners not to worry about taking detailed notes during the four scheduled plenary sessions but to concentrate instead on absorbing the general ideas and basic principles of management's new approach to the securities business. Branch managers were assured that they would receive within a week a complete transcript of the entire proceedings – a document that totaled nearly 250 pages of double-spaced type.

In his opening remarks in the morning session, Charlie cited the valuable lessons he had learned from his long association with Safeway Stores. "Although I am supposed to be an investment banker," he confessed, "I think I am really and truly a grocery man at heart. . . . I have been in the chain store business, you know, ever since 1912."[3] At one time in the late 1920s, Charlie lightheartedly bragged, he thought he knew everything there was to know about the grocery trade, but he "awoke with an awful thud in 1931 with the very irritating and humiliating discovery that I didn't know a damn thing about it." The reason for his ignorance and for that of virtually everybody in the business was that they had been deluged for years with "reams and reams of misinformation." Executives had administered their stores on the basis of "memory, hunch, intuition, tradition, and the general feel of the business; but they had nothing, I assure you, to support their conclusions." Grocery managers in the past had been obsessed with maintaining a standard markup on various lines of merchandise; depending on the item, they insisted on a 20, 30, or 40 percent margin over the wholesale cost.

After analyzing the problems facing chain stores more systematically in the early 1930s, Charlie and Safeway's top executives decided to scrap tradition and take a completely new approach to pricing. Having discovered the true facts, "we said that, as merchants, all we are entitled to expect . . . was not a profit in accordance with our expenses, not a profit in accordance with our hopes, not a profit in proportion to our avarice, but what was left in our pockets after meeting the lowest competitive prices in town."[4] By the same token, the securities business needed to reassess its approach to merchandising and customer relations, for it had much to learn from advancements in other sectors of the economy. Charlie continued: "I hope you will bear with me . . . , because I consider it absolutely basic if you are going to understand my theory of merchandising. When a

---

3. "Conference of Branch Managers," 6.   4. "Conference of Branch Managers," 7.

customer comes into the Safeway Store, . . . she is entitled to buy with confidence [knowing] that she is getting full value at the lowest possible price. . . . And the difference between what she pays, item by item, and our cost, by George, is our gross profit, and not some percent." The same guidelines would henceforth rule at Merrill Lynch: "When we open our doors to all classes of customers, we have simply got to nail the policy to the mast that anybody who comes into this shop is going to receive the squarest and best treatment on the lowest competitive terms."[5] This principle was especially true with respect to handling the accounts of unsophisticated investors. With respect to the firm's fiduciary responsibilities, Charlie added: "You can't cheat a person who trusts you." Trust, reliability, superior service, and low fees all became watchwords at Merrill Lynch in the 1940s and 1950s.

In a second trip to the podium later that morning, Charlie focused on an analysis of the revenues and expenses associated with processing various transactions. By 1939, the average cost of handling orders was estimated at $14.29 versus commission revenues of $10.17, which translated into a loss of more than $4 on every order executed, large and small combined. Round lot orders, in multiples of one hundred shares, generated revenues of approximately $16 per transaction, and were thus marginally profitable. But fractional orders, the so-called odd lots of fewer than one hundred shares, produced revenues in the range of only $5 to $6; as a consequence, small orders were a drag on profits, because the clerical expenses and fixed costs associated with handling odd lot and round lot orders were more or less the same. Despite the negative impact, Charlie had no intention of discouraging small accounts and fractional trades. In the brokerage field, odd lot transactions had many of the characteristics of loss leaders in the retailing sector; the justification for soliciting small accounts, especially from young people in their twenties and thirties, was the prospect that a reasonable percentage of these customers, given more wealth and confidence, would eventually generate a steady volume of round lot orders and thus be transformed into a source of substantial revenues.

One of the startling revelations of the internal analysis of costs and revenues was that the net interest earned on customers' margin accounts was sufficiently high to offset a large share of the recurring losses on routine transactions services. In the late 1930s, as Charlie explained, the annual interest revenue "has provided a cushion of between $700,000 and $1 million, and has concealed the real operating losses."[6] Indeed, the firm was staying afloat principally from the earnings produced by the extension of loans to customers with debit balances who bought securities on margin.

5. "Conference of Branch Managers," 9.   6. "Conference of Branch Managers," 5.

For more than a century, brokerage firms had acted as important financial intermediaries that connected the credit markets with the capital markets. Many customers, not just speculators but long-term investors as well, used borrowed funds to finance a portion of their portfolios. The main sources of loanable funds were, first, the commercial banks that advanced monies to brokerage houses at the prevailing "call rate," a comparatively low market rate commonly applied to loans fully collateralized by securities, and, second, the credit balances of customers, who were typically paid no interest on their idle monies. Customers who bought securities on margin were usually assessed interest rates that were one or two percentage points above the call rate. The managers of brokerage houses called this markup over their cost of funds the "interest override."

After he had completed the introductory pep talk early that morning, Charlie introduced Braun as the man who had produced the facts that had become the cornerstone for a series of innovative managerial decisions. Braun reported in detail on his consulting firm's review of the operations of the Pierce branch in Los Angeles in 1939 and early 1940. The office employed nine brokers who handled a total of 2,828 customer accounts, an average of more than 300 customers per broker. Approximately 90 percent of all customers traded only securities; 6 percent dealt strictly in commodities; and 4 percent were involved in both commodities and securities. Women maintained 25 percent of the branch's accounts. The volume of trading activity varied greatly: more than 15 percent of all customers had initiated no trades at all over the past year; 55 percent had recorded from one to five transactions; and 30 percent had generated six or more transactions. The slowest 70 percent of accounts produced a mere 15 percent of commissions, while the more active accounts were responsible for 85 percent of commission revenues.

Braun's analysis highlighted the importance of customers who maintained accounts either with debit balances or with credit balances to the firm's profitability and, in turn, to the income of its brokers. The most active trading accounts were margin accounts. Customers who bought securities in part with borrowed funds generated average annual commissions of $165 versus only $50 for customers who paid for securities fully in cash. Moreover, the average margin customer produced more than $70 annually in interest revenue. The largest revenue sources were a handful of margin accounts with debit balances in excess of $5,000; these customers had generated more than $500 in commissions and $440 in interest revenue in 1939. On the other side of the ledger, customers who regularly left on hand large cash balances to finance future transactions were also among the profitable accounts; they averaged $175 annually in commissions – more than three times greater than cash customers without credit balances.

The report revealed that long-term customers tended to initiate more transactions than newer accounts. About one-third of the branch's accounts had been on the books for more than five years, and these customers were responsible for nearly one-half of commission revenues. New accounts, while they contributed only modestly to current volume, were nonetheless desirable, because in time they matured into older accounts that possessed greater profit potential.

The second day of the meeting was devoted to discussions of organizational, structural, and procedural matters. To members of the audience, the most crucial presentations addressed the new policies related to broker compensation, customer service, and public relations. The big news was that annual fixed salaries would replace fluctuating commissions in compensating brokers. No longer would there be any incentive, or, equally important, the public suspicion of an incentive, for brokers to churn customer accounts. In conjunction with the announcement of its new policies, the firm made the following pledge in conspicuous lettering to attract the attention of its current accounts and to all prospective clients: "THE INTERESTS OF OUR CUSTOMERS MUST COME FIRST." The minimum salary for brokers was set at $2,400, and for about 15 percent of the sales force of around three hundred that figure represented a boost over their earnings in 1939. All brokers who had earned higher than the minimum were automatically granted a $25 monthly increase over their current earnings for the remainder of 1940. No broker was asked to take a cut in take-home pay. The salary program placed limits on how much a given broker could earn in the upcoming year, but that negative feature was offset by the security of a steady income and the prospect of salary increases in future years, if and when volume improved.

In addition to changes in the compensation package, the firm instituted a significant reorganization of work assignments and responsibilities at the branch level. Based on what had been learned from Braun's in-depth analysis of the Los Angeles office, Charlie and his key advisers decided to make dramatic changes in the traditional system of servicing accounts. These changes had dual purposes that were viewed as complementary – to provide better service for a varied clientele, while simultaneously boosting volume and improving the firm's overall profitability. The standard method of assigning accounts at every brokerage house in the nation had always been based on individualistic and competitive principles. Managers usually granted the originating broker – the employee who had recruited or opened a new account – the option of retaining that customer's future business on a more or less exclusive basis. The result of this traditional mechanism was that almost every broker at Merrill Lynch (and elsewhere) laid claim to a mixed bag of customers. In most instances the majority of names on a broker's client list were small, relatively inactive, and unprofitable accounts. From one-fourth to one-third of the typical broker's accounts were moderately active, but only marginally profitable. Just a few names on the client list, typically persons with large portfolios financed in part by margin loans, regularly placed orders for securities on a monthly or weekly basis.

In addition to differences in trading volume, almost every broker also handled a wide range of customers with varying objectives: bond investors were primarily interested in capital preservation; common stock investors bought and held securities for long-term growth; and speculators in puts and calls (options to buy and sell securities at a fixed price) sought to maximize capital gains in the short to intermediate term. Every broker, then, was expected to be a jack-of-all-trades with respect to their knowledge and range of services. To improve efficiency and effectiveness, Merrill Lynch elected to modify the concept of the all-purpose, all-knowing broker and the haphazard system of account allocation.

The new rationale for improved customer service was based on specialization and employee expertise. The task of reassigning accounts fell to the branch manager, who, except in the smaller offices, was no longer expected to act as a part-time broker. To assist in the realignment of customers with brokers – an evolutionary process that was expected to take several years before full implementation – the branch manager was given a new tool for decision making. At Braun's urging, Merrill Lynch executives decided to circulate a customer questionnaire designed to pinpoint the aims and goals of every client. The partners introduced to the brokerage field the personalized financial profile sheet – a universal form that, when completed, identified every client's financial objectives and the jointly agreed upon strategy for achieving them. The customer filled out the questionnaire, preferably during a face-to-face meeting with a Merrill Lynch broker, and then signed on the dotted line. The central idea was to give each customer the opportunity to tell the firm precisely what level of service he or she wanted from Merrill Lynch; and the firm, in turn, pledged to provide nothing more, and nothing less, than the customer desired. For example, customers were asked whether they routinely wanted brokers to offer opinions and advice about specific securities. Some customers indicated on the survey sheet that all they desired was reliable information on business trends and the finances of certain corporations, and that unsolicited advice was unwelcome.

Drawing on the information in the completed questionnaires, the branch manager divided customers into several categories and tried to match them with the most appropriate broker to serve their individual requirements.

All the small and inactive accounts in a given branch office were, over time, to be transferred to just one or two brokers, usually the most inexperienced men in the office, who now specialized in maintaining and nurturing the accounts of marginal customers. These small account brokers handled mostly odd lot orders and performed what was viewed, at least from one standpoint, as essentially a public service to the local community; at the same time, these brokers were instructed to remain alert to the fact that some previously inactive clients were on the verge of increasing their trading volume and were therefore eligible to graduate into the ranks of profitable accounts. After the transfer of small accounts took effect, the client list of brokers with the responsibility for handling the genuinely profitable accounts was expected to drop significantly – in the Los Angeles branch most client lists declined by about half, from around 300 names to only 150 names or thereabouts. The mainstream brokers now had more time to concentrate on providing superior services to accounts that were already generating a profitable volume of trades.

In a further effort to match clients with brokers, branch managers used the information on the surveys to divide customers into three broad groups: investors, speculators, and persons who periodically alternated between prudent investing and speculation depending on current market trends. In the Los Angeles office about one-third of active accounts seemed to fall into each category. Based on this data, those brokers who were more oriented toward capital preservation and long-term growth in their selection of securities were matched with clients in the investor group. Brokers who were comfortable with high risks and volatile price movements served customers who indicated a speculative bent. These brokers usually also handled the 5 percent or so of active accounts that traded commodities on a regular basis. Customers who fit most logically in the alternating investor-speculator group were assigned to brokers who were reasonably at home in both camps. There was, in other words, still a place in the organization for all-purpose brokers, but they now became a minority within the office rather than the overwhelming majority.

Under the new compensation and account allocation plans, the personnel in each branch office were encouraged to act as a team in meeting the needs of local customers and in developing new business. Brokers in the same office no longer had a strong incentive to compete with each other for new accounts – at least not for small or modest accounts; now they could concentrate on explaining to business prospects why Merrill Lynch services were superior to those of its competitors. Executives in New York planned to judge the performance of each branch as a unit, and the local manager had the power to adjust salaries to reflect each employee's contribution to the overall success of the branch.

To support their brokers in the field, Charlie and his new partners planned to break with the old taboos on Wall Street and launch an aggressive advertising and public relations campaign. In a lighthearted comment to the assembled managers, he remarked: "If R. H. Macy had the same approach toward . . . business-getting expenses that all members of the New York Stock Exchange have, I assure you R. H. Macy & Co. would be out of business by next April – and it wouldn't be April Fool's Day either."[7] The new emphasis was to be on educating the public about the functioning of the exchanges and the benefits arising from long-term investments in selected securities of profitable and growing corporations. The NYSE itself had parted with tradition and started running a series of generic advertisements in the late 1930s but the impact on trading volume had been minimal. At Charlie's insistence, his partners allocated $100,000 to the advertising budget over the next year. An analysis of income and wealth patterns indicated that there were approximately five million households nationwide – mostly upper-middle-class households in midsize cities – that owned few, if any, securities and were considered likely prospects for solicitation. Braun announced on the second day of the conference that the firm had contracted to place advertisements covering two-thirds of a page in *Time* magazine, with a circulation of more than 750,000, for twenty-eight weeks. According to Braun, *Time* was "the best single medium in the United States to reach the maximum number of potential customers for this business."[8] The firm also scheduled ads to run in newspapers with a combined circulation of fourteen million in cities with branch offices.

With regard to public relations, which, like advertising, was unapologetically identified as a handmaiden to sales, Charlie had in mind the creation of a speakers bureau that would reach citizens in a myriad of local settings. Charlie envisioned that in this soft-sell approach, representatives of the firm would regularly appear before groups such as the Kiwanis, Rotary, and Chamber of Commerce to discuss trends in business and developments in the financial markets. Women's groups were targeted, too, since up to one-quarter of the firm's existing customers were women, including substantial numbers of widows, professionals, and housewives. The emphasis was to be on educating the audience about investment opportunities in securities; the presentation would be generic in tone and favorable toward all brokerage and investment houses rather than heavily slanted toward Merrill Lynch. Even when other brokerage houses, the free riders, garnered a share of the new business, Charlie still believed the time spent was worthwhile since reinvigorating the stock market was in everyone's best

---

7. "Conference of Branch Managers," 50.   8. "Conference of Branch Managers," 217.

interest. Under the circumstances, Merrill Lynch executives concluded that they could not implement plans to help themselves without in many instances also boosting the public image of competitors as well. Because of his participation in numerous public forums that focused on reform of the capital markets during the 1930s, Pierce was given broad supervisory responsibility for the speakers bureau.

The public relations thrust was important in itself but it had organizational ramifications as well. Branch managers in the Pierce chain in the 1930s – and the same was true at virtually every other brokerage office in the nation – typically wore two hats. After receiving a promotion from the ranks of full-time brokers, managers split their time between administrative duties and the provision of routine brokerage services for a shrinking list of old and reliable customers. Indeed, many highly successful brokers resisted for years all efforts to draw them into management because they feared a loss of earning power if too much of their time was diverted away from handling transactions for active accounts.

Under the organizational restructuring at Merrill Lynch, the branch managers' main responsibilities became administration, sales promotion, and public relations. Although there was greater centralization of backroom operations under the new plan, branch managers retained a great deal of autonomy with respect to the hiring and firing of personnel – including clerks, secretaries, and brokers; managers were responsible for assigning, and occasionally reassigning, customer accounts and for determining the salary structure in their offices. With respect to the new speakers bureau, the manager became in most instances the primary spokesperson for the firm before local audiences. One consequence of the altered role for managers was that the possession of outstanding public speaking abilities, a skill that had not been highly valued under the old system, now became more critical for employees who aspired to managerial positions.

Branch managers were also expected to make regular annual visits to the offices or homes of good customers for no specific purpose other than to express in a friendly manner the firm's appreciation for the business generated over the past year or so. During these informal visits, customers were gently queried about any large or small complaints, and they were given the chance to be candid about which services might be expanded or improved to meet their needs or readjusted to ease their concerns. Branch managers, in short, were constantly in contact with the public and with regular customers, and they functioned in part as de facto market researchers. No overt solicitation of business was truly necessary in these private sessions; customers got the clear message that their account was vital to the long-term success of Merrill Lynch.

To provide more tangible support for brokers in the far reaches of the branch network, Charlie wanted to beef up the research and communications capabilities of the staff at the firm's headquarters in New York. A news department attuned to important business and financial developments would, through wire messages and bulletins, keep Merrill Lynch brokers more informed than their counterparts about breaking national and international events. Studies indicated that increases in the flow of pertinent news – whether good, bad, or indifferent – encouraged customers to initiate more trades. The research department that analyzed publicly traded corporations was scheduled for strengthening as well; its task was to provide more frequent and more accurate reports on a broad range of securities. For knowledgeable customers who wanted to make their own trading decisions independent of any broker's input, Merrill Lynch aimed to achieve competitive advantage by creating a superior information system. "Investigate, then invest," one of Charlie's favorite expressions dating back to his first career on Wall Street, became another of the firm's famous mottoes – short, sensible, memorable, and wonderfully quotable.

Not forgotten in the comprehensive review of future operations, Charlie and his close associates outlined a plan for reducing operating costs. The goal was to cut expenses by $1 million or about 15 percent of the costs incurred during the previous year. Some savings were anticipated from a consolidation and centralization of order processing, bookkeeping, and account maintenance in the New York office – cost reductions linked to the economies of scale and scope. The partners vowed to share a portion of these savings with customers by eliminating service fees that brokerage houses had traditionally assessed on relatively inactive accounts. The abolition of "irritating" service fees gave the firm another edge over the competition and something else to cite in advertisements. Large savings were also anticipated in renting office space. Since up to 85 percent of customer orders came in over telephone lines, Charlie saw no reason to incur the expense of locating branch offices in high-rent districts; as leases expired, offices would move to more modest surroundings – sometimes within the same building but on the second floor rather than street level. Charlie spoke pointedly on this matter: "It is perfect damned nonsense for us to maintain a gilded palace and take care of 15 percent of the people who infest it; we are through with running a club and charging no initiation or monthly dues."[9] Presumably, Braun's analysis of the Los Angeles branch had shown that office visitors accounted for only a small percentage of the profitable round lot trades. The emphasis on more spartan quarters was in harmony with the firm's commitment to serving middle-class households. It also drew on improvements in communications technology. Bro-

9. "Conference of Branch Managers," 50.

kerage was among the earliest business activities to be conducted with the general public almost exclusively by phone, and Merrill Lynch was among the first large enterprises to take this into account in formulating its business strategies.

With respect to the division of responsibilities among key executives in New York, Charlie made Smith his right hand-man and put him in charge of day-to-day operations and the implementation of all new plans and policies. Because Charlie came to his office on an irregular basis, Smith acted as deputy CEO. Magowan became head of the sales department. His job was to work with brokers individually and as a group to seek ways to add new customers and generate more volume. Because Pierce had a reputation as a maverick financier who had supported the SEC and done battle with the Old Guard at the NYSE, he was assigned responsibility for handling government relations. At an annual salary of $24,000, Pierce was by far the highest-paid member of the firm in 1940; by comparison, Smith drew $10,000 and Charlie allotted himself just $6,000, a sum he may never have actually withdrawn. Pierce lived to be one hundred years old and arrived at the office regularly well into his mid-nineties; after the merger in 1940, he played a supporting role in the firm's management but was not usually included in the inner circle of decision makers.

A holdover from the Pierce organization, George Hyslop was named manager of backstage operations – the terminology applied to processing orders and maintaining customer records. A few months later, in August 1940, Charlie drafted Michael McCarthy, who had an accounting background, from the Safeway organization in California to take over the backstage duties.[10] Like Braun, McCarthy had no prior experience in the securities field, but he soon learned the ropes and joined the inner circle. Hyslop transferred to the sales division. For himself, Charlie reserved investment banking and public relations; in the latter role, he consulted frequently with Braun, who became essentially a consultant on permanent retainer. Over the next decade and a half, Charlie focused much of his attention on advertising campaigns and various educational programs – including large investments of time and money in internal training programs for employees and the publication and widespread dissemination of facts and figures related to the overall economy, various industrial groups, and specific companies to both current and potential investors.

The discussions during the first three months of 1940 and the decisions announced at the meeting of branch managers in April set the tone and

---

10. McCarthy was an Irish Catholic born in Minnesota and educated in North Dakota. He moved to Oakland in 1924 and went to work in the grocery trade. Like Merrill, he was an outsider who made his mark on Wall Street. McCarthy succeeded Smith as CEO of Merrill Lynch in December 1957 and stayed in office until July 1966.

direction for Merrill Lynch over the next quarter century. A blueprint for a new corporate culture that differed dramatically from the atmosphere prevailing on Wall Street and in other brokerage firms across the nation was unveiled. Competition among brokers at the branch level was modulated, and teamwork and cooperation became guiding principles for employees in the network of branch offices. Confessing at the outset that the new concepts were experimental and might need to be adjusted or even abandoned altogether, Charlie was nonetheless optimistic about the practicality of the reforms. In retrospect, one of the remarkable aspects of the implementation of the new policies was how little of the original plan required modification as the months and years passed.

Late into the 1930s, the investment banking field was still feeling the negative effects of the Great Depression. Charlie had little hope that underwritings would do any more than make marginal contributions to the firm's revenues and profits. By assuming responsibility for more than fifty branch offices and over three hundred retail brokers, who now received fixed annual salaries, he was involved in a line of business very different from what he had experienced during his earlier career on Wall Street. In many ways the parallels that he had drawn with Safeway in his opening remarks to the assembled managers were highly appropriate; Charlie was now committed in terms of his time and capital to the retail end of the securities business. If trading volume failed to increase significantly and backstage costs could not be contained, the capital of $5 million that he and his partners had put at risk in the merged enterprise might be lost or severely dissipated within one or two years.

IO

TESTING NEW STRATEGIES:
THE WAR YEARS

Although most sectors of the U.S. economy experienced renewed prosperity during World War II, investment banking and brokerage houses benefited only modestly from the general upsurge in economic activity. While the volume of trading on the New York Stock Exchange had risen by the end of the war beyond the extremely low levels prevailing in the late 1930s and early 1940s, the overall increases for Wall Street firms were relatively small compared to those enjoyed by other business enterprises. Investment bankers were not critical in arranging the financing for the accelerated production of war matériel. Most industrial firms failed to rely heavily on the capital markets for two key reasons: first, many already had substantial excess capacity and, second, the U.S. government, in an attempt to expedite the war effort, voluntarily assumed the burden of financing the construction of many new plants that military leaders deemed necessary to boost output.[1] Through its massive bond programs and bank loan guarantees, the federal government, in essence, became the main intermediary between savers and the corporations that invested in new plant and equipment. Industrial leaders were also reluctant to raise new capital from private sources because they feared the possibility of a sharp postwar recession – as had occurred in the early 1920s after the previous world war. Meanwhile, many individual investors, still spooked by the disastrous decline in stock prices in the 1930s, were equally concerned about the consequences of a postwar crash.

The persistently low volume of activity on the nation's stock exchanges threatened the future of the enterprise created through the merger of the two firms headed by Charles E. Merrill and E. A. Pierce. With war raging in Europe, investors were hesitant to take positions in common stocks. Trading on the NYSE dropped continuously from 1939 to 1942; over the same period stock prices fared no better, with the Dow-Jones industrials

---

1. See White, "Government Financing."

dropping over 25 percent. As it happened, neither of Charlie's entries into the financial services sector in 1914 and 1940 had come at the most opportune times. He started separate business ventures near the outbreak of both world wars, and he was fortunate to survive the disruption of financial markets in both instances.

During the last years of the depression decade, Pierce & Company had consistently produced losses, and its capital, which totaled $15 million in 1930, was steadily being depleted. Recollections vary, but the best evidence suggests that both the Merrill and the Lynch families had lost about $1.5 million each – or about 85 percent – of their investment in the Pierce firm by the end of 1939.[2] After the merger, the downward trend in profits continued. Starting with a capital of only $5 million, the new enterprise lost just over $300,000 in the first nine months of operations. The outlook for future profitability was more encouraging than the bottom line indicated, however, because gross income was just $40,000 shy of operating expenses; the net loss was a higher figure because of the negative impact of more than $270,000 in nonrecurring expenses and write-offs.

In 1941 the firm finally turned the corner, earning a profit of $459,000. In 1943, the last year that Charlie came to his New York office on a regular basis, the firm earned $4.8 million in pretax income. The imposition of

---

2. When the two partners went into semiretirement in 1930, each invested $1.9 million in the Pierce firm in their respective mother's names – Octavia Merrill and Jennifer Lynch. In an interview conducted in 1982, Edmund Lynch Jr. asserted that virtually all of his grandmother's investment in the Pierce firm had been lost, but that Octavia Merrill's losses were eventually recouped after the firm became profitable in the late 1940s. Lynch Jr. also claimed that, in violation of his father's instructions prior to his untimely death in 1938, Charlie, acting as trustee of his former partner's assets, had failed to reinvest any of the Lynch family's monies in the firm after 1940. In response to a request for written records to support his claims of questionable treatment and Merrill's failure to live up to the highest ethical standards, Lynch Jr. was unable to produce any documentation, although he thought he had recalled examining an old letter containing pertinent facts at his sister's home a few years earlier. Having reviewed more of the accumulated evidence in a more dispassionate manner over a longer period of time, I suspect that Lynch Jr.'s allegations were untrue. Sometime in 1938, in the light of persistent operating losses, Charlie arranged the transfer of his mother's investment in the Pierce firm from its original equity position to creditor status in an effort to prevent the further erosion of the remaining principal. I suspect the same transfer was made for Jennifer Lynch's account. When the merger went through in 1940, Charlie left the Merrill family monies in the firm, but, believing the investment too risky for Lynch's widow, he arranged for the withdrawal of Jennifer Lynch's remaining funds from the firm and channeled them into other investments. I never saw any correspondence in the files indicating that Charlie had pledged to maintain Lynch's funds in all subsequent business enterprises. If, in truth, Charlie actually violated his partner's wishes, I believe he acted in what he thought was a prudent manner given the precarious times. Although the merged enterprise ultimately generated substantial profits, it was in a very dangerous financial position in 1940. The interview with Lynch Jr. was conducted by Edward Engberg in July 1982, and a copy of the transcript is located in the ML Files. After reviewing an early draft of this chapter, Henry Hecht, a former employee of Merrill Lynch, checked the old partnership records dated March 1940 and noted that both Octavia Merrill and Jennifer Lynch each had a remaining $250,000 interest in the Pierce firm – or about 15 percent of their original investment. Author's private correspondence, June 1995.

income taxes, which were applied to the partners' accounts at wartime rates of over 75 percent, brought the after-tax income down to $1.1 million. The final result was a respectable 16 percent return on the firm's net worth. We know these pertinent facts because the financial records were made public and thus became readily accessible to contemporaries and historians.

Among the many innovative policies that Charlie Merrill introduced to Wall Street during his career, few rank higher than his decision in 1940 to publish a comprehensive annual report for widespread public dissemination. The firm's annual report, which included an abbreviated income statement and a more detailed balance sheet, began with a statement that highlighted nine guiding principles for future operations; heading the list of the partners' so-called nine commandments was "Our customer's interest MUST come first." No law, federal or state, and no stock exchange regulation required any businesses organized as a partnership to make available its financial records to public scrutiny. Neither SEC nor NYSE officials had taken any action to encourage such unprecedented openness. Indeed, no other partnership or proprietorship in either the brokerage or investment banking sector had ever published a similar report – not in the United States nor anywhere else around the globe.[3]

Charlie voluntarily took this bold step because he believed it would communicate to the widest possible audience his commitment to removing another layer of the veil of secrecy that had prevailed in Wall Street circles for more than a century. In this era, only corporations routinely issued annual reports, and the main purpose was to inform bondholders and shareholders about the company's recent performance. Merrill Lynch's annual report differed, in part, because it addressed primarily the concerns of customers and, of course, a huge body of potential customers. Charlie believed, correctly as it happened, that the publication of an annual report would attract the attention of the financial press. Having long ago recognized the power of advertising, he wanted to generate as much publicity as possible in a medium that was essentially free – favorable stories in newspapers and magazines by friendly journalists. In a story in the *New York World Telegram* dated March 25, 1941, financial editor Ralph Hendershot hailed the publication; since the firm "deals with the public, the public has a right to know something about its financial affairs. . . . Merrill is to be congratulated on recognizing this fact."

---

3. This generalization may be too sweeping since some small partnership in the brokerage field somewhere may have issued an annual report in an effort to gain competitive advantage. But none of the firms that were members of the NYSE had ever taken such bold action. In 1940 only proprietorships and partners in nonincorporated firms were allowed on the floor of the nation's major stock exchanges.

Charlie also sought competitive advantage. Opening the books for inspection conveyed a subtle message to the investing public that other brokerage firms might have something to hide and, consequently, their brokers were perhaps less trustworthy in dealing with investors. Most partners in other Wall Street firms were not pleased with Charlie's disregard of a tradition that had always protected the privacy of their internal records. The NYSE had long-standing rules against admitting corporations to membership, but Merrill Lynch defied the spirit of that regulation by behaving as if it had been transformed into a corporate entity. In due course many competitors felt compelled to follow Charlie's lead and publish annual reports in order to dispel any lingering concerns about the probity of their operations. In the 1930s, the SEC had, by law, forced investment bankers to divulge more facts about new issues of securities to prospective investors; in the next decade, Charlie Merrill, by example rather than fiat, opened the door even wider to allow more light to penetrate the internal operations of Wall Street firms.

The first year was exceedingly difficult despite the partners' carefully laid plans. Not only did Charlie and his top lieutenants have to wrestle with the implementation of a totally new system of salaried compensation for brokers, but they had to move forward in the face of revenues that fell $1.2 million, or more than 20 percent from the previous year. Declining trading volume on the nation's stock markets, over which Merrill Lynch had no effective control, accounted for most of the lost revenue, but about $300,000 of the total reduction came as a result of internal reforms. Living up to the pledges announced at the April 1940 conference of branch managers, Charlie insisted on the elimination, or lowering, of numerous fees for routine services. Nuisance charges on small and inactive accounts went by the wayside.[4]

Customers on the West Coast were the prime beneficiaries of the fee reductions. For decades, a cartel of brokerage houses in the far western states, organized as the Pacific Coast Association of New York Stock Exchange Firms, had routinely charged customers additional fees that ranged as high as 50 percent above the prevailing rates for executing trades in eastern markets. Their justification for these extra fees was the high cost of leasing long-distance telephone and telegraph lines to the East Coast. Merrill Lynch, which now possessed the nation's largest chain of branch offices, broke ranks with the competition; the partners announced their intention to withdraw from the local cartel and, soon thereafter, to lower commission rates on all trades on the West Coast, and elsewhere, to the

---

4. These service fees were reinstituted at Merrill Lynch in the last quarter of the twentieth century after deregulation led to more price competition in the securities markets.

minimum levels set by the nation's various exchanges. When Charlie pulled the plug on that regional inequity, he immediately became the most unpopular man in rival brokerage houses from San Diego to Seattle. The cartel eventually collapsed. To remain competitive, other brokerage houses were forced to cut commissions by up to one-third. Some small firms did not possess the scale economies to survive the loss of revenue, and they folded or negotiated a merger with a larger organization. Charlie projected that, when fully implemented, the new fee schedule would save Merrill Lynch's West Coast clients $150,000 annually, and even more savings would accrue when trading volume improved.

In addition to reductions in service fees, the firm adopted more liberal policies with regard to the interest rates applied to credit and debit balances. Ted Braun's analysis of branch operations in early 1940 had shown conclusively that customers who borrowed from the firm to finance a portion of their portfolio or, alternatively, left cash on deposit for future investment were, in combination, responsible for the largest volume of profitable trades. In an effort to attract more margin accounts in every regional market, Charlie vowed that the firm would lower the interest rate applied to debit balances at every office in the branch network to a level that matched the rates of all legitimate competitors – whether rival brokerage houses, local banks, or other alternative lenders. To draw customers willing to leave idle cash with the firm between trades, he broke another taboo on Wall Street and pledged to pay interest on outstanding credit balances. The rate of 0.5 percent was low, but most financial institutions at the time were not paying much higher rates on saving accounts.

The solicitation of accounts that maintained credit balances was good business from two standpoints. First, these customers initiated more trades than cash customers, who never left idle money with the firm. Second, in performing its function as a financial intermediary, the firm realized wider spreads when it acquired loanable funds from customers rather than from outside sources. The partners paid lower interest rates on customers' credit balances than what it cost to access funds in the impersonal call loan market. To use the language of contemporaries, the interest override was greater when credit balances rather than call loans supported margin accounts. During 1941, credit balances rose from $9 to $22 million and provided the funds to cover about 40 percent of the outstanding debit balances of customers acquiring securities in part with borrowed money.

To cover the marked decline in gross revenues, which stemmed from the reduction in commissions and service fees and from the lower volume of trading on the nation's exchanges, the partners ordered a massive cost-cutting program throughout the system. When Charlie was first approached about returning to the financial services sector in late 1939, Win

Smith had argued that substantial cost reductions were possible without drastically affecting the quality of customer service and that losses could be converted into profits. Those assurances were among the key factors that convinced Charlie to launch his third career by venturing into the brokerage field. During the first year of operations, the partners reduced operating expenses $1.3 million, or about 20 percent of the total costs incurred by Pierce during the previous year. These savings were realized without lowering the salaries of brokers or backstage workers – an employee group that numbered about one thousand; only the partners accepted a lower monthly salary draw than had prevailed in 1939.

The main cost reductions came in three categories: office space, equipment rentals, and communications. In line with his proclamations at the April 1940 meeting, Charlie ordered the relocation of numerous brokerage offices away from high-rent districts and into more modest and less expensive surroundings. He decided that the telephone was a far more important sales tool than a fancy office at a fashionable address. To set a good example, Charlie moved the headquarters in New York City to a less expensive building at 70 Pine Street, which produced a savings of $50,000 annually in rental fees. Communications and record-keeping costs were reduced after the firm took fuller advantage of scale economies to consolidate backstage operations under the supervision of Mike McCarthy, who transferred from Safeway Stores to Merrill Lynch in the summer of 1940.

More savings were realized after Smith took responsibility for canceling a series of correspondent agreements with a group of independent brokerage firms located mainly in remote, medium-sized cities. During the 1930s, cooperative agreements had been negotiated with independent brokerage houses in locales where the Pierce chain offered no direct competition – mostly in the western states. For a split of the commissions and fees, Pierce provided transactions services for correspondents in the New York market. A closer examination of these arrangements in 1940 indicated that the cost of maintaining communications equipment and processing orders exceeded the revenues generated from these transactions. The decision to terminate the correspondent program was another reflection of management's effort to study more closely the costs of backstage operations and to adopt more efficient systems and procedures.

During the summer of 1941, the partners took advantage of a golden opportunity to nearly double the size of the branch network by merging with Fenner & Beane, a rival firm that possessed the nation's second largest chain of brokerage offices. Like most brokerage houses in the late 1930s and early 1940s, Fenner & Beane was feeling the effects of the low trading volume on the nation's exchanges. Discouraged about future prospects, top management approached Merrill Lynch about a possible merger.

Founded in 1916 in New Orleans by Charles Fenner and Alpheus Beane, this aggressive firm expanded throughout the southern states and into parts of the Midwest. Fenner & Beane differed from the Pierce firm in that the former drew a much larger percentage of its revenues from handling transactions in commodities – primarily cotton and grain futures. Much of its business was channeled through the regional commodity exchanges in Chicago, Memphis, and New Orleans.

In July 1941, Charles Fenner, his son Darwin, Alpheus Beane Jr., and several other partners met with Win Smith to discuss the possibility of a merger. Alpheus Beane Sr. had died in September 1937, and his death was one of the many factors that had contributed to the firm's misfortunes. The underlying problem was, of course, the low trading volume that affected every firm in the brokerage sector. According to the recollections of Darwin Fenner, Charlie was very enthusiastic about the proposed merger in a subsequent meeting. "Without any hesitation, Charlie said he favored the idea. He then reached into his desk drawer and drew out a blank piece of paper. Handing it across the desk to my father, he said: 'Write your own ticket.' "⁵ What he meant was that he wanted his prospective partners to invest as much of their own money in the firm as they were willing to put at risk. In less than a month all the details were worked out. The Fenner & Beane investors contributed around $1.5 million and were granted more than a one-fifth share in the partnership; Charlie retained about 55 percent of the ownership and Magowan was responsible for another 5 percent or so.⁶ During the deliberations the senior Fenner suggested that the new firm be titled simply the Merrill Company; but Charlie, still loyal to the memory of Lynch, thought otherwise. "I prefer the full name of Merrill Lynch, Pierce, Fenner & Beane," he remarked. "A name like that will be a challenge to anyone's memory and everyone will make an effort to remember it." After the merger in August 1941, journalists, in jest, frequently referred to the firm as "We the People" or "The Thundering Herd of Wall Street." The jibes were mostly good-natured, however, and on balance the decision to stick with a long string of names was successful in generating a great deal of public awareness about the firm's activities. In time, *We the People* became the title of the firm's in-house publication for employees.

5. Quoted in Keenan, "Chain of Fortune," 537.
6. The source for the ownership percentages after the merger with Fenner & Beane in 1941 is an interview an employee conducted with Robert Magowan, Nov. 19, 1982, in the ML Files. Magowan was specific about the numbers despite the passage of more than four decades. The firm's net worth rose $2.1 million in 1941, with $460,000 reported as the annual income; capital contributions thus rose $1.6 million during the year, but Merrill may have gotten some additional monies from his existing partners or from outside investors who joined the firm as limited partners.

Some partners and department heads at Merrill Lynch were not initially enthusiastic about the proposed merger with Fenner & Beane because they felt uncomfortable about the fact that commodities trading would account for a larger share of the firm's overall business. In 1942 this service generated 24 percent of the firm's total revenues, up from 17 percent in 1940. The commodities markets attracted two dramatically different types of customers: those with primarily defensive motives and speculators aggressively on the offense. Farmers and manufacturers routinely used the markets to hedge their positions and thereby protect themselves against the possibility of rapid price movements. Commodity traders, on the other hand, were primarily raw speculators hoping to make a killing when unexpected events periodically caused prices to move sharply upward or downward. The regular buying and selling of commodity contracts by active traders undeniably mimicked some of the basic elements of outright gambling. Fenner & Beane's internal records indicated that only a fraction of commodity traders consistently earned profits from these speculative ventures. Like the buyers of lottery tickets, a few speculators were occasionally big winners, but most holders of commodity contracts and options never profited. Many Americans, perhaps a substantial majority by 1940, had a similar perception of common stocks and the risks associated with their ownership.

An emphasis on commodities, internal critics argued, was incompatible with the new image that Merrill Lynch was trying to project. One of the key strategies in 1940 and the first half of 1941 had been to downplay the speculative aspects of the financial markets by explaining to potential investors the relative safety of investments in blue-chip stocks and in well-capitalized growth companies. An emphasis on commodity trades seemed potentially at odds with the goal of attracting a higher percentage of upper-middle-class households that were leery of overenthusiastic brokers promoting various get-rich-quick schemes.

But Charlie decided that he was comfortable with the concept of a full-service firm – an enterprise that would have a major presence in all three of the most important financial markets: trading in stocks and bonds, trading commodities, and underwriting new issues of securities. He was prepared to provide transactions services for long-term investors and raw speculators, as well as for anyone anywhere between those poles. Critics' concerns were alleviated when the partners agreed that the new offices acquired through the merger with Fenner & Beane would direct their efforts primarily at cultivating the securities end of the business. Indeed, Merrill Lynch brokers were an important catalyst for the emergence of a broader class of investors in securities in the southern states, a region where investors in common stocks had lagged the rest of the nation since colonial times.[7] By the end of 1943, income from commodities trades had fallen to less than 10 percent of the firm's aggregate commission revenues.

In the weeks before the merger, there were many doubters in the Fenner & Beane camp as well. Victor Cook and Norman Weiden, two partners in middle-level management positions at Fenner & Beane, were extremely skeptical about the proposed union, and they announced to peers their intention to withdraw from the partnership and investigate other employment opportunities. Charlie scheduled a fifteen-minute joint interview with the two men that ended up lasting seven hours and included an evening meal. According to Cook, Charlie greeted them in his usual disarming style: "Well, here are the two renegades! What is it about the firm you don't like?" Then item by item, Charlie overcame every objection. By the end of the meeting, Cook recalled, Charlie had convinced them that "his radical ideas were not a public relations man's dream but were based on strong personal conviction and great knowledge of Wall Street." After Charlie convinced Cook and Weiden to remain with the firm, the other key partners at Fenner & Beane fell in line. Merrill Lynch not only acquired a large network of branch offices, it strengthened its management core as well. Years later, Cook remembered Charlie as an executive who had the rare ability to "judge quickly but still very shrewdly."[8]

The integration of the Fenner & Beane branch system with Merrill Lynch's existing system was another daunting challenge, but the process went forward rather smoothly. The two formerly independent brokerage chains had only twelve competing offices in the same cities; thus, the main task was to educate Fenner & Beane employees about the parent's policies and procedures rather than the consolidation of duplicate facilities. Charlie viewed the merger as an offensive move that would broaden the firm's market penetration and, in one fell swoop, complete the task of creating a chain that reached the "Main Streets" in most of the nation's largest cities. After the merger, the firm possessed a chain of offices that served ninety cities in thirty states, plus outlets in Washington, D.C., and Havana, Cuba.[9] The states with the most offices were Texas with ten; California with eight; and Florida and Pennsylvania with seven apiece. Long before the term had entered the American vocabulary, Merrill Lynch had adopted the strategy of focusing a substantial share of its resources on the so-called Sun Belt states. Charlie, of course, always felt at home in either Florida or California. A breakdown of commission revenues in 1942 revealed that the firm had achieved a nice geographical balance: the Northeast accounted

---

7. Perkins, *American Public Finance*, 85–172.   8. Cook interview, ML Files.
9. In the mid-1930s, Fenner & Beane had two offices in London and one in Paris, but they were closed before the merger took effect.

for 27 percent of gross revenues; the Midwest, 25 percent; the Southeast and Southwest, 19 percent each; and the West, the remaining 10 percent.

In addition to the problems associated with the merger, another serious problem confronting management in the early 1940s was the continued decline in trading activity on the major stock exchanges. The federal government's campaign to sell war bonds provided competition for brokerage houses because it diverted the public's attention from corporate securities. Indeed, approximately 90 percent of Merrill Lynch's own employees participated in programs that encouraged regular investments in government bonds. With so much attention on financing the war, volume on the NYSE fell 18 percent in 1941 and another 25 percent the next year. The 126 million shares traded in 1942 was a figure so low that it actually dropped below the number recorded more than four decades earlier in 1900. The only bright spot was that, after three years of steady decline, the Dow-Jones industrial average climbed 7 percent in 1942, hitting a high for the year in late December, which augured well for 1943. Even with aggregate trading volume down by more than 25 percent, Merrill Lynch managed to squeeze out a small profit of $146,600 in 1942; those earnings translated into a meager 2 percent return on the capital base of $6 million.

As was true for all the nation's largest employers, the war caused changes in the composition of Merrill Lynch's workforce. After the initial personnel cutbacks in 1940, which reduced the number of employees to just under 1,000, the tide soon reversed, and employment rose steadily to meet the service demands generated by the increasing number of new accounts. Within five years, the firm had more than 2,500 employees. Brokers as an occupational group were not greatly affected by wartime demands because most of these men (and all the firm's brokers were male to my knowledge) were already forty-five or older and thus not prime candidates for the draft. Among several departures into the officer ranks from the administrative staff, Charlie's son-in-law Robert Magowan, age thirty-nine, joined the U.S. Navy and served in the Pacific theater. Most of the departures to join the armed services came from the backstage departments. In all, a total of 373 employees left to fight in World War II. Merrill Lynch adopted the liberal policy of paying all employees who left for military service a stipend of $25 per month (about $230 in 1995 prices) beyond their regular military pay. The partners' motivations were partly patriotic and in part designed to maintain the allegiance of workers, most of whom the firm hoped to reemploy when the war ended.

In an effort to replace lost workers and fill the new jobs that were constantly opening, the firm increased dramatically the number of women employees. The partners introduced numerous educational programs, lasting in some cases up to three or four months, that taught women the procedures required to process orders and maintain customer accounts. According to Mike McCarthy, the partner in charge of backstage operations, women employees met the challenges and showed that they could perform their tasks just as well or even better than men.[10] By the end of 1945 nearly half of the firm's employees were women, and virtually all worked in clerical and other backstage positions. Women employed as brokers, traders, and high-level managers came much later – long after Charlie Merrill had passed from the scene.[11]

Among the areas to which Charlie devoted considerable attention in the early 1940s were various research, educational, advertising, and public relations programs. Indeed, he saw these functions as overlapping and reinforcing – and essential for the firm's long-term success. Generating more reliable information for customers received a high priority, and the firm increased the size of its staff of securities analysts and the volume of reports on broad industries and specific firms.

In the past, most investment banking and brokerage houses had assumed a generally paternalistic attitude toward investors. Financial advisers and brokers made blind recommendations to clients about which securities to buy and sell on the presumption that people beyond the pale of Wall Street possessed neither the time nor the skills to digest business news and corporate reports and then make prudent decisions. Most Wall Street firms were also very secretive with respect to sharing information with the customers of rival brokerage houses and the financial press. As a rule, a stock analyst's recommendations to buy or sell were communicated exclusively to persons maintaining active accounts with a given firm. That way, valued customers would be able to move in or out of stocks at advantageous prices – meaning the prices prevailing before other investors or traders became aware of any pertinent new information. Customers with the most profitable accounts got the word first; lesser customers received the news hours or days later, with the interval depending on the value of their account. When customers insisted on written reports that discussed the advisability of trading certain securities, Wall Street firms typically charged a fee for the service. Outsiders without an active brokerage account usually received nothing at all in terms of either recommendations or relevant information – nothing but a cold shoulder.

Charlie disagreed with the prevailing attitude on Wall Street about the dissemination of information. Some customers, he thought, were fully

---

10. Author's interview with McCarthy, October 1994.
11. A few women had successful careers as securities analysts in the 1950s.

capable of making sensible investment decisions if they were given adequate data and a little guidance. He was also convinced that, by providing customers with reliable information about various industries and specific companies, brokers would find it easier to generate increased trading volume through telephone solicitations. To repeat one of Merrill Lynch's favorite advertising slogans, customers were encouraged to "investigate, then invest," and the partners were committed to provide the tools required to carry out a whole series of investigations. The research department sent out a bulletin called *Stock Comments* about twice a week; it gave investors timely analyses of corporate securities. At regular intervals the firm published special, more detailed reports on selected industries such as railroads, public utilities, and chain stores. The *Monthly Letter* concentrated on broader topics such as inflation, taxation, and similar issues pertinent to investors.

Most important, Charlie believed that the information generated by the firm's securities analysts and research staff should be widely disseminated on a nonexclusive basis. Persons with small accounts were granted access to the same information as the wealthiest clients. Regular customers were no longer assessed a service fee for printed reports. But even more revolutionary in concept, Merrill Lynch initiated the policy of sending free information to virtually all individuals who inquired – not just existing accounts. Charlie wanted everyone to become aware of the outstanding performance of the Merrill Lynch research staff, both the securities analysts and the compilers and conveyors of important business news. Financial journalists, who were usually brushed off and denied access to inside information at other respectable Wall Street firms, received a warm reception at Merrill Lynch. In routine stories and opinion columns, they often passed on the gist of the research staff's latest discoveries in newspapers and magazines that reached millions of readers.

As usual, there was a drive for competitive advantage in Charlie's decision to disregard long-standing tradition. From his perspective, the secrecy and exclusiveness that had prevailed in Wall Street circles for decades had been fundamentally self-defeating because they had unduly restricted the size of the pool of investors. Admittedly, the tight policies of Wall Street firms had probably made sense in the nineteenth and early twentieth centuries, when the amount of information available from corporate sources was limited and not always reliable, but as the nation approached midcentury, federal laws had altered dramatically the financial environment. The SEC and other government agencies had established new regulations that guaranteed access to much more detailed information about all corporations with outstanding securities. After 1940, Merrill Lynch became an important intermediary that helped to increase the flow of information from corporations to investors.[12]

The only downside of this open policy was the unavoidable problem of attracting free riders. Competitive brokerage firms were able to gain easy access to the valuable information produced by the firm's talented research staff, and they had no obligation to grant reciprocity. The concerns about free riders were legitimate, of course, but Charlie concluded that these reservations should not become an obstacle to the wide distribution of timely reports on traded securities. If competitive firms took advantage of the opportunity to rely on the capabilities of the Merrill Lynch staff, it was simply another cost of doing business. Charlie felt the same way, incidentally, about competitors who raided the firm and hired away skilled employees in which the firm had invested substantial amounts in formal training programs.

The main purpose of increasing public access to the information generated by the Merrill Lynch staff was to attract new brokerage accounts and generate more trades. Charlie hoped to lure customers from rival firms, of course. Ted Braun's survey in 1940 had revealed that it was not uncommon for active investors to maintain accounts with two or three brokerage houses. Before initiating a transaction, many investors wanted to solicit the opinion of several brokers. Equally important, Charlie wanted to attract the attention of disillusioned investors who had exited the market in the 1930s, as well as millions of skeptical savers in upper-middle-class households who theretofore had never felt comfortable about channeling a portion of their investments into common stocks. Once investors and potential investors became aware of the availability and reliability of Merrill Lynch's reports on corporate securities, Charlie concluded, they would be more inclined to open an account at one of the firm's branch offices, which were conveniently located in more than eighty cities.

In addition to weekly and monthly reports on various corporations and business sectors, Charlie asked the research division to produce two publications for a broad audience of investors. Both were distributed free of charge. In *Security and Industry Survey*, the firm's analysts rated hundreds of widely held stocks according to various investment objectives ranging from very conservative to highly speculative. The quarterly guide was automatically sent to customers with active accounts; other customers with less active accounts received copies upon the recommendation of their

---

12. Securities analysts formed a professional organization in New York in 1937 and began publishing a journal in 1945. James Burk cites Merrill Lynch as a firm that emphasized security analysis and the wide distribution of information to investors; see *Values in the Marketplace*, 62–64.

assigned broker. Outsiders could usually obtain a copy simply by requesting one over the phone or in writing. This publication was in many ways the successor to the regularly updated industry surveys that Fenner & Beane had begun producing several years earlier.[13] Before its introduction in 1935, most Wall Street analysts had concentrated on assessing the market potential of individual stocks without giving much attention to the outlook for entire groups of firms in broad industry groups.

In 1943, Charlie launched *Investor's Reader,* a biweekly magazine that focused on business news. La Rue Applegate, editor of the financial pages at *Time,* the general news magazine to which Merrill Lynch had been directing a substantial share of its advertising dollars, was hired to oversee the project. Typically twenty-four pages in length, the magazine featured articles on major business sectors and large corporations with outstanding securities. The editorial staff sought to maintain the highest journalistic standards; news accounts were objective, and none was slanted in an effort to induce customers to invest their monies in the companies under review. Advertising by Merrill Lynch was low key. Starting with a press run of 6,000 in July 1943, the magazine proved popular with customers and was continually expanded. By the mid-1950s *Investor's Reader* had a mailing list with more than 125,000 names. The readership included not only customers with active accounts but business leaders and academicians as well. The magazine helped to shape Merrill Lynch's public image as an organization that collected and disseminated business news in a responsible and trustworthy manner.

Roughly corresponding to the two major mergers in the early 1940s, generic titles like broker and customers' man were replaced in all internal communications and outgoing advertising copy with a more sophisticated title: account executive. The change in language was motivated by several considerations, both defensive and offensive in nature. To the vast majority of American citizens, the word *stockbroker* was closely associated with rampant speculation, biased information from unreliable sources, and high-pressure sales tactics. The Securities and Exchange Commission had used its prestige to help improve the public image of stockbrokers when it adopted the term *registered representative* to identify sales personnel who were licensed and authorized to deal with the general public. Some secu-

---

13. *Proceedings of First Managers Convention,* Fenner & Beane, 1935, 69–81. These survey publications were not distributed to the general public, however, but kept for reference purposes at the firm's branch offices. Customers were free to drop by and consult the so-called bible, but except in unusual circumstances the firm kept tight control on the information generated by its statistical staff. Before Charlie's bold departure from the Wall Street norm, few investment and brokerage houses wanted competitors to gain easy access to the diligent labors of their securities analysts.

rities firms latched on to *registered representative* as a good substitute for *stockbroker*, but in many instances the new, abstract title confused potential customers more than it enlightened them.

In tune with the SEC's effort to reshape the image of securities salesmen in a more regulated environment, Charlie, in an attempt to redefine public perceptions of the brokerage house and its employees, settled on *account executive* as the official terminology at Merrill Lynch. He borrowed a title commonly used in advertising and applied it to financial services. Early in the century the leading advertising agencies had universally adopted the title to enhance the status of employees who designed campaigns, implemented advertising programs, and were accountable to business clients for sales results. Neutral and nonthreatening, elitist but not snobbish, *account executive* had a reassuring ring: it communicated the desire to provide careful personal service to each and every customer; it had some of the same connotations as the word *trustee*. The ultimate purpose of the change in nomenclature was to upgrade the status of sales personnel to something more akin to accountants, lawyers, medical advisers, and other respectable professionals and to break the derogatory linkage to used car salesmen and other questionable sales occupations. Another argument for the change was that the firm's sales people were not just "ticker hounds" on the lookout for highly speculative issues but qualified professionals who drew on the support of a reliable staff of securities analysts to offer sensible recommendations for prudent investing.

The new title and status were designed for internal as well as external purposes. Given the shift in compensation policy from commission splitting to salaries, the partnership wanted employees who were regularly in contact with the public to maintain higher ethical standards than the industry norm. Charlie envisioned the sales staff as a group of trusted advisers to valued clients; he believed the distribution of reliable and timely information to thousands of customers would produce a sufficient volume of trades to keep the enterprise afloat and make it prosper. As the job title implied, the account executive's responsibility was to maximize the financial performance of individual portfolios from the customer's perspective. For example, the recommendation to "buy and hold" a collection of blue-chip stocks was an investment strategy fully in accord with the firm's guiding principles. Or stated more plainly: whereas old-fashioned stockbrokers were biased toward generating trades and churning their customers' portfolios, account executives at Merrill Lynch were expected to help customers invest in securities that increased wealth gradually.

At first the account executive terminology seemed outrageously pretentious to cynics who doubted the sincerity of all sales personnel in the securities field. In time, however, the title was adopted by competitive houses, and it eventually became the industry standard. Long before janitors were elevated to the rank of maintenance engineers and every midlevel bank employee became a vice president, stockbrokers at Merrill Lynch were upgraded to account executives. Through a costless retitling of a key occupational group, Charlie sought another competitive edge, and the strategy worked internally to boost employee morale and externally to promote customer confidence. Merrill Lynch salespeople, in truth, differed significantly from their counterparts in other brokerage houses; by assigning every customer an account executive, the firm signaled its fresh approach to prudent investing.

The new approach to sales and marketing produced the desired results in terms of growth. In the first nine months of operations in 1940, the number of accounts rose by one-third to approximately 50,000. The next year, in addition to the thousands of accounts inherited from Fenner & Beane, brokers signed up another 30,000 new customers. The next three years saw more growth: 27,000 new accounts in 1942; 49,000 in 1943; and 46,000 in 1944. By the end of World War II, Merrill Lynch served approximately 250,000 customers. Throughout the period, the firm's share of the trading volume on the NYSE remained fairly steady, fluctuating between 8 and 12 percent, which indicates that the main sources of growth were newcomers to the stock market rather than the disenchanted customers of rival brokerage houses. Not only was Merrill Lynch prospering, but other brokerage houses were also getting back on their feet and helping to strengthen the stock market. In 1945, the Dow-Jones average rose to its highest point since 1929, and the annual volume on the NYSE passed the 300 million mark for the first time since 1937.

Another department that Charlie headed in the merged firm was investment banking. Neither the Pierce nor the Fenner & Beane organization had acted as the principal underwriters for major corporations, so these duties fell in 1940 to the only person with a fair amount of prior experience. Despite his successes in the 1920s, Charlie did not make a major push to solicit underwriting clients during the war years. Underwriting was still in the doldrums, as it had been since 1929. Given the powerful role of the federal government in financing wartime expansion, not many large corporations were issuing new securities. Nonetheless, Merrill Lynch did participate in the new-issue market in two ways. First, the firm continued to serve valued clients that Charlie and Eddie Lynch had cultivated in the period from 1914 to 1929; many were chain stores in various retail sectors. One service for old clients was to act as one of the principal underwriters in refunding their maturing corporate bonds and in refinancing high coupon bonds or preferred stock with new bonds that carried the low interest rates prevailing in the early 1940s. Second, because the firm possessed the nation's largest chain of brokerage offices, prominent Wall Street investment bankers, who normally functioned strictly as wholesalers, often solicited Merrill Lynch to act as a major distributor of new issues – whether bonds, preferred stocks, or common stocks. Commissions were higher on the sales of new issues than on routine trades, so the partners and their employees were invariably delighted to be invited to participate in these transactions. Indeed, given its size, Merrill Lynch often received the largest allotment of securities for distribution to individual investors from the leading New York underwriters.

Charlie's role in the investment banking field in the 1940s was much different from his role in the 1920s. Previously, he had not only acted as a prime issuer of new securities for chain stores and other assorted entrepreneurial enterprises, he had also become deeply involved in merchant banking activities. He and Eddie Lynch held substantial amounts of common stock in many of the companies for which they had provided underwriting services. Both men became multimillionaires as a result. Charlie continued to maintain a controlling interest in Safeway Stores throughout his lifetime.

In the new firm, however, the merchant banking strategy never re-emerged during Charlie's lifetime. Merrill Lynch was a large organization whose primary function was the handling of a huge volume of mostly small to medium-sized trades in secondary markets. No longer in the glamour end of the business, Charlie had become the directing partner of a plebeian brokerage house. As he told the assembled branch managers in April 1940, by the time he had reached his mid-fifties, he saw himself primarily as a chain store executive, not a Wall Street financier. That altered status had not deflated his ego since, for years, he had expressed disdain for most of the aristocratic highbrows in pinstriped suits who managed the leading investment banking houses. While he thought Merrill Lynch might have the opportunity to expand its range of financial services at some point in the future, for the moment he and his partners needed to concentrate on the immediate challenge: the delivery of high-quality brokerage services to tens of thousands of customers at fair and reasonable prices. In this financial sector, none expected to acquire great wealth overnight. Most brokers and backstage personnel hoped merely to earn sufficient income to maintain a middle-class lifestyle, or, at best, to rise a notch or two and join the upper middle class.

In 1943, when trading volume on the exchanges had finally rebounded and the firm seemed on the path to sustained profitability, Charlie began to think more seriously about trying to test the waters in the investment banking field. He recruited George Leness, an employee of First Boston, which was then and has remained one of the top five or ten Wall Street investment banking firms, to assume leadership of Merrill Lynch's underwriting department. Born in Massachusetts and the holder of degrees from MIT and Harvard, the forty-year-old Leness was something of a blue blood and thus not someone who readily fit the less sophisticated Merrill Lynch mold. Nevertheless, he knew the underwriting business thoroughly, had good contacts with other powerful figures on Wall Street, and was willing to take his chances with an untested enterprise that seemed to have unlimited upside potential but equally great risk.

Charlie believed the firm could only enter this market by hiring a proven performer with undeniable expertise and a solid track record. Leness had the right credentials even if he possessed a rather stuffy and condescending personality. Over the past century, many ambitious brokerage houses had tried to diversify into underwriting for major corporate clients; but the barriers were formidable and the majority of these upstarts had been stymied and never even approached the elite ranks of this oligopolistic market. Leness planned to take advantage of Merrill Lynch's unprecedented access to hundreds of thousands of eager investors in the retail end of the securities business to attract major underwriting clients. In 1944, his first year on the job, the firm ranked twenty-first on the list of investment banking houses with the largest underwritings – a sharp improvement over its ranking of forty-second in 1943. In due time, and before Charlie's death in 1956, Leness had carried Merrill Lynch much closer to the heights of the investment banking field.

The renewed outbreak of war in Europe affected Charlie's private life as well. A strong defender of Great Britain in the fight against Nazi Germany, he and Kinta agreed in 1940 to assume temporary custody of three children belonging to the family of Dr. J. A. Elliot, who resided in Hoylake, a suburb of Liverpool on the Irish Sea. Under the care of a governess, the children – Alistair, eight; Ann, six; and Jean, four – stayed with the Merrill family until the end of the war. Meanwhile, Charles Jr., after marrying his college sweetheart, Mary Klohr, in Chicago less than two weeks after the bombing of Pearl Harbor, joined the army in early 1942 and later served with the infantry in North Africa and in the invasion of Italy. Their daughter Catherine was born in April 1943. Jimmy, the youngest son, served briefly in the army in 1944; after a few months in training camp, he left with a medical discharge and returned to his studies at Amherst College, where he had a distinguished academic record. At Amherst, Jimmy experimented with the poetry that later led to prestigious awards and international fame in literary circles. Robert Magowan joined the navy in 1942, leaving behind Charlie's daughter, Doris, and three young sons. Both Charles Jr. and Robert survived the war and returned to their families in good health.

After heading for Merrill's Landing in Palm Beach in November 1943 for his regular winter vacation, Charlie traveled to California the next spring to spend time with CEO Ling Warren and other members of Safeway's management team. He returned to New York on April 28, 1944, and the very next day suffered a heart attack. He spent more than a month in St. Luke's Hospital and returned to the Orchard in Southampton on June 10. In July, he had a second attack and spent three more months in St. Luke's before leaving for Florida for the winter. During the Labor Day weekend of 1945, Charlie suffered his third heart attack. He never fully recovered his health, and during nine of his last twelve years he experienced varying degrees of angina pain.

For a decade Charlie rarely visited his New York office. Win Smith became de facto directing partner of the firm throughout Charlie's remaining years. Although his physical health was tarnished, Charlie's mental faculties remained intact, and he continued to play an active role in setting the strategies and policies for Merrill Lynch throughout the remainder of the 1940s and into the 1950s. Through telephone calls, long memorandums, and frequent meetings at his Long Island residence with other top managers, Charlie remained involved in the myriad activities of Merrill Lynch.

II

SHARING POWER WITH WIN SMITH

In the months following Charlie's initial heart attack in April 1944, Merrill Lynch, Pierce, Fenner & Beane was forced to make a major adjustment in its administrative system. To assist other top managers in dealing with an unexpected crisis on the home front, son-in-law Robert Magowan, then on active duty in the Pacific theater, was expeditiously processed out of the Navy and promptly returned to the firm's New York headquarters. Once he had readjusted to civilian life, Magowan concentrated his energies on sales and public relations. With the directing partner incapacitated for long stretches of time for an indefinite period, Win Smith, the managing partner and second in the chain of command on the organizational chart, took on added responsibilities. Mike McCarthy, who headed the operations end of the business, also moved up a notch in the managerial hierarchy. Smith, McCarthy, and Magowan were the trio that effectively ran the firm on a day-to-day basis after Charlie's failing health had limited his participation in business affairs.

Overall, Charlie spent four and a half months in the hospital in 1944. After his release in late fall, Charlie, Kinta, and his personal nurse traveled to Merrill's Landing in Palm Beach. For most of the next twelve years his main residence was somewhere in the southern climes, first Florida and later Barbados. During the summer months he typically planned a long visit to the New York area that often extended into fall.

For the last eight months of 1944 and throughout 1945, Charlie's involvement in the firm's internal affairs was minimal and haphazard. Doctors feared for his life, and they severely restricted both his physical and his intellectual activities. The angina attacks were constant and painful, and they left the patient alternating between exhaustion and frustration. Cardiologists in that era had few tools at their disposal in fighting heart disease; surgery and other invasive procedures were not yet feasible options. The recommended treatment was restful peace and quiet. All forms of vigorous exercise, including sexual activity, were off limits. Nitroglycerin tablets under the tongue brought swift relief from a surge of angina pain, but they did nothing to reduce the frequency of the attacks, nor did they address the underlying problem of partially blocked arteries.

Because angina attacks could also be triggered by mental stress, Charlie was initially prevented from learning too much about anything that might prove unduly upsetting. Doris Magowan recalled years later that Kinta had been very protective during the early stages of Charlie's convalescence and often refused entrance to all outsiders, including business associates. Irritated about his isolation, Charlie complained to Doris on at least one occasion that his wife had assumed excessive control over his daily schedule.[1] Kinta decided who would have access and for how long, and all with the doctors' blessings. It was a bitter experience for a man accustomed to ruling the roost in his own home for the last three decades.

After a third heart attack in September 1945, Charlie was more reconciled to living with the dangers of overstimulation – mental or physical. Not an invalid, since he was permitted to leave his bed, eat meals with family and friends, take a leisurely swim in the pool, stroll around the grounds of his estates, and go out fishing in his motorboat, Charlie nonetheless stayed fairly close to his own surroundings during the last dozen years of his life. One exception was the trip that he made to Italy in 1950 to visit his son Jimmy.[2] His daily pleasures were cigarettes, one or two highballs in the evening (since moderate alcohol consumption was considered therapeutic, both mentally and physically), and a few rubbers of bridge with friends – mostly wealthy retirees and their spouses who were members of the local country club set.

After surviving more than eighteen months from the date of his initial seizure and with his condition fundamentally stable if not improving, the doctors granted Charlie permission to devote more of his time and his limited energies to business affairs. With the restrictions on his activities eased somewhat, he began to monitor more closely the situation at Merrill Lynch. But he was careful not to go overboard. In February 1946, Charlie admitted to Smith that the effort to reacquaint himself with the business sometimes took its toll. "Every time I attempt to stick my nose into something that has to do with the firm, I end up by getting worried and upset." He added: "This is really just silly of me, and so far as humanly possible I am just going to let you and your gang run the business and let the 'chips fall where they may.' "[3]

Despite the disclaimer, Charlie was more than a mere figurehead from

---

1. Doris Magowan to author, Sept. 8, 1995.
2. James described the circumstances of his father's Italian tour in his autobiographical *A Different Person: A Memoir* (1993), 30–43. Charlie traveled with a nurse; Kinta did not accompany him.
3. Merrill to Smith, Feb. 18, 1946, ML Files.

1946 to 1956. His evolving role became reasonably similar to the position of an activist chair of the board of directors in a large corporate enterprise – a chair who had only recently relinquished his CEO duties to protégés, but who still tried to stay apprised of recent developments and to influence decision making. Charlie was an absentee directing partner, but nonetheless he remained directly involved in the firm's internal affairs. Since Charlie had the largest capital investment in the firm, his opinions, when offered, could not be ignored or easily dismissed.

Beginning in 1946, weekly profit and loss statements for the entire branch system plus other important internal information flowed regularly from the New York office to his household. When his health was good and his mood upbeat, he communicated with Smith on a regular basis. If important initiatives related to sales, advertising, and public relations were under review, he usually demanded the right of prior consultation before any final decision was reached. Backstage operations and investment banking, in contrast, rarely came under his purview after 1944. Overall, his involvement in decision making was irregular, depending on the state of his health and whether he was settled in a location where communication with New York was easy and practical. Meanwhile, in all his written communications, Charlie continued to exhibit his former lucidity and vibrancy, and his business judgment, based in many cases on limited information, remained essentially sound and always consistent with his long-standing principles. Quality service at the lowest possible prices for customers who maintained brokerage accounts, whether large or small, was always his primary goal.

The focus here is primarily on the relationship between Charlie and his trusted aide, Win Smith, from 1944 to the founder's death in 1956. Because the narrative returns in the next chapter to a discussion of important events in the history of Merrill Lynch in the period from 1945 to 1950, the discussion here departs significantly from the standard chronological format because there appeared to be a fundamental unity with respect to how these two men performed their managerial tasks for more than fifteen years. Readers will also gain a fuller understanding of the critical role that Win Smith played in the firm's development after World War II and why his name was later substituted for that of Alpheus Beane in the firm's formal title.

Throughout the twelve years of Charlie's illness, Smith's position in the organization was decidedly awkward. Given the unusual circumstances of the directing partner's partial incapacitation, Smith fell short of possessing the authority of a full-fledged CEO. When Charlie had the energy to become involved in the firm's affairs, he exercised veto power over all major – and even some fairly minor – business decisions. After Charlie's health had stabilized in 1946, one of Smith's key roles was to serve as intermediary between the directing partner and the other general partners and department heads. At the same time, Smith had an enormous influence over decision making. For long periods, especially in 1944 and 1945, Charlie was not available for regular consultation, and Smith was free to act as the final arbitrator. Even when Charlie provided regular input, Smith wielded considerable power because in most instances he set the agenda for the exchange of views, and he, in turn, actually implemented policy. Smith was the only partner with direct access to Charlie; and, except in rare instances, others had to go through him to communicate with the directing partner. Magowan had access too, of course, since he was a member of the family, but the surviving records suggest that he rarely, if ever, tried to take advantage of his privileged status as the boss's son-in-law to undermine Smith's authority in any systematic way.[4]

As the chief spokesman for Merrill within the organization, Smith's authority was supreme, and few, if any, of the other active partners ever questioned his privileged status. An analogy to the world of politics may seen inappropriate to some readers, but in many ways Smith was cast in a role similar to that of a loyal prime minister who devotedly served an ailing and aging, but still strong-willed, monarch – an enlightened leader who had been forced by circumstances to reside permanently at a distance from the seat of power.[5]

Because of their contrasting styles and differing personalities, Smith and Merrill made a more effective management team than the former duo of Merrill and Lynch. Beginning with the dispute about liquidating a large

---

4. Since Magowan had more opportunities to discuss business matters with Charlie than other partners and employees, there must have been occasions when he exerted more influence on the directing partner than other department heads in the organization. On the other hand, he made no significant effort to abuse his family status and advance his own career to the detriment of other members of the organization – or at least nothing that I could detect in reviewing Merrill's correspondence. For example, I never saw any letters in the files from Smith complaining about undue interference by Magowan, or by anyone else for that matter. In his communications with Smith, Charlie occasionally mentioned Magowan's name but no more often than he mentioned Mike McCarthy and the other heads of important divisions and departments. The letters make it clear that Smith was Charlie's undisputed liaison with the firm, and there was no internal competition for Charlie's allegiance. As far as I could deduce from the surviving records, Magowan went about his business like a patient heir and expended his energies on impressing his peers rather than in buttering up his father-in-law. In 1955, Charlie installed Magowan as CEO of Safeway Stores, unquestionably a promotion based on raw financial and family power, but I do not believe Charlie ever seriously contemplated elevating his son-in-law to the top position at Merrill Lynch over either Smith or McCarthy.
5. In 1957, James Merrill published a first novel, titled *The Seraglio* (the Italian word for a large harem or a sultan's palace), that was based not all that loosely on the functioning of his father's household in the 1950s. The author exaggerated the excesses, but there was still an element of truth about the imperial atmosphere that prevailed.

share of the firm's investment portfolio in 1928, the two original partners were at odds about various matters, large and small, until Lynch's death in 1938. Charlie and Win Smith were complementary and mutually supportive rather than competitive and contradictory. Robert Rooke, a partner of all three men at various times from the 1920s through the 1950s, recalled that Smith was "not bombastic" like Merrill and Lynch, but a "pacifier and consolidator" – an executive who deliberated at length, considered all the options, and then acted methodically but decisively.[6]

Eight years younger than Charlie, Smith began his career at Merrill Lynch in a low-paying, entry-level position. Although he steadily advanced in the organization and became after 1939 the number two executive in the firm, he never abandoned his deferential attitude toward his mentor and benefactor. Charlie had lent Smith the money necessary to cover the junior partner's capital contribution to the firm in the late 1920s – a service Charlie performed for many new partners who had received promotions over the years. In an interview not long after the founder's death in 1956, Smith explained: "My early relationship with him was a combination of boss and father; later it developed into an older brother relationship and then as a partner and close friend."[7] According to the testimony of nearly everyone in the organization, Smith was the one executive who held things together in the postwar era after Charlie's illness threatened the firm's continuance. A careful and sympathetic listener, Smith was a master at negotiating compromises – among the many partners, as well as among the partners and the numerous employees working within this vast enterprise. Whenever Charlie became agitated and unsettled, usually about matters related to the brokerage firm but sometimes about personal conflicts within the family, Smith was invariably a calming influence. Patience and the exercise of uncommon good sense in a wide range of difficult situations were two qualities that ranked high on the list of his most notable attributes, and they were recognized in the 1940s and 1950s, and later in retrospect, by virtually everyone with whom he was ever associated in the Merrill Lynch organization.[8]

---

6. Rooke interview, Nov. 27, 1956, ML Files.
7. Smith, "Reminiscences," undated, ML Files.
8. The numerous testimonials about Smith's character in the firm's files are uniformly praiseworthy, and they all have the ring of utter sincerity. If anyone had anything critical to say about Smith, they were careful to keep it out of the archives. Smith was a saint, pure and simple, in the minds of most Merrill Lynch personnel. Of course, some of the people he fired for allegedly poor performance might not have felt so positively about him. A sentimental loyalist, Charlie had a hard time firing employees who had been with the firm for several years – even the indisputably incompetent. Smith, in contrast, could handle these unpleasant situations without lingering pangs of guilt if the facts clearly warranted a dismissal.

Winthrop Smith was born in 1893 into an old New England family that cherished its Puritan heritage; he grew up in South Hadley Falls, Massachusetts, a village just northeast of Springfield in the Connecticut River valley. His father was a local manufacturer. Smith attended Andover Academy and then enrolled at Amherst College, which was conveniently located just a few miles from his parents' residence. Finally settling on English literature as his college major, he never took any courses in economics, accounting, or business. His preparation for the business world was a broad liberal education. Graduating in 1916, he decided to investigate the securities field. "Not knowing anything about it, I thought I would like it," he remembered; "it was just a hunch, but my hunch was good."[9] A college chum had an uncle who was associated with Bonnbright & Company, and during the spring vacation of his senior year, Smith traveled to New York City and accepted an offer to start that summer as a messenger boy. After spending a few weeks at a citizens' military training camp in Plattsburg, New York, he reported for work at Bonnbright. Only then did he learn that the "living wage" he had been promised was a mere seven dollars per week (about one hundred dollars in 1995 prices).

While out delivering securities a few weeks later, Smith ran across another college friend who was returning to Amherst in the fall and was therefore planning to relinquish his summer job at Merrill, Lynch. The friend's pay was ten dollars per week for roughly similar work. Smith seized the opportunity. A few days later, he switched employers and received, in turn, an immediate 40 percent wage hike; Herbert Williams, the office manager at Merrill, Lynch, soon promoted him to a clerk's position in the cashier's cage. That November, Smith was sorting prospect cards for the sales force, "when I sensed someone was standing behind me, watching me." Smith turned around and was greeted by a "young little chap; . . . we chatted, then CEM asked me to go to the Amherst-Williams game." For the two loyal Amherst alumni, it was the beginning of a friendship that endured for nearly forty years, and included annual homecomings and occasional football games as late as the mid-1950s.[10]

In May 1917, soon after President Woodrow Wilson asked Congress for a declaration of war against Germany, Smith requested a leave of absence, joined the army, and reported to officers' candidate school at Plattsburg. When the war ended, he rejoined Merrill, Lynch: "I came back as a salesman at $100 a month versus $140 in the army as a second lieutenant." (His army pay was about $16,000 annually in 1995 prices.) After a decade

---

9. Smith interview, Nov. 16, 1956, ML Files.

10. Although Charlie did not graduate from Amherst College, he was later presented with an honorary degree because of his generous financial contributions. His son James was a graduate of Amherst. James Merrill died in February 1995.

in stock and bond sales, Eddie Lynch told Smith in December 1928 that he had been recommended for a junior partnership. Within a year of his promotion, the stock market crashed. When Charlie decided to sharply curtail his involvement in the financial services sector, Smith transferred, along with most of the Merrill, Lynch staff, to E. A. Pierce. Dispatched initially to Boston, he was appointed manager of the Chicago brokerage office in the early 1930s. Smith remained in that post until he became the principal instigator of the merger between Merrill Lynch and Pierce in the fall of 1939. Later, he recalled the circumstances: "It took three months of intensive study, which I coordinated, to persuade CEM to come into the merger. He had been interested to start with, but he wanted figures from every standpoint." Once the merger was arranged, Smith, rather than Pierce, became second in command within the new organization. Smith moved back to New York with the title of managing partner. Charlie was the sole directing partner; he was also the investor with the most money at stake in the enterprise.

After the doctors granted Charlie more freedom to participate in business affairs in 1946, the directing partner and the managing partner created an information system that fostered communications. Unless Charlie was temporarily incapacitated or had traveled to some remote location, he and Smith exchanged memos, telegrams, and phone calls on a regular basis – often daily. Charlie retained a personal secretary, usually Esther King, who traveled with him; her presence made it possible for him to dictate letters and memos whenever opportunities arose. While Charlie was in New York during the summer months and early fall, Smith often dropped by the Manhattan apartment for consultation or he took the family out to Charlie's estate in Southampton for the weekend. The two men, and members of their families, frequently spent some time together during the winter at Merrill's Landing in Palm Beach. In addition to Smith, Charlie periodically invited other key partners and business associates and their families to Southampton for the weekend, and occasionally to Florida for a week or so during the winter. At his residences in Palm Beach and Southampton, guests had many recreational opportunities, plus abundant free time to relax and enjoy the good life.

While Charlie continued to pursue his amusements and social diversions to the extent that his health and the doctors allowed, he maintained a keen interest in reading updates from Smith and in reviewing the firm's financial statements. For Charlie, business and pleasure overlapped and often were indistinguishable. He was extremely devoted to the brokerage firm; Merrill Lynch became simultaneously his main hobby and his most serious endeavor, and it remained so until his very last days. In a memorandum drafted for the firm's historical files in the early 1950s, Smith outlined the general nature of Charlie's relationship with his partners over the preceding decade.[11] "He has remained in almost constant touch with the affairs of the firm and has read and studied the reports with as much interest and clarity as had been his former practice," Smith explained. Although he was not physically present at headquarters, "in some ways this was an advantage," Smith added, "because he had a better perspective of what was happening to the business as a whole, and to our firm in particular, than he might have had if he had been actually participating in the day-to-day events."

Not surprisingly, Charlie was constantly frustrated because his infirmities prevented him from participating fully in the management of the firm. Like many people in similar situations, he lost much of his personal independence; in what cardiologists of that era believed was in the patient's best interests, they assumed control over his daily schedule. They dictated what he could eat, how many cigarettes he could smoke, how much alcohol he could consume, when he took a nap, and when he went to bed at night – usually around 9:30. Equally important, they regulated how many hours Charlie could devote to business matters in any given day. A registered nurse was always present to enforce the rules and monitor his condition.

In a revealing letter to one correspondent who had written in September 1949 to complain about the bonuses paid to executives and store managers at Safeway Stores, Charlie explained his overall situation. Because of his heart condition, he had not been permitted to go to his office for the past five years. "This enforced 'sitting-on-the-sidelines' has been a great disappointment to me, for I like to work; . . . the amount of time that I can give to business matters is rationed." As a consequence, he told this correspondent, he had not been paying as much attention to the progress of Safeway Stores, in which he remained by far the largest stockholder, as in past years. All the precious time allotted for business concerns was devoted to the brokerage firm. Although his participation had been limited, he nonetheless boasted that "I have been able, I believe, to influence and guide my partners and associates in Merrill Lynch to set an example for others to follow."[12]

While directing a large organization in absentia had its limitations, it also had some advantages. With fewer distractions, Charlie was able to concentrate on the problems and issues that interested him the most. As a rule, he focused on long-term strategies and intermediate tactical decisions. Smith took care of routine organizational disruptions, unless, of course,

11. Smith, "Reminiscences," undated, ML Files.
12. Merrill to Judge E. F. Langford, a resident of Nashville, Tenn., Sept. 13, 1949, ML Files.

they persisted and required action by the directing partner. In a 1946 letter to Dean Witter, who headed a competitive brokerage chain on the West Coast, Charlie was philosophical: "In many ways I think I am much more helpful to the firm by not being engaged in the hurly burly of day-to-day business." He added: "Now I have the opportunity to look at matters objectively, to study the more fundamental and important aspects of both our own business and the industry in general."[13] Another advantage of his limited involvement was that younger men with top management potential assumed more responsibility in the firm than might have otherwise been the case – in particular, Mike McCarthy, Bob Magowan, and a generation of postwar managers such as Don Regan. McCarthy and Regan later became CEOs of Merrill Lynch, and Magowan headed Safeway Stores. Because Charlie was incapacitated for more than a decade, other executives had the opportunity to develop their administrative talents at an earlier stage in their careers. Another consequence of his absence was that the potential organizational problem of a difficult management succession after Charlie's death was muted – and, indeed, that problem never arose.

In 1952, after roughly thirteen years of marriage, about the same time span as his previous two marriages, Charlie and Kinta were divorced. Whether the decision to file for divorce was a mutual decision, or something instigated primarily by one of the parties, is unknown. Unlike the pattern in his two previous divorces, Charlie actually initiated the legal proceedings, although in the end the Florida judge granted Kinta the divorce. The exact reasons for the marital breakdown are unclear. The contemporary records are sparse, and the surviving transcripts of interviews with family members and friends are surprisingly unrevealing. Charlie's two children by his first wife, Doris and Charles Jr., were young adults no longer living at home, and their contact with Kinta was sporadic. Son Jimmy, born to Charlie's second wife, was away at boarding school and college most of the time following his father's third marriage. Most interviewees who agreed to share their memories with Merrill Lynch personnel at various times from the 1950s to the 1980s were neutral in their descriptions of Kinta; few expressed any strongly negative or positive views about her behavior toward the partners, their families, members of the Merrill family, or her husband. Interviews with all three children in the early 1990s yielded much the same inconclusive results. Most respondents reported that Kinta had a pretty face and a shapely figure, but beyond those superficial descriptions of her physical attributes, other facets of her personality and demeanor

---

13. Merrill to Witter, no precise date but early in 1946, ML Files. Witter had written Charlie to compliment him and his partners on the contents of the firm's annual report for 1945.

remain to date largely a puzzle – an essentially blank slate. During the early years of the marriage, she was more compliant than Hellen had been in adjusting her life to conform to her husband's demands. After Charlie's heart problems limited his activities, she became more independent and less compromising. While some observers occasionally hinted that Kinta was, perhaps from the start, an insincere gold digger with designs on a huge share of a wealthy man's riches in future divorce proceedings, no family member felt sufficiently strong about her likely motives to make a definitive accusation.[14]

As a result of the lack of solid information, we can only make informed guesses about the sources of conflict and marital dissatisfaction. When Kinta married Charlie in 1939, it was just prior to his decision to emerge from semiretirement and take on the challenges and responsibilities of CEO at a revitalized Merrill Lynch. The second unanticipated event, five years into their marriage, was Charlie's initial heart attack in 1944 – and, of course, its aftermath. In the divorce papers filed in 1952, Charlie asserted that he had not engaged in sexual relations with his wife at any point in the past eight years.[15]

After a series of legal maneuverings, with numerous charges and countercharges, Kinta was granted a divorce on the grounds of desertion in December 1952. The financial settlement required Charlie to pay his ex-wife $640,000 in cash over a period of ten years. She also kept several thousand shares of Safeway Stores common stock that her husband had registered in her name in the early 1940s. After the divorce, Charlie resided most of the year on Barbados, which was at the time still a British possession. He purchased a home called Canfield House that was located near the residence of his good friends, Sir Sidney John and Lady Constance Saint.[16]

14. While no member of the Merrill family ever made such a stark accusation, I did hear derisive comments from retired employees of Merrill Lynch in casual conversations at the firm's New York headquarters. In response to my request for comments on a first draft of this chapter, Charlie's daughter, Doris, described Kinta as "extremely self-centered" and "a consummate shopper." Charles reported that his father's third wife "was almost uniformly disliked." According to Charles, she was "quick to take offense . . . strident . . . bossy." In an effort to be evenhanded, he added that his father "respected her close, sustained friendships with other women"; but that was about the only positive statement about her that I encountered during the entire research project. If I had sought information from some of Kinta's friends and relatives, it seems likely that I would have ended up with a more rounded picture. Since I envisioned this project as fundamentally a career biography, I never pursued that trail of evidence. Given the one-sidedness of my sources, I tried to soften my critique of Kinta and bury the details in the footnotes.
15. Details of the divorce motion and the financial settlement are spelled out in a letter from lawyer Robert Anderson to Terrance Keenan, an earlier Merrill biographer, Oct. 19, 1955, ML Files.
16. I ran across rumors that Charlie was having an affair with Lady Constance at some point in the mid-1950s. They were undeniably close friends and frequent companions. Whether there

In September 1952, Charlie consulted a new cardiologist, Dr. Samuel Levine, whose practice was centered in Boston, with professional connections to the nearby Harvard Medical School. In June 1953, at Dr. Levine's suggestion, Charlie agreed to submit to a radically new experimental treatment that, if successful, promised to alleviate the angina pains that had plagued him for so many years. The procedure required no surgery; the patient simply drank an "atomic cocktail."[17] The drink contained a small amount of radioactive iodine suspended in a liquid that, according to Charlie, "looked and tasted just like plain ordinary water."[18] A few days later his neck began to swell and swallowing was difficult, but these threatening side effects subsided within a few hours. Back at his Southampton estate, Charlie initially experienced no improvement in his condition; instead, it temporarily worsened. "The first week . . . I had about 76 pains, the next week over a hundred and the last week in June I had 127 pains." He felt extremely discouraged. "For the first time in my long illness I really and truly cried," he confessed. "I didn't cry so much from the pain as I did from being worn out with the whole God damn thing and disgusted because after all I'd gone through – this was my reaction."

From a low point in late June 1953, however, Charlie's health took a sharp upturn. The radioactive iodine treatment finally began to show positive results. Beginning in July, the angina attacks started to taper off. By the end of the month, they had ceased altogether, and by mid-September he could report that "for the last four weeks, I haven't had one single solitary heart pain night or day." Not surprisingly, Charlie praised Dr. Levine to the heavens and thanked his lucky stars for the favorable outcome of the experimental treatment: "It's almost incredible now to realize that I was able to go through the past nine and a half years. I can

was ever anything sexual between them is a matter for speculation; after the success of the treatment for his angina pains in 1953, the possibility of something more than friendship suddenly arose. If they were lovers, her husband seems to have been very tolerant and perhaps even approving of the liaison. In *The Seraglio*, which was based more than loosely on his father's opulent lifestyle, James Merrill certainly implied that the lead character pursued sexual adventures with unmarried and married women.

17. Ablation of the thyroid gland, which reduced its production of hormones, was a promising experimental treatment for angina sufferers in the mid-1950s. The goal was to lower the patient's metabolism, thereby diminishing oxygen demands and reducing the heart rate. Although the treatment worked extremely well for Charles Merrill, it was subsequently abandoned by the medical profession after the emergence of other superior treatments with fewer potential side effects. Author's correspondence with Richard J. Bing, M.D., professor emeritus of medicine, University of Southern California, October and November 1995. For more information on this general procedure, see Bing and Schelbert, "Isotopes in Cardiology." My thanks to Professor Doyce Nunis for providing easy access to the expertise of Dr. Bing. I also received useful input from Dr. Carol Mangione, the wife of USC colleague Phil Ethington.

18. Charlie explained the treatment and its aftermath in a letter to his friends Jack and Stella Little in England and cited in Keenan, "Chain of Fortune," 617–18.

play bridge, I can dance, I can swim, I can laugh, and above all, I can plan." He added: "As a matter of fact, I can plan too damn well." What he had in mind were the plans he was making to attend the huge gathering of Merrill Lynch managers from all across the nation in New York to celebrate his sixty-eighth birthday in October. At the formal dinner, he made a grand entrance, speaking at length to a crowd that, for the most part, had not heard his voice for nearly a decade. The occasion was the capstone of his long career in financial services. Free from the burden of constant pain and worrisome uncertainty, Charlie spent most of the last three years of his life in happier circumstances; indeed, both his physical condition and his mental outlook were positively affected by the healing powers of the experimental atomic cocktail.

Although he now had renewed capacity to participate more fully in the management of Merrill Lynch, Charlie failed to alter his lifestyle or his work schedule in any significant way after the summer of 1953. He had been away from the office routine for so long, and he wanted to take advantage of the opportunity to enjoy his final years absent the pain and suffering; in this instance, his quasi retirement was voluntary rather than imposed. Win Smith had performed outstandingly as the firm's de facto CEO since 1944; commission revenues and profits kept rising at a steady pace. A logical management succession had unofficially occurred. It had become Smith's firm in the postwar era in everything but name. Charlie's debt to Smith for keeping the enterprise moving forward was profound, and he often expressed his appreciation and gratitude, both in person and in their routine correspondence. These two men were charter members of a mutual admiration society, and the sentiments flowed frequently and profusely – and with utter sincerity – in both directions.

Over the years, Charlie became, in essence, a management consultant to his own enterprise. After a period of adjustment in the months immediately after his three major heart attacks, he discovered that his outsider role was workable and tolerable – and in certain ways advantageous. Charlie provided written and verbal advice on the issues that caught his attention, while Smith carried out policy and dealt with a variety of problems on a daily basis. Together, they created a management team that carried the firm to new heights in the late 1940s and early 1950s.

Charles Merrill in his World War I Army Air Corps uniform, 1918.
Merrill Lynch & Co. Archives.

Daughter, Doris, mother, Octavia, and Merrill, ca. 1931.
Merrill Lynch & Co. Archives.

Merrill and Winthrop Smith, ca. 1952. Merrill Lynch & Co. Archives.

Visit with operations managers, 1950. *Left to right*: George Young, Joe Benning, Al Horvath, Merrill, John Hennigan, and Win Callan. Merrill Lynch & Co. Archives.

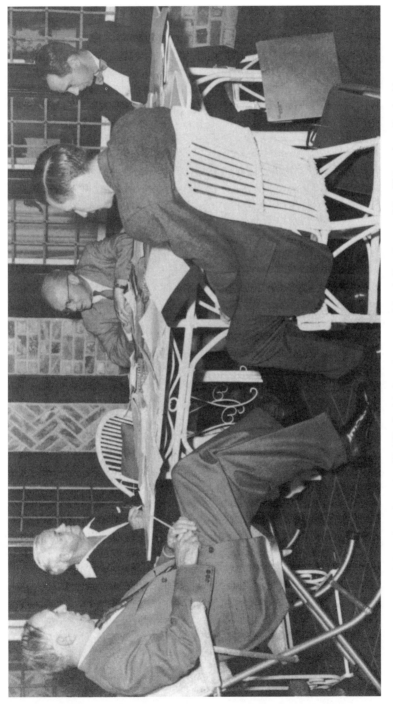

Left to right: Milija Rubezanian, Merrill, Win Smith, Don Regan, and Louis Engel, 1953. Merrill Lynch & Co. Archives.

Left to right: Winthrop Smith, Charles Merrill, Edmund Lynch, Jr., Edward Pierce, Darwin Fenner, and Alpheus Beane Jr., 1955. Merrill Lynch & Co. Archives.

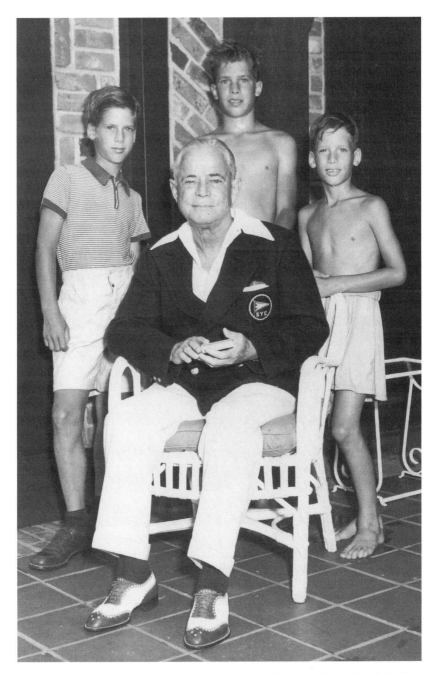

Merrill with three of his grandsons, 1950s. *Left to right*: Peter, Merrill, and Stephen Magowan. Merrill Lynch & Co. Archives.

Merrill in his sixties. Merrill Lynch & Co. Archives.

12

THE POSTWAR YEARS, 1945–1950

In the years immediately following World War II, Merrill Lynch moved forward to consolidate its leadership position in the brokerage field. As in the past, the partners introduced a series of innovative policies that benefited customers and employees alike. One milestone reached in 1949 was the opening of the one hundredth branch office; the site was Omaha, Nebraska, a fitting midwestern locale for an enterprise that had set its sights on cultivating upper-middle-class households in midsize cities distant from Wall Street. One clear indication of the success of the firm's growth strategy was its increased share of the trading volume on the New York Stock Exchange. From 1942, the first full year of operations after the merger with Fenner & Beane, until 1950, the partnership's share of round lot trading rose from 8.1 to 10.2 percent, up 26 percent, while its share of odd lot trading climbed from 10.2 to 14.7 percent, an increase of 44 percent. The huge jump in the odd lot market indicated that Merrill Lynch was attracting the business of thousands of middle-income households that were committed to building diversified investment portfolios.[1]

Although Charlie was no longer involved in the daily management of the firm, he monitored events from his summer home in Southampton and his winter retreat in Palm Beach. After doctors relaxed the restrictions on his daily schedule in 1946, he was in regular contact with Win Smith through frequent exchanges of financial reports and memorandums, and the two men talked on the telephone when necessity arose.[2] In keeping with the pattern established before his heart attack, Charlie focused most

---

1. Contrary to what most people at the time probably believed about the differences between odd lot trading and round lot trading, including the author until last year, the latter did not typically require greater financial resources. The firm's analysis of transactions in the early 1950s showed quite the opposite, namely, that odd lot trades on average involved higher totals than round lot trades. The explanation for this outcome is that many round lot trades were for stocks with low market prices, under forty dollars for example, whereas odd lot trades often involved stocks trading at fifty dollars and higher, sometimes much higher.
2. Smith, "Reminiscences," memorandum prepared for Stanton Griffis in 1954, ML Files.

of his attention on sales, public relations, and advertising, but he was occasionally drawn into deliberations about other matters as well.

The major organizational initiative after the war was the creation of a formal school to prepare trainees for careers as sales representatives at the various branch offices. Since the depths of the depression, the brokerage field had been a shrinking sector, and it had failed to attract more than a handful of replacements for hundreds of retirees. The economic revival during the war led to an upturn in trading volume, but the improvement was modest at best. By 1945, the median age of brokers at Merrill Lynch and other competitive brokerage houses was fifty and higher. Every executive in the brokerage field knew a critical labor shortage was looming, but many firms were reluctant to recruit and train younger employees because of persistent fears about the probability of a postwar recession similar to the sharp downturn after World War I.

Charlie thought the future of the U.S. economy looked bright, and he was prepared to expand the firm's work force, although he was quick to acknowledge that a postwar recession might lead to setbacks and retrenchments. He was likewise convinced that the shortage of well-trained brokers and branch managers presented a formidable challenge that required an unorthodox response. The partners' solution was to launch a training school at the firm's New York headquarters for successive classes of ambitious men, and a few unmarried women, in their early twenties to mid-thirties. The main purpose of the school was to prepare enrollees to become successful sales representatives at the branch offices scattered across the nation; a few trainees were destined for positions as security analysts or operations specialists.

In the past, new employees at virtually all brokerage houses had learned the ropes through ad hoc apprenticeships. Some new hires learned sales techniques firsthand by assisting established brokers; others started in the back office and later transferred to sales. For aspiring brokers, this on-the-job training regimen often extended over a period of four or five years – or even longer. Young people working in the New York financial district could advance their careers by attending courses sponsored by the NYSE Institute, but everyone living outside of the Wall Street area could only participate in that educational program through unstructured correspondence courses. Smith thought highly of that educational program, and he wrote a memo to Charlie in December 1940, in which he advocated making the "Security Analysis" course mandatory for all sales personnel.[3] Gaining

---

3. Smith to Merrill, Dec. 27, 1940, ML Files. The course consisted of eighteen lessons; Smith believed it would take the average student three nights of intense study to complete each lesson. He recommended that employees complete these assignments over a three-year period.

detailed knowledge about securities markets through alternative educational systems was more difficult than today; for example, only a few colleges and universities offered courses on financial markets in the 1940s.[4] The Merrill Lynch training school filled a glaring gap in the U.S. educational system, and it dramatically accelerated the business careers of most participants. Persons hired for sales at the various branch offices and sent to the training school usually became productive brokers within a year or two of completing the program.

Prior to World War II, only a few companies in the United States, or overseas, had instituted formal training programs that paid a select group of new employees a regular salary for several months while they devoted all their energies to essentially educational pursuits.[5] According to historian Timothy Spears, the National Cash Register Company established a training school at its plant in Dayton, Ohio, in 1894, "where salesmen, old and new, received an education in how to demonstrate and sell cash registers."[6] Classes lasted a week or two at most, however. In the early 1930s, Standard Oil of New Jersey (Exxon) organized a training school in New York City with formal classroom instruction that ran for several months; the trainees were sales personnel in various lubrication products.[7] As these examples attest, there were clearly precedents, but few American business firms regularly paid groups of twenty or more recent hires a living wage for three to six months while they attended an in-house training school.

Another radical departure from past practices in the brokerage field was the emphasis on recruiting sales trainees with some college background – men who possessed outstanding communication and analytical skills. The emphasis on hiring college graduates was a key element in the plan to professionalize the brokerage occupation and convert salesmen into account executives. In the late 1940s, a few years of business or military experience was also deemed valuable. By the 1950s the ideal candidate was a man twenty-four or twenty-five years old who had graduated from college and

4. As a rule, colleges and universities offered few, if any, courses in business subjects at the undergraduate or graduate level. An undergraduate business major was uncommon before the 1960s.
5. An exception to this generalization might be found among firms hiring specialized sales engineers and others who needed additional instruction beyond college about technologically complex products. But I doubt if any of these on-the-job training programs involved the expense of six months of schooling.
6. Spears, *100 Years on the Road*, 211.
7. My source is an interview of a close relative in June 1996. My father, Paul Perkins, earned an undergraduate degree in chemistry from the University of Virginia in 1929 and later attended a three-month lubrication school for about twenty trainees organized by Standard Oil in New York in the early 1930s. Thereafter, he sold lubricants, waxes, and other petroleum derivatives to manufacturing firms and dairies in Virginia. He believes the organization of the special school was an isolated event, and not an instructional program repeated on a regular basis.

spent eighteen to twenty-four months as a junior officer in the military.[8] Generally speaking, Merrill Lynch was a true pioneer in providing extensive educational programs and training for new employees in the sales division long before they were asked to make a significant contribution toward generating commission revenues.

The impetus for the inauguration of a formal training school is difficult to pinpoint. Like many successful new ideas in the business world, it had several antecedents. Charlie was exposed to the merits of an accelerated instructional program during his military service in World War I. Before prospective pilots sat in the cockpit for their first lesson, the Army Air Corps provided a month or so of introductory classroom instruction. In 1918, Charlie attended flight school in Austin, Texas, before receiving pilot training at an airfield near San Antonio. After earning his wings, he was assigned the task of training other young pilots for combat at an airfield in Florida. Charlie later realized that a roughly similar mixture of classroom education and on-the-job training would benefit entrants into the securities field. Son-in-law Robert Magowan was another executive who knew something about the value of training programs for employees who were targeted for upper-level sales or managerial positions since he had participated in one at Macy's in the early 1930s.[9] Win Smith was a third executive who, according to reliable sources, was also an advocate of the training school concept and perhaps its true progenitor.[10] Most likely, the concept emerged from conversations among these three key partners, plus the probable input of consultant Ted Braun.

To organize the curriculum and supervise instruction at the New York training school, the firm hired Dr. Birl Shultz, who had headed the NYSE Institute.[11] Alpheus Beane Jr., son of the Fenner & Beane cofounder and just returning from military service, was named director of the school. The first class of twenty-three entered the six-month program in December 1945. Most of the men chosen for accelerated training during the

---

8. In the late 1940s, the firm also instituted a junior training program for recent college graduates with no business or military experience. The two-year program included on-the-job training at a local branch office plus three months of formal schooling in New York City. Future CEO William Schreyer joined the firm as a member of one of the very early "junior" classes.

9. In a letter to the author in May 1996, Doris Magowan asserted that her husband had been the originator of the training school concept.

10. In an in-house interview in 1982, CEO Don Regan recalled that both Merrill and Smith had claimed to be the original source of the training school concept.

11. According to the transcripts of an interview with Don Regan in the 1980s, the firm's Chicago office, managed by Homer Hargrave, ran its own training school for a few years in the postwar era. Presumably, the curriculum focused more on commodities than securities since the nation's most active commodities exchange was located in Chicago, and up to one-quarter of customer trades were in commodities.

immediate postwar years were recently discharged veterans. Two of the seventy trainees in the first three classes were women who aimed for careers as security analysts. Among the most notable members of the second class of trainees that entered the school in March 1946 was ex-marine Donald Regan; after a series of rapid promotions, he became CEO in the 1970s and then served in Washington as Treasury secretary and chief of staff under President Ronald Reagan in the 1980s. At one point Birl Shultz reportedly tried to recruit his son George for the Merrill Lynch training program, but George decided to attend graduate school and pursue a career in academia and government service. In a strange twist of fate, George Shultz eventually became secretary of state under President Reagan, and he and Don Regan, his father's former student, served together in the same cabinet.

The training school initiative was an expensive gamble. In addition to the salaries of Shultz and Beane, a small staff, and several part-time instructors, the partners were obligated to pay twenty trainees an entry-level salary for six months. During this entire period none was generating commission revenues or contributing significantly to the ongoing workload. But Smith, Magowan, and Charlie decided the training school was a necessary expense to create a base for the firm's development.

Recalling his experiences in the program years later, Don Regan underlined the positive interaction between trainees and departmental managers at headquarters: "This gave those coming out of the training school an understanding of New York, an understanding of the home office, . . . and it got them off to a much faster start." The benefits flowed in both directions: "Another strength was it gave many home office people their initial contact with those who were to be the firm's salesmen of the future and allowed them to put the full flavor of the firm into hundreds of younger people." Regan also remembered some shortcomings: "Six months in New York was much too long. It gave people too much time to play. Some of the instruction was uneven."[12] Based on the criticisms of participants, the school term was subsequently reduced from six to three months. By the late 1940s, the typical sales trainee was given two or three months to become familiar with procedures at the local branch office before leaving for New York to join classmates from across the nation in the program. When the trainee returned to the originating branch, he was set to work soliciting customers and servicing small and medium-sized accounts; in time, a portion of those accounts usually generated a sufficient volume of trades to cover his salary and generate profits for the partnership.

12. Regan interview, April 1983, ML Files.

One of the main risks associated with investing so much time and money in training was the possibility that many new hires would be lured away by other employers, in the brokerage field or other industry sectors, who paid straight commissions rather than annual salaries supplemented by year-end bonuses and profit-sharing. This free rider problem was unavoidable given that the partners had no legal way of forcing employees to remain with the firm for a specific number of years after graduating from the training school.[13] Under a worst-case scenario, other brokerage houses would have the luxury of devoting modest resources to hiring and training new employees; instead, they could realize dramatic savings by recruiting sales personnel pretrained by Merrill Lynch. Few competitors, including other large brokerage chains, tried to emulate the Merrill Lynch system for training new employees. Some large brokerage houses, like Bache, occasionally started formal training schools in highly profitable years, but then eliminated them during the next business downturn.[14] As a rule, however, most firms ran no elaborate in-house training programs, much less organized schools in financial centers with extensive classroom instruction.

Charlie was prepared to assume the risk of desertions to competitors. And, indeed, when competitors sought to raid other firms for sales personnel, they usually looked to Merrill Lynch first because it possessed the largest pool of talent. As it happened, some brokers did seek greener pastures; about one-quarter of them left the securities business altogether. Losses averaged around 25 percent of training school graduates during the first two decades. Because of competitive raids in the 1950s and 1960s, a significant portion of all licensed brokers had received their initial training at Merrill Lynch. The outstanding education provided to hundreds of trainees was another valuable contribution that Charlie and his partners made to reviving the public's confidence in the nation's capital markets after the dislocations of the depression years and World War II. Despite the occasional defections, most trainees remained with Merrill Lynch throughout their careers. In short, the expensive recruitment gamble paid off: it provided the partnership with a steady supply of freshly trained brokers for its more than one hundred branch offices. As a result, the firm had the manpower to handle the increased volume of trading in the 1950s and thereafter.

13. The firm instituted a "no-return" employment policy in an effort to discourage marginal defections. Brokers who left Merrill Lynch to join competitive firms were not allowed to return to the fold in the event the greener pastures turned brown. Some ship jumpers soon discovered that they no longer had ready access to reliable research information and regretted their departure; others enjoyed successful careers elsewhere and earned high incomes through the prevailing system of splitting commissions.

14. John Fitzgerald interview, Aug. 10, 1983, ML Files.

At Charlie's insistence, Merrill Lynch created a profit-sharing plan. He had been introduced to the concept by the entrepreneurs who managed the pioneering chain stores that Merrill Lynch had financed in the late 1910s and the 1920s. During the first quarter of the twentieth century, numerous corporations with growing white-collar staffs had added attractive fringe benefit programs, including retirement and pension plans, to their overall compensation packages. The primary motive for more liberal fringe benefits was to attract and retain the loyalty of well-qualified and highly motivated employees.[15] Some firms chose profit sharing as an alternative to a well-defined pension program. At Merrill Lynch, the partners went further than most contemporary enterprises: they extended the benefit program below the middle-management level to include all full-time employees – brokers, research staff, and clerical personnel.

Before the 1929 crash, the partners in most Wall Street firms had typically given their valued employees year-end bonuses when profits met expectations. In the 1930s and early 1940s, however, bonuses were few and far between because of low trading volume and persistent operating losses. With business on the upswing after 1942, Merrill Lynch resumed the practice of paying regular year-end bonuses. As a rule, these bonuses were not trivial amounts but cash payments that boosted an employee's annual income by 10 to 15 percent. The most effective branch managers and brokers received even larger financial rewards.

In addition to bonuses, employees were offered a share of the partnership's net profits. Charlie opted for profit sharing rather than a formalized pension plan for future retirees because profit sharing was inherently a more flexible system. Annual contributions to a profit-sharing account were not mandated when earnings sank, a feature some partners viewed as advantageous given the unpredictability of the brokerage business over the past several decades.

Another positive feature of the profit-sharing plan from Charlie's perspective was that these monies stayed within the firm and boosted its capital resources. A large portion of the retirement fund was invested in an issue of the partnership's subordinate debt, where it earned generous interest. With the overall volume of transactions constantly rising and the level of current liabilities proportionately growing, the partnership regularly required additional capital to meet and exceed by a healthy margin the minimum requirements established by the NYSE. Charlie assumed responsibility for soliciting outside investors who might be willing to par-

15. Both Zunz, *Making America Corporate*, and my former student, Clark Davis, "Living on the Ladder," explore the expansion of fringe benefits for white-collar employees. A few large firms added retirement programs to the overall compensation package in the first half of the twentieth century.

ticipate in the enterprise as limited partners. When his efforts came up short, he was occasionally forced to liquidate a portion of his personal investment portfolio and channel the proceeds into his partnership account at Merrill Lynch.

All partners still active in management were, under normal circumstances, never allowed to withdraw more than very small portions of their original capital and accumulated profits from the firm. The only exception to this rule was the privilege of diverting for other purposes the 6 percent annual "interest" payment on every partner's accumulated capital.[16] Unless they had outside sources of income – and few did – Merrill Lynch executives lived mainly on their salaries until retirement; only at retirement were they free to begin withdrawing huge chunks of capital from their partnership accounts. Over the years, several key executives, including CEOs Win Smith and Mike McCarthy, accumulated a fair amount of wealth in their partnership accounts, but their salary allotments were, compared to those of most executives on Wall Street, nothing spectacular. As a result, their lifestyles remained surprisingly modest given their status and net worth. These financial constraints and other complex considerations eventually led the partnership to convert to the corporate form of ownership, but that change came several years after Charlie's death.[17]

According to the profit-sharing program adopted in 1945, the partners agreed to allocate from 8 to 12 percent of net profits to a permanent fund for the future benefit of all eligible employees. No employee was asked to make a matching contribution; the partners absorbed the entire cost of the program. Employees could start drawing on their share of profits within five to ten years of joining the firm. Some eligible employees made withdrawals to buy a new home, cover unexpected medical expenses, or pay the cost of a college education for their children, but many just let the profits accumulate to provide supplemental income during their retirement years.

In the first year the partners allocated $942,000 to the profit-sharing fund. Thereafter annual contributions during Charlie's lifetime ranged from a low of $154,000 in 1947 to a high of $2.3 million in 1954. In the

16. The firm's system of dividing the annual increase in a given partner's account into two discrete portions – a nominal interest payment on the outstanding balance in the capital account and the remainder as net earnings – was strictly an internal accounting decision. The Internal Revenue Service, for example, failed to recognize any artificial split between interest income and profits in assessing taxes. As far as the IRS was concerned, both additions to individual capital accounts were income streams taxable at the same progressive rates. The 6 percent interest allocation to capital accounts was not a true business expense because there was no payment to outsiders. A partner's weekly or monthly salary draw was likewise taxed at the same progressive rate.

17. Merrill was a longtime supporter of the proposal to allow brokerage and investment banking houses to incorporate.

mid-1950s, aggregate payments into the fund totaled approximately $10 million, or just over $2,000 per employee. Significantly, the profits set aside for employees added up to about one-fifth percent of the partners' combined capital accounts. Sometime prior to Charlie's death in 1956, the firm's employees, through profit sharing, had assumed a greater financial stake in Merrill Lynch than any single partner, including the founder himself, and that result corresponded perfectly to Charlie's beliefs about the importance of employee participation and a mutual commitment to a common enterprise.

One of the main areas in which vast improvement was noticeable at Merrill Lynch during the late 1940s was in the formulation and execution of the advertising program. Charlie had long been an advocate of more vigorous promotional activities, but, because of the restraints and restrictions imposed by the NYSE and lingering questions about the propriety of advertising by Wall Street firms, the leading securities houses had done little to advertise their products and services. Other providers of competitive financial services were less restrained, however. Life insurance companies, for example, had effectively used advertising campaigns to steadily increase their volume of business.[18] Something on the order of fifty million American households owned at least one life insurance policy by 1950, whereas estimates of common stock ownership were, at best, no more than one-eighth of that figure. The lesson to be drawn, Charlie concluded after noting the success of insurance companies, was that convincing large numbers of Americans to forgo consumption and put aside a portion of their current income to finance a more secure retirement was not an impossible task. Most insurance policies sold in this era were so-called whole-life policies: the premium combined low "term" rates to cover the risk of an untimely death with a wealth-building savings plan that generated cash value over time.

Charlie was not reticent in borrowing from the life insurance sector to stress the prudence of a long-term, life-cycle perspective, but he thought a financial plan that included a substantial portion of common stocks was the most sensible vehicle for achieving an individual's long-term financial goals. Common stocks were admittedly riskier than the savings component in insurance packages over the short to intermediate run, but the rates of return over periods of ten years or longer were typically much higher. Some insurance products barely kept ahead of the inflation rate. The equities of growth companies had the potential of increasing real inflation-

18. Historian J. Owen Stalson published a massive review and analysis of the marketing of life insurance, including coverage of advertising programs, in 1942; see Stalson, *Marketing Life Insurance,* and its nearly 900 pages of text and appendixes.

adjusted wealth over time, and that was an especially important factor for investors looking toward a comfortable retirement. In confidential discussions with customers, Merrill Lynch brokers usually recommended that households possess a prudent mix of savings accounts, insurance policies, and marketable securities.

As the firm's revenues and profits grew, the advertising budget expanded, and the character and tone of the message changed as well. The key person responsible for the new momentum was Louis Engel, head of the advertising department. Engel came to Merrill Lynch through a familiar intermediary: consultant Ted Braun. A reporter working for *Business Week* magazine in the mid-1930s, Engel drew the assignment of covering the chain stores' fight against the proposal by mom-and-pop grocery stores to impose prohibitively high taxes on multiple retail outlets in California. Braun's firm played a prominent role in helping Safeway Stores and the other grocery chains defeat the tax plan in a statewide referendum. While the story was unfolding, Braun proved a reliable source of information for Engel, and the two men became fast friends. In 1940, when the Los Angeles consulting firm was drawn into the merger negotiations between Merrill Lynch and E. A. Pierce, Braun urged Engel to apply for a staff position at the rejuvenated brokerage house. Braun knew Charlie intended to put greater emphasis on public relations and advertising, and he thought Engel's inventiveness and ingenuity would produce a mutually advantageous arrangement. But the journalist, in the meantime, had become managing editor of *Business Week,* and content with the progress of his career, he ignored Braun's urgings.

Then, in early 1946, managerial changes at *Business Week* prompted Engel, then thirty-seven, to resign and pursue other employment opportunities. That summer, he arranged an interview with Win Smith. "I remember saying to him," Engel recalled, " 'Now look, let me tell you quite honestly, I don't know a stock from a bond.' " One reason for his poor understanding, Engel speculated, was the lamentable performance of the brokerage sector in explaining investment principles to millions of potential customers. "Maybe you're the problem," he bluntly told Smith. "You're trying to sell your product to people who are just as ignorant about it as I am."[19] Despite his involvement in the business world for more than a decade, Engel was not knowledgeable about securities, because, as managing editor of one of the nation's leading business magazines, he had routinely assigned stories dealing with Wall Street topics to other members of the editorial staff. Engel not only felt inadequate with respect to his understanding of financial principles, he also, like millions of Americans,

19. Engel interview with Engberg, p. 5, ML Files.

remained skeptical about the fairness and honesty of financial markets. With those reservations in mind, Engel decided to stick with a field he already knew – publishing. He agreed to serve as editor and correspondent for *Changing Times,* a new publication launched by the Kiplinger family with its headquarters in the nation's capital. Within weeks, Engel realized his new job was not working out as anticipated. Kiplinger kept pressing his new employee to move to Washington. Engel resisted because he wanted to work and reside in New York City.

Engel later recalled with gusto the story about how he finally joined Merrill Lynch. Walking through Grand Central Station late one afternoon, he spontaneously phoned Smith and asked if the job as advertising and sales promotion manager was still open. Smith replied that the partners had finally identified a seemingly qualified candidate, and they were hoping to fill the spot within a day or two. "Are you interested?" Smith inquired. "I said, yes; I am definitely interested," Engel replied. Smith told him to hold the phone so that he could consult quickly with some of his advisers. "I still don't know what he did," Engel explained. "He went away five or ten minutes – I just barely made it on my nickel supply; . . . I guess he called Ted Braun out in Los Angeles." When Smith got back on the line, he simply said, "All right, you're hired. When can you report?" Engel responded: "I said two weeks, or something. And that's how I came to Merrill Lynch . . . on November 15, 1946."

Engel designed the type of aggressive advertising program that Charlie had been advocating for years. Imaginatively using his own naïveté to create more genuinely informative advertisements, Engel wrote purposefully unsophisticated copy that addressed the questions and concerns of persons geographically and intellectually distant from Wall Street. He presumed that most readers glancing at a brokerage ad knew as little – or even less – about stocks and bonds as he himself had known prior to joining Merrill Lynch. In his copy he tried to explain investing principles in plain and simple language.

Engel's unorthodox ideas and his desire for creative independence soon produced conflicts with George Hyslop, his immediate superior. Hyslop, a partner inherited from the Pierce organization, had been assigned primary responsibility for advertising and public relations soon after the merger in 1940. Engel found he could not make a move without checking every little detail with Hyslop, and the policy irritated him no end. "He insisted on seeing every little two-by-two ad even if it was for hog bellies in the *National Butcher* magazine," Engel jokingly recalled. Charlie and Smith soon realized that Hyslop's managerial philosophy had become an obstacle to progress, and he was eased out of the partnership. After Robert Magowan assumed most of Hyslop's duties, the advertising department func-

tioned more harmoniously, since Magowan granted Engel far greater latitude in decision making. Magowan was also a supportive ally in internal
conflicts with other departments.

One technique that Engel favored was inviting potential customers to
respond promptly through the mail – either by writing a personal letter or
by filling out a coupon requesting free and objective information.[20] At one
point he told the partners: "We have a research department to analyze
people's portfolios and you never advertise it; . . . it's the best thing you've
got to sell, for God's sake." Given the green light, Engel launched a major
campaign to inform the public about the availability of portfolio analysts
on the Merrill Lynch staff. When magazine and newspaper readers responded eagerly to ads inviting them to mail a list of their holdings to the
New York office for analysis, the personnel in the research department
complained bitterly about the extra workload. An overworked staff argued
that Engel's initiatives had gone too far – another case of "too much of a
good thing." They pressured Magowan to force Engel to scale back the
placement of ads proclaiming their services – services for which neither
they nor the partners were receiving any direct monetary compensation.

With Charlie's blessing, Magowan backed Engel to the hilt, and the ads
ran on schedule. Magowan told the research department that coping with
the heavy inflow of mail was an internal problem that required an internal
solution. The advertising department, he reminded the complainers, was
producing remarkable results in generating thousands of solid leads for
Merrill Lynch brokers nationwide. Engel had demonstrated beyond all
doubt that, with the proper advertising, a brokerage firm could attract the
attention of thousands of households that were interested in planning for
their financial security – households that were expressing a new willingness
to consider something other than whole-life insurance policies with modest
rates of return. When the onslaught of letters continued, the partners
authorized the head of the research department to add more staff to handle
the deluge. Charlie and Smith concluded that the maintenance of a large
research department was another inescapable high cost of doing business
if they wanted to provide reliable services on a mass scale and in a thoroughly professional manner.

Engel's most innovative advertisement, one that often turns up on lists
of the one hundred most influential ads in the nation's history, appeared
in the fall of 1948, approximately two years after he had joined Merrill
Lynch. Titled "What Everybody Ought to Know about This Stock and

---

20. For interesting reading on the use of advertising coupons and similar techniques in market
research, I recommend the collection of essays by Alfred Politz; see Hardy, ed., *The Politz
Papers*.

Bond Business," the ad consisted of six thousand words of very small print squeezed onto a full-size newspaper page. The copy was informational and educational – and textbook dry in tone. There were no explicit references to the firm's own brokerage services in the entire text, but at the bottom right of the page was a small calling card that identified Merrill Lynch as the sponsor and invited readers to request free reprints of the ad in pamphlet form. In the history of print media, no single advertisement with so much seemingly boring copy had ever been published for any product or service.

At first Charlie, Smith, and Magowan were only lukewarm about this questionable marketing concept. At five thousand dollars, the cost of running the full-page ad in the *New York Times* was extremely high relative to the size of the advertising budget (2 percent of the annual appropriation, to be exact). How many people, the partners wondered, would actually make the effort to read the text and how many, in turn, would respond by asking for reprints of a text that could easily be clipped right out of the newspaper? The partners also debated whether to spend so much money for an essentially generic advertisement that was likely to benefit rival firms. Despite his superiors' reservations, Engel insisted on gambling a portion of his annual budget on the innovative concept.

Finally, a compromise was reached. The partners agreed to allow Engel to run a trial advertisement in the *Cleveland Plain Dealer*, where the cost of space was much lower than in New York. If the ad bombed, they could drop the whole idea without wasting another nickel of the advertising budget. When the public response to the Cleveland experiment proved encouraging, Engel received permission to test the ad in the *New York Times*. During the week or so after publication, the firm received more than five thousand requests for pamphlet reprints. "What was most amazing," Engel recalled, "was that we got hundreds and hundreds of long and thoughtful letters." Some respondents were profusely appreciative. One person wrote: "God bless Merrill Lynch; . . . I have been wanting to know this all my life; . . . I owned stocks and bonds and I never really knew what I owned." The firm ran the same advertisement, or slightly revised versions, in newspapers across the country, not only during the next few months, but, indeed, for years thereafter. The total number of responses exceeded three million, and those returns translated into millions of prospective customers for the firm's eager brokers. With that one concept alone, Engel proved himself a promotional genius. His subsequent aggressive campaigns, which were typically both educational and eye-catching, set new standards for brokerage firms and other enterprises in the financial services sector.

Attracting new accounts was vital to the firm's continued success because so many customers curtailed their activity or redirected the bulk of their trading to other brokerage houses in any given year. In the late 1930s, long-term customers were the main source of commission revenues, but a decade later the reverse was true. An internal analysis of revenue sources in 1950 revealed that 45 percent of trading commissions could be traced to accounts that had been on the books for two years or less. Engel's advertisements and promotional ideas attracted the attention of a raft of new prospects and thus helped Merrill Lynch maintain its position as the nation's leading brokerage house. A few years after the publication of his famous full-page advertisement, Engel received an invitation from Charlie to join the partnership. And, as frequently happened in this organization, Charlie volunteered to lend Engel the ten thousand dollars to cover his initial capital contribution, which amounted to a meager one-quarter of 1 percent of the partners' total investment.

In 1950, the partners authorized a second, in-depth analysis of their customer base with the aim of improving service and increasing profits. The project was roughly similar in content and direction to the survey conducted by Ted Braun's management consulting firm a decade earlier when Charlie was deciding whether he should return to the struggling financial services sector. The previous analysis had concentrated on a single branch office in Los Angeles; the new study drew on a sample of six thousand accounts drawn from branch offices across the nation – about 2 or 3 percent of all active accounts. The Braun analysis had pinpointed the critical importance of a small percentage of very active accounts in generating genuinely profitable trading volume. Particularly crucial, Braun had revealed, were two types of customers: those who maintained margin accounts and routinely purchased securities with borrowed funds, and those who left monies on deposit with the firm to finance future purchases.

The 1950 study was more comprehensive and more statistically reliable, but it essentially reinforced the conclusions of its predecessor.[21] The data proved that just 6 percent of active accounts generated 52 percent of all commission revenues. As in the past, the brokerage field remained a strange, lopsided business since only a fraction of the active customers – the cream of the crop – were responsible for almost all the profits. On the other hand, any brokerage house with a bright future required thousands of small and medium-sized accounts, because, out of that vast pool, some customers were likely to become very active traders at some later date.

The 1950 survey elicited information from customers on income levels,

---

21. "Managers' Conference Transcript," 1953, ML Files. The contents of the 1950 survey were discussed in detail at the 1953 meeting. Why top executives took so long to communicate the findings of the survey to branch mangers is unknown.

occupations, age, and other characteristics, and these data were analyzed in conjunction with the commission revenues from various categories. Persons in the highest income bracket (over $15,000 annually; $90,000 in 1995 prices) constituted 16 percent of active accounts and generated 37 percent of commission revenues. At the other end of the spectrum, persons with incomes under $5,000 annually ($31,500 in 1995 prices) made up approximately one-quarter of accounts and generated 12 percent of the commissions. The five occupational groups with the most active trading patterns were business owners (12 percent of accounts and 20 percent of commissions); salaried executives (17 percent of accounts and 19 percent of commissions); retirees (14 percent of accounts and 18 percent of commissions); professionals (18 percent of accounts and 17 percent of commissions); and housewives (16 percent of accounts and 13 percent of commissions). The top five groups combined were responsible for three-quarters of all active accounts and more than 85 percent of commission revenues. An analysis of the age distribution of customers produced other interesting results: persons over 65 (6 percent of accounts and 6 percent of commissions); persons 56–65 (20 percent of accounts and 26 percent of commissions); persons 46–55 (31 percent of accounts and 37 percent of commissions); persons 36–45 (27 percent of accounts and 21 percent of commissions); and persons 35 or younger (15 percent of accounts and 9 percent of commissions). The data revealed that trading activity rose progressively as a customer matured, peaked between ages 50 and 55, and then tailed off gradually. At Merrill Lynch, persons under 36 had opened more than twice as many accounts as those over 65, and they generated 3 percent more in commission revenue. This critical statistic indicates that, in addition to its small-town orientation, the firm was becoming more successful in attracting younger households who had the vision to plan ahead for their financial futures. Based on educational public relations programs and informative advertising, the partners were beginning to make inroads on the long-term savings market that aggressive life insurance companies had dominated since early in the twentieth century. Charlie's goal, and the goal of every forward-looking person in the capital markets, was to convince more Americans to invest a significant portion of their retirement funds in blue-chip stocks rather than strictly in whole-life insurance policies and savings accounts with low rates of return.

In the aftermath of World War II, the U.S. economy surprised many forecasters by performing surprisingly well. There were minor dips in output but no serious postwar recession. The stock market, fearing a downturn that never materialized, experienced falling prices from 1945 to 1948, but then rebounded in 1949 and 1950 following the election of President Harry Truman. Over the five-year period, the closing Dow-

Jones industrial average climbed a modest 4.5 percent annually. Meanwhile, the volume of stock trading, the one statistic most vital to the success of the nation's brokerage houses, remained thoroughly discouraging throughout the late 1940s. Volume on the NYSE fell from 363 million shares in 1946 to just 272 million shares in 1949. Then, in 1950, trading volume surged to 524 million shares, the highest level of activity in more than fifteen years. It was an encouraging breakthrough year for the entire brokerage sector. The persistent depression in the field, which began in the 1930s and was never fully alleviated during the war years, finally ended.

Numerous external factors produced a friendly economic environment that contributed to the firm's success in the postwar era. Many households, including many middle-class households, were unusually liquid after 1945 because rationing and shortages had reduced their opportunities to acquire tangible goods. Low interest rates on government bonds encouraged numerous savers to seek higher returns on alternative investments. The common shares of many leading corporations regularly paid dividends that yielded, at existing stock prices, as much as 5 to 7 percent annually and also held out the promise of capital gains. Meanwhile, the financial reforms of the 1930s had given the public greater confidence in the fundamental fairness of the securities market. Merrill Lynch's advertising and its various promotional activities provided a measure of reassurance and helped overcome the reluctance of doubters with fading memories of plummeting stock prices. Throughout the war years, Charlie and his partners had been making elaborate preparations to take advantage of any and all favorable opportunities that might arise in the U.S. economy, and immediate postwar conditions were extremely conducive to the realization of that goal. Charlie had been prescient about an economic downturn in the late 1920s, and he was prescient again about the continuation of the economic expansion after 1945.

Aided tremendously by the renewed interest of American investors in trading common stocks, Merrill Lynch's annual report at midcentury listed some enviable numbers in several important categories. Revenues climbed to a record $45 million, more than 50 percent higher than the previous record in 1946. Net profits before taxes totaled $17 million, another new high, and nearly $4 million of that figure went to employees in the form of bonuses and contributions to profit sharing. Customer credit balances of $145 million nearly equaled the $152 million lent to customers who maintained margin accounts and financed a portion of their portfolios with borrowed funds. The favorable balance between debits and credits meant that the interest override was substantial, somewhere in the range of $2.5 million. About 15 percent of the firm's net profit thus arose from acting as a financial intermediary and performing essentially commercial banking functions. The remaining 85 percent came from transaction services and underwriting. In terms of the partners' return on capital, the final profits realized in 1950 – after deducting bonuses and profit sharing, charitable contributions, and federal taxes at a 70 percent rate – translated into a return of about 30 percent on the previous year's net worth of $14 million.[22]

After a long decade of struggle and only modest financial success, Merrill Lynch reached a new plateau in 1950. All the previous work in honing the organization, establishing sound principles, improving customer relations, training personnel, and spreading the word through advertising finally started to pay off at higher and more sustainable levels. At long last, the firm's overall performance met Charlie's and Win Smith's rosiest expectations back in 1940. The timetable was slower than anticipated, but the firm nonetheless entered the second half of the century in exceptionally sound condition. Its market share in stock trading, commodities trading, and underwriting was either the highest or among the highest in all three sectors. By midcentury, Merrill Lynch had developed the organizational capacity to take full advantage of any upswing in trading on the nation's stock and commodity exchanges.

22. Included in the rate-of-return calculation are the interest allocations to partners on their outstanding balances at the end of 1949.

of additions to the staff. In 1943, the typical branch had six sales personnel and seven clerical workers; by 1952 the same office employed eleven people in sales and twelve backstage clerks. In step with its aggressive strategy, Merrill Lynch was routinely adding new employees a year or so in advance of proven customer demand for their services; as a consequence, the employee workload had eased. The typical branch employee handled about 15 percent fewer orders in 1952 than in 1943. Meanwhile, salaries had increased by one-fifth to one-quarter. Other expenses at the local level (office rents, communications equipment, and miscellaneous items) had nearly doubled. With salaries and other costs rising at a faster clip than revenues, the typical branch office, after adjusting for price changes, was actually 15 percent less profitable in 1952 than a decade earlier.

The main problem for all brokerage houses in 1952 was a familiar lament – low trading volume. Following the pattern established during the two world wars, cautious investors curtailed their transactions after the outbreak of the Korean War. (Despite what many leftist critics of the capitalist system have sometimes alleged about the militaristic motives of bankers and securities dealers, wartime years have rarely been rewarding for Wall Street firms.) Volume on the NYSE dropped from 524 million shares in 1950 to 337 million shares in 1952. Taking into account periodic fluctuations, trading volume on the NYSE between 1943 and 1952 climbed at a rate of only 2.5 percent annually – or 30 percent overall. During this same period, Merrill Lynch had doubled its work force and granted most employees modest raises in terms of buying power. With employment levels up and productivity falling, perhaps the most surprising fact revealed by an analysis of the financial statements was the partners' ability to maintain profitability.

With stock trading subdued during the Korean War, the partnership kept its head above water by diversifying its sources of revenue. One area where improvement was most visible was in handling trades of common stocks that were not listed on the organized exchanges. Before proceeding, we should pause briefly and reflect on the investing public's more favorable attitude toward unlisted stocks in recent years. Aided by high-speed computer technology, the volume of trading in unlisted stocks on the NASDAQ market in the 1990s has surpassed the level of activity in listed securities on the renowned NYSE. Back in the 1950s, the unlisted sector of the securities market was referred to as the over-the-counter sector, or off-board, and trading volume was much, much lower than today. Most stocks traded over the counter were (and remain) the issues of small to medium-sized firms with modest or nonexistent dividend payments but outstanding growth potential in terms of future earnings. Younger investors seeking long-term capital gains and with a tolerance for fluctuating

Table 13.1. *Financial data for Merrill Lynch, 1940–1956*
(in millions of dollars)

	Income	Net profits before taxes	Capital account
1940[a]	4.2	(0.3)	4.0
1941	8.6	.5	6.1
1942	9.4	.2	6.0
1943	17.3	4.8	7.8
1944	18.6	4.4	10.0
1945	28.1	8.8	12.5
1946	29.5	6.2	14.0
1947	22.4	1.8	14.6
1948	26.7	3.7	15.5
1949	25.1	2.4	16.0
1950	45.6	12.5	18.0
1951	44.3	9.5	21.0
1952	43.6	6.3	23.0
1953	47.7	6.7	24.0
1954	73.3	19.3	30.0
1955/56[b]	82.0	18.7	36.0

[a] 1940: Nine months.
[b] 1955/56: Fourteen months (change in end of fiscal year from December to February).
Source: Merrill Lynch annual reports, 1940–1956.

market prices were frequently attracted to unlisted stocks, and the firm's research department had a good record in identifying the winning issues and avoiding the losers. Merrill Lynch acted as the primary market maker for numerous over-the-counter stocks that traded nationally, or sometimes just in local and regional markets. In 1943, revenues from over-the-counter transactions totaled around 10 percent of the aggregate commissions earned on trades in listed stocks, but by 1952 that percentage had climbed to more than 16 percent.

Another sector that exhibited noticeable improvement was the underwriting and retail distribution of securities. Partner George Leness, who headed underwriting, reported that his department had reached a new high in terms of annual revenues, generating $3.9 million in gross income in 1952; the improvement came after six rather flat and disappointing years from 1945 to 1951. The firm's financial commitments to corporate clients reached $130 million in 1952. In comparison with its competitors, Merrill Lynch ranked seventh on Wall Street in the management of new corporate issues behind (1) First Boston; (2) Morgan, Stanley; (3) Halsey, Stuart; (4) Blyth; (5) Harriman, Ripley; and (6) Smith, Barney. The firm also ranked seventh in dollar volume of participations in securities syndicates managed by other underwriters. A top-ten ranking in the second category was not surprising because retail distribution, given the size of the branch network, was one of Merrill Lynch's greatest strengths, and the leading underwriters were usually eager to include the firm in their syndicates. The unprecedented climb into the top ten of syndicate managers was much more noteworthy.

Leness discussed some of the reasons why it had taken so many years for his department to earn a high ranking among the leading syndicate managers: "To compete successfully for underwriting business, our first job was to create a competent, well-trained organization. This cannot be done overnight, especially when you are competing for new business with long-established underwriting houses who have a continuity of management, training, and client relationships going back, in some cases, for seventy-five or one hundred years."[2] Leness and his staff had discovered few shortcuts in their pursuit of new clients. "Endless patience and persistency is needed in dealing with corporations," he concluded. The effort to attract more underwriting business by advertising in the nation's most widely read financial publications had proved ineffective. Relationship banking, which ignored most pricing considerations, was still the norm on Wall Street in the 1950s. Consequently, cultivating personal contacts with important corporate executives was a prerequisite for success. With that thought in mind, Leness urged all branch managers to remind their brokers to be constantly on the lookout for opportunities to initiate underwriting deals with new clients.[3]

Leness pointed to an earlier change in federal securities laws that had allowed the firm to quickly enter one important market. The SEC had ruled in May 1941 that all new debt issues by regulated public utilities were henceforth open to competitive bidding by all legitimate underwriters.[4] The explicit purpose of the ruling was to reduce the commissions linked to the flotation of new bond issues to the lowest possible level, thereby benefiting the utility companies and their millions of customers. The implementation of the new procedure was a disaster for many competitors, Leness noted, but luckily "a boon for us." Before the law took

---

2. Leness, "Managers' Conference Transcript," 119–29, ML Files.
3. In rewarding salaried brokers who identified new underwriting clients, the firm deviated openly from its normal compensation policy. Any employee who identified and solicited an underwriting customer received a generous commission when the transaction was complete, and fellow employees in the same branch office usually got a little extra money, too.
4. Seligman, *Transformation of Wall Street*, 211–22.

Table 13.2. *Underwriting standings (by dollar volume)*

	1943		1949		1952	
	A	B	A	B	A	B
Merrill Lynch	42	–	12	21	7	7
Blyth	2	7	4	2	4	4
First Boston	1	3	2	3	2	1
Halsey, Stuart	3	1	1	1	1	3
Harriman, Ripley	5	10	5	5	11	5
Kidder, Peabody	4	12	3	10	5	10
Lehman	14	2	6	8	8	12
Morgan, Stanley	34	6	14	4	12	2
Smith, Barney	6	5	10	15	13	9
White, Weld	13	–	16	17	10	6

A: Corporate underwriting participations.
B: Underwritings managed, including railroad and municipal bonds.
Source: Managers' conference transcript, 1953, p. 122, ML Files.

effect, Morgan, Stanley had dominated the underwriting market for public utilities, garnering up to 70 percent of the available business in the late 1930s. The SEC rule was designed to produce more competition, and Merrill Lynch seized the opportunity. Leness noted that twenty-six of the seventy-nine corporate issues in which the firm had been the primary underwriter in the period from 1950 to 1952 had come as a direct result of competitive bidding.

Many municipal bond issues across the nation were subject to similar competitive bidding rules. Leness presented data showing that his department had made 163 successful bids for municipal bonds in 1952, more than double the total a year earlier. The partners had participated in $44.5 million of municipal underwritings, the highest dollar volume in the firm's history, and more than twice the annual average from 1945 to 1951. Municipal underwriting was a more geographically diverse market than corporate underwriting. Leness identified sizable regional markets in nine cities – Chicago, Omaha, San Francisco, Los Angeles, Dallas, Indianapolis, Kansas City, New Orleans, and Philadelphia – where Merrill Lynch was active in the issuance and secondary trading of municipal securities.

Another major surprise in the early 1950s was the stellar performance of the firm's commodities division. When Fenner & Beane, which had strength in commodities trading, had joined the enterprise in the 1941 merger, Charlie and his close associates had reservations about whether they wanted to maintain a strong presence in a market where short-term speculation was undeniably a driving force. The image of commodities traders making or losing thousands of dollars in a few days, or just a few hours, was one aspect of the financial markets that Charlie hoped to downplay because he wanted the public to distinguish between investments in the common stocks of reliable corporations and those monies risked on the wild gyrations of commodity contracts. As a result of steadily falling stock prices in the early 1930s, the differences between the ownership of common stocks and commodity contracts had been further blurred in the public mind. In the end, Charlie settled on a broad and comprehensive marketing strategy: the firm would try to meet the needs of every customer seeking legitimate brokerage services, whether their transactions reflected an obsession with absolute safety or the desire to engage in speculation – or more typically something between those two poles.

Once committed to remaining active in handling commodity transactions, the partners directed the department's research staff to provide timely reports and other services for customers interested in price trends for important foodstuffs and raw materials. Brokers were expected to make certain that customers eager to profit from price fluctuations were knowledgeable about the risks associated with commodities and possessed the financial resources to withstand setbacks.[5] Although the partners decided to continue providing transactions services for customers with speculative leanings, Merrill Lynch took few steps to expand its volume of commodity trades after the merger with Fenner & Beane. In 1943, for example, commissions on commodity trades generated a mere 8 percent of branch revenues.

A decade later, however, commissions from commodity transactions had risen sharply. In 1952, the branch network generated more than 20 percent of its revenues from commodity trades; commodity transactions produced commissions equal to one-third of the revenues arising from trades in listed stocks. Several factors explain the upsurge in commodity trading. The New York partners had become more aware that a substantial number of commodity transactions were initiated by so-called trade accounts, meaning insiders directly involved in growing, processing, or mining various foodstuffs and raw materials. The motives of this group of participants in the commodity markets were essentially defensive, not speculative. The producers and processors of traded goods were seeking to protect themselves, a practice usually termed "hedging" by financial experts, against the possibility of unfavorable price movements during the upcoming months. To accomplish this goal, they either purchased or sold futures

5. That group included speculators interested in puts and calls on common stocks as well as commodity contracts.

contracts. Indeed, the commodity markets had two distinct types of regular participants: safety-first insiders and speculative outsiders. Both groups needed each other to keep the commodity markets functioning, and brokerage houses could not adequately serve one group without simultaneously serving the other.[6]

Perhaps another important reason for the increased volume of commodity transactions at Merrill Lynch offices was the unprecedented advertising and public relations program launched by the head of advertising, Lou Engel, in the late 1940s. Even before the widespread dissemination of his famous full-page advertisement explaining the basic facts about stocks and bonds, Engel had produced ads and promotional literature that explained in unsophisticated language the principal features of futures and option contracts. In response to the partners' fears in 1948 that a congressional investigating committee might actually recommend a new law that would make illegal the trading of futures contracts involving foodstuffs and raw materials not yet produced, Engel quickly consulted an introductory economics textbook for help in drafting advertising copy that justified the functioning of the commodity exchanges and argued their importance for the continuance of the free market system.[7] Congress later dropped the investigation of the commodity markets and turned its attention to other matters.

In his presentation at the conference, division head Harry Anderson reported that $3 million, or more than 40 percent of total commodity revenues, had arisen from trade accounts during 1952. He was optimistic about reaching $5 million in annual commissions from trade customers a few years down the road. One reason for the improved outlook was expanded trading in commodities other than the old mainstays – grains, livestock, and cotton. Anderson cited increased activity in less traditional markets, including hides, metals, wool, eggs, potatoes, and burlap. The research department had identified more than 25,000 potential trade prospects across the nation; out of that pool, Merrill Lynch brokers maintained only 1,500 active accounts, mostly in southern and midwestern cities. If the partnership could raise its market share from approximately 6 percent to something over 10 percent, revenues, commissions, and profits would climb significantly.

Meanwhile, Anderson assured his listeners that the firm had no inten-

6. The legitimacy of futures contracts has been debated for centuries. One outstanding book that focuses on speculation in both stocks and commodities is Cedric Cowing's *Populists, Plungers, and Progressives.*

7. Engel interview with Engberg, p. 27, ML Files. Homer Hargrave, the key partner in the commodities sector, traveled to New York from his Chicago office to review Engel's advertising copy; he suggested only a few minor changes – allegedly over a two-martini luncheon that Engel hosted.

tion of ignoring the speculators who still generated 60 percent of commodity commissions. In fact, these customers were especially valuable because most were highly active traders. Speculators who regularly traded commodities tended to generate about four times more commission revenue per account than customers who concentrated on securities. Commodity contracts usually expired in a matter of weeks or months, which stimulated regular market participants to initiate frequent transactions. Anderson urged branch managers in localities remote from Chicago, New York, Memphis, and New Orleans (four cities with organized commodity exchanges) to think more seriously about developing their commodity business. To prepare sales personnel more thoroughly in this specialized sector, the Chicago branch, managed by Homer Hargrave, had recently created a supplementary training program for new hires interested in commodities. In addition, the branch welcomed prolonged visits by seasoned brokers throughout the network who wanted to improve their understanding of the booming commodity markets.

In a lengthy segment of his presentation during the first morning session, McCarthy carefully analyzed the changing profile of the sales force over the past decade. In the early 1940s, after years of low trading volume, brokerage was dominated by older men; the median age at Merrill Lynch and elsewhere was fifty or higher. By 1952, fueled in part by graduates of the formal training program and the retirement of aging brokers, youth ruled at Merrill Lynch. The median age for brokers had dropped to thirty-five. Encouraged by the upswing in trading volume in 1950, the branches had started hiring at a rapid pace, and they concentrated on young men just a few years out of college. By 1952, one-quarter of the sales force was between the ages of twenty-six and thirty, and most in that group had been at their desks for less than eighteen months. The youth movement was not confined to the broker ranks but extended to managerial positions as well. Some offices were run by branch managers not yet forty. Indeed, Charlie made a habit of proclaiming that there was no job in the organization, excluding senior management, which could not be filled by someone as young as thirty-two.

Disregarding the performance of brokers just starting their careers, McCarthy cited data that revealed that the typical compensation package for the 824 brokers with more than one year of experience compared favorably, first, with the earnings of their counterparts in the early 1940s, and, second, with the reported earnings of brokers currently employed by competing firms. In 1943, only a handful of Merrill Lynch brokers, no more than 2 or 3 percent of the sales force, had earned more than $15,000 annually in 1952 dollars; a decade later, more than sixty brokers exceeded that level, and they represented about 8 percent of the sales force. Exclud-

Table 13.3. *Expansion in offices and sales personnel*

	Merrill Lynch	Other NYSE member firms	ML % of total
	Number of offices		
1943	88	657	11.8
1947	92	806	10.3
1952	102	1,057	8.8
	Number of sales personnel		
1943	506	6,213	7.5
1947	718	8,900	7.5
1952	1,186	11,147	9.6

Source: Managers' conference transcript, 1953, p. 37, ML Files.

ing this elite group, the typical Merrill Lynch broker generated $33,500 in commission revenues and earned a salary of $8,400 annually. (Adjusting for inflation, brokers earned about $48,000 in 1995 prices; the typical broker today earns around $80,000.)[8] For purposes of comparison, Merrill Lynch's innovative and unduplicated "salary" policy was roughly the equivalent of granting its brokers a 25 percent split of gross commissions. Most competing firms granted their brokers splits ranging from 28 to 35 percent of gross commissions. McCarthy cited statistics from the NYSE, indicating that Merrill Lynch brokers generated about 50 percent more in annual commissions from transactions on the Big Board than the registered representatives of other member firms. As a consequence, competing brokers who received a generous one-third split of gross commissions working for other houses usually still earned less than their counterparts at Merrill Lynch. The high volume at Merrill Lynch translated into the most lucrative compensation packages in the brokerage sector.

McCarthy explained that the partners' immediate goal was to bring every broker with five years of experience up to the $40,000 level in gross commissions. Under normal circumstances, that production level merited a salary in the range of $9,000 to $11,000. If experienced brokers fell significantly short of that production standard, then branch managers needed to investigate the situation and exercise more supervision. "If it's below $40,000, I'd want to know why," McCarthy remarked.[9] Because so

8. Data released by the Securities Industries Association showed that the median earnings for all stockbrokers who served individual accounts was $78,856 in 1995; the mean average was much higher at $123,839. *Los Angeles Times,* Aug. 6, 1996.
9. "Managers' Conference Transcript," p. 36.

many new hires had been with the firm for less than five years, only 20 percent of the sales force in 1952 was actually meeting the suggested standard. With maturation and greater experience, McCarthy anticipated that a majority of brokers, responding positively to the incentive of increased salaries, would soon meet the production guidelines. When that goal was accomplished, he envisioned substantial financial rewards for everyone associated with the firm – not only individual brokers, but branch managers, staff personnel, and all partners with invested capital. Since most of the brokerage firm's operating costs were fixed rather than variable, high volume was essential for continued success.

As it happened, the modest sales goals that McCarthy announced at the 1953 conference were exceeded by a wide margin just two years later. An analysis of the performance of the sales division in 1954 revealed that the typical Merrill Lynch broker generated $53,000 in commissions, which, under normal circumstances, merited a salary in the neighborhood of $12,500 to $14,000.[10] Profits were strong in 1954, too. After allocating $7.5 million to the profit-sharing fund, which translated into more than $1,600 per employee, and paying $13 million in federal income taxes, the partners realized a return of nearly 25 percent on their invested capital of $26 million.

In wide-ranging remarks at the end of both days of the conference, Charlie discussed a variety of issues related to the broad market for investment capital in the United States. Unlike other speakers at the conference, he focused more on the status of the entire securities sector and less on partnership issues. In an assessment of recent trends, he expressed "dismay and disappointment" that so little had been done by the NYSE and its member firms to draw a wider swath of the general public into the stock market. "Wall Street is still doing business at the old stand; . . . to me it is incredible that there has been so little change in almost a decade." With rhetorical flair, he challenged the audience: "Can you think of any business that has changed less in that period? The railroad industry has become dieselized; the automakers have gotten rid of the gear shift; and the aviation industry has developed jet power. But the securities business still appears satisfied with the horse and buggy." To support his allegations, Charlie cited a Brookings Institution report that put the number of U.S. stockholders at just 6.5 million, not the 10 to 15 million many so-called experts had supposed. Particularly depressing was the news that only half of all American families with incomes over $10,000 ($55,000 in 1995 prices) owned any common stocks at all. Charlie noted despairingly that all firms

10. Notes on regional conference no. 4, Dec. 12, 1955, ML Files.

in the securities field combined spent a mere $3 million annually on promotional advertising, whereas insurance companies combined spent $22 million.

Too many people on Wall Street, Charlie lamented, still thought about securities "in terms of their speculative possibilities." Too few of the leaders in the brokerage field had come to the realization that millions of prospective buyers were no longer interested primarily in speculation but rather in making genuinely long term investments in the common stocks of reliable blue-chip corporations and growth-oriented companies. Although Merrill Lynch was doing its best to alter the perceptions of peers, other elements on Wall Street remained skeptical and therefore hesitated to embrace sales strategies that targeted thousands of professionals, technicians, and midlevel executives in upper-middle-class households. "The job we have got to do is a basic job of education," Charlie concluded. "It's probably the biggest job of mass education that has ever been confronted by any business at any time in history." More help was needed not only from other firms in the securities field, he asserted, but also from American corporations that regularly floated new issues of stocks and bonds. Charlie suggested that large corporations divert a portion of their advertising budgets away from specific products and institutional statements about the virtues of capitalism and redirect their money toward making "a determined effort to sell their shares to the public." He added: "I can think of nothing that would build a stronger democratic capitalism, nothing which would provide a stronger defense against the threat of Communism, than the wider ownership of stocks in the country."

Before saying good-bye and sounding the gavel for the last time, Charlie reassured everyone attending the conference that when he died – whatever the date – the $4.5 million in his capital account would stay invested in the firm for at least another five years and possibly longer. After providing several key details about the general terms of his will, he mused: "It's a funny thing about the United States and the people that live in it; they work like hell – they fight like hell – they scratch, they bite, they yell, and they scream – and when they kick the bucket, they give it all away." He continued: "That is something that the English and French simply can't get through their heads. What makes us tick? I think the only thing that makes us tick is that we love our country, we love our fellow man, and we love to serve our neighbors and make them happy; just as well as we serve the members of our family." Charlie may have gone overboard in citing a series of generalities as motivating factors, but he was certainly right about the generous character of American philanthropy, which proudly traces its roots to Carnegie and Rockefeller and even further back in time to other less well known business leaders.[11] Charlie left substantial sums directly to Amherst College and Harvard University, and many other educational institutions and charities benefited from the Merrill Trust, which disbursed gifts for more than twenty years after his death.

Before leaving the podium, Charlie profusely thanked the group for the birthday gift presented to him the previous night. "I just don't want to break down and cry – I came close to crying last night; I did wipe my face four or five times." Maintaining his composure, he continued: "I can't think of anything that has touched me quite as much as to have you endow a scholarship at Amherst College in my name. . . . it's one of the most sweet, generous, and touching things that has ever happened to me." Given his wealth at the time, the funds involved in creating the endowment were not all that consequential, but the thought behind the gift made a tremendous impact on the thankful recipient. Charlie was genuinely appreciative of the respect and support of his business associates, some of whom had also been his closest and most valued friends for many, many years.

While Charlie Merrill possessed incredible foresight with regard to the development of U.S. capital markets and what products and services would likely prove beneficial to millions of investors of all stripes, he was not infallible or uniformly prescient. His one major strategic miscalculation was his inability to comprehend the vast potential of mutual funds as a vehicle for prudent long-term investment, particularly for small and medium-sized accounts, in the post–World War II era. Some of the younger members on the Merrill Lynch staff tried to enlighten the directing partner about the many positive aspects of mutual funds, but Charlie remained unpersuaded. He rejected what, in retrospect, was sound advice from subordinates with their ears close to the ground; one anecdote is indicative of the prevailing atmosphere at that time.

In the early 1950s, Don Regan, the whiz kid who had become Robert Magowan's top assistant in the sales department, studied the whole mutual fund sector in depth and concluded that certain types of funds would be highly appropriate for any brokerage firm that was striving to reach millions of middle-class households with limited financial resources. Regan drafted a lengthy report recommending that the firm recognize the legitimacy of mutual funds and start promoting their sale to customers as an

11. Stephen Girard, a Philadelphia banker, left more than $6 million to establish a school for the education of orphans in 1831; adjusting for inflation, that sum would exceed $100 million in 1995 dollars and place him in about the same league as Merrill. Indeed, American millionaires have been especially generous with their gifts to colleges and universities. The same charitable attitude toward educational institutions is less evident in other nations and cultures.

alternative to direct investments in the common stocks of individual corporations. Charlie, Smith, and Magowan were all privy to the confidential report. A few days after handing the file over to his boss, Regan became restless waiting for some response from the senior partners. Finally, Magowan agreed to broach the topic of mutual funds and the contents of Regan's report during a weekend gathering at Charlie's residence on Long Island, an informal setting where business and recreational activities routinely intermixed. Early the next Monday, Regan popped into Magowan's office and inquired about the outcome of the discussion. Magowan explained that Charlie had rejected the idea out of hand, arguing that the firm had never had any success with mutual funds. Smith echoed those sentiments, citing his experience with the Pierce organization in the 1930s. Regan then asked, "And how about you? Didn't you speak up?" Magowan responded sheepishly, "No, I agreed with them." Regan irreverently blurted out: "Christ – shot down by the Father, Son, and Holy Ghost!"[12]

Regan was hugely disappointed by the reaction of the two senior partners because he knew Magowan was sympathetic toward his mutual funds initiative. The written report had been a trial balloon launched by Regan, with Magowan acting as a noncommittal accomplice; they gambled that Charlie and Smith might be willing to reconsider their outlook about what was certain to be a controversial topic. Although Charlie usually thought he knew all the answers when it came to sound investment principles, he was occasionally willing to contemplate new concepts that ran against the grain or challenged prevailing taboos. Ted Braun had more luck in redirecting his thinking about crucial matters than probably anybody else either in or outside of the organization. But Regan lacked such clout. When the sales department's trial balloon was summarily pricked at Charlie's Southampton home, Magowan judiciously decided to avoid a confrontation and wait for another, more propitious opportunity to press the issue. Some years later, Regan became CEO, and he was more successful in forcing his partners to wake up to the changing realities of the marketplace and to respond more positively to the undeniable revolution in mutual funds. In time, the firm sponsored a series of mutual funds under the Merrill Lynch banner. But nothing along those lines emerged in the 1950s.

To be completely fair in this context, Charlie's reservations about the prudence of promoting the sale of mutual funds were justifiable given the uneven performance of that financial sector during the first half of the twentieth century. We need to keep in mind that most mutual funds were a much, much different breed of animal in the 1930s and 1940s than what most of us are familiar with today. The origins of modern mutual funds

12. Regan interview conducted by Engberg, Sept. 1982, ML Files.

can be traced to innovations in the London and Amsterdam capital markets in the nineteenth century.[13] The term commonly accepted in British circles to describe this type of financial vehicle was *investment trust*. Most of the early mutuals were so-called closed-end funds. The sponsors sold shares to the general public with the assistance of a prominent underwriter and then invested the capital not in plant, equipment, or inventories but rather in the stocks and bonds of other corporations.

The purported advantages to investors in the funds were primarily twofold. First, buyers achieved instant diversification even with a modest investment because the fund typically held the securities of numerous corporations in several industries. Second, a fund was continuously monitored by financial experts who, in theory, bought the shares of companies with a profitable outlook and, equally important, routinely removed from the portfolio the securities of companies with declining prospects. The investor in a mutual fund was, therefore, relieved of the burden of trying to analyze reams of information and then deciding at what price to buy or sell a specific stock or bond. Fund managers usually received fees for their services based on the aggregate value of the securities in the portfolio; annual fees varied but were usually a moderate figure such as 1 percent or less of total assets.

Closed-end funds, past and present, possessed one negative characteristic that dismayed critics and limited their long-term popularity. Since they traded on the stock exchanges in auction markets like other securities, fluctuating opinions about the direction of the broader stock market could drive the prices of mutual shares either higher (premium) or lower (discount) than the underlying value of the securities in their portfolios.

To illustrate the principle briefly, let us consider the following example: suppose a closed-end mutual fund held the stocks of several hundred companies, which, if sold separately, would likely generate sufficient cash to return $100 per share to investors. Simple logic would suggest that, if the probable liquidating value of a fund's portfolio was $100 per share, then the fund's share would likely trade on the exchanges at a price very close to that $100 – maybe just a few dollars above or below that figure. Unfortunately, in many instances the shares of closed-end funds defied the rules of logic. While the prices of certain funds on the exchanges did hover close to their probable liquidation value, many funds, in contrast, traded at substantial discounts or premiums. Indeed, it was not uncommon for

---

13. In his recent book on Dutch investment in American railroads, Veenendaal claims that the first modern mutual fund was created in Amsterdam in 1774 to invest in a portfolio of ten foreign bonds; see *Slow Train*, 153–63.

closed-end funds to change hands in secondary markets at premiums or discounts ranging from 5 to 15 percent.

The main danger in these deviations from liquidating value was that, during a prolonged stock market boom, the premium on certain funds with strong performance records would occasionally rise to 30 or 40 percent, which put them at risk of a potentially tremendous downfall when sentiments on Wall Street shifted from bull to bear. In an unfavorable market, premiums on mutual fund shares could quickly disappear and even be converted into heavy discounts within just a few months. When that happened, persons who had invested in a closed-end fund at a very high premium often suffered more severe capital losses during a sharp downturn than would have been the case if they had actually owned the underlying corporate shares in the fund's portfolio. In short, the closed-end mutual fund, rather than functioning as a prudent investment vehicle, in many cases produced more uncertainty and displayed more price volatility than individual stocks. Closed-end funds, under certain circumstances, could become highly speculative investments.

In the late stages of the stock market boom of the 1920s, the number of new closed-end mutual funds rose dramatically. As late as March 1927, about fifty funds regularly traded on Wall Street. A year later, their number had risen more than threefold. The total value of all mutual fund portfolios in 1924 was less than $10 million; before the crash in October 1929 their portfolio values had skyrocketed to $3 billion.[14] The typical fund traded at nearly a 50 percent premium above liquidation value. A year later, in the aftermath of the crash, the average fund traded instead at a 25 percent discount. While the Dow-Jones industrials had dropped about 40 percent, the typical mutual fund was down more than 70 percent. By the low point in 1932, most closed-end mutual funds had fallen 80 to 90 percent below their previous highs, and the majority were soon defunct.[15]

Meanwhile, the popularity of closed-end funds was so great in the late 1920s that none other than Charlie Merrill was at one point busy formulating an ambitious plan to join the crowd. Energized by the growth prospects of Safeway Stores, in which he was the controlling stockholder, and the success of other chain store operators in the food retailing sector,

---

14. Rottersman and Zweig, "Early History of Mutual Funds," 14. This excellent article appeared in a publication sponsored by the Museum of American Financial History; the magazine title is *Friends of Financial History: Chronicling the History of America's Capital Markets.*

15. One closed-end fund that performed reasonably well, relative to its competition, from 1925 to 1935 was State Street Investment Trust managed by Paul Cabot. The fund shifted into highly liquid assets after the 1929 crash and then reinvested heavily in common stocks near their lows in 1933. For a capsule biography of Cabot, see the insert by Alan Levine in *Friends of Financial History* (Spring 1994), 13–14.

Charlie and his business partners actually drafted a formal prospectus for a new closed-end fund. To be underwritten and subsequently managed by Merrill, Lynch, it proposed to attract investors by accumulating a diversified portfolio of securities issued by major grocery chains across the United States. But when equity prices on the NYSE failed to recover in 1930, Charlie scotched the whole project. Charlie probably thanked his lucky stars for his good timing on that missed opportunity. If he had proceeded at a faster clip and actually sold fund shares to the general public, he might easily have been stigmatized in the 1930s as the irresponsible promoter of a closed-end mutual fund that produced tremendous losses for thousands of unsophisticated investors.[16] Having dodged a speeding bullet once with respect to the lure of mutual funds, Charlie was extremely careful not to put himself directly in the line of fire on a second occasion. The poor performance of mutual funds in the early 1930s and his own near miss with the grocery chain project left him skeptical about their viability, and he was not about to reassess this attitude in his waning years.

What complicated the debate in the early 1950s, when Regan and Magowan wanted to explore opportunities in a new light, was the growing popularity of a different type of mutual fund that had previously attracted only a tiny fraction of American investors: the "open-end" mutual fund. (The vast majority of mutual funds in the United States today, including those managed by Fidelity, Dreyfus, T. Rowe Price, and Vanguard, are open-end funds.) These funds differed in several ways from their closed-end cousins. For example, the shares of open-end funds, once issued to investors, never traded in secondary markets. The issuing companies agreed in advance to redeem shares promptly in response to customer requests at the portfolio's current liquidation value, a policy that instantaneously eliminated the potential problem of rising premiums or falling discounts. The redemption of shares was a transaction service performed by the fund managers for fairly modest fees.[17]

The number of shares outstanding in open-end funds were not limited to any preset figure but could be easily expanded or reduced in response to customer demand. To acquire shares, investors paid commissions ranging from 8 to 12 percent (about two or three times more than the standard rate for transactions involving regularly traded common stocks). These up-

16. The irony here is that at the same time Charlie was warning customers to reduce their exposure to equity markets in 1928 and 1929, he was actively pursuing the opportunities associated with the creation of a closed-end fund linked to Merrill, Lynch. Perhaps he thought grocery chains would be less vulnerable than industrials and railroads in a bear market. Many grocery chains did hold up better than the broad indexes if measured on a relative basis, but most nonetheless lost more than 50 percent of their precrash value.
17. Most of the early mutual fund issuers charged what today we call "backend fees" – for example, a flat two dollars per share or a payment based on a percentage of liquidation value.

front fees became known in financial lingo as the "load." In some cases the issuers sold shares directly to investors; in other instances, the issuers arranged to distribute their funds through cooperating brokerage houses, with the sales commission divided according to some prearranged formula. Investors in open-end funds received the advantages of diversification and professional portfolio management, and, like the owners of closed-end funds, they usually paid an annual management fee of 1 percent or less based on the aggregate value of the portfolio. After making a minimal threshold investment, say $200 to $500, customers usually had the opportunity to purchase additional shares, or even fractional shares, at regular intervals with payments as low as $10 to $25. The issuers of open-end mutual funds directed their promotional materials at investors seeking a reliable stream of future income plus capital appreciation over the long term whether the sums committed by customers were small, medium-sized, or exceedingly large. The antithesis of active traders, mutual fund investors typically held their shares for years or decades.

The first investment vehicle in the United States with most of the characteristics of the modern open-end fund was the Alexander Fund, established in Philadelphia in 1907. Other funds based on similar principles, but usually with different issuance and redemption procedures, followed over the next two decades. Launched in 1924, Massachusetts Investors Trust was among the first to proclaim its intention of investing exclusively in the common stocks of established corporations, forgoing completely bonds and preferred stocks. Seeking to attract new customers through the established brokerage network, the issuers signed an agreement in 1927 with Learoyd, Foster & Company to distribute shares to interested investors. The minimum investment, five shares in this instance, cost $250 plus the sales commission of $12.50; the total of $262.50 was about the price of a new Model T Ford and well within the range of most upper-middle-class households.

Massachusetts Investors Trust boasted 5,000 shareholders and $14 million invested in the common stocks of more than one hundred corporations at the end of 1929. Hammered like all other common stock investors by the bear market, the fund's portfolio lost in excess of 80 percent of its value from 1929 to 1932, although the managers continued to pay token dividends. Given similarly huge declines in the market value of private holdings of common stocks, a still small but growing number of individual investors decided to entrust their savings to professional management. One beneficiary of this trend was Massachusetts Investors Trust, which grew to more than 20,000 investors and $30 million in assets by the end of 1934. When stock prices rebounded from their lows in 1932, many unflinching investors recouped a significant portion of their paper losses. The fund survived the depression, and its managers produced solid returns during the 1940s. They demonstrated that open-end funds, properly administered, were a sensible option for common stock investors who sought a steady income from dividends plus the benefits of consistent capital gains. Many brokerage firms agreed to become distribution agents not only for Massachusetts Investors Trust but also for other new open-end funds that entered the market in the late 1940s and early 1950s. Merrill Lynch, however, brushed aside all mutual fund inquiries from mutual fund executives about the use of its unparalleled distribution system.

In addition to his fading memories of one close call with the scuttled proposal for a closed-end fund devoted to chain stores, Charlie, at various times in the early 1950s, expressed additional reasons for opposing the sale of open-end mutual funds. He was concerned that if the funds became too popular, the demand for the transaction services routinely performed by brokerage firms would correspondingly diminish. Admittedly, the commissions that brokers at competing firms were reportedly earning on the sale of mutual funds were generous, but thereafter the normal routine of selling securities with deteriorating prospects and buying more promising replacements – the broker's normal repeat business – was bound to suffer. Mutual fund investors had the reputation of rarely reducing or shifting their assets to alternative investments; moreover, when investors decided to liquidate shares, the transaction was handled internally by the original issuer rather than through a negotiated exchange in secondary markets. Brokerage would become a less remunerative occupation if the services performed became increasingly one-dimensional – arranging purchases of mutual fund shares and doing little else. From Charlie's perspective, the firm's endorsement of mutual funds would be the equivalent of advising all investors to adopt a rigid buy and hold policy. In that altered atmosphere, brokerage houses would steadily lose volume and might not generate sufficient revenues to stay afloat.

Charlie likewise believed that the individual investor could achieve all the benefits usually associated with mutual funds by working closely with Merrill Lynch brokers to build a personal portfolio designed to meet very specific needs. To obtain the proper amount of diversification, for example, investment experts had long argued that a medium-sized portfolio, containing the common stocks of no more than eight to twenty leading companies, with each selected from a different business sector, was normally sufficient. It typically carried no greater risk of price volatility than a large portfolio composed of hundreds of different securities.[18] Except for begin-

---

18. The validity of this claim about an adequate degree of diversification in portfolios containing eight to twenty stocks has come under scholarly attack in recent years. In a study at the

ning investors with little money, adequate diversification was within the grasp of most customers. Finally, Charlie was unwilling to concede that the managers of mutual funds had any better sources of timely financial information than the typical Merrill Lynch customer. By the 1950s the firm had assembled one of the best, if not the very best, staff of security analysts anywhere in the country. By discussing their specific financial goals with their regular broker and listening to sound advice, Merrill Lynch customers could successfully manage their own personalized portfolios. Indeed, in most cases the customer could tailor an investment program designed to perform even more effectively than what could be achieved by sinking money into an amorphous mutual fund, in which portfolio managers marshaled a varied pool of stocks designed to satisfy the multifaceted, and often incompatible, requirements of thousands of disconnected investors.

Charlie's advocacy of the Merrill Lynch approach to long-term financial success versus the mutual fund route had much to recommend it. Few of his arguments could be easily dismissed or contradicted, which explains why Regan and Magowan, the two junior revolutionaries, had no luck in getting to first base with their aging mentor. From a certain perspective Charlie was standing on unassailable ground. In the early 1950s, the number of open-end mutual funds was limited and front-loan commission rates were relatively high, often 8 to 12 percent. While mutual funds admittedly had the potential of providing adequate financial returns to unsophisticated customers, Charlie sincerely believed that experienced investors who wanted superior performance were better served by traditional methods. A well-trained Merrill Lynch broker could help a customer accumulate the most appropriate types of financial assets, and then reshape that portfolio periodically with judicious sales and substitutions.

What Charlie failed to fully comprehend, however, was that these two fundamental approaches to investing were not mutually exclusive but were instead potentially complementary and reinforcing. For the beginning investor with limited resources, mutual funds were a sensible starting point because they provided instant diversification for even the smallest portfolio. Because he himself was so fascinated with the challenges of the stock market, Charlie also failed to understand that many otherwise successful people were painfully uncomfortable in dealing with balance sheets, income statements, and everything associated with the selection and rejection of

---

University of Nevada, Gerald Newbould and Percy Poon demonstrated that investors seeking to stay within 10 percent of the average market volatility and within 10 percent of average market return over the long term needed to hold roughly equal proportions of at least 60 large-capitalization stocks or somewhat more than 100 small-cap stocks. "Portfolio Strategy," *Market Logic* (July 3, 1996), p. 7.

securities. They wanted to entrust other professionals with the ultimate authority and responsibility, and mutual fund managers were more than willing to perform those duties. Another attribute of mutual funds was that they tended to attract investors who were committed to seeking financial rewards over the long haul; mutual fund investors were not speculators chasing easy money. Most were long-term, life-cycle savers with the patience to ride out the unpredictable gyrations of the stock market over a period of years. According to Merrill Lynch's promotional material, these were the very same type of customers Charlie and his partners were supposedly trying to solicit and serve.

Charlie's thinking was also way below par with respect to how the rise of independent mutual funds might impact the volume of trades on the organized exchanges and over the counter. He concentrated on the potential downside: the possibility of fewer trades by individuals who decided to sell their entire inventory of stocks and shift their capital permanently into mutual funds. In the early 1950s at least 90 percent of the trading volume was initiated by private individuals, so there was a great deal at stake in the rivalry between brokerage houses and mutual fund issuers. Again, Charlie was slow to grasp that even if the funds claimed an increasing share of the total equities market, the securities themselves would not cease to circulate but simply come under the tighter control of a smaller group of decision makers – the fund managers. Since there were, at the time, no pure index funds that were wedded to a buy and hold investment strategy, the various fund managers were free to exercise their judgment about the purchase and sale of huge blocks of securities in their portfolios. In an effort to demonstrate superior performance and attract more accounts, many fund managers had high turnover rates. In short, trading itself did not halt once individuals had moved out of stocks and bonds and into mutual funds; instead, the trading occurred under different circumstances, and those circumstances were likely to produce tremendous economies of scale for brokerage houses since the prevailing rules and regulations on Wall Street prevented any discounts to customers such as the managers of mutual funds who authorized extraordinarily large transactions. Indeed, the largest brokerage houses, including Merrill Lynch, were in the most favorable position to serve the transactions needs of fund managers because they had the resources to execute orders involving tens of thousands of shares quickly and efficiently.

Ironically, Merrill Lynch had already responded in a thoroughly positive manner to the requirements of other types of institutional investors that employed professional money managers. By the early 1950s, the firm had assigned special sales representatives at its New York headquarters to service exclusively institutional customers. Insurance companies and independent pension funds were the main accounts. Both groups were swamped with regular inflows of cash that they invested in a mixture of securities that depended, first, on certain legal requirements and, second, on the judgment of professional money managers. After shocking revelations of unregulated imprudence in the early twentieth century, many states had passed new laws that stipulated institutional investments in a restricted class of securities such as government and corporate bonds that stressed safety rather than extra income and capital gains. The preferred stocks of corporations with solid dividend records sometimes turned up on eligibility lists. By midcentury, however, some states had relaxed the rules and allowed money managers more latitude in the selection of securities, including the option of adding a certain percentage of common stocks, usually in the blue-chip category, to institutional portfolios. Thus, Merrill Lynch already had experience in dealing with the expectations of institutional money managers, and, in retrospect, we can safely conclude that they almost certainly had all the skills necessary to assist the managers of open-end mutual funds in the selection of common stocks with outstanding appreciation potential.

In one of the very few instances in his long and distinguished career, Charlie simply failed to consider what type of service might be in the best interest of certain groups of serious investors. Instead, he placed the welfare of the firm – his partners and loyal employees – on a higher plane than the dictates of those impersonal market forces so clearly identified as paramount two centuries earlier by the political economist Adam Smith. In the past, Charlie had usually ranked the requirements of individual investors – outstanding service at fair prices – as the top priority in decision making, but when it came to mutual funds, his vision blurred. Charlie saw mutual funds as rivals that threatened his enterprise and other responsible firms in the brokerage sector. He probably hoped that during the next stock market downturn, investors would lose confidence in the managers of open-end funds, and that these upstarts would go the way of most closed-end funds after the 1929 crash: completely out of business. And if some competitors (the brokerage houses that greedily sold mutual funds to boost their earnings) were discredited as well, so much the better. Charlie's adamant opposition to mutual funds influenced the outlook of Smith and McCarthy as well. As a consequence, the firm was slow to recognize the legitimate appeal of mutual funds to small accounts and, in time, to more substantial investors with vast sums available for permanent investment.

As a result of Charlie's biases, the firm's policy during his lifetime was to avoid suggesting mutual funds to customers as prudent investments. In conformity with that policy, the research staff did not monitor the performance of the portfolio managers of open-end mutual funds, and, as a consequence, it was unable to offer anything in the way of buy and sell recommendations to inquiring customers. Brokers were instructed to arrange purchases of mutual funds for customers who absolutely insisted on their inclusion in investment portfolios, but those customers were flying blind as far as the Merrill Lynch staff was concerned. Presumably, customers who were strongly attracted to the diversification and trusteeship aspects of open-end mutual funds took their business to competing brokerage houses that had a more accommodating attitude toward what in the 1950s remained a fairly novel investment vehicle in the U.S. market.

Because the leaders in the brokerage field were slow to recognize the tremendous growth potential in the mutual fund sector, other organizations – outsiders in Wall Street circles, just as Charlie Merrill had been at the start of his long career – took advantage of the window of opportunity and responded more positively to market signals. By the end of the twentieth century, approximately one-third of U.S. households owned mutual funds, and Fidelity Investments, a Boston-based firm that launched its first open-end fund in the 1930s, had become the recognized leader in the field. In the mid-1990s, the assets in Fidelity's numerous funds accounted for approximately 3 percent of the entire U.S. equities market and 1.5 percent of the global equities market. Merrill Lynch eventually became a major player in the mutual funds sector but did not rule the roost as it had in underwriting and stock brokerage.

Charlie missed the boat on open-end mutual funds, but he was among the first to endorse one fresh idea with somewhat similar goals that came from a most unlikely source – the bowels of the New York Stock Exchange. Victor Cook, who joined Merrill Lynch at the time of the Fenner & Beane merger in 1941 and who almost left the firm until Charlie turned him around during the scheduled exit interview, was a member of the NYSE committee that worked out the details for the Monthly Investment Plan. MIP was an innovative program that allowed people with modest incomes to invest a small amount of money in common stocks listed on the exchange on a monthly or quarterly basis without incurring prohibitively high minimum commissions on odd-lot transactions.

After years of complaining loudly that the NYSE was a suicidal institution mired in outdated traditions and out of touch with the changing needs of the investing public, Charlie was elated to witness the unprecedented initiatives taken by exchange officials. More than three decades earlier, soon after U.S. entry into World War I, he had been slapped on the wrist by NYSE officials for challenging long-standing advertising codes. After the scandal involving NYSE president Richard Whitney in the late 1930s, the new leadership had dramatically shifted course and adopted policies designed to drag member firms into modern times, but from Charlie's viewpoint, the commitment to attracting new customers was insufficient. Merrill Lynch fought continuously for lower minimum commissions on stock transactions with the goal of signing up thousands of new accounts, but peers with lower volume usually lobbied instead to raise the minimum limits, and they usually prevailed. Other firms tended to view investor demand for transaction services as essentially inelastic over the short, intermediate, and long run. Charlie and his partners believed that lower minimum fees would attract enough new business to produce greater gross revenues and higher profits in the long run. By the mid-1950s Merrill Lynch had sufficient clout on Wall Street that its highly publicized campaign to allow interested investors on limited budgets to systematically acquire stocks could not be easily ignored by Keith Funston, president of the NYSE, and other powerful figures on Wall Street.

The Monthly Investment Plan, introduced in January 1954, was a compromise between competing groups – namely, Merrill Lynch and the majority of member firms. Minimum rates for routine trades by regular customers were maintained at prevailing levels, which satisfied the majority; the reduced fees applied strictly to predominantly odd lot trades by a small group of beginning investors who took the trouble to sign up in advance for the special program. Enrollees could accumulate stocks, including fractional shares, by investing as little as $40 quarterly, which translated into $160 annually (about $900 in 1995 prices). Customers of any age and occupation were eligible, but the fundamental concept was roughly similar to the discount prices some automobile dealers and real estate developers offer to "first-time buyers," usually people in their twenties or early thirties. Minors were also eligible. The minimum annual investment was about the same as the premiums many households were paying to maintain whole-life policies. The brokerage sector was finally becoming more competitive with its main rival for investment dollars in the twentieth century.

NYSE officials forecast that Merrill Lynch would likely handle the lion's share of the money-losing transactions, and their expectations were fulfilled. During the first calendar year, the firm signed up nearly one-half of all participants. A few years later Merrill Lynch serviced about 70 percent of all MIP accounts. By the end of the decade, most competitors were no longer enrolling new MIP accounts. Years later, after the deregulation of fees and prices, Merrill Lynch transferred the remaining MIP accounts to its own Sharebuilder Plan, which permitted customers to buy and sell just a few shares of stock at low commissions. Whether MIP, given the high cost of record keeping for thousands of small accounts, was a profitable venture over the long term is difficult to assess. Some enrollees built a sizable portfolio within two to five years and eventually became active traders. Many new customers found the $40 monthly minimum a greater sum than they were either able or willing to devote to investments, and their accounts went inactive. One thing we can say with certainty is that the fundamental concept of the MIP was compatible with Charlie's strategy of involving thousands of young adults who seemed headed for the upper middle class, or higher, in the expanding capital markets.

Perhaps the most important benefit of the MIP was how the firm used its endorsement of the program in advertising campaigns to complement its other promotional efforts. For example, in 1956, the partners placed an informational booth in the middle of Grand Central Station, the hub of New York City's rail transportation system, to publicize their commitment to "People's Capitalism," a purposely all-inclusive term. Lou Engel created a series of advertisements to assure potential customers of modest means that they could anticipate a warm welcome at more than one hundred branch offices from coast to coast. Meanwhile, the NYSE spent a fair portion of its institutional advertising budget to hype the program. Potential participants were encouraged to inquire about the details at any convenient brokerage office of any member firm. The prime beneficiary of NYSE advertising was, in this instance, Merrill Lynch. Competitors may have been displeased about that outcome, but justice was unquestionably served; for more than a decade Merrill Lynch had spent millions of dollars on advertisements that reassured the public about the long-term safety and superior performance of common stocks. The promotional campaigns of Charlie and his partners had generated business, not only for their own enterprise, but indirectly for other brokerage houses as well. In rising waters, all boats float higher, and Merrill Lynch had done more since 1940 than any other private institution, including the NYSE itself, to help the brokerage sector overcome its tarnished public image. By the early 1950s everyone on Wall Street, including legions of former skeptics, recognized what Charlie and his organization had accomplished in terms of enhancing the status and reputation of brokers, irrespective of employer or affiliation.

The advertising for the MIP was effective in attracting new accounts from many previously reticent prospects who had been intimidated by the frightening mysteries surrounding the financial markets or who were simply distrustful of brokers. The $40 quarterly investment was the minimum commitment; there were no restrictions on investing larger amounts. Many upper-middle-class households with the financial resources to acquire securities beyond the minimal level finally realized that Merrill Lynch was genuinely interested in providing sound guidance to a wide range of customers, not just those who were already fabulously wealthy. Indeed, all the publicity about the MIP probably had its greatest impact on households somewhat higher on the economic scale than the targeted audience. The MIP served the interests of Merrill Lynch over the long run because it made an indelible impression on investors who had increasing amounts of discretionary income and the resolve to supplement the cash surrender value in life insurance policies with sensible and sound investments that could produce annual returns of 10 to 12 percent rather than a mere 4 to 6 percent. By 1956, Merrill Lynch was handling 19 percent of the odd lot volume on the NYSE, a new high in terms of market share.

In his last years, Charlie's most critical business decision was only indirectly related to the affairs of Merrill Lynch. In 1955, he decided to replace Ling Warren, the CEO at Safeway Stores since the mid-1930s. Charlie was still the controlling stockholder, and the Merrill family, including all the various trusts, actually had a greater financial stake in Safeway Stores than any other business enterprise. When Charlie returned to the financial services sector in 1940, he put his faith in Warren, a fellow Floridian, and granted him a great deal of autonomy. Within a few years, Charlie was hearing complaints from several sources about Safeway's management, but poor health kept him from paying close attention to events in distant Oakland. Warren came east to confer about important matters on a regular basis, but Charlie never traveled to the West Coast after 1944. Following the improvement in his physical condition in 1953, Charlie began to investigate the Safeway situation in greater depth and to ponder the wisdom of a change in leadership. Charlie discovered that Warren had progressively centralized the decision-making system and had become a minor autocrat; for example, regional managers were not permitted to discuss matters of common interest without first gaining permission from the CEO.[19] Warren also made a strategic miscalculation by overemphasizing Safeway's private label brands.

The only two contenders for the job at Safeway in Charlie's mind were Mike McCarthy and Robert Magowan. McCarthy was Win Smith's top assistant and had been third in the chain of command since Charlie's first heart attack in 1944. McCarthy started his career in California with a grocery chain that was absorbed by Safeway in the early 1930s, and it seemed possible that he might welcome a return to the more casual lifestyle in California. At Merrill Lynch, he would have to defer to Smith before gaining promotion to the top spot in the organization. Magowan had also spent some time in California working for Safeway in the mid-1930s and thus was familiar with the region and its climate. Neither man had any

19. Magowan interview with Engberg, Nov. 1982, ML Files.

experience as a top executive in the grocery field, so they were on fairly equal terms on that score. Whether Charlie chose Magowan because McCarthy demurred, or because Magowan actively campaigned for the position, or because Charlie favored Magowan from the outset is unclear from surviving records, but this transfer of executive power between the two largest organizations under Charlie's direct control had tremendous long-run implications. Safeway and the grocery trade, not Merrill Lynch and securities, became the enterprise most closely associated with the wealth and power of the Merrill family from 1955 forward.

While wintering at Canfield House in Barbados in 1956, Charlie developed a series of irritating skin diseases that persisted for months. In June and July, he spent nearly a month at the Peter Bent Brigham Hospital in Boston, where a group of physicians under the direction of Dr. Samuel Levine addressed all his various infirmities, including progressive kidney failure. He left the hospital feeling fairly fit but his underlying health and his general attitude about his unstable condition waxed and waned over the next several months. Charlie was making plans to travel south for the fall season when he suddenly developed uremia; wastes that were normally processed by his kidneys rose to toxic levels and irritated his brain. On October 5, he lapsed into a coma; he died the following afternoon, just a few days short of his seventy-first birthday. After the funeral at the Church of the Ascension in New York, attended by more than seven hundred mourners, his body was sent to Palm Beach for burial. His grandparents, parents, and two sisters were already interred in Florida. In conformity with his wishes, he was buried wearing his army air corps uniform from World War I.

14

———— • ————

MERRILL'S LEGACY

Charles Merrill deserves high ranking on any list of the most influential entrepreneurs in American history. Because of his unparalleled contributions to the development and democratization of twentieth-century capital markets, future historians should place him in the same rarefied company with such familiar names as Andrew Carnegie, John D. Rockefeller, Thomas Edison, Henry Ford, Sam Walton, Bill Gates, and John Pierpont Morgan. The main reason for his lack of public recognition has been the paucity of information about his monumental accomplishments.

In the realm of financial services, Merrill has no peer in the twentieth century with respect to the broad impact of his entrepreneurship. J. P. Morgan, the acknowledged American leader in the investment banking field by the late nineteenth century, immediately comes to mind as the best-known Wall Street figure. But, Morgan was, in truth, less the entrepreneur since his main contribution to the development of the nation's financial sector was the expansion of an already successful firm started by his father, Junius Spencer Morgan, a decade before the Civil War. Operating out of a solitary office on Wall Street, Morgan catered to the capital requirements of railroads and industrial clients and, in tandem, to the income requirements of wealthy households with millions of dollars available for permanent investment in corporate and government bonds – plus a sprinkling of preferred and common stocks. Morgan was primarily interested in preserving the status quo, not in institutional innovation.

Merrill, in contrast, was the directing partner of a sprawling enterprise with branch offices in 108 cities that provided a full range of investment services, including securities transactions on secondary markets, commodities trading, and an increasing volume of underwriting for medium-sized corporations with outstanding growth prospects. Merrill was instrumental in initiating a series of private sector reforms on Wall Street in the 1940s that complemented the activities of the Securities and Exchange Commission, established by Congress in the 1930s. Together, these private and

public reforms set the stage for a rejuvenation of the capital markets after
the devastating effects of the Great Depression. Brokerage firms, not the
established investment banking houses, became the innovators on Wall
Street in the middle decades of the twentieth century; their marketing
strategies paralleled the initiatives of the leading companies in the retail
sector of the economy. Beginning in the 1950s millions of middle-class
households became regular investors in common stocks, and Merrill Lynch
led the way in providing services and guidance.

Merrill aimed his message about the prudence of long-term investments
in common stocks primarily at two groups that had participated only
marginally in capital markets prior to World War II. First, he targeted
households headed by younger people, many with roots in the middle
class, who were upwardly mobile and thus open to fresh ideas about how
best to accumulate greater wealth for a more secure future. Second, he
tried to reach every household, irrespective of age or occupation, that
already possessed the wherewithal to afford an upper-middle-class lifestyle
but had avoided equities and stockbrokers because of ignorance or fear.
Most of the people in these two categories had the capacity and the
commitment to regularly save a portion of their annual income; their main
investment vehicles had been bank savings accounts, U.S. savings bonds,
and whole-life insurance policies. Some had invested in stocks in the 1920s.
After the dismal performance of the stock market in the early 1930s,
cautious households were reluctant to venture into equities. In an effort to
alter perceptions and, in turn, investment patterns, Merrill strove to develop an organization with the capacity to draw a significant fraction of the
nation's hesitant households into the securities markets. While the firm
was prepared to help a wide range of customers meet varying financial
goals, the partners encouraged investors to build and maintain portfolios
containing largely the common stocks of well-managed corporations with
outstanding growth potential.

Through aggressive advertising and sales promotion, Merrill advanced
the concept that a well-chosen portfolio of common stocks promised
better-than-average total returns to patient investors – and without incurring undue risk – when both increased dividends and capital appreciation
were taken into account. By adhering to a systematic investment program
in common stocks over periods of ten, fifteen, or twenty-five years, households could accumulate sizable financial assets and move up several notches
on the economic scale. Following the pattern of Henry Ford, who set out
to build a reliable automobile that every middle-class American family,
urban or rural, could afford to buy and operate, Charlie Merrill dreamed
of creating a service organization that would educate millions of ordinary
Americans about sound investment principles and show them the path to

greater wealth and higher economic status through the accumulation of common stocks.

Merrill differed from other prominent American entrepreneurs in that his most meaningful contributions came late in his career. He also differed in that he failed to concentrate his energies on one business sector throughout his lifetime but abruptly shifted careers – not just once, but twice. Merrill actually had three successful business careers: the first, as underwriter and merchant banker (1914–29); the second, as chain store grocer (1930–39); and the third, as the leader of the nation's largest brokerage firm (1940–56).

Merrill's first solo venture was launched in 1914 when he rented office space, hired a secretary, and recruited a few securities salesmen. Edmund Lynch joined the firm within the year, and the partnership of Merrill, Lynch was born in 1914. Like many struggling firms on the fringes of Wall Street, it provided brokerage services for individual investors, and, when opportunities arose, solicited corporate clients that were seeking additional capital for expansion. The partners acted as underwriters for small and medium-sized companies that were unable to attract the attention of prominent investment banking houses like J. P. Morgan and Kuhn Loeb. Charlie formed close business ties with a number of entrepreneurs who were building regional chains of retail stores that offered customers reliable merchandise at low prices. Through the sale of bonds and preferred stock, plus limited issues of common stock in certain cases, Merrill, Lynch helped the CEOs of these corporations raise the capital to expand their operations. In many instances, the underwriter's compensation package included a sizable block of common stock or, alternatively, option contracts to buy shares of the corporation's common stock when, and if, prices rose. In one highly unusual transaction after the end of World War I, the partnership purchased controlling interest in the American division of Pathé, the French film producer and distributor. Lynch spent much of his time in the early 1920s managing the movie company, which distributed silent films, many with European casts, from its headquarters in New York City.

From 1915 to 1930, Merrill, Lynch engaged primarily in what today we call merchant banking. The partnership held large blocks of common stock issued by a number of its underwriting clients. Most of these corporations prospered, and their stocks soared. The partner's paper profits during the 1920s totaled in the millions. Merrill developed a particularly close relationship with Safeway Stores, a grocery chain originally based in Los Angeles. In one crucial transaction in 1926, Merrill convinced Lynch to sell the partnership's financial interest in Pathé to Joseph Kennedy, then a budding movie mogul, and to reinvest the proceeds in Safeway Stores.

Soon thereafter, Charlie had the foresight to predict as early as 1928 a probable sharp downturn in the stock market. He advised all the firm's brokerage customers to cease buying securities on margin and to curtail their indebtedness. After much prodding, he finally forced a reluctant Lynch and a majority of the firm's junior partners to heed similar advice. As a consequence, the partnership liquidated a large portion of its stock portfolio in the weeks before the crash in October 1929.

In the aftermath of the stock market crash, Charlie, at age forty-four, made a dramatic career shift. He decided to withdraw largely, but not entirely, from his involvement in the financial services sector. He and Lynch worked out an agreement to transfer the retail end of their business to E. A. Pierce, a respected brokerage firm with one of the nation's largest chains of branch offices covering about forty cities. Winthrop Smith, an Amherst alumnus who had been with Merrill, Lynch since 1916, was among the sales personnel who agreed to join the Pierce organization in 1930. Confident that the stock market would soon recover its momentum and that the retail end of the securities business had a bright future, Merrill and Lynch each agreed to invest $1.9 million of their personal funds in E. A. Pierce for a period of ten years. Meanwhile, Merrill, Lynch was downsized dramatically; its only significant transactions in the 1930s were underwritings that merely refinanced maturing bonds for long-standing corporate clients.

During his first career in the financial services sector, Charlie Merrill was already advocating many of the concepts and principles that, decades later, became well known to a wider public. From the outset, he instructed all the brokers employed by his firm to refrain from enticing customers with questionable rumors, hot tips, and the possibility of quick profits. He believed a broker's primary responsibility was to help every customer reach his or her stated financial objectives. Churning accounts (the common practice of recommending trades for no legitimate purpose other than the generation of lucrative brokerage commissions) was roundly condemned, and brokers who failed to obey the house rules were invited to resign. Charlie argued that before recommending the purchase of any class of securities, a broker should determine exactly what types of investments were genuinely appropriate for a specific customer. Retired persons living primarily on interest and dividends, for example, should never be sold anything of a speculative nature. For customers who could legitimately accept elements of stock market volatility, Charlie demanded that his staff make every effort to gather reliable information on well-managed companies with legitimate growth prospects. Charlie favored full disclosure of pertinent information to every customer, whether large or small. "Investigate, then invest" was one of the slogans he repeated in promotional materials from 1911 on. Straightforward dealing, he argued, was the only policy likely to generate the repeat business on which every sales representative thrived, and stock brokerage was no exception to that general principle.

In yet another departure from industry norms, he became an early advocate of informative advertising and sales promotion techniques. Merrill, Lynch had positive results with direct mail solicitations of prospective investors. The leadership on Wall Street, hoping to preserve the status quo, viewed all advertising, however reserved and restrained, as essentially a deviation from accepted professional standards, and the NYSE applied strict rules to member firms in an effort to limit its scope. Merrill was also an early advocate of the strategy of attracting a diverse group of customers even if the volume of trading that some customers generated was, on average, fairly modest. There was safety in numbers, he proclaimed; in a business where customer turnover was typically very high, the most sensible policy was to work constantly to add new accounts.

In short, Merrill was a prescient maverick. Many of the ideas that seemed unconventional and suspiciously unprofessional to contemporaries in the 1920s, he later had the opportunity to implement on a wider scale with profound and positive effects. In due time, he unmasked the hypocrisy of many of the self-serving "professional ethics" of the Wall Street establishment. These restrictive rules had been imposed, not to further the public interest, but simply to maintain the establishment's hegemony over the capital markets.

In his second career, Merrill was closely linked with the ascendancy of one of the nation's largest grocery chains. He devoted much energy in the late 1920s and early 1930s to overseeing the tremendous expansion of Safeway Stores from its regional base on the West Coast to other areas of the country. For three or four years, he was frequently on the road, arranging a series of mergers and acquisitions. When, in the mid-1930s, Safeway shifted to an emphasis on consolidation and the search for internal efficiencies, Merrill spent a greater percentage of his time in recreational pursuits – tennis, boating, bridge games, and improving his properties. He lived at the palatial Merrill's Landing in Palm Beach for about half the year, and at the Orchard, his Long Island home, during the other six months. Semiretirement is probably the most appropriate term to describe his occupational status from his late forties to his mid-fifties.

After Safeway's expansion phase had wound down, Merrill visited California two or three times annually to confer with CEO Ling Warren, whom he had installed in the early 1930s, and with other Safeway executives. Warren was also a frequent guest at Merrill's Landing and at the Orchard. Merrill's work pattern varied considerably during the late 1930s.

Sometimes he went several weeks without focusing closely on business matters; at other times, he devoted weeks of intense activity to addressing corporate problems or formulating new strategies. Although he held no official position in the Safeway hierarchy, not even heading the board of directors, Merrill owned a controlling interest in the corporation, and he called the shots on most critical issues.

Two developments during his Safeway decade were particularly noteworthy. First, Merrill was exposed to the challenges of merchandising staple goods through a network of thousands of retail outlets. Chains like Safeway took advantage of the economies of scale and scope to provide careful consumers with basic foodstuffs that offered genuine value. The modern supermarket, which allowed customers to roam the aisles and select items off the shelves, was changing the whole system of grocery retailing in some regions in the late 1930s, and Safeway was among the grocers in the forefront of this transition. There was something fundamentally egalitarian about the grocery business since almost everyone, irrespective of income level, was a steady customer, and that democratic element appealed strongly to Charlie Merrill's sense of self-worth. When he told friends and relatives that he wanted to be remembered by future generations as a man who helped millions of American consumers save a few pennies on the purchase of every quart of milk, he was quite sincere in his sentiments. Merrill also learned to appreciate the merchandising technique that relied on loss leaders – a few basic products sold at cost or sightly less than cost – to generate store traffic and produce higher volume overall. He rejected the concept, which had long dominated the thinking of most executives in the grocery trade, that every store manager should try to maintain rigid percentage markups on every product line.

During the political battle in California over the proposal to impose prohibitive taxes on multiple chain store outlets, Merrill met Ted Braun. The owner-manager of a small public relations consulting firm in Los Angeles, Braun was one of the few practitioners in the 1930s to employ truly reliable polling methodologies to assess public opinion. Once Braun gained an understanding of why so many consumers had so many negative feelings about chain stores, he helped craft a long-term advertising and promotional campaign that tried to educate citizens about fundamental issues. When all the votes in a statewide referendum were tallied, the chain stores won an overwhelming victory. The public chose low prices for good-quality products over the survival of thousands of high-priced and low-volume retail stores. Merrill was extremely impressed by Braun's performance, and the two men maintained a close business relationship over the next two decades. Together, they later introduced a series of fresh and revolutionary ideas to the Wall Street community.

At the urging of Win Smith, Merrill launched his third and final career in 1940. Smith persuaded his longtime friend and former partner to accept an invitation to return to Wall Street on a full-time basis. The ten-year partnership agreement that had governed E. A. Pierce since 1930 was about to expire, and the struggling brokerage firm was on the verge of dissolution. After incurring heavy losses in the second half of the 1930s, when trading volume on the stock exchanges shrank dramatically, its net worth was precariously low. The money that Merrill had committed to the Pierce firm in 1930 was largely dissipated. Smith had lost all, or almost all, of his personal savings as a consequence of his investment in the failing partnership. Although security prices on the NYSE had recovered from their horrendous lows of the early 1930s, citizens were nonetheless extremely reluctant to trade common stocks. With the possibility of American military involvement in another world war looming on the horizon, the outlook for the entire brokerage sector was bleak in 1940.

Given the circumstances, Charlie Merrill's motivations for coming out of semiretirement at age fifty-five and returning to the financial services sector to rescue a threatened enterprise deserve consideration. Most of his friends and long-term business associates advised, in no uncertain terms, that he avoid active participation. The mundane brokerage business was vastly different, they warned, from the glamorous merchant banking activities with which he had been associated in the 1920s. Despite a series of New Deal reforms, the public was leery of equities and the stockbrokers who encouraged their ownership. Trading volume on the NYSE was extremely low. Almost every brokerage house in the nation had realized losses from 1937 to 1939. With conditions generally deteriorating rather than improving, the prospects for a turnaround seemed slim to most impartial observers. Kinta Merrill, who had only recently become Charlie's third wife, was unenthusiastic about the prospect of any drastic change in her husband's work schedule and relaxed lifestyle.

Why Merrill chose to ignore a chorus of cautionary advice is open to speculation, and a thoroughly convincing explanation will likely remain elusive. His pronouncements for the historical record about his motivations consist mostly of abstractions and generalities. With the exception of confidences, confessions, and regrets expressed in letters to his daughter, Doris, with respect to marital problems with Hellen, his second wife, and occasionally in correspondence with his two sons, Charles Jr. and Jimmy, Charlie was not typically self-reflective. His vagueness may not, however, present an overwhelming handicap for useful historical analysis. Relying on the insights of Freudian psychology, all modern biographers realize that their subjects were not always fully aware of all the factors influencing their behavior.

We can quickly dismiss any burning desire to add materially to his personal fortune as the critical factor. Already a multimillionaire, with a substantial cash inflow from dividends on portfolio investments, he had little practical use for an enhanced income or additional assets. Since neither son had expressed any interest in pursuing a business career and both had disavowed most aspects of an upper-class lifestyle, increasing the size of his inheritable estate was a low priority.

The most plausible explanation for his entrepreneurial activity from 1940 to 1956 was his unquenchable desire to tackle an enormous challenge and emerge victorious. Merrill was presented with the perfect opportunity to test his boldest ideas on a grand scale in a real-world setting. An ambitious business leader, he set his sights on the equivalent of ascending Mt. Everest to the accomplished mountain climber: creating a nationwide organization with the capacity to provide reliable brokerage services for thousands of households in a forthright and honest manner at sensible prices; simultaneously, this revitalized enterprise would need to generate adequate compensation for its employees and also produce competitive returns for the investors who provided the capital. More than half the starting capital for the partnership came from Merrill alone. Fortunately, he possessed adequate financial resources to keep the enterprise afloat long enough to give his dreams, and Win Smith's dreams, too, a fair test in the marketplace.

Merrill had a vision of the future that his contemporaries on Wall Street generally lacked. Others allowed outmoded attitudes and traditions to govern their actions. For decades, the leadership in the financial district believed the gulf between the brokerage houses, which provided routine transaction services in secondary markets, and investment banking houses, which underwrote new issues of securities, was unbridgeable. Since the emergence of capital markets in the United States in the last decade of the eighteenth century, the primary focus of the leading underwriters had been on governmental and corporate indebtedness. The elite investment banking firms placed bonds with upper-class households, plus institutions like banks and insurance companies, that sought a steady, secure, and predictable income – and little more. Investors were encouraged to hold their bonds until their maturity dates, disregarding all intervening fluctuations in bond prices. For customers who absolutely insisted on acquiring securities with the potential for better-than-average returns, staid investment houses recommended the common stocks of a few choice railroads and large industrials. These investors anticipated that, when earnings increased, dividends on the outstanding common stock would rise at a roughly corresponding rate. For the prudent customer determined to invest in equities, the reward, which compensated for the extra risk of fluctuating prices on the stock exchanges, was the prospect of a steadily increasing cash flow from higher dividend rates plus, at best, modest capital gains.

Those persons seeking greater wealth from sharp advances in equity prices, whether in the short run or over the long term, were forced to turn to other providers of financial services in the securities field. These investors were uniformly labeled as speculators – persons with a penchant for reckless gambling; they interacted with the less respectable elements on Wall Street. Speculators transacted business exclusively with the retail brokerage houses that handled transfers in the secondary markets. To sum up the overall situation, the functioning capital markets represented a seemingly undissolvable marriage of extremes: cautious investors seeking safety and expressing a willingness to settle for modest returns existed in more or less harmony with allegedly irresponsible speculators who made fortunes or, alternatively, lost everything, by reacting quickly to inside information or responding to unconfirmed rumors about the direction of stock prices.

Charlie Merrill set out to bridge the chasm between prudence and speculation, and thereby expand the number of participants in the capital markets. He sought a middle way for households that hoped to realize higher returns over the long term and were willing to accept a modest increase in risk. He wanted to show millions of reluctant and fearful citizens that carefully selected equity investments in growing corporations could translate into substantial additions to household wealth over horizons of ten to twenty years or more. By the first half of the twentieth century, many middle-class households had sufficient resources, plus a strong motivation, to divert a portion of their income into various financial assets with the potential of providing a more secure retirement.

To supplement the monies invested in low-interest savings accounts at chartered financial institutions, many middle-class households turned increasingly to life insurance companies. The premium paid on a whole-life policy served two distinct purposes; it combined term coverage, which provided lump-sum payments to beneficiaries in the event of death, with a regimented savings program. This second feature led to steadily increasing cash surrender values with only a slight risk of loss. If the insured avoided an untimely death, policyholders had the option of collecting the accumulated cash value. Just as promised by the issuing companies, whole-life policies allowed households to accumulate financial assets over time, but the returns on the monies invested were relatively low – usually 3 to 4 percent annually. Merrill knew that sensible investments in common stocks could produce returns that were at least double and often triple the rates available from investments in whole-life policies, and the risk of loss was only slightly higher if the customer concentrated on blue-chip companies and held for at least ten years. For example, $500 invested annually in the savings feature of a whole-life policy earning 4 percent produced $6,245 after ten years, but the same amount invested regularly in common stocks that returned 10 percent (appreciation plus dividends) produced $8,765 – a sum 40 percent greater. Moreover, some common stocks returned 12 to 15 percent annually, and a few growth stocks even exceeded 20 percent. In short, the returns on whole-life policies were modest and limited, whereas the returns on common stocks were typically higher and open-ended.

In addition to the lessons he had learned about mass merchandising in the grocery trade, which were in some measure transferable to the moribund brokerage business, external developments in the 1930s were also important in creating an inviting atmosphere for Merrill's return to the financial services sector. Building on the precedents established by the Interstate Commerce Commission and various state commissions that regulated the activities of railroads and utilities, New Deal securities laws pried open previously closed doors and promoted the flow of straightforward information to curious investors, as well as to millions of potential investors. The playing field on Wall Street became more level – not perfectly level since insiders still had access to more reliable information, but more tolerably level. Corporate officials who broke the new laws either by withholding critical news or by releasing incorrect or misleading information were subject to criminal prosecution. Unethical brokers who misled or cheated customers could likewise be fined and sent to jail – the ultimate humiliation for the white-collar criminal. Federal regulation inspired trust, and it laid the necessary groundwork for the mass participation of American households in the equity markets. Merrill saw the opportunity, and he made it happen.

Although he agreed with the advocates of these new rules and regulations, Merrill was not actively involved in promoting governmental reform in the 1930s. It should be mentioned, however, that one of his partners, Edward Pierce, was among the handful of Wall Street figures to appear before congressional committees and urge tighter federal laws. The vast majority of prominent underwriters and representatives of the major stock exchanges opposed federal regulation. Pierce and Merrill concurred about the investor's need for greater access to pertinent financial data and about the advisability of new rules requiring security dealers and their representatives to adhere to the highest ethical principles. The two men became partners in 1930 when Merrill became a passive investor in E. A. Pierce. In 1940, they merged their two firms into a single enterprise. Pierce and Merrill were an outstanding duo; the former concentrated on the public, governmental sector, while the latter focused on reforming procedures in the private, unregulated financial sector through voluntary initiatives.

Given his critical role in promoting the reform of the nation's capital markets in the 1930s, Pierce, like Merrill, has not always received his full due from historians.

According to his three children, Merrill was not active in public affairs and was, indeed, rarely a contributor to any political party or to any political candidate's campaign. Like most of his friends and business associates, he was a registered Republican. And like millions of his fellow citizens, Charlie never hesitated to express political opinions at the dinner table or during social gatherings; mostly he espoused conservative views that stressed independence and self-reliance. On an abstract plane, Merrill disapproved of all "unnecessary" government intervention in the economy, although he voiced no serious objections to the regulatory policies of the SEC, which presumably met the Constitution's "necessary and proper" qualification. Merrill gave some money to fellow businessman Wendell Willkie during the presidential campaign of 1940, but that gesture was atypical. Except for a few mild jabs at President Franklin Roosevelt in speeches to Merrill Lynch employees in the early 1940s, Merrill generally avoided political topics in discussions of business strategy. In reading hundreds of letters and memorandums covering his entire career, I came across only isolated complaints about obstructionist politicians or misguided political organizations. While many of his peers in the business world frequently criticized the Democratic Party and President Roosevelt for promoting allegedly socialistic policies and thereby undermining the U.S. economy, Merrill kept his eyes focused narrowly on the immediate problems facing his enterprise in the marketplace.

Indeed, when he periodically turned his attention to the obstacles created by outside forces, Merrill reserved most of his animus for the "dinosaurs" running the NYSE, plus other Wall Street insiders who seemed incapable of comprehending what policies and programs were genuinely in their own best interest over the long term. The main conflict with the NYSE related to the enforcement of minimum commission rates on trades. The other brokerage houses, believing the demand for their services was essentially inelastic, regularly lobbied for higher minimum rates. Merrill and his partners thought the opposite; they battled to hold the line and advocated instead the lowering of minimum rates. Merrill, in short, was once again ahead of his time, and his vindication came in the last quarter of the century when rates and prices were subject to widespread deregulation.

Like many wealthy citizens in his income tax bracket, Merrill groused in private about the high rates, ranging from 70 to 90 percent for the top categories, that had been imposed during World War II. In public pronouncements, he was extremely vocal about reducing the taxes applied to capital gains arising from securities transactions, since these rates impacted negatively on his customers. In messages published in the firm's annual reports, the directing partner often advocated reductions in capital gains taxes as a spur to investment.

While he felt more comfortable with the self-reliance rhetoric of the Republican Party, Merrill must have felt grudging respect for Roosevelt and congressional Democrats since they had actually succeeded in reforming the financial markets. The self-reform platitudes of Wall Street conservatives had proved inadequate; stronger medicine was required, and only the federal government had the power to clean up the mess. Although Merrill and Joseph Kennedy, the Democratic businessman who was surprisingly named the first head of the SEC, never maintained a personal or business relationship after completing the transaction involving the sale of Pathé Studios in 1926, the two men had reasonably parallel views about what steps were necessary to revive the U.S. capital markets. No one working for Merrill Lynch from 1940 forward was required to pass muster with regard to their political or religious beliefs.[1] Despite his Republican leanings, Merrill embraced an aggressive strategy that aimed to democratize the market for common stocks. He welcomed a more inclusive society where tens of millions owned equities and where sharp differences between the wealth accumulation strategies of the already rich and ordinary middle-class people were less pronounced.

During the most entrepreneurial phase of his long career, Merrill, in the early 1940s, spearheaded a whole series of private sector reforms on Wall Street. By agreeing to a merger, Merrill assumed responsibility for a nationwide network of branch offices that, after the union with Fenner & Beane, totaled around ninety locations, many of them in mid-sized cities. In a deliberate strategy aimed at bringing Wall Street to Main Street, Merrill Lynch concentrated on soliciting customers whose status was upper middle class – store owners, supervisors, professionals, skilled blue-collar workers, and anyone else with the means and desire to build wealth over time through a judicious investment program in common stocks. Previously, when other brokerage houses had sought to broaden their customer base, they had done so primarily by dangling before the public the lure of quick profits through active trading. In contrast, Merrill Lynch stressed the advantages of adopting a long-term horizon; this outlook was especially emphasized when the firm attempted to attract new accounts from households of modest means.

---

1. Barriers did not fall for minorities at most Wall Street brokerage firms, except for clerical and janitorial workers, until long after Merrill had passed from the scene. Women were occasionally hired and trained as security analysts in the 1940s and 1950s; a few became account executives.

At the urging of consultant Ted Braun, whose input deserves greater recognition by financial historians, Merrill decided to scrap the traditional commission-driven system for compensating stockbrokers. Sales personnel at Merrill Lynch were put on a fixed salary that was subject to periodic review by local branch managers. By dampening internal rivalries for the most active accounts, brokers at the local level were encouraged to work in a more complementary manner; they promoted the advantages of doing business with Merrill Lynch and thereby gaining access to the reports and opinions of its outstanding research staff. This radical new compensation program was a crucial element in a comprehensive marketing plan that, according to Braun, would help to reassure the public that Merrill Lynch brokers only recommended the purchase or sale of securities when a proposed transaction was genuinely in the customer's financial best interest. The broker's incentive for churning accounts to generate commissions was greatly diminished. With the adoption of this overarching compensation and marketing strategy, the firm immediately created a major competitive advantage over its main rivals in the brokerage field.

The decision to restructure the employment contract between the partners and their sales representatives was extremely risky from several perspectives. First, it converted what had been a significant variable expense, the standard commission split with brokers, which typically ranged from 25 to 40 percent of the gross commission on trades, into a fixed cost. After this policy took effect in 1940, the fixed-cost component in the partnership's total operating budget jumped from around 50 percent to about 85 percent. If trading volume on the stock exchanges, which fell every year from 1938 to 1942, had continued to shrink in the mid-1940s, Merrill Lynch might not have survived; at the very least the partners would have been forced to reassess the viability of the experimental compensation program.

The second risk was that the firm's most productive brokers would resign and join competitive houses, all of whom still retained the traditional split commission system. A few valuable employees did seek greener pastures, but most stayed. In every case a given broker's salary in 1940 equaled or exceeded the amount earned in the previous year from commissions alone. Moreover, Merrill assured every employee that, if the volume of future business met the expectations of the senior partners, salaries would climb steadily and on average stay competitive with other brokerage houses.[2] The loyalty of employees, brokers and support personnel, was also

---

2. The salary program for sales personnel remained in place throughout Merrill's lifetime, but after the deregulation initiatives of the 1970s led to wholesale rate cuts, the firm reverted to a compensation system more closely linked to individual performance.

strengthened by the payment of year-end bonuses and the partners' contributions to an innovative and generous profit-sharing program. By his death in 1956, the firm's employees, through the funds accumulated in the plan, laid claim to a greater share of the partnership's capital than any single investor, including the founder, Charles Merrill.

Among Merrill's other important innovations in the early 1940s was the publication of an annual report that included an income statement and balance sheet. No law or SEC rule prompted this initiative. Merrill Lynch became the first partnership in the brokerage field to voluntarily reveal this critical information to employees, customers, and financial journalists. Merrill decided that the demystification process, which had been proceeding apace on Wall Street since the mid-1930s, needed another boost. He believed that he and his business partners had nothing to hide from interested parties, and a published annual report was an effective means of communicating that fundamental principle to a wider audience, which included, most prominently, hundreds of financial journalists.

In another bold move, the partners eliminated incidental service fees that had been routinely applied to customer accounts; equally important, they started paying interest on customers' credit balances – the idle cash left with the firm after the sale of securities. Braun's survey of the operations of the Los Angeles branch in 1940 had demonstrated that customers who maintained either debit or credit balances generated the highest volume of trades and were invariably the most profitable accounts. Granting interest on all credit balances was an innovative and unprecedented policy on Wall Street that was designed to attract new accounts. Simultaneously, Merrill Lynch recruited a corps of expert security analysts and distributed their reports and recommendations to customers, and to potential customers, free of charge in most instances. The department also responded as soon as possible to a customer's request for a written analysis of his or her financial portfolio, again free of charge. This upgrading of the research department was, over the long term, one of the most critical factors in the firm's success since active traders naturally drifted toward brokerage houses with the most current and reliable information.

Merrill's lifestyle changed radically after 1944, when he suffered the first of a series of heart attacks. Throughout the next year, he played a minor role in the firm's affairs. Win Smith assumed most of the directing partner's former duties. Smith and Merrill generally saw eye-to-eye on issues, large and small. In this earlier era, the best medical advice for heart attack victims was complete rest and the avoidance of stress. Merrill's health stabilized in 1945 and thereafter he stayed on a fairly even keel, but persistent angina pains, day and night, were a constant annoyance.

When the doctors finally allowed their recovering patient to spend several hours each day reading reports, analyzing data, and drafting memorandums, Merrill, who was bored and depressed because of the lack of mental stimulation, dived back into the fray. He and Smith were in communication on a more or less daily basis through the mails or by telephone. With the exception of special celebratory events, Merrill rarely visited his office at headquarters after 1944. When residing in the New York area from late spring to early fall, he met regularly on weekends with Smith and other top executives, including his son-in-law, Robert Magowan. When living in Palm Beach during the winter months, he frequently invited business associates and their families to Florida for lengthy working vacations.

In certain ways this arrangement, which, with occasional gaps, continued for the next decade, was highly advantageous. Merrill was free to focus his attention on high-level policies and strategic planning, while Smith dutifully and expertly administered day-to-day operations. After the founder's death in 1956, Smith succeeded as directing partner, but deteriorating health forced him to retire about a year later. Mike McCarthy, who first managed backstage operations and later became assistant managing partner, became the firm's new leader. In recognition of Smith's invaluable contributions to the enterprise, the partnership changed its name to Merrill Lynch, Pierce, Fenner & Smith.[3]

In their lengthy correspondence, Merrill and Smith rarely discussed the policies and activities of competitive brokerage houses. Presumably, the firm was so far ahead of competitors that comparisons to tradition-bound firms were not deemed pertinent. In reams of memos written over more than a decade, Merrill cited the practices of grocers and other aggressive retailers far more often than other financial service providers. In its solicitation of accounts from middle-class households through a national network of branch offices – an effort supported by an aggressive advertising and promotion program – Merrill Lynch had little serious competition in the 1940s and 1950s, and a careful examination of top management's internal correspondence makes that point abundantly clear. The only standard that Merrill Lynch executives strived to surpass was what their own firm had accomplished during the previous twelve months.

Merrill finally got relief from the agony of angina pains in 1953 after

---

3. Alpheus Beane Jr. desperately wanted to succeed Smith as directing partner, and when his ambitions were thwarted, he threatened at a partnership meeting to leave the firm and peddle the Beane name to a competitive brokerage house. An unpopular figure, Beane thereby burned his bridges. The other partners unanimously voted to substitute Smith's name for Beane's in the firm's title. Beane, in turn, withdrew from the partnership and did, in fact, join another firm.

agreeing, at age sixty-seven, to undergo an experimental medical treatment using radioactive iodine. Despite his improved health and renewed energy, he decided to perpetuate the arrangement with Smith regarding the division of managerial responsibilities. The directing partner confined his involvement to deliberations about broad policy issues. On ceremonial occasions, Merrill periodically returned to headquarters for brief intervals. In 1953, he participated actively in a two-day conference attended by the managers of the firm's 108 branch offices, plus important department heads stationed in New York. In October 1955, he was feted at a huge gala that his partners had arranged to celebrate his seventieth birthday.

At the end of World War II, Merrill and his partners were ready with a second round of fresh initiatives. The firm established a formal training program that included three to six months of classroom instruction in New York. The school enrolled primarily new hires in their middle to late twenties. Most of the trainees were pointed toward careers as stockbrokers, although the upgraded job description at Merrill Lynch identified them as "account executives," a more sophisticated title that Merrill had imposed in the early 1940s. The program trained hundreds in the fundamentals of prudent investing, and along the way it acclimated graduates to the distinct business culture that permeated Merrill Lynch. By the mid-1950s more than half of the sales force was younger than forty, and several branches were administered by managers in their mid-thirties.

With few exceptions, everything worked largely according to plan at Merrill Lynch from 1940 on, and in many cases the results exceeded the partners' rosiest expectations. After languishing in the early years, trading on the stock exchanges revived in the mid-1940s, and, despite a few down years, volume continued to reach new heights. Stock prices fluctuated, but no sell-off like the debacle from 1929 to 1932 revisited the American market. Brokerage again became a profitable line of business for firms with viable organizational capacities. The public image of stockbrokers softened; the account executive nomenclature became the industry norm, and persons in this occupational category were increasingly perceived as genuine professionals. At Merrill Lynch, the strategy of soliciting accounts from middle-class households from coast to coast paid off handsomely for everyone involved: for repeat customers, for loyal employees, and for investors with capital at risk.

Under the direction of George Leness, the investment banking department used its leverage as a mass distributor of new issues to attract new underwriting clients, and within a decade it ranked among the ten leading syndicate managers on Wall Street.

Even the commodities business, which at one point seemed destined for the chopping block because of its inherently speculative aura, was rekindled in the postwar era and emerged as a vital profit center. In short, Merrill Lynch was successful in a whole range of financial markets, validating Merrill's decision at the outset to provide a full array of services for a variety of customers, from safety-oriented trust fund administrators to wild-eyed speculators. Meanwhile, the partners and their employees were dedicated to providing superior services at fee schedules that equaled, or slightly undercut, competitors.[4] Customers with limited financial resources were treated with the same courtesies usually reserved elsewhere for the rich and powerful. Over time, word-of-mouth endorsements by existing customers generated thousands of new accounts.

The work culture that pervaded the Merrill Lynch organization was upbeat, friendly, and constructive. Merrill's influence as a leader and role model in the 1940s and 1950s cannot be overstated. Employees were imbued with certain values – ethical and practical – that reflected the missionary zeal of the founder. Customer service was always a top priority. Other business enterprises in almost every sector of the U.S. economy adopted that "service" motto in the fourth quarter of the twentieth century, and especially after foreign competition made inroads with millions of American consumers, but an emphasis on maintaining outstanding customer relations reigned at Merrill Lynch from its very inception. Few account executives labored with the expectation that they and their families could, or should, anticipate astronomical upward economic and social mobility. The personal goal of most brokers was to achieve upper-middle-class status by midcareer and then enjoy the benefits of a secure lifestyle. A majority of the firm's regular customers had similar aspirations, which created a compatible synergy. Some extremely ambitious account executives, eager for the opportunity to maximize their income potential, decided to leave the firm, but the majority identified with the stated goals of the organization and stuck around until retirement. Merrill Lynch employees in whatever occupational category typically earned more than their peers at other brokerage houses. A generous profit-sharing program complemented the salary compensation system. Bringing the fruits of Wall Street to Main Street gave many employees, not just the directing partner, a great deal of personal satisfaction. Merrill felt he had achieved something truly worthwhile by showing previously unsophisticated savers how to

---

4. Commission rates on trades were fixed and uniform throughout the brokerage sector, but Merrill Lynch eliminated most of the supplemental fees that other brokerage houses frequently applied to customer accounts, especially small accounts.

optimize their returns on financial assets by taking sensible risks in the common stocks of sound and growing corporations, and most of the firm's employees had similar feelings about their helpfulness to customers.

Merrill's only serious misreading of future trends in the financial markets came with respect to his uncompromising attitude toward open-end mutual funds. Donald Regan proposed in the early 1950s that the firm enter this emerging market by agreeing to sell the shares of open-end funds to interested customers.[5] But Merrill rejected the idea immediately, and without giving proper consideration to the significant advantages of the still relatively new open-end format. He failed to envision the merits of open-end funds for millions of savers, not just those in the middle class but upper-class investors as well, who wanted to delegate to professional portfolio managers the responsibility for selecting and rejecting individual securities. His notable failure to act on sound advice from a trusted subordinate with innovative ideas came very late in his long career; perhaps the years had taken their toll and sapped a portion of his entrepreneurial spirit.

Of course, Merrill never claimed infallibility. Indeed, he occasionally ignored some of his own best advice with respect to the wisdom of carefully investigating any proposal before investing hard-earned money. "If I made a decision fast I was right 60 percent of the time," he once remarked. "If I made a decision carefully I'd be right 70 percent – but it wasn't always worth it."[6] Luckily, Merrill was actually right about most things more often than three-quarters of the time. Win Smith had tremendous respect for his mentor's negotiating style:

> Charlie was a genius in laying down the basic terms of an agreement in a delicate, intricate transaction. The sincerity and logic of his proposals convinced the other side of his candor from the outset, always the first essential in any business deal. He could be awfully tough on a pleasant level in jockeying for a position favorable to him[self], but he immediately compromised if he saw the other fellow had a valid argument.[7]

Merrill received a fair number of kudos from the business press in the final stages of his career. His name popped up on lists of the top fifty to one hundred U.S. business leaders, and he was often one of the few, if not the only one, to stand as a representative of the entire financial services sector. Probably the most widely circulated of many accolades came from the pen of Martin Mayer, a financial journalist-historian, who published *Wall Street: Men and Money* in 1955:

5. The firm continued to execute orders for closed-end funds because they traded on the NYSE.
6. Quoted in Charles Merrill Jr., *Checkbook*, 7.
7. Quoted in Engberg manuscript, chap. 7, p. 11.

He is the first authentically great man produced by the financial market in 150 years. The Drews and Goulds, . . . the Morgans and the Livermores – these men existed in a tight little island of their own making, where the public were sheep to be shorn. . . . Merrill brought in the public, not as lambs to be fleeced but as partners in the benefits. . . . The climate of the 1930s helped, the New Deal laws helped, and many individuals helped, but the prime mover was Charlie Merrill.[8]

Merrill's legacy endured. He established the principles, strategies, and policies that carried the firm to the pinnacle of success. Before he died, Merrill Lynch was the undisputed leader in two key financial markets: stock brokerage and commodities. Several decades later, the firm bypassed all competitors to become the leading investment banking house on Wall Street. It earned the top position in both the wholesale and the retail ends of the securities business – an unprecedented accomplishment. By the end of the twentieth century Merrill Lynch, no longer a partnership but now a corporation, had extended its reach to financial markets around the globe – from London to Hong Kong. As a result of these achievements, Merrill's influence equaled the impact of all previous American financiers, including his only legitimate rival, J. P. Morgan. In democratizing the stock market, Merrill created an enterprise that gave middle-class households access to a far wider range of investment opportunities. He truly brought Wall Street to Main Street. Because of his many contributions, Charlie Merrill deserves recognition as the nation's premier entrepreneur in the thriving financial services sector.

8. Quoted from a reprint in *We the People* of an article titled "The Fabulous Firm of Merrill Lynch" that Mayer published in March 1955 in the *Reporter*.

EPILOGUE
MERRILL LYNCH IN THE 1990s

During the last four decades of the twentieth century, the legacy of the founder continued to influence the institutional development of Merrill Lynch and the broader securities markets, including stock and bond markets at home and abroad. Charlie Merrill wanted his firm to keep growing by providing superior services to customers at fair prices, and for the most part that dream has been realized. By the 1990s, Merrill Lynch was a market force not just on Wall Street, but in London, Tokyo, and in many other money centers around the globe. The democratization of the stock market, originally fostered by Merrill, has been inexorably expanding to new locales, drawing in new investors ranging in economic status from the middle class to the superrich. In the United States, where commercial banking is typically less concentrated than in other nations, Merrill Lynch has emerged as the single most recognizable name in the financial services sector; and it may be the most recognizable name around the globe.[1]

As Charlie had envisioned, Wall Street has beaten an ever widening path to millions of customers on Main Streets coast-to-coast and established a strong foothold. A clear majority of American households now own common stocks – either outright or indirectly through myriad pension plans and mutual funds. Currently, there is talk in Congress about investing a certain portion of Social Security funds in common stocks to meet the accelerating retirement demands of baby boomers after 2015. If that happens, virtually every working American will have a link to Wall Street.

Meanwhile, the upbeat, customer-oriented corporate culture that Charlie promoted within Merrill Lynch during his long career has persisted. Unwilling to rest on past achievements, executives and devoted employees are continually striving to expand and improve the firm's broad range of financial services. With the twenty-first century beckoning, Merrill Lynch

---

1. The key sources for this chapter are the firm's annual report for 1996 and a supplementary fact book.

remains the market leader in providing brokerage services, a ranking held since the early 1940s. It has a network of more than 475 offices in the United States. After the acquisition of White Weld & Company in 1978 and a major push in the 1980s, Merrill Lynch seized the coveted leadership position in underwriting new issues of stocks and bonds in both national and international securities markets. By almost any conceivable standard, Charlie's entrepreneurial creation ranked number one in more of the leading money centers around the world in the 1990s than any other competitive enterprise.

Perhaps the most dramatic change at Merrill Lynch over the past four decades has been its aggressive expansion into overseas markets. At Charlie's death in 1956, the firm had just three foreign offices, and two were a mere stone's throw from the U.S. border: in Toronto, Canada, and in Havana, Cuba. The latter closed soon after the revolution brought Fidel Castro to power in January 1959. The only other foreign office was in Geneva, Switzerland, which was opened as a window on Europe in 1951. Today, Merrill Lynch has offices in forty-five countries, including representatives on every continent except Antarctica. One of the newest offices, opened in 1997, is in Moscow, Russia, once the capital of the Soviet Union. The 7,600 people stationed overseas represent about 15 percent of total personnel. More than half of the nearly 600 research analysts, residing in New York and thirty other locations throughout the world, concentrate on monitoring the performance of securities issued by corporations headquartered outside the United States. In 1996, the foreign branches contributed 30 percent of total revenues and accounted for 45 percent of total assets. Winthrop Smith Jr., son of the founder's closest business associate in the 1940s and 1950s and the directing partner for a few years immediately after Charlie's death, serves as the current chairman of Merrill Lynch International. He is the only blood relative drawn from the pool of Charles Merrill, Edmund Lynch, Edward Pierce, Charles Fenner, and Winthrop Smith (and earlier Alpheus Beane) to hold a prominent executive position with the firm. Like almost all U.S. business enterprises, Merrill Lynch is a thriving meritocracy that promotes people strictly on the basis of performance.

The second most notable change at Merrill Lynch since the 1950s has been the major shift in its sources of revenue and profit. During Charlie's lifetime, individuals trading the stocks of specific corporations generated more than 75 percent of revenues, with commissions on commodity trading contributing significantly in certain years. Underwriting and distribution fees were merely supplemental revenue sources. Individuals paid full commissions for basic transaction services at fixed minimum rates regardless of the size of the trade; in addition, customers maintaining margin accounts produced net inflows of interest income. By the 1990s, transactions linked to individual accounts were far less important in the overall picture, and not just at Merrill Lynch but at all the full-service brokerage houses. On the major U.S. stock exchanges, individuals accounted for only one-quarter or less of daily trading volume, and their share has been constantly shrinking. The professional managers of large portfolios initiate the largest volume of trades in equity markets today; moreover, the commissions paid are variable and negotiable.[2]

At present Merrill Lynch relies on mutual fund commissions and fund management fees to enhance its profitability. That statement could not have been made a quarter century ago. Charlie was an adamant opponent of mutual funds, and his hostile attitude colored the outlook of his immediate successors in executive positions. Given the firm's inaction, the Fidelity organization, based in Boston rather than New York, was presented with the opportunity to seize the initiative in a market with only token competition. Not until Don Regan became CEO in 1971 did Merrill Lynch venture into mutual funds. Over the next two decades, Merrill Lynch drew on its unparalleled retail distribution system to make up a good deal of lost ground. At the end of 1996, the firm offered customers more than two hundred different mutual funds with aggregate portfolios of over $230 billion. Merrill Lynch ranked first in market share among rival brokerage houses and third overall behind Fidelity and Vanguard, two issuers that specialize in mutual fund distribution and fund management. At Merrill Lynch commissions from the sale and redemption of mutual funds totaled more than 60 percent of the gross commissions linked to customer trades of listed securities. These commissions combined, however, accounted for less than 15 percent of total revenues. Although Merrill Lynch has more than eight million retail customers, brokerage in secondary markets, once the lifeblood of the firm, has become less important in producing sales and income.

Commodity commissions in 1996 generated less than 1 percent of total revenues, a clear indication of how this phase of the business has declined on a relative scale in recent decades. Internal critics of commodity trading argued as early as 1941 that this activity was, by its very nature, excessively speculative and should be downplayed in formulating long-term plans. Periodic news reports about huge customer losses resulting from unexpected gyrations in commodity prices damaged the reputation of the firm,

---

2. Burk, *Values in the Marketplace,* 139–41. The author argues that changes in federal and state laws since 1930 have contributed significantly to increased institutional participation in the stock market. The adoption of revised prudent-man laws at the state level allowed trustees and fund managers to invest more extensively in equities. Meanwhile, federal regulation enhanced the flow and accuracy of financial data about listed stocks.

the critics alleged; they believed news reports about commodity losses dampened efforts to convince a whole generation of reluctant savers to invest in common stocks. But Charlie was attracted to the concept of an all-purpose enterprise with universal service. As it happened, the rise of new revenue sources in other sectors has reduced the firm's reliance on commodity commissions.

In the 1970s, Merrill Lynch was among the leaders in weakening barriers that, in the first instance, had limited the ability of banks, brokers, and other enterprises to provide convenient and reliable transactions services for retail customers residing in distant states, and that, in the second instance, had prevented a single business entity from performing under one roof both commercial banking and investment banking functions. Most states in the 1950s had laws that made it difficult, if not impossible, for commercial banks to create extensive branch networks, even within a given state. There were exceptions to this generalization, most notably in California, where Bank of America had hundreds of offices; nonetheless, because of haphazard rules and regulations, a commercial bank could not use a uniform and widely recognizable name to create an interstate banking system in any regional market, much less the wider national market. Commercial banks were always allowed to solicit and maintain out-of-state checking accounts, but most households were reluctant to open an account with a bank across the state border because of the absence of local offices to answer routine questions and solve minor problems. Compounding the issue, banks were prevented from paying interest on any account that was subject to withdrawal by check, which meant that customers with savings accounts in financial institutions hundreds of miles from their residences could not conveniently draw on those accounts to make payments to third parties.

The first major crack in the prevailing system occurred in 1969 when the obscure Five Cents Savings Bank of Worcester, Massachusetts, began offering customers with savings accounts a new type of transactions service. Rather than withdrawing money in person at the teller window or through the mail, the account holder could prepare a "negotiable order of withdrawal" and deliver it to any third party. The so-called NOW accounts and their progeny caused a minor revolution in financial services.[3] In 1977, Merrill Lynch inaugurated its Cash Management Account (CMA), the first effort by any brokerage house to offer everyday transactions services to account holders. Customers received check-writing privileges plus a VISA credit card, and their idle credit balances earned money

3. Wriston, *Risk,* 176.

market interest rates. The firm's advertising department hyped the convenience of an all-purpose brokerage/bank account, but customers were slow in responding. One year after launch, a management review panel concluded that the unpopular program was a costly mistake, and it recommended pulling out. But CEO Don Regan was adamant about continuance: "My hand still stings from banging on the table," he later recalled. He told subordinates: "There are several ways you can do this; one is over my dead body."[4] Regan was right, of course, just as he had been about mutual funds two decades earlier.

Several years later, aided by rising interest rates, which made money market returns especially attractive, the public response to CMA was enthusiastic. Given the success of brokerage houses in attracting customers to cash management accounts and their near cousins, commercial banks in the United States have been pleading with Congress, state legislatures, and bank regulators to allow them, in turn, to perform a wider range of brokerage and investment banking functions on the grounds that Merrill Lynch and other Wall Street firms have already effectively entered their domain. Commercial banks have sought reciprocity and equal advantages. In reality, brokerage houses have always performed one critical commercial banking function: for decades they have acted as financial intermediaries, lending to customers who maintained margin accounts and profiting from interest overrides. For example, E. A. Pierce survived (barely) in the late 1930s, largely because of the net income generated from loans to customers with margin accounts.

Other barriers between commercial banking and investment banking have likewise been crumbling. The Glass-Steagall Act of 1933, a cornerstone of New Deal reform legislation, had, according to contemporaries, institutionally isolated the customers of commercial banks from the potential corruptions of the unpredictable stock market.[5] In the regulatory environment created in the 1930s, commercial banks were expected to stress safety above all other concerns and thereby protect depositors, while Wall Street firms were granted the leeway to engage in riskier ventures. In the 1960s, that hard-and-fast dividing line began to fade, and by the 1990s it had become a faint blur. Congress had not repealed Glass-Steagall by the mid-1990s, but bank supervisors and administrators of the Federal Reserve System reinterpreted the law in an increasingly liberal fashion and thereby steadily undermined the original intent of congressional legislators. Under

4. Hecht, *Legacy of Leadership*, 138.
5. For a survey of the secondary literature related to the controversy over Glass-Steagall, the best source is Benston, *Separation of Commercial and Investment Banking.*

the regulations operable today, commercial banks are permitted to engage more actively in underwriting corporate debt issues and in promoting the sale of mutual funds than they were a quarter century ago.

Given the evolution of financial regulation in the domestic market and the expanded opportunities overseas, the strategies that Merrill Lynch pursued in the 1980s, and into the 1990s, paralleled strategies in the 1920s to a greater extent than those that were operative in the 1950s. Immediately after World War II, the firm was primarily a brokerage house, living off commissions linked to secondary markets, with all other financial services merely complementary. In the 1920s, in contrast, Charlie Merrill and Eddie Lynch became successful mainly because of their merchant banking activities; they invested their own capital in the common stocks of a series of chain stores that had become underwriting clients.

The modern firm's reentry into various types of merchant banking activities occurred in 1972 with a linkage to the venerable British investment banking house of Brown Shipley, which traced its roots back to the early nineteenth century. (My first book, published in 1975, focused on Brown Brothers, an Anglo-American enterprise with offices on both sides of the Atlantic; thus I have, through the merger route, come full circle.) British rules are typically more permissive than U.S. regulations with respect to allowing underwriters and dealers to maintain substantial equity positions in other types of nonfinancial business enterprises. In 1995, Merrill Lynch acquired Smith New Court, one of the leading securities dealers in the London market.

Given the less restrictive legal environment at home and abroad, Merrill Lynch has broadened the scope of its activities by expanding into new financial markets. The firm is now active in trading various types of derivatives linked to financial instruments and in arranging corporate mergers and acquisitions, including some uninvited takeovers. In the 1920s, Charlie had routinely handled mergers and acquisitions for grocery chains, especially Safeway Stores after 1926, with staff assistance from less than a dozen people; today, the firm's expanded M&A department employs hundreds of specia-lists. As a result of the expanding scope of operations, by the mid-1990s Merrill Lynch earned greater revenues from activities financed with its own capital for the benefit of its own account than from commissions on trades in secondary markets for millions of retail customers, large and small.

From an internal perspective, another of the major changes at Merrill Lynch since the founder's death was the abandonment of the salary system for compensating sales personnel. The implementation of the salary system in 1940 made the firm unique among peers in the brokerage field, and this distinction was emphasized in the solicitation of new accounts. The salaries of brokers were typically adjusted on a yearly or semiannual basis to reflect the recent productiveness of individuals, but they were not directly tied to specific trades. Elsewhere the broker and employer split the commission on all trades, which occasionally led to the unscrupulous churning of accounts.

The elimination of fixed rates on trades by the NYSE in 1975 was one factor that hastened the change in the compensation system at Merrill Lynch. Brokerage firms were granted the right to compete on the basis of price for all types of business, ranging from huge block trades to the smallest odd lot transactions. This alteration in the competitive climate on Wall Street was one of the factors that accelerated the decline of relationship banking, particularly in the underwriting field. Prior to deregulation, corporate clients and institutional buyers tended to remain loyal to underwriters who had performed adequately in the past since no competitor could offer lower fees or substantially better deals for similar services. Merrill Lynch was never a member of the tight, oligopolistic club of syndicate managers, but rather one of its primary challengers, and particularly in the post–World War II era. For example, in the federal government's highly publicized antitrust suit, filed in October 1947, seventeen investment banking firms were cited for restricting competition in underwriting, but Merrill Lynch was not on that list.[6]

After 1975, a range of financial inducements undermined the long-standing gentlemanly relationships among the elite investment banking houses and their clients. Suddenly, vigorous competition ruled the day. Even formerly staid firms like Morgan Stanley joined the fray. Merrill Lynch was one beneficiary of this fresh start on Wall Street because it was often in a position to offer clients and customers the most attractive deals on the basis of service and price. The expertise of the research staff, which had been one of the firm's hallmarks since the early 1940s, was an important element in moving Merrill Lynch into a leadership position in underwriting, mergers, and acquisitions by the 1990s.

Another policy change that had an impact on customer relations was the reimposition of service fees on routine retail accounts. In 1940 Charlie had loudly broadcast the firm's elimination of a series of minor nuisance fees on customer accounts. The absence of service fees gave Merrill Lynch another competitive edge in an era when minimum rates on security transactions were dictated by the stock exchanges. But one thrust of the deregulation movement was to discourage mindless uniformity in pricing decisions; each customer, whether large or small, should be billed, ac-

---

6. The government ultimately lost the case against the principal underwriters. For an excellent summary of the trial, see Carosso, *Investment Banking in America*, 458–95.

cording to popular marginal costing theories, precisely for the cost of the services used – never billed too much, of course, but also never billed too little. In this atmosphere of more accurate costing and reflective pricing, Merrill Lynch executives finally decided to abandon the long-standing policy and begin assessing annual maintenance fees on most retail accounts to cover the cost of routine record keeping. Initially, many customers with small or medium-sized accounts howled in protest, but in time most accepted the rationale for the fees.

Under the increasing liberal rules of the NYSE, Merrill Lynch shifted from partnership status to corporate status in January 1959. Twelve years later, in 1971, it became the first of the major brokerage houses to go public, offering its own stock to outside investors.[7] Together these two alterations in legal and organizational status helped solve a whole series of persistent problems. Before incorporation, the death of a general partner might lead to the withdrawal of a substantial amount of capital at an inconvenient time. In the mid-1950s, Charlie told his partners that he had arranged his will to guarantee that his personal capital would remain with the firm for five years after his death, but beyond that date he could make no commitment. By going public, all stockholders would have access to an active market where they could liquidate their holdings in an orderly fashion, whether through block trades or incremental sales. After 1971, customers had the opportunity to place an order with a Merrill Lynch account executive to buy Merrill Lynch common stock, thereby instantaneously becoming the employer of the agent handling the transaction and presumably receiving a fractional rebate on the commission in the next dividend payment.

Going public was perhaps the ultimate realization of Charlie Merrill's vision. The democratization of the stock market reached another milepost; customers and owners were no longer distinct categories but potentially overlapping groups. Customers could still obtain outstanding service at reasonable prices, and, in addition, by acquiring just a few shares of stock in Merrill Lynch itself, they could become part owners of the enterprise launched in 1914 by the nation's preeminent entrepreneur in the financial services sector.

7. Donaldson, Lufkin and Jenrette, a smaller house, was actually the very first Wall Street firm to go public.

APPENDIX
UNPUBLISHED MANUSCRIPTS

Resting in the Merrill Lynch corporate archives are five valuable unpublished manuscripts: three separate biographies of Charles Merrill, one biography of Edmund Lynch, and one broad survey of the firm's history through the mid-1980s. The last was written by Edward Engberg, an outside author working under contract; the research project pointed toward the publication of a book to celebrate an important anniversary date, but for various reasons that idea was finally scrapped.

The four biographies go back further in time and require more discussion. In the long period of recovery after his three heart attacks in 1944, Charlie, facing the reality of his own mortality, began to think more seriously about perpetuating a small measure of immortality for himself and some of his former business associates by means of a carefully researched biography. His doctors, believing that such a project would be less taxing and life-threatening than a deepening involvement in the firm's ongoing business affairs, endorsed the concept as a good outlet for his pent-up energies. Charlie first decided to sponsor a commemorative biography of Edmund Lynch, who had died prematurely in 1938 at age fifty-two. The Lynch biography, like several subsequent historical projects that focused on Merrill's own life, was not well thought out – either in terms of engaging the services of a qualified author or in terms of identifying the prospective audience for a book-length manuscript.

In a nostalgic mood in the fall of 1946, Charlie noticed, or had called to his attention, a short story titled "Little Victory" by Robert Lewis in the October issue of the *Atlantic,* a popular magazine in the postwar era. After consulting with a few friends about financing a Lynch biography, Charlie's personal secretary, Marguerite Francis, wrote Lewis an exploratory letter in early November. She closed portentously: "Mr. Lynch was quite a character in the financial world, his memory being fresh in the minds of many who knew him, some of whom loved him, and many of whom could not stand the sight of him.'"[1] Lewis responded favorably, and after a cordial meeting with Charlie, a deal was struck. The author was to receive $5,000 (about $40,000 in 1995 prices), plus travel expenses to New York, for researching and writing the biography. While Lewis was an experienced researcher and an outstanding stylist, he had no background in finance or economics.

Whether Lewis would act as a ghost writer or write under his own name was deliberately left up in the air. Under the terms of the contract, Charlie reserved the right, first, to substitute his own name on the title page as the accredited author and, second, to determine at the end of the project whether publication would be pursued. In a November 1946 letter, Charlie told Lewis that, while he would not "interfere with you as to your style and strategy in working out this story," he nonetheless believed they had reached an agreement that "you would not slant the writing in a manner to which I objected."[2] In other words, Lewis was working from the outset in the twilight zone between disinterested objectivity and the threat of heavy censorship.

Charlie told Lewis to gather all the pertinent information available from internal and external sources related to Lynch's career and then to write a chronicle that would set the record straight. In other words, the project began with laudable ideals and unrestricted access to reliable data. However, Charlie's plan for establishing historical accuracy was essentially to collect as many amusing or embarrassing incidents from the past as possible; recounting a long series of human interest stories against a backdrop of critical dates was his concept of good history, and his unsophisticated outlook was shared, of course, by a majority of the American public. While he realized that certain fellow employees were likely to be at least mildly critical of Lynch's ungenerous behavior toward subordinates, Charlie had no idea of the depth of the lingering antagonism toward his former business associate. Lynch had his faults, Charlie had no illusions about that, but in his selective memory, Lynch was overwhelmingly a genuine business hero. Indeed, as a result of Charlie's esteem, Lynch's name has been perpetuated on the masthead right up to the present.

Lewis took just over two years to produce a draft manuscript that ran to thirteen chapters and 194 pages. After sending out chapters to several of Lynch's former personal secretaries, to Win Smith, and to other executives at Merrill Lynch, and assessing their feedback, Charlie expressed strong dissatisfaction with the author's performance. Critics cited a number

---

1. Francis to Lewis, Nov. 8, 1946, ML Files. The files contain substantial correspondence on the Lynch biography; only a few of many letters are cited in the notes.
2. Merrill to Lewis, Nov. 26, 1946, ML Files.

of alleged inaccuracies; most of them were, in truth, minor errors or interpretive quibbles, but they were nonetheless sufficient in the eyes of several readers to discredit the author and his entire manuscript. Charlie asked Lewis for a thorough rewrite but he failed to offer any clear instructions about how to proceed, other than some generalities about making the biography broader and more comprehensive. The bewildered Lewis had received no helpful guidance about how to proceed; in response, he simply threw up his hands and refused to do any further work. After a series of acrimonious letters regarding the quality of the manuscript and the financial terms of the contract, the whole project ground to a halt. Lewis was paid, and that was the end of it.

Fifty years have passed since this perplexing episode, and it is now possible to make an informed judgment about what really happened to sour the relationship between Merrill and Lewis. In retrospect, the fundamental problem was not that Lewis had done an inferior job. On the contrary, he had performed his task all too well. He drew liberally on the information made available to him from reliable sources to paint an accurate portrait of Edmund Lynch. Rather than acknowledging the unflattering reality about Lynch, Charlie blamed the messenger. Rather naively, Charlie thought at the beginning that he wanted a biography that would include the proverbial "warts and all," but when he saw the final draft, the warts covered from one-quarter to perhaps one-third of Lynch's exposed body. His former partner was not always a lovable or admirable character; instead, he was exposed as a hard-nosed and occasionally ruthless businessman who regularly treated underlings like contemptible peasants.

Faced with the truth about Lynch, Charlie concluded that he could not in good conscience reveal the whole story to his inner circle of friends and family nor to the outside world. If he arranged publication by a vanity press or even decided to circulate the manuscript privately, he could easily be accused of egregious disloyalty to his former partner. The manuscript, as it stood, was not a sentimental memorial to his dead colleague but something that seemed closer to an investigative report by a muckraking journalist. Another option – to engage a second writer to cull out the worst examples of Lynch's excesses and sanitize the text – was an alternative, since he, as the contractor, owned all rights to the contents of the text, but that notion ran counter to Charlie's principles regarding full disclosure. Finally, he decided to bury the manuscript and forget about it as quickly as possible. In all likelihood, few members of the Lynch or Merrill families ever read the manuscript in its entirety or even large sections of it. My guess is that readers today have a more tolerant attitude about the personality quirks of biographical subjects, and they would accept the Lynch manuscript with hardly a murmur. Lewis was, in short, a conscientious biographer who was ahead of his time. It is to be hoped that something scholarly will be published at some future date about Lynch's accomplishments, which, as Charlie always maintained, were genuine. For persons unwilling to wait for a fuller treatment, a five-part article by Bill Loughran in the *Boston Irish Echo* covers in a fair amount of detail the highlights of Lynch's life; I suspect Loughran had access to a copy of the Lewis manuscript.

During the months that Lewis was writing former employees and encouraging them to put down on paper their memories of Lynch, many respondents simultaneously wrote to Charlie suggesting that he too was a viable candidate for a full-scale biography. Some sent him carbon copies of their recollections, and the receipt of this material stimulated his juices and led him to consider a second biographical project. The nasty episode with Lewis was not unduly discouraging because Charlie calculated, first, that the stories reflecting badly on his character and judgment would be fewer in number and less vicious in tone, and, second, that whenever the biographer felt obligated to turn up the heat a little, he would be able to handle the consequences with grace and good humor. Recounting amusing, if mildly unflattering, anecdotes about himself, which he did quite voluntarily in regaling visitors, was far different from broadcasting demeaning stories about Lynch, or indeed about any third party, living or dead.

In a letter to Robert Magowan in May 1949, Charlie authorized the gathering of material about his life for a biography.[3] In discussing the selection of a biographer, Charlie mentioned Frederick Lewis Allen, who had just published a book about John Pierpont Morgan that was favorably reviewed by general readers and scholars alike.[4] "This man, at least, can write and he knows more than most authors about business and Wall Street." (There is no evidence in the files that Lewis was subsequently contacted.) While Charlie thought the research phase could proceed, he added a few caveats: "I have learned from experience that books of this sort should be written, or in any event, published, after the subject is dead." In July 1949, Charlie sent Smith a long memo in which he named about fifty people, with identifying comments, from his past; he wanted all of them contacted, with invitations to contribute their recollections of memorable events.[5]

Regarding the principle of objectivity, Charlie made it quite clear that he wanted a full and forthright accounting of his life and career, not a

---

3. Merrill to Magowan, May 5, 1949, ML Files.
4. John Blum, chair of the Department of History at Yale University, was quoted on the back of the later paperback edition: "The best biography of its subject; distinguished alike for its literary merit and its historical insight."
5. Merrill to Smith, July 15, 1949, ML Files.

whitewash. He ordered Smith to seek out all the pertinent information, both good and bad: "It is just silly to try to side-step, or soft-pedal, the disasters and mistakes – such as Waring Hat and Saxon Motors." Fortunately for future historians, the firm made numerous good-faith efforts in the decade from 1945 to 1955 to collect a substantial amount of information, including transcripts of oral interviews, from many people who had crossed paths with the founder from childhood through adulthood. The data gathered remain invaluable and constituted the research base for this book.

For the last five years of his life, Charlie devoted a great deal of his energies to orchestrating the ongoing biography project. Elizabeth Fowler, an employee working on the staff of *Investor's Reader,* was asked to oversee the marshaling of pertinent material, and she wrote preliminary drafts of a few early chapters.[6] The first author to attempt a full-length manuscript was Stanton Griffis, a longtime friend who had been associated with the investment firm of Hemphill Noyes and later Paramount Pictures. Griffis had served as U.S. ambassador to several countries, including Egypt. Having recently published his memoirs, entitled *Lying in State,* the prospective author had experience with preparing a book-length manuscript. He was on good terms with Hellen Merrill, Charlie's second wife. Details of the arrangement between Charlie and Griffis have not survived, but the general tone of subsequent correspondence suggests that Griffis, in retirement, was looking for an interesting project to fill the idle hours, and he solicited the assignment. A huge admirer of Charlie's accomplishments on Wall Street, this well-intentioned, but amateur, historian volunteered his services, and Charlie, at Hellen's urging, accepted.

Griffis drew on the mass of data collected in the early 1950s and in late 1953 or early 1954 produced a 260-page manuscript titled "Biography of Charles Merrill: A Saga of Wall Street." Not a polished work of art, the manuscript nonetheless possessed one great virtue – at least from the viewpoint of modern researchers. Griffis quoted liberally from Charlie's own writings: frequently the uninterrupted quotations run for several pages. One or two of the letters and memos reproduced by Griffis were items that I was never able to relocate in the archives; the originals may be lost or possibly misfiled.

The internal assessment of the Griffis manuscript followed the pattern established in handling Lewis's biography of Lynch. Charlie sent draft chapters for evaluation to insiders, including Win Smith, and even to his ex-wife Hellen. The critics cited a number of minor factual errors that

---

6. Fowler was involved in the biography project for several years; Jeff Avirett also spent some time on it.

seemed to them to represent a major drawback. Hellen focused on the errors of omission.[7] According to her damning critique, Griffis had failed to include numerous stories for which she knew Charlie had a particular fondness. In the end, Griffis's manuscript was judged incomplete and inadequate, and it was set aside.

Throughout the process of planning and executing the Griffis biography – plus two additional efforts by different authors – no one intimately involved in the project seemed to demonstrate any comprehension of the importance of framing the narrative in the most appropriate context, namely, the profound impact of Merrill both on the institutional development of the financial services sector and on the retail grocery trade. All the participants in these biographical projects seemed utterly clueless about the broad significance of Charlie's career achievements and his influence on the capital markets and the national economy. In general, the authors were too reticent; they were reluctant to make grandiose claims about the importance of their subject for the historical record. None had any deep understanding or appreciation of financial history, nor did they seek to educate themselves, except superficially, about the evolution of U.S. capital markets over the past century. Instead, everyone saw the biography as primarily the recounting of a fascinating story about an obscure physician's son from Florida who migrated to Wall Street and, against all odds, became enormously successful. In telling the Merrill story, they were encouraged to give more or less equal billing to friends, relatives, business associates, important underwriting clients, and intimate members of the family who had interacted with Charlie over the years. In short, anecdotes received priority over substance and analysis.

Charlie took Hellen's complaints about the lack of complete and full disclosure in the Griffis manuscript to heart, and he sought someone to fill in all the missing blanks. A much younger man who had recently joined the firm's editorial staff was tabbed for the assignment. In 1955, Terrance Keenan began work on a detailed 684-page manuscript titled "Chain of Fortune: The Life and Work of Charles E. Merrill." The author covered all the bases and included just about every colorful anecdote anyone could recall with any specificity. Given the parameters of the project, Keenan's performance was highly professional. He drafted an outstanding manuscript both in terms of organization and style. If he had submitted the project as a completed dissertation in a contemporary graduate history program, I am confident that he would have been awarded a doctoral degree at most American universities. I will always be extremely grateful for his care and diligence in laying out the facts surrounding the life of

7. Hellen to Merrill, April 30, 1954, ML Files.

Charles Merrill. Much of my information on Charlie's childhood and teenage years was drawn from Keenan's masterful text.

Family and friends were by and large delighted with the contents of the Keenan manuscript, which was not available for review until just before Charlie's death in October 1956. Unfortunately, outside readers in the publishing world were less enthusiastic. They cited the length and unnecessary details as stumbling blocks to publication for a trade audience. In a last effort to produce something more acceptable to publishers, Stanley Frank, an experienced New York writer with ties to the *Saturday Evening Post*, then a large-circulation magazine, was hired to tighten the prose and reduce the Keenan text to a manageable size. He produced a highly readable manuscript of 330 pages. Frank did an excellent job of abridging Keenan, but commercial publishers again expressed no serious interest in the text – maybe the lack of titillating scandalous material, except for Charlie's three divorces, was the main deterrent. Presumably, no university presses were contacted, probably because there were no notes or bibliography, although such documentation could have been easily provided without too much additional effort. In any event, nothing much happened with respect to the Merrill biography until I became involved in the late 1980s. For more on that story, please refer to the introduction.

In 1985, Henry Hecht, an employee who had worked on the editorial staff of *Investor's Reader* and other in-house publications since the 1940s, wrote *A Legacy of Leadership: Merrill Lynch, 1885–1985*, a 150-page commemorative paperback filled with interesting black-and-white photos, numerous sidebars, and an engaging text that met the highest professional standards for accuracy and objectivity. The firm financed publication and distributed tens of thousands of copies to employees and other interested parties.

BIBLIOGRAPHY

Primary Sources

Amherst College Archives. Alumni Biographical Files. File on Charles E. Merrill.
Merrill Lynch Corporate Archives, World Financial Center, New York City. Included in the historical files are five book-length manuscripts: three separate biographies of Charles Merrill by Stanton Griffis, Terrance Keenan, and Stanley Frank; one biography of Edmund Lynch by Robert Lewis; and a history of the firm by Edward Engberg.

Author's Interviews

Doris Merrill Magowan, Charles Merrill Jr., James Merrill, Michael McCarthy, I. Paul Perkins

Transcripts of Interviews

Transcripts of interviews in ML Files include William Dunkak, Louis Engel, John Fitzgerald, Edmund Lynch Jr., Donald Regan, Robert Rooke, Vivian Smith, Winthrop Smith Sr., and Winthrop Smith Jr. There are also multiple interviews, conducted at different times, with Charles Merrill's three children: Doris Merrill Magowan, Charles Merrill Jr., and James Merrill.

Government Documents

U.S. Census, 1860. Manuscript records, Holmes County, Lexington Post Office, Miss. Reels 653.582 and 653.598. National Archives.
U.S. Census, 1870. Manuscript records, Holmes County, Lexington Post Office, Miss. Reel 593.731. National Archives.
U.S. Census, 1880. Manuscript records, Clay County, Fla. Microfilm roll, 79–126. National Archives.

Secondary Materials

Akin, Edward. *Flagler: Rockefeller Partner and Florida Baron.* Kent, Ohio: Kent State University Press, 1988.

Alicoote, Jack, ed. *The 1927 Film Yearbook*. Film Daily, 1928.

Amherst Catalog. Amherst College. 1904–5, 1905–6.

Ayres, Arthur. "Governmental Regulation of Securities Issues," *Political Science Quarterly* (1913), 586–92.

Barbour, George. *Florida for Tourists, Invalids, and Settlers*. New York: Appleton, 1882.

Baskin, Jonathan. "The Development of Corporate Financial Markets in Britain and the United States, 1600–1914: Overcoming Asymmetric Information," *Business History Review* (1988), 199–237.

Baskin, Jonathan, and Paul Miranti. *A History of Corporate Finance*. Cambridge: Cambridge University Press, 1997.

Benston, George. *The Separation of Commercial and Investment Banking: The Glass-Steagall Act Revisited and Reconsidered*. New York: Oxford University Press, 1990.

Bernheim, Alfred, ed. *The Security Markets: Findings and Recommendation of a Special Staff of the Twentieth Century Fund*. New York: Twentieth Century Fund, 1935.

Bill, Ledyard. *A Winter in Florida*. 4th ed. New York: Wood & Holbrook, 1870.

Bilstein, Roger. *The American Aerospace Industry: From Workshop to Global Enterprise*. New York: Twayne, 1996.

Bing, Dr. Richard J., M.D., and Dr. H. Schelbert. "Isotopes in Cardiology," in Richard J. Bing, ed., *Cardiology: The Evolution of the Science and the Art*, 181–99. Harwood, 1992.

Bowser, Eileen. *The Transformation of Cinema, 1907–1915*. New York: Charles Scribner's Sons, 1990.

Brandeis, Louis. *Other People's Money and How the Bankers Use It*. Edited by Melvin Urofsky. 1913. New York: Bedford/St. Martin's, 1995.

Brooks, John. *Once in Golconda: A True Drama of Wall Street, 1920–1938*. New York: Harper & Row, 1969.

Burk, James. *Values in the Marketplace: The American Stock Market under Federal Securities Law*. Berlin and New York: Walter de Gruyter, 1988.

Cabell, Branch, and A. J. Hanna. *The St. Johns: A Paradise of Diversities*. New York: Farrar & Rinehart, 1943.

Carosso, Vincent. *Investment Banking in America: A History*. Cambridge, Mass.: Harvard University Press, 1970.

  More Than a Century of Investment Banking: The Kidder, Peabody & Co. Story. New York: McGraw-Hill, 1979.

  The Morgans: Private International Bankers, 1854–1913. Cambridge, Mass.: Harvard University Press, 1987.

Cassady, Ralph, and Wylie Jones. *The Changing Competitive Structure in the Wholesale Grocery Trade: A Case Study of the Los Angeles Market, 1920– 1946*. Berkeley and Los Angeles: University of California Press, 1949.

Chandler, Alfred D., and Stephen Salsbury. *Pierre S. du Pont and the Making of the Modern Corporation*. New York: Harper & Row, 1971.

Chapman, Stanley. *The Rise of Merchant Banking*. London: George Allen & Unwin, 1984.

Chernow, Ron. *The House of Morgan: An American Banking Dynasty and the Rise of Modern Finance*. New York: Atlantic Monthly Press, 1990.

Clarke, Sally. "Consumer Negotiations," paper presented at conference focusing on new directions in business history at Hagley Library, April 1997, Wilmington, Del.

"Conference of Branch Managers, 1940." Transcript of proceedings, April 1940. ML Files.

Cowing, Cedric. *Populists, Plungers, and Progressives: A Social History of Stock and Commodity Speculation.* Princeton: Princeton University Press, 1965.

Crooks, James. *Jacksonville after the Fire, 1901–1919.* Jacksonville: University of North Florida Press, 1991.

Cunningham, William. *American Railroads: Government Control and Reconstruction Policies.* Chicago: A. W. Shaw, 1922.

Davis, Clark. "Living on the Ladder: Work and Culture in the Emerging Corporate Order, Los Angeles, 1900–1930," Ph.D. dissertation, University of Southern California, 1994.

Davis, Lance, and Robert Gallman. "International Capital Flows in the Nineteenth Century," manuscript presented at April 1993 meeting of All-U.C. Economic History Group, Pasadena, California.

Davis, Thomas. *History of Early Jacksonville.* Jacksonville, Florida: W. B. Drew, 1911.

Deaderick, Lucile, ed. *Heart of the Valley: A History of Knoxville, Tennessee.* Knoxville: East Tennessee Historical Society, 1976.

De Bedts, Ralph. *The New Deal's SEC: The Formative Years.* New York: Columbia University Press, 1964.

De Long, Bradford. "Did J. P. Morgan's Men Add Value? An Economist's Perspective on Financial Capitalism," in Peter Temin, ed., *Inside the Business Enterprise: Historical Perspectives on the Use of Information,* 205–36. Chicago: University of Chicago Press, 1995.

Derr, Mark. *Some Kind of Paradise: A Chronicle of Man and the Land in Florida.* New York: William Morrow, 1989.

Edwards, J. R. "Company Legislation and Changing Patterns of Disclosure in British Company Accounts, 1900–1940," manuscript prepared for Institute of Chartered Accountants in England and Wales, 1981.

Engel, Louis. Transcribed interview conducted by E. Engberg, in 1980s, ML Files.

Engel, Louis, and Henry Hecht. *How to Buy Stocks.* 8th ed. Boston: Little Brown, 1994.

Engle, N. H. "Gaps in Marketing Research," *Journal of Marketing* (April 1940), 345–53.

"Enterprise and Evangelism," *Investor's Reader,* Oct. 19, 1953. (A business magazine published regularly by Merrill Lynch for distribution to customers.)

Factbook: Merrill Lynch & Co. New York, 1996.

Farrell, Maurice, ed. *The Dow Jones Averages, 1885–1970.* New York: Dow Jones, 1972.

Florida: A Guide to the Southernmost State, no named author, Federal Writers' Project. New York: Oxford University Press, 1939.

Foley, William. "The Organization and Management of a Bond House" and "Bond Salesmanship," *Annals of American Academy of Political and Social Science* (September 1907), 257–63, 264–68.

Frank, Stanley. "Chain of Fortune." ML Files.

Friedricks, William. *Henry E. Huntington and the Creation of Southern California.* Columbus: Ohio State University Press, 1992.

"A Metropolitan Entrepreneur Par Excellence: Henry E. Huntington and the Growth of Southern California, 1898–1927," *Business History Review* (1989), 329–55.

Geisst, Charles. *Visionary Capitalism: Financial Markets and the American Dream in the Twentieth Century*. New York: Praeger, 1990.

Griffis, Stanton. "Biography of Charles Merrill: A Saga of Wall Street." ML Files.

Grunning, Wid, ed. *Wid's Year Book: 1918*. Reprinted by Arno Press, New York, 1971.

Guide to Florida. Authored by anonymous "Rambler," privately printed, 1875. (New edition in Floridiana Facsimile Reprint Series, introduction by Rembert Patrick. Gainesville: University of Florida Press, 1964.)

Hampton, Benjamin. *History of the American Film Industry: From Its Beginnings to 1931*. New York: Dover, 1931.

Hardy, Charles Oscar. *Odd-Lot Trading on the New York Stock Exchange*. Washington, D.C.: Brookings Institution, 1939.

Hardy, Hugh, ed. *The Politz Papers: Science and Truth in Marketing Research*. Chicago: American Marketing Association, 1990.

Hawkins, David. "The Development of Modern Financial Reporting Practices among American Manufacturing Corporations," *Business History Review* (1963), 135–68.

Hayes, Samuel, III, et al. *Competition in the Investment Banking Industry*. Cambridge, Mass.: Harvard University Press, 1983.

Hecht, Henry. *A Legacy of Leadership: Merrill Lynch, 1885–1985*. New York: Privately printed, 1985.

Hoisington, Harland. *Wall Street 1920–1970: Five Fabulous Decades*. New York: Vantage Press, 1972.

Hoogenboom, Ari and Olive. *A History of the ICC: From Panacea to Palliative*. New York: W. W. Norton, 1976.

Horowitz, Helen Lefkowitz. *Campus Life: Undergraduate Cultures from the End of the Eighteenth Century to the Present*. New York: Knopf, 1987.

Hoyt, Edwin. *The Supersalesmen*. Cleveland and New York: World, 1962.

Huertas, Thomas, and Joan Silverman, "Charles E. Mitchell: Scapegoat of the Crash?" *Business History Review* (1986), 81–103.

Huertas, Thomas, and Harold van B. Cleveland. *Citibank, 1812–1970*. Cambridge, Mass.: Harvard University Press, 1985.

Izod, John. *Hollywood and the Box Office, 1895–1986*. New York: Columbia University Press, 1988.

Jencks, Christopher, and David Riesman. *The Academic Revolution*. Garden City, N.Y.: Doubleday, 1968.

Keenan, Terrance. "Chain of Fortune: The Life and Work of Charles E. Merrill." Book-length manuscript, 684 typed pages, ML Files.

Kerr, K. Austin. *American Railroad Politics, 1914–1920: Rates, Wages, and Efficiency*. Pittsburgh: University of Pittsburgh Press, 1968.

Kerwin, Charles. "Haphazard Buying or Sound Investment?" *System: The Magazine of Business* (February 1926), 232–96.

Klein, Maury. *The Life and Legend of Jay Gould*. Baltimore: Johns Hopkins University Press, 1986.

Koszarski, Richard. *An Evening's Entertainment: The Age of the Silent Feature Picture, 1915–1928*. New York: Charles Scribner's Sons, 1990.

Lebhar, Godfrey. *Chain Stores in America, 1859–1962*. 3d ed. New York: Chain Store Publishing Corporation, 1963.

Levine, Alan. "Paul Cabot and State Street Investment Trust," *Friends of Financial History* (1994), 13–14.

Lewis, Robert. "Life of Edmund Lynch." ML Files.

Loeser, John C. *The Over-the-Counter Securities Market: What It Is and How It Operates*. New York: National Quotation Bureau, 1940.

Loll, Leo, and Julian Buckley. *The Over-the-Counter Securities Market*. 3d ed. Englewood Cliffs, N.J.: Prentice Hall, 1973.

Loughran, Bill. "The Gael behind the Merrill Lynch Empire," *Boston Irish Echo*. Five-part series, October–November 1985/6.

Lovejoy, Clarence. *Lovejoy's College Guide*. New York: Simon and Schuster, 1968.

Magowan, Robert. Transcribed interview, November 19, 1982, ML Files.

"Managers' Conference Transcript," October 1953, ML Files.

Marchand, Roland. *Advertising the American Dream: Making Way for Modernity, 1920–1940*. Berkeley: University of California Press, 1985.

Matthews, John. *Struggle and Survival on Wall Street: The Economics of Competition among Securities Firms*. New York: Oxford University Press, 1994.

McCraw, Thomas. *Prophets of Regulation*. Cambridge, Mass.: Harvard University Press, 1984.

Michie, Ranald C. *The London and New York Stock Exchanges, 1850–1914*. London: Allen & Unwin, 1987.

Merrill, Charles, Jr. *The Checkbook: The Politics and Ethics of Foundation Philanthropy*. Boston: Oelgeschlager, Gunn & Hain, 1986.

Merrill, James. *A Different Person: A Memoir*. New York: Knopf, 1993.

    The Seraglio. 2d. ed. New York: Atheneum, 1987. First published in 1957.

    From the First Nine: Poems 1946–1976. New York: Atheneum, 1981.

Merrill Lynch Annual Reports. 1940–57, 1996.

Miranti, Paul. *Accountancy Comes of Age: The Development of an American Profession, 1886–1940*. Chapel Hill: University of North Carolina Press, 1990.

    "Associationalism, Statism, and Professional Regulation: Public Accountants and the Reform of the Financial Markets, 1896–1940," *Business History Review* (1986), 438–68.

    "The Mind's Eye of Reform: The ICC's Bureau of Statistics and Accounts and a Vision of Regulation, 1887–1940," *Business History Review* (1989), 469–509.

Myers, Philip. "I Soldiered with Charlie," *American Heritage* (1973), 73–75.

Navin, Thomas, and Marian Sears. "The Rise of a Market for Industrial Securities, 1887–1902," *Business History Review* (1955), 105–38.

New York Stock Exchange. Official record of listed securities for 1910 and 1917.

Newbould, Gerald, and Percy Poun. "Portfolio Strategy," *Market Logic* (July 3, 1996), 7.

Nicolson, Harold. *Dwight Morrow*. New York: Harcourt, Brace, 1935.

Nocera, Joseph. *A Piece of the Action: How the Middle Class Joined the Money Class*. New York: Simon & Schuster, 1994.

"Charlie Merrill and His Stock," *Gentlemen's Quarterly* (October 1994), 223–29, 269–78.

Norden, Martin. "The Pathé Frères Company during the Trust Era," *Journal of the University Film Association* (1981), 15–32.

Parrish, Michael. *Securities Regulation and the New Deal*. New Haven: Yale University Press, 1970.

Pechman, Joseph. *Federal Tax Policy*. 4th ed. Washington, D.C.: Brookings Institution, 1983.

Pecora, Ferdinand. *Wall Street under Oath*. New York: Simon & Schuster, 1939.

Perkins, Edwin J. *American Public Finance and Financial Services, 1700–1815*. Columbus: Ohio State University Press, 1994.

"The Divorce of Commercial and Investment Banking: A History," *Banking Law Journal* (1971), 483–528.

Plummer, Hellen (formerly Hellen Merrill). "An Old Wives' Tale." Manuscript drafted in mid-1950s. ML Files.

"Portfolio Strategy," *Market Logic* (July 3, 1996).

Pressly, Thomas, and William Scofield, eds. *Farm Real Estate Values in the United States by Counties, 1850–1959*. Seattle: University of Washington Press, 1965.

Rae, John. *The American Automobile Industry*. Boston: Twayne, 1984.

Raucher, Alan R. "Dime Store Chains: The Making of Organization Men, 1880–1940," *Business History Review* (1991), 130–63.

Regan, Donald. *A View from the Street*. New York: New American Library, 1972.

Rinehart, Floyd, and Marian Rinehart. *Victorian Florida: America's Last Frontier*. Atlanta: Peachtree, 1986.

Ripley, William Z. *Railroads: Finance and Organization*. New York: Longmans, Green, 1915.

Railroads: Rates and Regulations. New York: Longmans, Green, 1916.

"Public Regulation of Railroad Issues," *American Economic Review* (1914), 541–64.

Rottersman, Max, and Jason Zweig, "An Early History of Mutual Funds," *Friends of Financial History* (Spring 1994), 12–20.

Samuel, Lawrence. *Pledging Allegiance: American Identity and the Bond Drive of World War II*. Washington, D.C.: Smithsonian Institution Press, 1997.

Seligman, Joel. *The Transformation of Wall Street: A History of the Securities and Exchange Commission and Modern Corporate Finance*. Boston: Houghton Mifflin, 1982.

Sheldon, Henry. *Student Life and Customs*. New York: Appleton, 1901.

Sicilia, David. "Supermarket Sweep," *Audacity* (1997), 10–19.

Siegel, Jeremy. "Equity vs. Fixed Income: Return Patterns since 1802," *American Association of Individual Investors Journal* (June 1992), 7–10.

Sirkin, Gerald. "The Stock Market of 1929 Revisited: A Note," *Business History Review* (1975), 223–31.

Slide, Anthony, ed. *The American Film Industry: A Historical Dictionary*. Westport, Conn.: Greenwood, 1986.

Smiley, Gene. "The Expansion of the New York Securities Market at the Turn of the Century," *Business History Review* (1981), 75–85.

Smiley, Gene, and Richard Keehn. "Margin Purchases, Brokers' Loans, and the Bull Market of the Twenties," *Business and Economic History* (1988), 129–42.

Smith, George David, and Richard Sylla. "The Transformation of Financial Capitalism: An Essay on the History of American Capital Markets," *Financial Markets, Institutions, and Instruments* (1993), 1– 62.

Smith, Winthrop. "Reminiscences of Charles E. Merrill." Memorandum drafted in mid-1950s. ML Files.

Snowden, Kenneth. "Amercian Stock Market Development and Performance, 1871–1929," *Explorations in Economic History* (1987), 327–53.

"Historical Returns and Security Market Development, 1872–1925," *Explorations in Economic History* (1990), 381–420.

Sobel, Robert. *N.Y.S.E.: A History of the New York Stock Exchange, 1935–1975.* New York: Weybright & Talley, 1975.

The Great Bull Market: Wall Street in the 1920s. New York: W. W. Norton, 1968.

Amex: A History of the American Stock Exchange, 1921– 1971. New York: Weybright & Talley, 1972.

The Big Board: A History of the New York Stock Market. New York: Free Press, 1965.

The Life and Times of Dillon Read. New York: Truman Talley/Dutton, 1991.

Dangerous Dreamers: The Financial Innovators from Charles Merrill to Michael Milken. New York: John Wiley & Sons, 1993.

Spears, Timothy B. *100 Years on the Road: The Traveling Salesman in American Culture.* New Haven: Yale University Press, 1995.

Stalson, J. Owen. *Marketing Life Insurance: Its History in America.* Cambridge, Mass.: Harvard University Press, 1942.

Stockbridge, Frank P., and John H. Perry. *Florida in the Making.* New York and Jacksonville: De Borver, 1926.

Strasser, Susan. *Satisfaction Guaranteed: The Making of the American Mass Market.* New York: Pantheon Books, 1989.

Tebeau, Charlton. *A History of Florida.* Coral Gables, Fla.: University of Miami Press, 1971.

Tedlow, Richard. *New and Improved: The Story of Mass Marketing in America.* New York: Basic Books, 1990.

"Theodore Braun: A Biographical Sketch," Public Relations Office, Braun and Company, Los Angeles, California.

Vance, Sandra, and Roy Scott. *Wal-Mart: A History of Sam Walton's Retail Phenomenon, 1962–1992.* New York: Twayne, 1994.

"Butler Brothers and the Rise and Decline of the Ben Franklin Variety Stores: A Study in Retail Franchising," *Essays in Economic and Business History* (1993), 258–71.

Varnum, John P. *Florida: Its Climate, Productions, and Characteristics.* New York: South Publishing, 1885.

Veenendaal, Augustus J. *Slow Train to Paradise: How Dutch Investment Helped Build American Railroads.* Stanford: Stanford University Press, 1996.

Vernon, J. R. "World War II Fiscal Policies and the End of the Great Depression," *Journal of Economic History* (1994), 850–68.

Waller-Zuckerman, Mary Ellen. "The Business Side of Media Development: Popular Women's Magazines in the Late Nineteenth Century," *Essays in Economic and Business History* (1989), 40–59.

"Marketing the Women's Journals, 1873–1900," *Business and Economic History* (1989), 99–108.

Walter, Ingo, ed. *Deregulating Wall Street: Commercial Bank Penetration of the Corporate Securities Market.* New York: John Wiley & Sons, 1985.

Wasko, Janet. *Movies and Money: Financing the American Film Industry.* Norwood, N.J.: Ablex, 1982.

Werner, Walter, and Steven Smith. *Wall Street.* New York: Columbia University Press, 1991.

"What Does the Public Know about the Stock Exchange? Roper Survey Reveals Extent of Misconceptions and Misinformation about the Services of the Exchange," *Exchange Magazine* (January 1940).

White, Gerald. "Government Financing of Industrial Facilities during World War II: Are There Energy Crisis Parallels?" *Essays in Economic and Business History* (1981), 109–20.

Wilkins, Mira. "French Multinationals in the United States: An Historical Perspective," *Entreprises et Histoire* (1993), 14–29.

Wriston, Walter. *Risk and Other Four-Letter Words.* New York: Harper & Row, 1986.

Wyckoff, Richard. *Wall Street Ventures and Adventures through Forty Years.* New York: Harper & Brothers, 1931.

Yenser, Stephen. *Consuming Myth: The Work of James Merrill.* Cambridge, Mass.: Harvard University Press, 1987.

Young Men's Christian Association of Amherst College. *Amherst Student Handbook.* 1904–5, 1905–6.

Zunz, Olivier. *Making America Corporate: 1870–1920.* Chicago: University of Chicago Press, 1990.

INDEX

DATE DUE
